Policy Studies Yearbook
Annual Review 2021

Also from Westphalia Press
westphaliapress.org

Policy Studies Yearbook

Annual Review 2021 • Volume 12, Issue 1

Emma R. Norman, editor

Westphalia Press
An imprint of Policy Studies Organization

Policy Studies Yearbook
Annual Review 2021 • Volume 12, Issue 1

Westphalia Press
An imprint of Policy Studies Organization
1367 Connecticut Ave., NW
Washington, D.C. 20036
info@ipsonet.org

ISBN: 978-1-63723-813-4

Cover and interior design by Jeffrey Barnes
jbarnesbook.design

Daniel Gutierrez-Sandoval, Executive Director
PSO and Westphalia Press

Updated material and comments on this edition
can be found at the Westphalia Press website:
www.westphaliapress.org

POLICY STUDIES YEARBOOK

ANNUAL REVIEW 2021 • VOLUME 12, ISSUE 1

© 2022 Policy Studies Organization

PSO

Policy Studies Yearbook Annual Review 2021
Note from the Editor

Emma R. Norman
Policy Studies Organization

Welcome to the *Policy Studies Yearbook Annual Review* 2021! Pioneered by the *Policy Studies Journal* over a decade ago, the *Policy Studies Yearbook* is a unique twin-pronged project designed to: first, connect a large, international, and multi-disciplinary body of policy scholars and practitioners via the *Yearbook* directory; and second, to disseminate the best of their research in contemporary policy developments, commentaries, and reviews of the policy literature in the *Yearbook* annual publication.

The *Yearbook* Directory

As the many members of the directory know, the growing needs of the *Yearbook* directory were fulfilled by moving it in 2021 to a new, updated, and stand-alone website at psoyearbook.org. Here, policy scholars, policy practitioners, and advanced graduate students can stay current on recent research in their subfield by uploading their profile, affiliations, research areas, and lists of publications—old and new. Members use the directory to get connected and stay that way. But the directory is far more than a simple contacts list. You can use its searchable database to promote your latest research to exactly the right people, find new colleagues and research collaborators, identify experts in highly specialized areas, establish your peer reviewer niche (and link it to other sites), identify potential peer review panel members,[1] nominate preferred peer reviewers when submitting articles to journals, send the right people copies of your latest publications, shortlist potential faculty, convene integrated conference panels, contact policy practitioners in your subfield, or select compatible graduate supervisors—among many other things. If you're not already a member, it is free and easy to sign up and get connected—just follow the simple instructions on the homepage at psoyearbook.org. We send out a yearly email to remind you to update your *Yearbook* directory profile to ensure it remains current and can get you in touch quickly and easily with the policy people you need to know (and those who need to know *you*)!

---

1   As an editor with a couple of the PSO's other journals for many years, the multidisciplinary nature of the policy studies field has always made it somewhat challenging to find the best reviewers for highly specialized policy areas. Years ago, I discovered that the searchable international listing of policy scholars in the *Yearbook* directory is also an invaluable resource for editors to find exactly the right peer-review panel for promising submissions.

Policy Studies Yearbook 12.1: vii-xiv. 10.18278/psy.12.1.1
©2022 Policy Studies Organization

The *Yearbook* Annual Publication

For eleven years, the Yearbook Annual Review was published by Wiley as a supplemental issue of the prestigious Policy Studies Journal (PSJ). All past issues of the Yearbook can now be accessed freely in one click on the homepage of the above web address. As the new editor, I am proud to present the twelfth issue of the Policy Studies Yearbook Annual Review. It expresses admirably the growth of our twin-pronged project in its wider aims and scope, while also offering the same detailed, rigorous, and highly engaging scholarly reviews of the literature for which the Yearbook became renowned under Hank Jenkins-Smith's editorship. As you will see, this year's expanded publication also includes commentaries, original research, and multidisciplinary policy connections that I hope you will find interesting, inspiring, and useful.

Yearbook Review 2021 Issue Summary

State-of-the-Policy-Art Literature Reviews

The past eleven *Yearbooks* all included review articles summarizing the most recent scholarship in specific policy subfields. In many cases, these were created and submitted by faculty members with stellar graduate students as coauthors. This year's *Yearbook Annual Review* will not disappoint readers looking for the same standard of rigorously peer-reviewed state-of-the-policy-art analytical reviews. Our first four articles comprise the most exceptional of the submissions we received in this area.

Regarding the editor's main selection criteria, *Yearbook* articles not only review the literature rigorously, widely, and underline its importance beyond the narrow subfield in question. They also draw a strong original contribution from those reviews. Our first article this year does all these things with considerable aplomb. In "A Systematic Review of Policy Learning: Tiptoeing through a Conceptual Minefield," Bishoy Louis Zaki, Ellen Wayenberg, and Bert George (2022) offer an impressive systematic study on the extant research regarding policy learning. Their findings point strongly to the continuing need for enhancing the conceptual and analytical value of policy learning, which lies at the heart of the policy process and its scholarship. Of course, the strength of exceptional review articles lies not merely in the breadth and depth of the literature reviews they contain, but in their ability to balance this by defining, justifying, and assisting future research agendas in the field. This article is particularly strong in these areas: from the breadth of its clearly elaborated coding scheme, to its problematization of areas of weak theorization and lack of clarity, to its well-considered and justified suggestions for avenues of future study. The authors emerge with a conceptual framework of policy learning designed to ameliorate what they call the 'persistent fragmentation' and conceptual clarity issues rife across this burgeoning subfield of policy studies.

Just as policy learning relates to many stages of the policy process, so too does collaboration theory—as our second article argues strongly. Madeleine W. McNamara and John C. Morris (2022) give a thorough review of the collaboration literature in "Expanding the Utility of Cross-Sectoral Collaboration in Policy Studies: Present and Future." They contend that its reach extends far beyond the usual focus on policy implementation and well into the realms of practical policy application at different stages of the policy cycle. Like Zaki, Wayenberg, and George (2022), their strongest contribution lies in the realms of developing theory and underlining new avenues for future research, leading them to flag opportunities for a greater inclusion of cross-sectoral collaboration theories (and practices informed by them) into policy research more broadly. To aid thinking about how cross-sector collaboration may relate strongly to the practice of policy studies beyond implementation, the contemporary policy examples and contexts the authors discuss, such as the COVID-19 pandemic, are particularly illuminating.

In the third article, Saahir Shafi and Daniel J. Mallinson (2022) focus on the shifting policy landscape in research and practice concerning "A Decade in Drug Policy and Research: Evaluating Trends from 2010 to 2020 and Presenting Major Policy Developments." This in-depth systematic review finds that research preferences have closely followed policy developments, especially in the United States in the wake of COVID-19 and the black lives movement. For example, the flow of states and countries toward more liberal drug policies is reflected in the growing body of literature on legalization and decriminalization. This article is particularly effective in showing not just a sense of how policy is changing over the years, but how well prevailing research trends match and trail, if not at times predict, such developments. Policy, as the authors underline, begets research—and research funding.

Fourth, in "Seeing the Visual: A Literature Review on Why and How Policy Scholars Would Do Well to Study Influential Visualizations," Eduardo Rojas-Padilla, Tamara Metze, and Katrien Termeer (2022) offer a technically sophisticated review of the literature on visualizations and justify its importance to negotiating and framing policy. The authors identify exactly how (and to whom) visual elements can and should be critical to both policy making and policy scholarship, though its prominence in the discipline has to date been patchy at best. An excellent example of the widening multidisciplinarity of the policy sciences, this article does much to persuade us that, despite our specialized subfield, embracing the 'visual turn' in future policy studies is not only beneficial to our discipline; it is fast becoming requisite in almost every area.

Policy Developments and Commentaries

Our last four pieces showcase the wider focus we hoped this year would contribute to the new format of the *Yearbook Annual Review*. Two comprise original research in, respectively, contemporary gender representation policy and defense policy, though each implicates and teases out other policy strands too. Our final two contributors offer extended commentary articles. One corrects foreign policy misperceptions regarding the Ukraine's position in the global landscape that appear to have been lost in translation. The other applies cultural studies to better understand party system change and its concomitant policy ramifications.

In our fifth article, Mahbub Prodip's (2022) comparative analysis of reserved seats identifies the main hindrances impeding policies designed to promote gender equality and women's political empowerment from a developing democracy perspective. In "Women's Political Empowerment in India and Bangladesh: Gender Quotas and Socio-economic Obstructions," Prodip provides a poignant counterpoint to the Western context in which quotas are most often discussed. The author and notes the multiple problems with the institutional design of gender equality policies in both countries. He argues that the socio-economic barriers experienced by women continue to stymie the formal institutional measures designed to level the political playing field when it comes to women's real policy influence at the local level.

John Ash's (2022) excellent contribution tackles a host of policy issues (environmental/economic, defense/military, political autonomy/democracy/sovereignty, cyber questions, and security/neutrality) as they intersect with the policy concerns surrounding the unique geopolitical case for Greenlandic independence. The island stands at the forefront of climate change and has brought the prospect of increased availability of Arctic natural resources as well as concerns that these might provide focal points for conflict in the region. In "An Arctic Promised Land: Greenlandic Independence and Security," Ash focuses on the most salient defense issues, taking theory/conceptual consonance, normative considerations, and practical economic/military perspectives on board. This in-depth study emerges with five detailed policy options and advice from a military and geopolitical perspective that account for the wide range of intersecting policy issues involved.

Our seventh piece is entitled "Misrepresenting Ukraine's Democracy, Misguiding U.S. Foreign Affairs—Afterthoughts on a Recent Debate in Washington and Nuclear Non-proliferation." In this commentary, Andreas Umland (2022) highlights recent challenges to Western foreign policy toward Eastern Europe, and particularly Ukraine, that informed debates in some important policy circles in 2021. Whether due to misinformation, stereotypes, or language barriers, Umland's critical commentary examines some of the most serious claims used as reasons to call for an end to U.S. support for Ukraine and offers counter evidence in each case.

Finally, Riccardo Pelizzo and Zim Nwokora (2022) bring both political science and cultural studies back into the policy spectrum in "The Cultural Determinants of Party System Change." Through their notion of the 'rise of the fluid self' derived from an entertaining exploration into key developments in popular culture in the 1960s, the authors provide an initial foray into the cultural basis of party system change/transformation/fluidity not customarily found in the canonical literature on the subject. The authors argue that the rise of the fluid self reduced the appeal of parties (as evidenced by the decline in party-membership levels) and that political parties' vanishing appeal contributed to the destabilization of west European party systems. Both have affected the policy offers made to electorates by parties and ensuing policy developments. The wide empirical evidence concerning party system fluidity since the 1960s offered in this commentary article suggests the point may be an important one for future studies to explore. Of particular note concerns whether and to what extent the correlation between fluid self and system fluidity may have a causal basis and, if so, whether the political and policy sciences ought to take cultural contexts more fully on board in future research.

Concluding Remarks

ACTION: Please bookmark the new Yearbook website at http://www.psoyearbook.org/directory/ and easily update your profile there.

I hope you enjoy our new *Policy Studies Yearbook* articles for 2021. The PSO and I express our sincere thanks to Hank Jenkins-Smith and the *PSJ* editors and staff for creating and running this extremely useful twin resource for policy experts for the last 12 years under the remit of the *PSJ*. Theirs are large shoes to fill! The directory is a fantastic online tool for scholars, practitioners, editors, journalists, and students to aid networking, scholarly collaboration and continued contact in the field—all the more important in today's socially distanced world.

Now our new website has been up and running for a year, it is even quicker and easier to use. I encourage you to create a profile in the *Yearbook* directory membership at psoyearbook.org (just click the link "Get Listed") to receive all our updates about the directory and annual publication projects. Or click on 'directory' on the homepage to add a new profile or update an existing profile on http://www.psoyearbook.org/directory/. As always, it's very simple: just click on Yearbook Members > Update Information, enter the email address associated with your profile and add your latest contact details and published works. If you no longer have access to that address, no problem. Just follow the instructions to reset. Please note that, for security reasons, Yearbook staff check and approve new profiles before they go live, but updates should be instantaneous. Please also ask your colleagues to add their profiles if they have not already done so.

I very much look forward to working together with you in the future! Our call for papers for the upcoming 2022 *Yearbook Annual Review* can be found below. If you have any queries or suggestions for new features you would like to see the *Yearbook* directory fulfill, or if you wish to submit a paper for consideration in the 2022 *Yearbook Annual Review*, please email me at psoyearbook@ipsonet.org.

Editor: Emma R. Norman
psoyearbook@ipsonet.org

References

Ash, John. 2022. "An Arctic Promised Land: Greenlandic Independence and Security." *Policy Studies Yearbook Annual Review* 12.

McNamara, Madeleine W., and John C. Morris. 2022. "Expanding the Utility of Cross-Sectoral Collaboration in Policy Studies: Present and Future." *Policy Studies Yearbook Annual Review* 12.

Pelizzo, Riccardo, and Zim Nwokora. 2022. "The Cultural Determinants of Party System Change." *Policy Studies Yearbook Annual Review* 12.

Prodip, Md. Mahbub Alam. 2022. "Women's Political Empowerment in India and Bangladesh: Gender Quotas and Socio-economic Obstructions." *Policy Studies Yearbook Annual Review* 12.

Rojas-Padilla, Eduardo, Tamara Metze, and Katrien Termeer. 2022. "Seeing the Visual: A Literature Review on Why and How Policy Scholars Would Do Well to Study Influential Visualizations." *Policy Studies Yearbook Annual Review* 12.

Shafi, Saahir, and Daniel J. Mallinson. 2022. "A Decade in Drug Policy and Research: Evaluating Trends from 2010 to 2020 and Presenting Major Policy Developments." *Policy Studies Yearbook Annual Review* 12.

Umland, Andreas. 2022. "Misrepresenting Ukraine's Democracy, Misguiding U.S. Foreign Affairs—Afterthoughts on a Recent Debate in Washington and Nuclear Non-proliferation." *Policy Studies Yearbook Annual Review* 12.

Zaki, Bishoy Louis, Ellen Wayenberg, and Bert George. 2022 "A Systematic Review of Policy Learning: Tiptoeing through a Conceptual Minefield." *Policy Studies Yearbook Annual Review* 12.

Call for Papers for the 2022 *Policy Studies Yearbook Annual Review*

We are now calling for papers for the 2022 *Yearbook Annual Review*. Review article submissions for the 2022 issue summarizing recent policy scholarship in specific policy subfields, or articles and shorter commentaries focusing on recent practical policy developments should be emailed to the editor at psoyearbook@ipsonet.org by no later than May 1, 2022.

Aims and Scope

In the past, the content of the *Yearbook Annual Review* included short review articles summarizing the most recent scholarship in specific policy subfields. We will continue to publish, now and in the future, such articles on the state of the academic literature. From 2021 the *Yearbook Annual Review* is broadening its aims and scope to also include articles and shorter commentaries that critically discuss key practical policy developments of the previous year (or last few years). Such articles and commentaries may focus on either one policy area across several countries or states, or policy developments in a single country or region (one policy area or related areas).

Many policy developments and mis-developments have been particularly momentous in 2020-22 concerning the global pandemic: international aid and cooperation, crisis response, democratic accountability, electoral procedures, vaccine and lockdown policies, viral variants, economic recovery, trade restrictions/opportunities, public diplomacy, global leadership, great powers and grand strategies, e-commerce, remote learning, border controls, freedom of movement/association, regional fragmentation, globalization and its discontents, and a host of other areas. The practical policy areas the editor is interested in considering include, but are not restricted to, these fields. There is, of course, much to be said concerning the lightning speed of many policy developments over the last three years, both within and between states. It is the aim of future *Yearbook Annual Reviews* to publish the best articles and commentaries in key policy areas and provide a spirited forum for future discussion, comment, critique, and careful connection to the most recent academic advancements in the literature.

Submission Requirements

Publication is open to all scholars who conduct research in public policy, including independent scholars, faculty professors, advanced graduate students, and policy practitioners. Submissions will undergo rigorous double-blind peer review. State of the literature and original research articles should be around 8-9,000 words in total, including abstracts and Chicago style Author-Date citations and reference list. Shorter commentaries are welcome but should be appropriately referenced throughout with the sources of all claims/data cited (reference list at the end); offer balanced and critical perspectives on a current policy issue and its handling (or mishandling); and conclude with practical policy suggestions drawn from the preceding discussion. Clear, clean, jargon-free writing is, of course, mandatory. Strictly, submissions should NOT be published or under consideration elsewhere. If in any doubt, please email the editor a proposal for consideration first.

Publication

Yearbook Annual Review articles will all be featured in the listings within the Yearbook to facilitate access to current policy research. They will also be featured on the Policy Studies Organization (PSO) website and listed in the PSO curriculum project searchable article database along with the many other articles published in PSO journals such as: the *Policy Studies Journal, Review of Policy Research, Politics & Policy, Policy & Internet,* and *Asian Politics & Policy.*

A Systematic Review of Policy Learning: Tiptoeing through a Conceptual Minefield

BISHOY LOUIS ZAKI

Department of Public Governance, University of Ghent

ELLEN WAYENBERG

Department of Public Governance, University of Ghent

BERT GEORGE

Department of Public Governance, University of Ghent

Policy learning is an increasingly salient concept in public policy research and practice. With growing theoretical advancements, it offers substantial value for policy analysis. However, the field's conceptual state calls for refinement, and its burgeoning literature calls for a much-needed synthesis. We address these calls by conducting a systematic literature review of empirical policy learning articles with a focus on synthesizing a growing, yet relatively fragmented, body of research and addressing inherent conceptual clarity issues. In total, 147 articles were analyzed and integrated into an overarching framework offering a background conceptualization of policy learning that complements and supplements existing conceptual approaches. This conceptualization is centered on understanding the interplay between policy issues, information and knowledge, systems and structures, and context. In conclusion, an extensive research agenda on policy learning is proposed to help advance public policy theory, research, and practice.

Keywords: Policy Learning, Systematic Literature Review, Public Policy, Public Administration, Policy Analysis, Concept Formation, Conceptual Clarity, Conceptualization in Policy Studies, Research Agenda.

---

* Acknowledgements: The first author would like to extend sincere thanks to Professor Claudio Radaelli, the School of Transnational Governance, European University Institute for the many interesting conversations, insights, and debates on policy learning over the past two years. Sincere thanks are also due to Professor Mike Jones, University of Tennessee Knoxville for the many stimulating reflections and debates on Policy Learning during several meetings in 2020. The authors would like to sincerely thank Professor Emma R. Norman and our anonymous reviewers at the *Policy Studies Yearbook* for their constructive feedback and support.

Policy Studies Yearbook 12.1: 1-52. 10.18278/psy.12.1.2

Una revisión sistemática del aprendizaje de políticas: Caminando de puntillas por un campo minado conceptual

El aprendizaje de políticas es un concepto cada vez más destacado en la investigación y la práctica de políticas públicas. Con crecientes avances teóricos, ofrece un valor sustancial para el análisis de políticas. Sin embargo, el estado conceptual del campo requiere refinamiento y su floreciente literatura requiere una síntesis muy necesaria. Abordamos estos llamados mediante la realización de una revisión bibliográfica sistemática de artículos de aprendizaje de políticas empíricas con un enfoque en sintetizar un cuerpo de investigación creciente, aunque relativamente fragmentado, y abordar cuestiones de claridad conceptual inherentes. En total, 147 artículos fueron analizados e integrados en un marco general que ofrece una conceptualización básica del aprendizaje de políticas que complementa y complementa los enfoques conceptuales existentes. Esta conceptualización se centra en comprender la interacción entre cuestiones de política, información y conocimiento, sistemas y estructuras, y contexto. En conclusión, se propone una amplia agenda de investigación sobre el aprendizaje de políticas para ayudar a promover la teoría, la investigación y la práctica de las políticas públicas.

Palabras clave: Aprendizaje de políticas, Revisión sistemática de la literatura, Políticas públicas, Formación de conceptos, Conceptualización en estudios de políticas, Agenda de investigación.

政策學習的系統回顧：通過概念雷區踮起腳尖

政策學習是公共政策研究和實踐中越來越突出的概念。隨著理論的不斷進步，它為政策分析提供了巨大的價值。然而，該領域的概念狀態需要完善，其蓬勃發展的文獻需要急需的綜合。我們通過對實證政策學習文章進行系統的文獻綜述來應對這些呼籲，重點是綜合不斷增長但相對分散的研究主體，並解決固有的概念清晰度問題。總共有 147 篇文章被分析並整合到一個總體框架中，提供了政策學習的背景概念，補充和補充了現有的概念方法。這種概念化的核心是理解政策問題、信息和知識、系統和結構以及背景之間的相互作用。總之，提出了關於政策學習的廣泛研究議程，以幫助推進公共政策理論、研究和實踐。

關鍵詞：政策學習，系統文獻回顧，公共政策，概念形成，政策研究中的概念化，研究議程。

Decades ago, leading scholars such as Karl Deutsch (1966) and John Dewey (1938) rejuvenated the discussion on learning as a form of context adaption and a supplementary understanding to power-based politics in public administration. In doing so, they laid a foundation for what we now know as "policy learning." From there on, championed by leading scholars, interest in policy learning has flourished (e.g., Sabatier 1988; Rose 1991; Bennett and Howlett 1992; Dunlop and Radaelli 2018). The allure of policy learning is undeniable as it yields instrumental transformations, from achieving policy objectives to improving public service performance and disaster management (see e.g., Wai Yip So 2012; O'Donovan 2017). The salience of learning is emphasized by the very nature of public administration and its longstanding tradition of responding to new challenges and shortcomings, particularly in an era of wicked and complex policy problems where varieties of learning can empower sense making and enable better responses to pressing challenges (Peters 2017; George *et al.* 2020; Zaki and Wayenberg 2021; Zaki and George 2021). The importance of learning has been further accentuated by relatively recent paradigmatic transformations such as Public Value and Digital Era Governance, which focus on continuous improvements with an orientation toward collaborative learning among actors, knowledge sharing, and engaging with new technology (see e.g., Bryson, Crosby, and Bloomberg 2014; Dunleavy *et al.* 2006).

With these foundational influences, interest in policy learning permeated the realms of theory, research, and practice. Scholars continuously engage in theory development and extension to enhance the yield of policy learning for public administration (see e.g., Dunlop and Radaelli 2018; Heikkila and Gerlak 20013). In a discursive process, theoretical contributions are rapidly employed to refine theory and garner insights for practice in critical areas from governance to disaster response and recovery (see e.g., O'Donovan 2017; Weissert and Scheller 2008; Zaki and Wayenberg 2021). With the growing role of Public International Organizations and transnational networks, policy learning also serves as a practice-oriented framework across the supra/subnational spectrum. Examples include large-scale efforts such as the European Union's Open Method of Coordination (OMC) (Tamtik 2016) and the OECD's transnational governance focus (Porter and Webb 2008). On the subnational and municipal levels, policy learning is key in in trans-municipal networks and local partnerships formed to foster learning and exchange of experiences (see e.g., Lee and Van de Meene 2012; Kern and Bulkeley 2009).

Ontologically, policy learning literature and theory have remarkably matured over the years. Robust theoretical refinements have emerged to illuminate various facets of policy learning, policy making, and their intersections. This included (among many others) refining our understanding of the interactions between individual and collective learning (see e.g., Heikkila and Gerlak 2013), systematizing different modes of policy learning and their boundary conditions (see e.g., Dunlop and Radaelli 2013), the operationalization of policy learning across multiple levels of analysis (see e.g., Dunlop and Radaelli 2017, 2020), and theorizing key relationships between policy learning and policy change (see e.g., Moyson, Scholten, and Weible 2017). This led to policy learning theoretically crystallizing at the heart of different theories of the policy process—such as the Narrative Policy or Institutional Analysis Development Frameworks, among others (see e.g., Jones and Radaelli 2015; Heikkila and Andersson 2018).

Despite this progress, several calls still echo the need for enhancing the conceptual and thus analytical value of policy learning (see e.g., Radaelli 2009; Dunlop and Radaelli 2018; Goyal and Howlett 2018). Policy learning literature still endures an array of interwoven theoretical, empirical, and practical challenges, mostly of a conceptual stemming. First: *theoretically*, the concept of policy learning remains shrouded in ambiguity and still warrants more clarity (Karlsen and Larrea 2016; Dunlop, Radaelli, and Trein 2018). It also endures conceptual fragmentation and stretching (Goyal and Howlett 2018). Thus, it comes as no surprise that research on policy learning is sometimes deemed synonymous with sweeping a "conceptual minefield" (Levy 1994) or treading a jungle with overlapping definitional contours and a dizzying array of definitions (Borrás 2011; Stark 2019). As conceptual clarity influences theory development (Gerring 1999; Alvesson and Blom 2021), such issues can also contribute to the relatively slowed theoretical development of policy learning (Gerlak *et al.* 2018). Second: *empirically*, conceptual, and definitional clarity issues have spill-over effects as they undermine research-based knowledge creation. Without some convergence on fundamentals, scientists face difficulties building on the work of each other (Kaplan and Haenlein 2006; Cole 1983). This can explain the relatively reduced cohesion and knowledge production and accumulation somewhat observable in policy learning and some of its subfields (see e.g., Stark 2019; Maggetti and Gilardi 2016). Consequently, with limited conceptual cohesion, attempts to operationalize learning have not been frequently tied to clear definitions (Pattison 2018). Third: *practically*, though highly encouraged, frameworks fostering policy learning rarely define it or agree how it can be identified and streamlined. Given those issues, practitioners and researchers can struggle to identify when learning takes place and discern its role in affecting change (Knoepfel and Kissling-Näf 1998; Dunlop and Radaelli 2016). Put together, this can render policy learning a "hembig," as such; a concept that is hegemonic, yet ambiguous and excessively scoped (Alvesson and Blom 2021). Furthermore, the burgeoning interest in policy learning has caused a notable growth of literature, with the concept being utilized across a variety of disciplines, policy areas, and using different approaches. As the literature grows, the need for synthesizing this sprouting body of knowledge becomes more pressing, particularly with concerns over body of knowledge fragmentation (Bennett and Howlett 1992; Bakır 2017).

As demonstrated, conceptual clarity, fragmentation, and knowledge accumulation issues underpin the field's trichotomy *of theoretical*, *empirical*, and *practical* challenges. Additionally, there is a growing need to synthesize this growing body of literature. Driven by this problematization, in this article we utilize a systematic literature review as a method for crafting state of the art field syntheses to support knowledge accumulation and reduce fragmentation. We employ the review results to propose a background conceptualization of policy learning and a future research agenda that builds on recent conceptual and theoretical refinements in emerging policy learning research (see e.g., Heikkila and Gerlak 2013; Moyson, Scholten, and Weible 2017; Dunlop and Radaelli 2013). In doing so, we are guided by the following pressing research questions:

1. *What is the current landscape of policy learning literature?*

2. *What is the current definitional state of policy learning in that literature?*

3. *How can policy learning be better conceptualized?*

4. *How can the answers to the above questions inform a future research agenda?*

In this review, we analyzed a total of 147 empirical articles published in journals included in the public administration category of the Web-of-Science Social Sciences Citation Index (SSCI). Following the Preferred Reporting Items for Systematic Reviews and Meta-Analyses (PRISMA) outlined by Moher and others (2009), we offer results using a replicable and transparent process aimed at taking stock of the field's empirical state of the art.

The contribution of this article is threefold. Theoretically, we employ theoretical triangulation by drawing on theories of the policy process, the policy learning literature, and our review findings to propose a conceptual framework of policy learning grounded in structural dimensions salient in extant literature. Thus, we contribute to addressing persistent fragmentation, cohesion, and conceptual clarity issues (see e.g., Dunlop and Radaelli 2018; Stark 2019). Methodologically, we use an innovative approach that first utilizes an integrative review to synthesize the body of literature. Then, we carry our empirically grounded findings into a problematized review that draws on interdisciplinary resources to scrutinize and reimagine literature toward a theoretically coherent background conceptualization of policy learning. Thus, we contribute to knowledge production and accumulation while avoiding *a priori* assumptions and yielding replicable and comparable results to inform future research agendas (see e.g., De Vries, Bekkers, and Tummers 2015; Pickering *et al.* 2014). To our current knowledge, there have been no full-fledged systematic literature reviews focusing on the conceptualization of policy learning to date. Our third contribution bridges the theoretical-practical divide. With ontology often being a dividing line in landscaping policy learning (Dunlop and Radaelli 2017), we argue that the field's currently dominant ontological position contributes to the field's conceptual challenges. We postulate that an ontological re-alignment toward an integrated, policy systems-grounded, multidimensional perspective can better leverage policy learning research and practice.

Hence, we elaborate on a proposed framework that sets to achieve such endeavor, thus meeting the two chief criteria for solid theoretical contributions: originality and utility (Corley and Gioia 2011).

This article proceeds as follows—we next elaborate on the methodological framework before providing a synthesis of the review findings; we then propose a background conceptualization for policy learning along with a future research agenda.

Methods and Research Design

Methodological Approach

Systematic literature reviews (SLRs) are ideally suited to synthesize a large body of literature, enhance the accumulation of knowledge, integrate insights, and inform future research agendas (Pickering *et al.* 2014; Post *et al.* 2020). In this review, we hybridize two relevant, yet seemingly opposing, approaches to SLRs: the integrative SLR (Elsbach and van Knippenberg 2020) and the problematizing SLR (Alvesson and Sandberg 2020). Integrative reviews lead to synthesis that lays the foundation for the creation of new frameworks and perspectives (Callahan 2014; Torraco 2005). Such reviews are highly justified when reconceptualization is needed in mature, yet fragmented, literatures. Hence, they are of value given the fragmented nature of the policy learning literature as they allow taking a full-stock inventory approach. On the other hand, problematized systematic reviews take a narrower approach aiming to reimagine literature through focused critical inter-rogation. This leads to enhanced perspectives on particular phenomena based on reflexivity, broad reading, focused selection, and problematizing, especially where conceptualization is sought (Alvesson and Sandberg 2020).

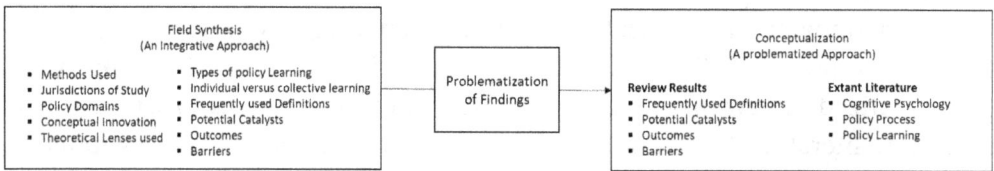

Figure 1: Methodological Overview

This inherently implies the potential for ontological re-alignment, thus is of value given the established influence of ontological positions in policy learning research. This problem-driven strand of SLRs also allows us to openly draw on a set of interdisciplinary intellectual resources otherwise not viable in integrative approaches (which is highly suited for our research objectives).

As the policy learning literature can be highly fragmented, heterogenous, yet also underpinned by a salient conceptual challenge, we find that an innovative phased hybridization of the two approaches (as demonstrated in Figure 1) to be valuable. An integrative approach to certain aspects of literature (e.g., research methods, regions of study, policy domains, definitions used, potential catalysts, outcomes, and barriers) can yield in-depth insights and for necessary synthesis. A problematized focus on the salient conceptual issue at hand is best suited for building a coherent background conceptualization of policy learning. Hence, after conducting a full-fledged integrative review, we identify and problematize the key results of our integrative review (the most frequently used definitions of policy learning) to critically interrogate underlying challenges and propose a conceptualization of policy learning. In this case, focused problematization allows analytical scrutiny of concepts and the identification of knowledge gaps. Thus, we "open up" the conceptualization of learning to insights from policy process, policy learning theory, and cognitive psychology literature.

Data Collection and Analysis

In addition to following Moher and others' (2009) PRISMA, we closely observe four key criteria of robust systematic approaches to literature reviews: *problem definitions* (as outlined in the introduction section), *search strategy, evaluation criteria*, and *data extraction and analysis* (Badger *et al.* 2000).

Search Strategy and Evaluation Criteria

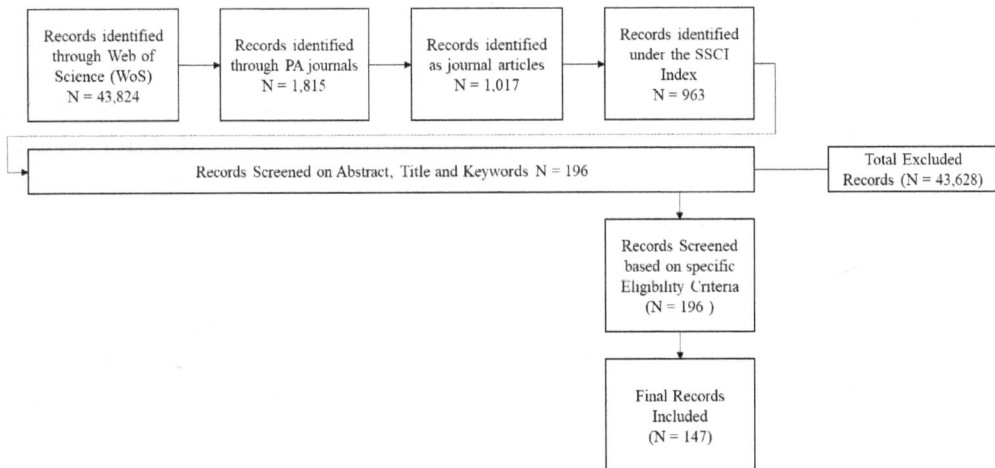

Figure 2: Data Collection Process

As illustrated in Figure 2, first, we conducted an electronic search in the Web of Science (WoS) database with "policy learning" as the keyword in the topic field (title, abstract, and keywords). Second, results were refined to include articles under the Public Administration category. Third, results were narrowed down to only include journal articles. The fourth step was identifying articles under the Web of Science Social Citation Index (SSCI) as a recognized benchmark for rigorous, high quality peer reviewed publications (Huijbregts, George, and Bekkers

2021; Bakır 2017). To ensure including all potentially relevant articles, no time constraint on publications was imposed. The last search update was conducted on September 23, 2020.

To evaluate articles for inclusion in the final dataset for coding, three steps were followed: First, non-English articles were excluded. Second, abstracts were screened to exclude non-empirical articles (in some cases, full article reads were required). Non-empirical articles (N = 21) were excluded from coding yet are used to enrich our discussion and analysis. We view non-empirical articles as purely conceptual or theoretical contributions that do not include an empirical case analysis.[1] Third, articles were fully read to exclude those with no tangible focus on, or implications for, policy learning. No removal of duplicates was necessary as the search was comprehensively conducted through the Web of Science (WoS) database. A final set of 147 articles was included for coding. A chronologically ordered list of included articles is available in Appendix I.

Data Extraction and Analysis

Developing coding categories was centered on linking research design with research questions and reducing the complexity of the coded attributes for meaningful insights and higher face validity. For that purpose, we developed two main coding categories allowing for the integration and problematization of our findings:

- Field synthesis attributes: A set of attributes focused on answering our first research question aimed at synthesizing the policy learning literature landscape. This category includes key identifiers of regions of study, policy domains, methodological approaches, novel conceptual/theoretical contributions, theoretical lenses used, types of policy learning, and instances of individual versus collective learning focus.

- Conceptual attributes: A set of attributes focused on answering our second research question aimed at identifying the current definitional state of policy learning by distilling key conceptual dimensions. This includes definitions used, potential catalysts, outcomes, and barriers. Selection of these attributes draws on the need to consider key bounding dimensions, characteristics, and entailments for conceptualizations in social sciences, particularly within issues of conceptual pluralism (Ansell 2019; Gerring 1999). Consistently, such attributes were used for similar purposes in earlier systematic reviews (see e.g., De Vries, Bekkers, and Tummers 2015).

---

1   Non-empirical (yet relevant) articles were excluded from the formal coding process to avoid introducing inconsistencies and imbalances in coding outputs given that several coding items do not necessarily apply to non-empirical/theoretical contributions (e.g., this includes regional jurisdiction of analysis and theoretical lens used). However, as above indicated these valuable and seminal contributions were still consistently used throughout the article. Examples include Bennett and Howlett (1992) and Dunlop and Radaelli (2017, 2018).

Using an integrative approach, results from the two coding categories are synthesized to showcase the empirical and conceptual landscape of policy learning research. This is followed by a problematized focus—through which conceptual attributes are triangulated with policy process, policy learning, and cognitive psychology literature (as a theoretical inspiration for widely used definitions of policy learning)—to scrutinize existing conceptualizations and propose a background conceptualization of policy learning. This addresses our third research question: how can policy learning be conceptualized? Finally, results from both coding items and the proposed conceptualization are used to formulate a future research agenda, thus addressing our fourth research question.

Coding was independently conducted by the first author to ensure uniformity. Iterative consultation, calibration, and alignment with co-authors was undertaken through regular meetings to ensure consistency. Coding was done over two stages to strengthen reliability. At the first stage, 20 percent of eligible articles were coded, then coding categories were refined and revisited. At the second stage, the remaining 80 percent of eligible articles were coded. All coded articles were then revisited to ensure uniformity. In the next section, we provide the results of our systematic review.

Results

In this section we present the results of the field synthesis attributes followed by the results of the conceptual attributes analysis.

Field Synthesis

Regions of Study

Coded articles represented empirical contributions from 29 regions of study (including cities, countries, local, national, and international collaborative/transnational frameworks). The five most frequently researched regions were: the United States (12 instances, 16.4 percent), the European Union (8 instances, 10.9 percent), the United Kingdom (8 instances, 10.9 percent), Australia (7 instances, 9.5 percent), and Canada and New Zealand (4 instances each, 5.48 percent). While several factors can contribute to region selection for empirical research, the existence of each of the most researched regions within some form of collaborative or federal governance arrangement can somewhat substantiate such configurations' role in catalyzing policy learning (see e.g., Kerber and Eckardt 2007; Weissert and Scheller 2008; Tamtik 2016). Consistently, regions within established networks or collaboration frameworks have been frequently studied in conjunction. For example, several studies with combinations of the United Kingdom, Canada, Australia, and New Zealand (see e.g., Legrand 2016; Stark 2019) or the European Union (see e.g., Bomberg 2007). Furthermore, 79 articles (53 percent) were presented within a comparative framework of more than one region or within a collaborative framework of multiple regions. This echoes findings by Dunlop and Radaelli (2020) on the instrumentality of comparative approaches for policy learning research and the value of policy learning as a theoretical lens for comparative policy analysis.

Policy Areas

We identified and grouped studies in 13 main policy areas. To facilitate analysis, each policy area has sub-categories of specific policy issues (see Appendix I for a full list of categories). The top five areas were consistent with the Primary Substantive Focus Areas" identified in the *Policy Studies Journal* public policy yearbook (Jenkins-Smith *et al.* 2020). Policy learning was most frequently studied in areas of: Environment (26 instances, 17.7 percent), Governance (23 instances, 15.6 percent), Economy (21 instances, 14.3 percent), Healthcare and Welfare (16 instances, 10.9 percent each).

Methodological Approaches

Our analysis shows that 125 articles (85 percent) used qualitative research methods, while 20 articles (13.6 percent) used quantitative methods, and two articles (1.4 percent) used mixed methods. Consistently, we observe a diverse set of data collection methods and sources. There is wide use of in-depth interviews (see e.g., Raudla *et al.* 2018; Dunlop, James, and Radaelli 2019), particularly semi-structured ones (see e.g., Thunus and Schoenaers 2017). This is methodologically known to allow for the exploration of expert and key informant insights. Given that most interviews are focused on experts and high-level officials, the number of interviewees was usually small, ranging from around 7-13 (see e.g., Marshall and Béland 2019; Dunlop, James, and Radaelli 2019) and going up to larger sets of around of 100 informants in exceptional cases (see e.g., Stark 2019). Additionally, there is consistent supplementary use of public documents and statements (see e.g., Crow *et al.* 2018), surveys and questionnaires ranging from 38 up to 666 respondents (see e.g., Lee and Van de Meene 2012; Pattison 2018; Montpetit 2009), and direct observations (see e.g., Thunus and Schoenaers 2017). Given these methodological choices, the case study form is most prominent (see e.g., Tavits 2003). This is consistent with what we know about policy learning research in terms of using multiple supplementary sources and thick descriptions to account for contextual factors (Moyson, Scholten, and Weible 2017). As for analytical methods, in addition to narrative case studies, there is some use of Process Tracing (see e.g., Motta 2018; Wilson 2019), and Qualitative Comparative Analysis (see e.g., Bandelow *et al.* 2017).

For quantitative studies, we observe the use of regressions and factor analysis, particularly with surveys and questionnaires (see e.g., Moyson, Scholten, and Weible 2017; Pattison 2018; Montpetit and Lachapelle 2017), multivariate regression analysis for historical data (see e.g., Lee 2017), and social Network Analysis (see e.g., Howlett, Mukherjee, and Koppenjan 2017; Lee and Van de Meene 2012).

Two articles using mixed methods adopted quantitative content and survey analyses with interviews and narrative case studies (Mossberger and Hale 2002; Baekkeskov and Öberg 2016).

Novel Conceptual and Theoretical Contributions

While most empirical articles naturally contribute to some refinement of theoretical understandings, we elect to focus on salient, clearly pronounced conceptual/theoretical contributions. Here, we identified 21 articles (14.2 percent) making both salient theoretical propositions grounded in empirical research. This closely converges with the 18 percent observed by Gerlak and others (2018) in the field of environmental research. Such contributions are usually in the form of new interdisciplinary theoretical propositions aimed at refining understandings of policy learning dynamics. For example, Kamkhaji and Radaelli (2017) reconceptualize causal mechanisms of policy change in crisis, and Nowlin (2020) offers a model of disproportionate information processing in policy-oriented learning. This also includes constructing analytical frameworks to streamline policy learning modalities such as Dunlop's (2009) typology of policy maker-expert exchanges in epistemic policy learning. Notably, 11 out of the 21 articles identified use multiple regions in their empirical analyses, thus substantiating the leverage of comparative approaches in conceptual synthesis and theory extension.

Theoretical Lenses Used

Our findings show that in 37 instances (25 percent), articles did not clearly establish a theoretical lens of inquiry. In the remaining set of articles, we observe the use of single and multiple theoretical lenses amounting to a total of 141 instances. Within this set, "policy learning" as an overarching (yet largely ambiguous lens) was employed in 32 instances (22.6 percent), the advocacy coalition framework (ACF) at 24 instances (17 percent), policy transfer at 17 instances (12 percent), policy diffusion at 8 instances (5.6 percent), epistemic communities, network theory, and organizational learning at 7 instances each (4.9 percent), social learning, lesson drawing, and policy convergence at 5 (3.5 percent), 4 (2.83 percent), and 3 (2.1 percent) instances, respectively.

Types of Policy Learning

Consistent with proliferating fragmentation, we observe a substantial set of policy learning types. In 48 instances (32.6 percent), there was no clearly articulated type or label for the policy learning variant studied. For the remaining instances, we identified a staggering set of 61 different policy learning types. Though these types of learning could be conceptually similar, they can be presented under different labels (seldom defined). Hence, it becomes highly subjective to discern whether they can be amalgamated, combined, or taxonomized. The ten most observed types of learning are presented in Table 1.

Table 1: Most Observed Policy Learning Types

Rank	Learning Type	Frequency	Percentage (%)	Examples
1	Instrumental Learning	26	14.86	(Lee and Van de Meene 2012)
2	Social Learning	25	14.29	(Mooney and Lee 1999)
3	Organizational and Institutional Learning	17	9.71	(Stark and Head 2019; Nilsson 2006)
4	Political Learning	14	8	(Jenkins-Smith 1988)
5	Individual Learning	8	4.57	(Dudley 2007)
6	Epistemic Learning	7	4	(Baekkeskov 2016)
7	Network Learning	5	2.86	(Tamtik 2016)
8	Lesson Drawing	4	2.29	(Klochikhin 2013)
9	Reflexive Learning	4	2.29	(Dunlop 2015)
10	Single Loop Learning	4	2.29	(Di Mascio et al. 2016)

The remaining types of learning were observed in very low frequencies: conceptual learning at three instances (1.71 percent), diffusion, governance learning, government learning, policy transfer, positive learning, self-directed learning, strategic learning, thick and thin learning at two instances each (1.14 percent) while the 40 remaining types each at one instance (0.57 percent). The findings on frequently used types of learning draw parallels with a recent review of learning in the environmental policy domain where social and organizational learning were also observed to be some of the most frequently used (see Gerlak et al. 2018).

Individual versus Collective Learning

In our dataset, 117 out of 147 articles (79.5 percent) discussed policy learning on the collective level (e.g., institutions, organizations, government, governance, coalitions, etc.). This included the use of theoretical frameworks such as the ACF (see e.g., Bandelow et al. 2017), Institutional and Organizational Learning (see e.g., Dunlop 2015), or networks (see e.g., Malkamäki et al. 2019). Eleven articles (7.5 percent) discussed policy learning on the individual level (offering a model of individual learning or studying—in some degree—the determinants or facets of learning behavior on the individual level). This also featured theoretical frameworks including the ACF (see e.g., Dudley 2007), and information processing theory (see e.g., Nowlin 2020). Nineteen articles (13 percent) discussed learning on both the individual and collective levels (e.g., focused on the relationships between levels, relationships between individual learning and collective learning outcomes, etc.). Those also featured a tangible use of the ACF as a theoretical framework (see e.g., Nedergaard 2009).

Conceptual Attributes

In this section, we elaborate on the synthesis of salient conceptual dimensions of policy learning by showcasing its potential catalysts, outcomes, barriers, and different definitions employed in literature. This is aimed at addressing our second research question on the current definitional state of policy learning.

Potential Catalysts, Outcomes, and Barriers

Given the field's established inclination toward qualitative methods, identifying such attributes from a causal or correlative standpoint can be challenging. Hence, we present a non-exhaustive set of potential catalysts, outcomes, and barriers associated with policy learning identified through an in-depth second cycle inductive coding (Miles and Huberman 1994). By drawing on policy process theory and policy learning literature, we find that potential catalysts, outcomes, and barriers fall under one of four distinct categories: Information and Knowledge-related, Systems and Structures-related, Actor-related, and Context-related. To ensure rigor and consistency, the inductively identified attributes (potential catalysts, outcomes, barriers) are vetted against an understanding of different theories of policy learning and the policy process. For example, the role of politically adversarial attitudes in light of Sabatier's ACF, or the certification of actors in light of Dunlop and Radaelli's (2013) scope conditions for the genera of learning, etc.

Tables 2, 3, and 4 list the main catalysts, outcomes, and barriers we collated.

Table 2: Potential Catalysts of Policy Learning[2]

Levels	Examples
Information and Knowledge	Information flow and communication, and transparency. Access to clear evidence and information, evaluations, and impact assessments, nature and analytical tractability of problems, framing, discourse, and narratives.
Systems and Structures	Networks and coordination frameworks, institutional structures, mandates and capacities, government structures and systems, political support, structured engagement with expertise, and learning governance, leadership support.
Actors	Actor learning and legal abilities, policy brokers and entrepreneurs, advocacy coalitions and lobbying, individual preferences, experiences and ties, engagement of stakeholders, and scope of affected groups.
Context	Public pressure, exogenous shocks, and intensity of focusing events, contextual factors and context similarities, level of political contestation, and conflict.

---

2   In this context, potential catalysts are viewed as conditions that can facilitate engaging in policy learning whether as preconditions, antecedents, or moderators (depending on the configuration of context).

Table 3: Outcomes Associated with Policy Learning

Levels	Examples
Information and Knowledge	Cognitive updates, changes of beliefs and attitudes.
Systems and Structures	Establishing new structures and systems, institutional change, discourse and policy institutionalization, administrative and general reforms, enhanced accountability, policy change and adoption, new legislation, policy failure, new policy initiatives.
Actors	Coalition formation, growth of collective intelligence, convergence for collective action, updated understanding of policy instruments, goal transformation, policy coordination and convergence.
Context	Adaptability to contexts and policy adaption.

Table 4: Potential Barriers to Policy Learning

Levels	Examples
Information and Knowledge	Issue complexity, diverging paradigms and ontological assumptions, echo chambers, belief entrenchments, lack of clear and reliable knowledge, lack of openness and transparency.
Systems and Structures	Lack of government support, rigid hierarchies with specific varieties of learning, lack and distortion of incentives, limited political and institutional capacity, absence of debate platforms, weak learning governance, institutional and policy amnesia, budgetary constraints.
Actors	Low certification of teaching actors, ambivalence toward expertise, policy makers' lack of time and attention, lack of influential interest groups, adversarial attitudes.
Context	Partisanship, and high political contestation, context dissimilarities, lack of scope conditions for proper learning typologies, conflict between learning outcomes and established norms.

Two necessary nuances exist here. First, the above tables should be viewed as guiding and overarching logical frames encompassing different parameters within commonly permeable dimensions. For example, parameters such as adversarial attitudes or contexts can be studied as internal properties of actors or as external properties of a policy environment (see e.g., Karlsen and Larrea 2016). Thus, the dimensions (and parameters therein) identified should be not viewed as rigid or non-permeable structures. Second, given the established features of policy learning research and the conceptual pluralism (and often ambiguity) of policy learning types in the above tables, we treat different types of policy learning as one in terms of their association to certain potential catalysts, outcomes, and barriers. Thus, we do not create tightly coupled associations between varieties of learning (e.g., social learning, single loop learning, instrumental learning, etc.) and certain potential catalysts, outcomes, and barriers.

Table 5: Frequently Used Definitions of Policy Learning

Sn.	Definition	Frequency	Percentage (%)	Examples
1	Policy learning is understood as the updating of policy beliefs based on knowledge and information on the policy problem at hand.	14	18.9	(Raudla *et al.* 2018)
2	Relatively enduring alterations of thought or behavioral intentions that result from experience and are concerned with the attainment or revision of policy objectives.	13	17.6	(Pattison 2018; Rough 2011)
3	A process in which knowledge about policies, administrative arrangements, institutions etc. in one time and/or place is used in the development of policies, administrative arrangements, and institutions in another time and/or place.	8	10.8	(Newman and Bird 2017; Bomberg 2007)
4	A deliberate attempt to adjust the goals or techniques of policy in response to past experience and new information.	7	9.5	(Kerber and Eckardt 2007)
5	The commonly described tendency for some policy decisions to be made on the basis of knowledge and past experiences and knowledge-based judgments as to future expectations.	2	2.7	(Karlsen and Larrea 2016)
5.1	Learning is associated with the "viability of policy interventions or implementation designs."[3]	2	2.7	(Yackee and Palus 2010)

---

3   Definitions 5 and 5.1 were both of the same frequency; given that this list is ordered by frequencies, we have listed both definitions at the 5th rank.

Definitions: A Definitional State of the Art

An analysis of policy learning definitions substantiates endemic conceptual ambiguity and fragmentation issues. Lending substantiation to claims of conceptual ambiguity, 81 (51 percent) articles identified provided no definition for policy learning. This also aligns with findings from Gerlak and others (2018), indicating that in their dataset on learning in environmental studies, 58 percent of articles did not provide a definition of policy learning. Lending substantiation to claims of conceptual fragmentation, we identified 34 distinct definitions in the remaining 66 articles. In Table 5, we list the most frequent approaches to defining policy learning (used for more than one instance each).

Discussion

In this article, we set out to conduct a systematic review of policy learning research driven by the need to address conceptual ambiguity, fragmentation, and cohesion issues. This is in addition to synthesizing the field's growing body of literature. In doing so, we aimed to answer four central questions:

What is the Current Landscape of Policy Learning Research?

Piecing together the results of our field synthesis attributes indeed confirms that policy learning is blossoming with scholarly and practical interest (Bakır 2017). Yet the debate around conceptual advancement has been often Sisyphean. On one hand, a scholarly stream calls for organizing research within existing frameworks and stepping back from adding new concepts to avoid further splintering (see e.g., Goyal and Howlett 2018), while another stream sees room for conceptual innovation and new approaches, yet grounded in existing categories (see e.g., Maggetti and Gilardi 2016; Dunlop and Radaelli 2018). There is a steady flow of theoretical and conceptual contributions (both offering new angles and re-organizing within existing literature) employed to address critical contemporary issues such as the environment, the economy, healthcare, and governance. Methodologically, the field is largely inclined toward qualitative research designs, particularly given their ability to consider contextual factors and elucidate underlying relationships. Consequently, there is significant reliance on data source triangulation from public documents and expert interviews. There is also a tendency to utilize comparative and multiple case studies. Most cases lie within collaborative governance/policy arrangements (e.g., the European Union, Commonwealth, etc.). Interestingly, though policy learning is known to positively influence governance and policy outcomes, research within developing economies and the global south is relatively scarce.

Theoretically, multiple theoretical lenses can elucidate novel aspects. However, their fragmentation and ambiguity can pose challenges for homogeneity, consistency, and knowledge accumulation, thus potentially obscuring causal relationships and inducing discrepancies in empirical findings (Garcia and Calantone 2002; Harmancioglu, Droge, and Calantone 2009). Similar findings on theoretical and analytical lens fragmentation and ambiguity have been observed within some sub-domains of policy learning literature (see e.g., Gerlak *et al.* 2018). Our results here show an obvious case of theoretical lens ambiguity and fragmentation. This can partly explain the field's restricted ability to organize, systematize, and taxonomize findings, particularly given its qualitative inclinations (see Collins and Stockton 2018).

What is the Current Definitional State of Policy Learning in Said Literature?

Piecing together our conceptual synthesis attributes creates a high-resolution image of the field's conceptual ambiguity and fragmentation. Our data shows that 51 percent of the articles did not offer a definition of policy learning, while the remaining 49 percent employed 34 different definitions. The most frequently employed definitions are based on the seminal ACF's definition of policy-oriented learning, largely centered on policy learning being an update of beliefs and behaviors (attitudes, positions, and actions) toward policy issues. This is consistent with our findings indicating that the ACF is one of the most frequently employed theoretical lenses of inquiry. We observe 61 different labels (indicating types of learning) that are seldom defined, and hence discerning their conceptual proximity to one another remains a challenging endeavor.

However, amid fragmentation and ambiguity, there are semblances of consistency. As key conceptual entailments: potential catalysts, outcomes, and barriers to policy learning can be viewed within four distinct categories highly consistent with our understanding of the policy process and policy learning theory. These are: knowledge, actors, systems and structures, and context. Thus, we postulate that drawing on the problematic issues of commonly used definitions, while leveraging underlying consistencies in the extant literature, can assist in offering a coherent background conceptualization of policy learning.

Implications for Theory: How Can Policy Learning be Better Conceptualized and Defined?

In this section, we conceptualize policy learning by adopting a three-stage process. First, we engaged in critical interrogation of the most frequently used definitions using a problematized approach. At this stage, we critically reflect on frequently used definitions in terms of their ability to act as background or overarching conceptualizations of policy learning while fully acknowledging their merits and appropriateness in their specific contexts. Second, we leveraged the results of this systematic review along with the extant policy learning and policy process literature to propose a conceptualization of policy learning. Third, we scrutinized our proposed conceptualization against the criteria of conceptual goodness by Gerring (1999).

A Problematized View

A Critical Interrogation of Definitions

An analysis of the most frequently used definitions shows two sets of epistemological issues (see Table 5): first, the underpinnings of ACF-driven definitions of policy learning (particularly definitions 1 and 2); and second, relatively limited acknowledgement of other frequently used definitions of the embeddedness of said learning within a nuanced policy process with salient structural dimensions (particularly definitions 3, 4, 5, and 5.1). Furthermore, a persisting issue among the most frequently used definitions is the conflation between the processual nature of policy learning and the outcomes of such a process. In this section, we elaborate on the implications of such issues and draw on an interdisciplinary set of resources to propose a conceptualization of policy learning.

ACF-Inspired Definitions

This set of definitions is centered on the notion of "policy-oriented learning" proposed by Sabatier (1988) in his seminal ACF, thus conceptualizing policy learning mainly as changes in beliefs sometimes leading to changes in behaviors. This is with the caveat of contingent learning highlighted by Kamkhaji and Radaelli (2017), indicating that genuine processes of learning can follow (and not precede) observable behavioral changes under certain conditions. While this approach can be suited for the adversarial nature of the ACF, its underlying hypotheses, and its micro foundational cognitive model of learning, we put forward two main critiques. First, it highlights the inherent limitations of this approach in capturing the nuances and complexity of individual learning in its discipline of origin (cognitive functional psychology), and how these limitations are exacerbated when this approach is used in the complex multilevel, multi-actor study of public policy. Second, it illuminates the relatively limited ability of this approach to function as an overarching definition or a background conceptualization that is able to capture the diverse meanings associated with the complex and diverse phenomena of policy learning, especially beyond the specific micro foundational approach it utilizes (for a discussion on background concepts, see Adcock and Collier 2001; Maggetti and Gilardi 2016).

ACF-inspired definitions draw on cognitive and functional definitions of learning nested in the creases of psychological studies. Thus, they view learning as an impact of experience on behavior or as "enduring changes in mechanisms of behavior" (Lachman 1997; Domjan 2010). Indeed, learning is an inherently cognitive process—this has been asserted through policy learning literature. However, an almost exclusive reliance on this approach to defining learning can be conceptually and empirically challenging, mainly due to the conflation between learning as a mechanistic or organic process and the outcomes or products of such learning (expressed as changes of thoughts or behaviors) (Ormrod 2008). This is given the commonly obscured causal pathways between experience, behavioral change, and learning on one hand, and the latencies between cues and perceived outcomes on the other (De Houwer, Barnes-Holmes, and Moors 2013). In a public policy environment, these issues become even more perplexing, particularly with the temporal space and causal relationships between learning and behavioral change being far more complex, obscured (and often delayed) given the density, diversity, and interconnectedness within modern policy systems (see Borrás 2011). Such approaches to learning (even in the less dense contexts of individual learning psychology) make it "unlikely that one can find an observable change in behavior that provides a proxy for the change in the organism that is assumed to define learning" and renders such functional definitions "overinclusive" (De Houwer, Barnes-Holmes, and Moors 2013; De Houwer 2011).

Overreliance on functional definitions has had evident implications for policy learning research. This manifests in policy learning being dubbed a "black box" (Lee and Van de Meene 2012), with researchers facing challenges ascertaining the learning inspirations of actors (Legrand 2012), identifying when learning has taken place, potentially confusing learning, and the products of learning as Malkamäki and others (2019) warn, or elucidating causal pathways between learning, the update of policy beliefs, and behavioral change or change in action (Leifeld 2013).

Another issue pertinent to such definitions is the conflation of policy learning as a multidimensional practice embedded within the policy process and a densely populated policy universe, with policy learning as a micro-foundational cognitive component process or "learning about policy." In that sense, we see a manifestation of how policy learning can become conceptually "overinclusive." This issue is exacerbated with the growing complexities of the "policy universe" as an aggregation of a vast array of interconnected private, public, social, local actors involved in the policy process where policy making spans multiple stakeholders (Howlett, Mukherjee, and Koppenjan 2017). Here, an ontological disconnect can be observed in using functional micro foundational conceptualizations of learning to research causal relationships in complex policy systems, which literature already shows has micro-meso-macro interactions as demonstrated by Dunlop and Radaelli (2017). Last, but not least, solely utilizing the ACF's approach to conceptualizing policy learning can somewhat mute the learning process. This is particularly so, given that the ACF's view of learning-driven policy change is mainly due to exogenous shocks or pressures. This constricts the space for other drivers and modes of learning such as experimental governance or reflexive learning (see e.g., Dunlop and Radaelli 2013). It is important to emphasize that our critique of this approach to conceptualizing policy learning does not argue against the inherent micro-foundational cognitive nature of learning. However, it pertains to the ability of such an approach to account for the complexity of learning in the policy process at the individual level, and to provide an overarching background concept that is able to capture the complexity and multi-levelness of such learning process.

Other Frequently Used Definitions

As background concepts, other frequently used definitions (3, 4, 5, and 5.1) draw relatively limited relevance to the structural dimensions salient in extant policy learning and policy process literatures. Thus, they risk empirical myopia or oversight of potentially relevant and central influences on learning. Furthermore, they also conflate the process of learning, with its products or outcomes. Thus, they do not offer an entirely internally consistent conceptual framework over which empirical designs can be built, and where knowledge can be streamlined. This can partly explain the field's limited conceptual cohesion, and restrained ability to systemize and cultivate findings across research lines (see e.g., Stark 2019; Maggetti and Gilardi 2016). These issues articulate the need for an internally consistent conceptualization of policy learning that is grounded in empirical realities of public policy and policy learning literature, while maneuvering shortcomings of existing conceptualizations.

Conceptualizing Policy Learning

Given our findings, we argue that an ontological re-alignment toward a policy-theory grounded conceptualization of learning can alleviate some of the field's conceptual burdens. This nudges the concept into "policy-embedded learning," where learning is submerged within the fabric and context of the policy process, rather than policy-oriented learning where overinclusive and cognitively functional phenomena of learning about policies occur. To do so, we leverage two main inputs, first: our findings on main conceptual dimensions of policy learning (i.e., potential catalysts, barriers, outcomes, and definitional themes), second: structural dimensions of conjointly governing literatures of the policy process and policy learning.

Structural Conceptual Dimensions

Drawing on our review results, we find that an inductive categorization of potential catalysts, outcomes, and barriers for policy learning into actors, systems and structures, information and knowledge, and context is consistent with key elements salient in major theories of the policy process and policy learning (even when expressed with occasionally varying labels). This, for example, includes the multiple streams framework (Kingdon 1984), the policy systems approach (Easton 1965), the Institutional Analysis Development Framework (Ostrom 2007), and the collective learning theory (Heikkila and Gerlak 2013). Policy learning literature also acknowledges the salience of these dimensions as inherent core features as we highlight below:

- *Information and Knowledge*: policy-related information and knowledge are the raw material for learning, thus they played a foundational role in the emergence of policy learning as a supplemental understanding to power-based policy making (Bennett and Howlett 1992; Heclo 1974). The role of information and knowledge has been salient in various conceptualizations under the umbrella of policy learning such as policy transfer and convergence among other theoretical approaches (see e.g., Casey and Gold 2006; Heikkila and Gerlak 2013; Nilsson 2006). Policy learning literature acknowledges that knowledge is highly interactive across various dimensions, actors, and contexts, and thus its presence permeates the structural dimensions of what constitutes a policy system (Montpetit and Lachapelle 2017).

- *Context Submergence*: policy learning is entwined with its context (Karlsen and Larrea 2016). The relationship between learning and its context is both dialectic and discursive and moves beyond sensitivity to full context submergence. In many cases, policy-making contexts provide conditions that significantly shape pathologies and outcomes of learning (see e.g., Dunlop 2017; Dunlop, James, and Radaelli 2019). Contextual factors can influence how policy learning is used, whether as means for political assertion, legitimization, or even survival (Toens and Landwehr 2009; Weiss 1986). Thus, policy makers also grapple with the political and power ramifications of learning outcomes within highly contested issues and contexts (Laffin and Ormston 2013). It follows that influences of power, political, and contextual factors are inseparable from policy learning, particularly given that learning emerged as a supplemental (and not a substitute) explanation for power-based politics.

- *Actor Centrality:* Agency perspectives have started taking some initial steps in the policy learning literature (see e.g., Borrás 2011; Zhang and Yu 2019). Various types of actors play central roles in shaping and directing learning. For example, the role of individual actors is critical to policy learning, not only as constructors and re-constructors of policy issues, but as cross-pollinators shaping issues across organizations and coalitions. This brings micro foundational cognitive biases, perceptions, and issue constructions to the forefront (see e.g., Dudley 2007; Heikkila and Gerlak 2013). Additionally, within policy learning, organizational actors interact with other individual and organizational actors, institutional norms, and discursive structures, in a manner that shapes and directs learning as well across policy contexts and levels; micro, meso, and macro (see e.g., Checkel 2001; Zito 2009; Stark and Head 2019).

- *Systems and Structures*: as the literature shows, policy learning does not occur in a vacuum, rather within institutional systems and structures (Moyson, Scholten, and Weible 2017). Such structures (organizational, institutional, or otherwise) have norms, tendencies, and preferences that can largely shape policy learning by interacting with various elements of policy systems (see e.g., Checkel 2001, 2009; Lee, Hwang, and Moon 2020). However, the embeddedness and interaction of policy learning within structures in policy systems still requires more emphasis (Bomberg 2007).

Based on the findings of our review of the extant policy learning and policy process literature, and the above identified dimensions distilled from empirical works, we offer an overarching and background conceptualization that can be used to supplement and complement existing definitions of particular modes of policy learning. Thus, we conceptualize policy learning as *the circulation and consumption of policy issue-related information and knowledge among actors in a policy system and structure, within a policy* context (see Figure 3).

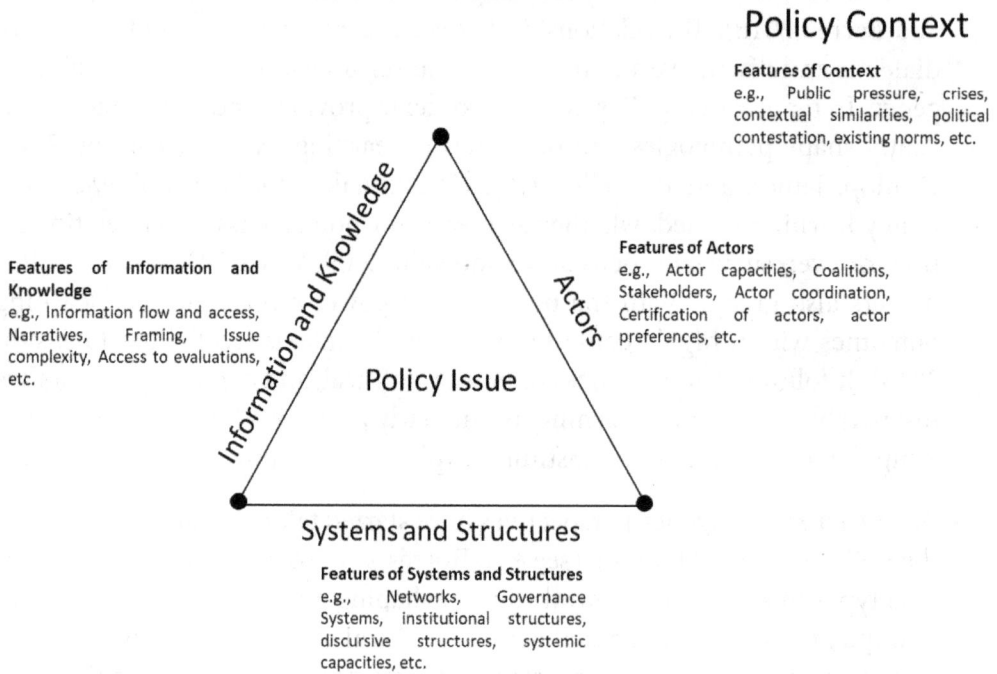

Policy Context

Features of Context
e.g., Public pressure, crises, contextual similarities, political contestation, existing norms, etc.

Features of Information and Knowledge
e.g., Information flow and access, Narratives, Framing, Issue complexity, Access to evaluations, etc.

Information and Knowledge

Policy Issue

Actors

Features of Actors
e.g., Actor capacities, Coalitions, Stakeholders, Actor coordination, Certification of actors, actor preferences, etc.

Systems and Structures

Features of Systems and Structures
e.g., Networks, Governance Systems, institutional structures, discursive structures, systemic capacities, etc.

Figure 3: A Background Conceptualization of Policy Learning

In this context, the circulation and consumption of knowledge and information express varying degrees of "depth of interaction." This ranges from a mere circulation of policy-related knowledge and information (known to increase awareness of policy issues or induce tangible implications for the policy-making agenda), to in-depth dialectic and discursive engagement with knowledge and information (across levels, systems, and structures) that spans different processes such as sense making, translation, negotiation, and institutionalization (see e.g., Heikkila and Gerlak 2013; Sabatier 1988).

We contrast this conceptualization against the key features of "conceptual goodness" proposed by Gerring (1999) as a guiding framework for concept formation in social sciences: *familiarity, resonance, parsimony, coherence, differentiation, depth, theoretical,* and *field utility.* While policy learning enjoys significant scholarly interest, rearranging the concept under the same label is preferrable to introducing a new conceptual label (Maggetti and Gilardi 2016; Goyal and Howlett 2018). This provides familiarity and resonance. The conceptual statement is also both syntactically and logically *parsimonious.* In terms of *coherence,* this conceptualization directly draws on the empirical attributes of policy learning as the phenomenon in question. Thus, it provides a non-coincidental typologically sensible grouping of policy learning's underlying dimensions (Gerring 1999; e.g., Hamilton 1987). With respect to *differentiation,* this conceptualization delimits and defines a policy process-embedded view of learning and separates policy learning from its outcomes, thus allowing a clear and theoretically consistent view of the phenomenon. Clearly bounding the concept allows for the distinction between policy learning and other seemingly similar and often confounding concepts and mechanisms (e.g., policy transfer, policy convergence, etc.). In ensuring differentiation, we also lay the groundwork for operationalization, given that the former is a precursor of the latter (Gerring 1999). The proposed conceptualization also meets the central criterion of *depth,* where we draw on and "bundle" core defining characteristics of the concept (Gerring 1999). In our case, such characteristics are grounded in empirical findings, policy process, and learning literatures—it is of *theoretical utility.* By adopting a classificatory view, this conceptualization creates a high-level hierarchal category that allows for the overlay and placement of existing policy learning theories and concepts (e.g., collective learning: Heikkila and Gerlak 2013; epistemic learning: Haas 1992; Policy Transfer: Dolowitz and Marsh 2002, etc.). This largely eliminates potential spillover effects on existing concepts within a field of study resulting from the introduction of novel conceptualizations (Ansell 2019). In doing so, we avoid compromising the conceptual integrity of other concepts in the field (i.e., through inducing or proposing changes to established concepts), thus achieving a substantial degree of *field utility.*

Conceptual Utility

The proposed conceptualization offers five main merits. *First,* it builds on a view of policy learning that is grounded in both theoretically and empirically substantial dimensions of policy learning and policy theory. *Second,* it offers an overarching, dynamic, and adaptable framework for modelling and weighing different case-sensitive contexts in policy learning research. *Third,* with clearly articulated dimensions, it allows for better systemization, accumulation, and mapping of findings serving as an analytical framework of policy learning processes. *Fourth,* it emphasizes the nuanced and interactive nature of policy learning. For example, the interaction between agency and structure has been previously pointed out in the literature (see e.g., Zhang and Yu 2019). However, modeling in other salient dimensions, such as context and knowledge, in an overarching conceptualization of policy learning has been lacking. This conceptualization embraces the highly interactive and dynamic nature of policy learning, particularly with growing tendencies toward networked governance, deliberation, collaborative partnerships, and complex networked spaces (Sanderson 2009; Malkamäki *et al.* 2019). It does so by illustrating the simultaneous interaction points between actors, systems and structures, information and knowledge, and context, particularly with the expansion of the policy universe and the growing influence of non-linear and non-hierarchal models of the policy process (Sotarauta 2012; Crozier 2008). Hence, as a background conceptualization, it falls in line with being "a general idea which, once having been tagged, substantially generalized, and explicated, can effectively guide inquiry into seemingly diverse phenomena" as explained by Merton (1984).

This conceptualization also advances the ongoing debate on what can constitute evidence of policy learning (see e.g., Montpetit and Lachapelle 2017; Bennett and Howlett 1992). The literature shows that outcomes of policy learning usually fall within two broad categories: *cognitive* or inward products, such as updates of cognition, intelligence, awareness, or beliefs; and *behavioral* or outward products, such as policy or narrative changes. In both categories, the outcomes of learning can be both confirmatory (thus affirming the *status quo*) or negatory (thus acting against the *status quo*). Linking the proposed conceptualization with the observable and potential manifestations of learning (cognitive and behavioral) can assist in discerning what constitutes evidence of learning. This, of course, does not speak to the quality, or utility of learning, as it can still be misdirected or failure-inducing (see e.g., Dunlop 2017). Establishing links to the proposed conceptualization can guard against the inclusion of non-genuine instances of learning, particularly given the long temporal frames often associated with policy learning research which can introduce potentially confounding or "learning-like" phenomena (see e.g., Radaelli 2009).

Conclusions: How Can the Results of Our Systematic Literature Review Inform a Future Research Agenda?

After carefully tiptoeing through the conceptual minefield, we now leverage our findings to offer two sets of conclusions to inform a future research agenda, hopefully clearing some mines. The first set is spurred by the results of our systematic field synthesis, and the second is inspired by our proposed conceptualization of policy learning.

First, results based on our field synthesis call on policy learning researchers to consider three main aspects. *Theoretically* articulating the definitions of policy learning (and the logics of choice) upon which empirical research is designed, and thus consolidating ontological positions and enhancing theoretical grounding (Gerlak *et al.* 2018). The same can be argued for theoretical lenses used to study policy learning, whether as the *explanandum* or the *explanans*, two main approaches to the study of policy learning outlined by Dunlop and Radaelli (2020).

This also applies to delineating the types and levels of learning and their interactions within studied cases. Clearly explicating those aspects can enhance synthesis and knowledge accumulation. This also can enable theory building and extension research by drawing on more nuanced and relatively less ambiguous empirical configurations. Such considerations pertinent to theoretical clarity can contribute to strengthening the field's theoretical cohesion (see Collins and Stockton 2018). This can also enhance our ability to conduct replication research as well as contextualize and extend research findings to different settings.

Methodologically, while qualitative methods in policy learning have significant exploratory leverage that can illuminate complex relationships and interactions (see e.g., Raudla *et al.* 2018; Dunlop, James, and Radaelli 2019; Thunus and Schoenaers 2017), the field is yet to garner the full potential of quantitative and mixed methods. Through this article, and by drawing on policy learning literature, we have argued for—and showcased—the complex, multi-leveled, and multi-actor nature of policy learning. We certainly observe that the largely qualitative methodological approaches to the empirical research analyzed are indeed rigorous and suitable for the respective research objectives. Yet if future scholarship is to engage in research endeavors that consider the multi-level, multi-actor, and complex features of policy learning (as we find is warranted), qualitative methods in standalone mode might not necessarily be sufficient in all cases. Thus, mixed-methods research can allow for broader understandings and interpretations, particularly for complex phenomena and systems (Molina-Azorin 2016; McKim 2015). This can contribute to enhancing structured knowledge accumulation and eventually enable the conduction of policy learning metanalyses. As our analysis offers an empirical toolkit of potential catalysts, outcomes, and barriers associated with policy learning. A first step on the path can be to map those relationships and their associations under different configurations building on existing frameworks using a range of context-sensitive quantitative and mixed methods.

Empirically, the geographical dispersion of research calls for more attention to empirical accounts on policy learning from developing and transitioning countries. The growing role of public international organizations and their learning influences within developing economies lends additional importance to conducting more research within such contexts as relatively vibrant and pristine environments with for potential policy learning. Future research in this avenue can illuminate key areas pertinent to the interplay between economic development, policy, and political legacies, politico-administrative traditions, and policy learning. This can enable nuanced comparative cross-national and cross-regional comparisons toward more in-depth understandings of causal mechanisms and the influence of policy learning (both as a cause and an effect) on policy design and outcomes within new contexts, as encouraged by Dunlop and Radaelli (2020).

Second, we leverage our proposed conceptualization of policy learning to propose a coherent future research agenda over three main lines of action. *The-*

oretically building on existing theories and concepts of policy learning (see e.g., Collective learning: Heikkila and Gerlak 2013; Advocacy coalitions: Sabatier 1988; Epistemic learning: Haas 1992; Policy transfer: Dolowitz and Marsh 2002; Genera of learning: Dunlop and Radaelli 2013) by elaborately plotting and mapping their positions from the proposed conceptualization. This includes using this conceptualization to unpack existing concepts into meaningful taxonomies that delineate their nature whether as super/sub-ordinate concepts, products/outcomes, types, or mechanisms, of learning. This is in addition to using the proposed conceptualization to scale existing approaches to defining and operationalizing policy learning across multiple levels of analysis complementarily.

Bridging the *theoretical-empirical divide*, the proposed conceptualization can be utilized as an analytical framework with three main foci on: illuminating multi-level interactions, clarifying the relationship between policy learning and policy change, and developing measurements. Here, we view an analytical framework as a structure of theoretically grounded simplifying ontological propositions (assumptions) that are useful to understanding complex phenomena with applicability across multiple contexts (Dunlop and Radaelli 2018).

We start by employing the proposed conceptualization to illuminate multi-level micro-meso-macro interactions (see: Dunlop and Radaelli 2017). Throughout this article, we have argued for the complex, interactive, and interconnected nature of policy learning, and that in many cases, learning types are seldom standalone or constant. We have also showcased that the structural dimensions identified in our conceptualization (i.e., actors, information and knowledge, systems and structures, and context) are often in a state of flux across multiple levels simultaneously (individual, organizational, systemic, etc.). As such, they can interact and vary even within single units of analysis (see Biegelbauer 2016). Thus, simultaneously scaling the proposed conceptualization across multiple levels of analysis can leverage more nuanced investigation of complex policy-learning phenomena. It also allows the overlay of different micro-meso-macro policy-learning theories and theoretical lenses and plotting their interactions across different levels within single and multiple cases. This can also help elaborate on (and taxonomize) the micro, meso, and macro level factors acting as catalysts or barriers to policy learning and establishing their relationships to outcomes under different configurations within existing frameworks. Doing so can contribute to a needed dialectic and discursive process of hypotheses formulation and testing in the policy-learning literature. Naturally, such an approach ties into our aforementioned call for more use of quantitative and mixed-methods research.

Another enticing prospect of using this conceptualization as a multi-leveled analytical framework pertains to exploring the enigmatic and "analytically blurred" causal relationship between policy learning and policy change. Stronger and more robust research designs can be achieved through mapping relationships between micro foundational, meso, and macro-level influences using the proposed conceptualization as a new and refined approach that allows for systematic comparisons across different levels of analysis (see e.g., Moyson, Scholten, and Weible 2017; Dunlop and Radaelli 2017). The proposed conceptualization's clear structural elements provide ample space for using configurational approaches and methods to unravel causal inferences, particularly those between policy learning and policy change (see e.g., Thomann and Maggetti 2017; Dunlop and Radaelli 2017). Once again, this ties into our earlier call for hypotheses generation and testing to be enabled through a wider range of methodological tools at different levels.

Last, but not least, with a growing research agenda on measuring policy learning, we call for future research that operationalizes this conceptualization to create multi-dimensional measurements and scales for policy learning while leveraging existing approaches to measurement (e.g., Radaelli 2009; Moyson, Scholten, and Weible 2017; Pattison 2018).

On the *practical* plane we call for utilizing the proposed conceptualization and toolkit of potential catalysts, outcomes, and barriers to offer policy makers and practitioners a framework for designing frameworks and processes that can facilitate effective and efficient policy learning. In doing so, we extend Dunlop and Radaelli's (2018) "wider audiences" call by opening up policy learning as a practice to exploring "what can go wrong" and identifying how can key factors be managed toward enhancing policy-learning processes within different contexts.

Finally, as we are naturally limited by the available analytical capacity to synthesize a manageable number of resources, future reviews, and syntheses can build on and extend our review by expanding the dataset for analysis. This can include non-SSCI publications and books. Furthermore, as policy learning is a highly practice-oriented endeavor, we call for future reviews to also include practitioner and practice-oriented resources such as reports and proceedings pertinent to learning from national governments or public international organizations and transnational networks (e.g., the European Union, African Union, WHO, OECD, World Bank, etc.).

On our endeavor to maneuver the complexities of the burgeoning policy-learning literature, we presented a theoretically coherent and empirically grounded background conceptualization of policy learning, we also provided a synthesis of its growing body of literature. We then proceeded to outline how this conceptualization can be leveraged to enhance the field's theoretical, empirical, and practical leverage. As this endeavor has further substantiated the centrality of policy learning for public policy research and practice, we further echo the calls for investing significant intellectual resources in the field in the years to come.

Appendix I: Supplementary Material

Substantive Areas of Focus Breakdown

Articles coded have been represented under different substantive areas of focus corresponding to those mentioned in the *Policy Studies Journal* public policy yearbook (Jenkins-Smith *et al.* 2020). To enable the analysis, several policy domains have been aggregated under the respective substantive areas of focus as follows:

Sn.	Substantive Area of Focus	Sub domains
1	Economic Policy	Labor Policy, Monetary Policy, Fiscal policy, Financial-Banking Policy, Minerals and Mining Policy, Competition Policy, and Industry Development Policy.
2	Energy Policy	Nuclear Policy, Wind Policy, Electricity, and Shale Gas
3	Environmental Policy	Dam Building, Disaster Management, Climate and Climate Change, Natural Disasters, Emissions, Nuclear Waste, and Marine Conservation.
4	Welfare Policy	Social Policy-Leaves, Social Policy-Pension, Social Policy-Welfare, Childcare, Family Violence, Disability, Discrimination, Indigenous Populations, LGBT, Basic Income, Social Service and Societal Design, Drunk Driving.
5	Healthcare Policy	Pandemic, and general Healthcare policy
6	Governance	Procurement, Open Method of Coordination, Administrative Reform, Open Governance, Public Performance, Regulation, Regulatory Assessments, Cluster Coordination, Governance Networks, and Evidence-based Policy Making.
7	Agricultural Policy	Food Safety, Biotechnology, Hormones, and Veterinary.
8	Urban Policy	Urban Studies, Land Claims, and Housing
9	International Affairs	Brexit, Foreign Policy, Refugees, Immigration, and International Committees.
10	Legislation	Freedom of Information, Death Penalty, Parliamentary Affairs, and Justice – Legal.
11	Transport	Railways
12	Education	School Buildings, General Policy on Education
13	Science and Technology	Innovation, ICT, Technology, Research Policy

List of Coded Articles

Sn.	Article Name	Year	Journal Name
1	Policy Learning and the Evolution of Federal Hazardous Waste Policy	1985	*Policy Studies Journal*
2	Urban Policy and the Myth of Progress	1997	*Policy and Politics*
3	Analytical Debates and Policy Learning: Analysis and Change in the Federal Bureaucracy	1998	*Policy Sciences*
4	The Temporal Diffusion of Morality Policy: The Case of Death Penalty Legislation in the American States	1999	*Policy Studies Journal*
5	Policy Feedback: The Comparison Effect and Small Business Procurement Policy	1999	*Policy Studies Journal*
6	Policy Networks and Policy Learning: UK Economic Policy in the 1960s and 1970s	2000	*Public Administration*
7	The Road to Innovation, Convergence or Inertia: Devolution in Housing Policy in Canada	2000	*Canadian Public Policy*
8	Policy Transfer and Policy Learning: A Study of the 1991 New Zealand Health Services Taskforce	2000	*Governance*
9	Social Benchmarking, Policy Making and New Governance in the EU	2001	*Journal of European Social Policy*
10	Environmental Policy as Learning: A New View of an Old Landscape	2001	*Public Administration Review*
11	Conceptual Innovation and Public Policy: Unemployment and Paid Leave Schemes in Denmark	2001	*Journal of European Social Policy*
12	Evaluation, Policy Learning and Evidence-based Policy Making	2002	*Public Administration*
13	European Governance and the Transfer of 'New' Environmental Policy Instruments (Nepis) in the European Union	2003	*Public Administration*
14	Institutional Choice and Policy Transfer: Reforming British and German Railway Regulation	2003	*Governance*
15	Policy Learning and Uncertainty: The Case of Pension Reform in Estonia and Latvia	2003	*Policy Studies Journal*
16	Managing Diversity in a System of Multi-level Governance: The Open Method of Co-ordination in Innovation Policy	2004	*Journal of European Public Policy*

17	Governing Informally: The Role of the Eurogroup in EMU and the Stability and Growth Pact	2004	*Journal of European Public Policy*
18	Peer Review of Labour Market Programmes in the European Union: What Can Countries Really Learn from One Another?	2005	*Journal of European Public Policy*
19	The Role of Assessments and Institutions for Policy Learning: A Study on Swedish Climate and Nuclear Policy Formation	2005	*Policy Sciences*
20	The Fertile Soil for Policy Learning	2005	*Policy Sciences*
21	Mass Production of Law. Routinization in the Transposition of European Directives: A Sociological-Institutionalist Account	2006	*Journal of European Public Policy*
22	Potential Focusing Projects and Policy Change	2006	*Policy Studies Journal*
23	Policy Learning in an Enlarged European Union: Environmental NGOs and New Policy Instruments	2007	*Journal of European Public Policy*
24	Policy Learning in Europe: The Open Method of Co-ordination and Laboratory Federalism Policy Learning in Europe	2007	*Journal of European Public Policy*
25	Disaster Management in the United States: Examining key political and policy challenges	2007	*Policy Studies Journal*
26	Individuals and the Dynamics of Policy Learning: The Case of the Third Battle of Newbury	2007	*Public Administration*
27	Restructuring Welfare for the Unemployed: The Hartz Legislation in Germany	2008	*Journal of European Social Policy*
28	Learning from the States? Federalism and National Health Policy	2008	*Public Administration Review*
29	Accountability Agreements in Ontario Hospitals: Are they Fair?	2008	*Journal of Public Administration Research and Theory*
30	Examining Perceived Honest Performance Reporting by Public Organizations: Bureaucratic Politics and Organizational Practice	2009	*Journal of Public Administration Research and Theory*

31	EU Policy toward Other Regions: Policy Learning in the External Promotion of Regional Integration	2009	*Journal of European Public Policy*
32	Patterns of Innovation in EU-25 Regions: A Typology and Policy Recommendations	2009	*Environment and Planning C: Politics and Space*
33	European Agencies as Agents of Governance and EU Learning	2009	*Journal of European Public Policy*
34	The Power of Institutionalized Learning: The Uses and Practices of Commissions to Generate Policy Change	2009	*Journal of European Public Policy*
35	Policy Learning and Transfer: The Experience of the Developmental State in East Asia	2009	*Policy and Politics*
36	Governance and Policy Learning in the European Union: A Comparison with North America	2009	*Journal of European Public Policy*
37	Old Wine in New Bottles? Instrumental Policy Learning and the Evolution of the Certainty Provision in Comprehensive Land Claims Agreements	2009	*Canadian Public Policy*
38	Policy Learning Processes in International Committees	2009	*Public Management Review*
39	Using Intermediate Indicators: Lessons for Climate Policy	2009	*Climate Policy*
40	So Near, Yet So Far: Connecting Welfare Regime Research to Policy Learning Research	2009	*Policy and Politics*
41	Policy-learning and Environmental Policy Integration in the Common Agricultural Policy, 1973–2003	2010	*Public Administration*
42	Bringing Interests Back In: Using Coalition Theories to Explain European Wind Power Policies	2010	*Journal of European Public Policy*
43	From "Smart Regulation" to "Regulatory Arrangements"	2010	*Policy Sciences*
44	Learning from Experience? Second-Order Policy Devolution and Government Responsiveness	2010	*Journal of Local Self Governance*
45	Policy Learning and Organizational Capacities in Innovation Policies	2011	*Science and Public Policy*
46	Conflicting Advocacy Coalitions in an Evolving Modern Biotechnology Regulatory Subsystem: Policy Learning and Influencing Kenya's Regulatory Policy Process	2011	*Science and Public Policy*

47	Policy Learning Through Public Inquiries? The Case of UK Nuclear Energy Policy 1955-61	2011	Environment and Planning C: Government and Policy
48	Who Teaches and Who Learns? Policy Learning Through the C40 Cities Climate Network	2012	Policy Sciences
49	Policy Transfer and Convergence within the UK: The Case of Local Government Performance Improvement Regimes	2012	Policy and Politics
50	Policy Learning and the 'Cluster-Flavoured Innovation Policy' in Finland	2012	Environment and Planning C: Government and Policy
51	Social Policy Learning and Diffusion in China: The Rise of Welfare Regions?	2012	Policy and Politics
52	The Merry Mandarins of Windsor: Policy Transfer and Transgovernmental Networks in the Anglosphere	2012	Policy Studies
53	Greening Growth through Strategic Environmental Assessment of Sector Reforms	2012	Public Administration and Development
54	Policy Learning? Crisis, Evidence, and Reinvention in the Making of Public Policy	2012	Policy and Politics
55	The Role of Experts in the European Union's Research Policy	2012	Review of Policy Research
56	Innovation System in Transition: Opportunities for Policy Learning between China and Russia	2013	Science and Public Policy
57	Learning as a Key to Citizen-centred Performance Improvement: A Comparison between the Health Service Centre and the Household Registration Office in Taipei City	2012	Australian Journal of Public Administration
58	Networked Learning in Complex Policy Spaces: A Practitioner's Reflection on the Open Method of Coordination	2013	Canadian Public Administration
59	Understanding the Eradication of Slave Labour in Contemporary Brazil - An Implementation Perspective	2013	Policy Studies
60	Discourse Coalitions and the Australian Climate Change Policy Network	2000	Environment and Planning C: Government and Policy

61	Learning and Change in 20th-century British Economic Policy	2004	*Governance*
62	Learning, Frames, and Environmental Policy Integration: The Case of Swedish Energy Policy	2005	*Environment and Planning C: Government and Policy*
63	Polydiffusion in Intergovernmental Programs - Information Diffusion in the School-to-work Network	2002	*The American Review of Public Administration*
64	Measuring Policy Learning: Regulatory Impact Assessment in Europe	2009	*Journal of European Public Policy*
65	Policy Transfer as Learning: Capturing Variation in What Decision-Makers Learn from Epistemic Communities	2009	*Policy Studies*
66	Policy Transfer Using the 'Gold Standard': Exploring Policy Tourism in Practice	2014	*Policy and Politics*
67	Policy Learning and Diffusion of Tokyo's metropolitan Cap-and-trade: Making a Mandatory Reduction of Total CO2 Emissions Work at Local Scales	2014	*Policy Studies*
68	Policy Learning, Aid Conditionality or Domestic Politics? The Europeanization of Dutch and Spanish Activation Policies through the European Social Fund	2014	*Journal of European Public Policy*
69	Participatory Evaluation: A Useful Tool for Contextualising Cluster Policy?	2014	*Policy Studies*
70	Comparative Strategic Behavior of Advocacy Coalitions and Policy Brokers: The Case of Kenya's Biosafety Regulatory Policy	2014	*Journal of Comparative Policy Analysis*
71	Freezing Deliberation through Public Expert Advice	2017	*Journal of European Public Policy*
72	Learning-Shaping Crises: A Longitudinal Comparison of Public Personnel Reforms in Italy, 19922014	2017	*Journal of Comparative Policy Analysis: Research and Practice*
73	Overcoming the Failure of 'Silicon Somewheres': Learning in Policy Transfer Processes	2017	*Policy and Politics*
74	Cognition and Policy Change: The Consistency of Policy Learning in the Advocacy Coalition Framework	2017	*Policy and Society*
75	British Columbia's Fast Ferries and Sydney's Airport Link: Partisan Barriers to Learning from Policy Failure	2017	*Policy and Politics*

76	Why Have Policies Often Remained Symbolic? Understanding the Reasons for Decoupling between Policy and Practice	2017	*Review of Policy Research*
77	Beyond Subsidiarity: The Indirect Effect of the Early Warning System on National Parliamentary Scrutiny in European Union Affairs	2017	*Journal of European Public Policy*
78	Policy Learning, Motivated Skepticism, and the Politics of Shale Gas Development in British Columbia and Quebec	2017	*Policy and Society*
79	The Limitations of Policy Learning: A Constructivist Perspective on Expertise and Policy Dynamics in Dutch Migrant Integration Policies	2017	*Policy and Society*
80	How Does Policy Learning Occur? The Case of Belgian Mental Health Care Reforms	2017	*Policy and Society*
81	Singular Memory or Institutional Memories? Toward a Dynamic Approach	2018	*Governance*
82	Policy Learning over a Decade or More and the Role of Interests Therein: The European Liberalization Policy Process of Belgian Network Industries	2018	*Public Policy and Administration*
83	Do Disasters Lead to Learning? Financial Policy Change in Local Government	2018	*Review of Policy Research*
84	Factors Shaping Policy Learning: A Study of Policy Actors in Subnational Climate and Energy Issues	2018	*Review of Policy Research*
85	Fiscal Policy Learning from Crisis: Comparative Analysis of the Baltic Countries	2018	*Journal of Comparative Policy Analysis: Research and Practice*
86	Policy Diffusion and Directionality: Tracing Early Adoption of Offshore Wind Policy	2018	*Review of Policy Research*
87	Comparative Analysis of State Policymaking in Child Welfare: Explaining Policy Choices	2018	*Journal of Comparative Policy Analysis: Research and Practice*
88	Defining Regional Climate Leadership: Learning from Comparative Analysis in the Asia Pacific	2018	*Journal of Comparative Policy Analysis: Research and Practice*

89	Learning as a Necessary but Not Sufficient Condition for Major Health Policy Change: A Qualitative Comparative Analysis Combining ACF and MSF	2019	*Journal of Comparative Policy Analysis: Research and Practice*
90	Multilevel Policy Implementation and the Where of Learning: The Case of the Information System for School Buildings in Italy	2019	*Policy Sciences*
91	Comparative Metrics and Policy Learning: End-of-Life Care in France and the US	2019	*Journal of Comparative Policy Analysis: Research and Practice*
92	Bounded Policy Learning? EU Efforts to Anticipate Unintended Consequences in Conflict Minerals Legislation	2019	*Journal of European Public Policy*
93	Evaluations as a Decent Knowledge Base? Describing and Explaining the Quality of the European Commission's Ex-post Legislative Evaluations	2019	*Policy Sciences*
94	Can't Get No Learning: The Brexit Fiasco through the Lens of Policy Learning	2019	*Journal of European Public Policy*
95	Street-level Bureaucrats, Policy Learning, and Refugee Resettlement: The Case of Syrian Refugees in Saskatoon, Canada	2019	*Canadian Public Administration*
96	Policy Learning and the Public Inquiry	2019	*Policy Sciences*
97	The Drivers of Regulatory Networking: Policy Learning between Homophily and Convergence	2019	*Journal of Public Policy*
98	Assessing Strategic Policy Transfer in Romanian Public Management	2019	*Public Policy and Administration*
99	Multi-stakeholder Initiatives, Policy Learning and Institutionalization: The Surprising Failure of Open Government in Norway	2019	*Policy Studies*
100	Reconceptualizing Major Policy Change in the Advocacy Coalition Framework: A Discourse Network Analysis of German Pension Politics	2013	*Policy Studies*
101	Policy Learning and Science Policy Innovation Adoption by Street-level Bureaucrats	2014	*Journal of Public Policy*
102	Development of the Environmental Taxes and Charges System in Estonia: International Convergence Mechanisms and Local Factors	2014	*Policy Studies*

103	Policy Learning in the Eurozone Crisis: Modes, Power and Functionality	2015	*Policy Sciences*
104	Organizational Political Capacity as Learning	2015	*Policy and Society*
105	Haven't We Been This Way Before? Evaluation and the Impediments to Policy Learning	2015	*Australian Journal of Public Administration*
106	Policy Ideas and Policy Learning about 'Basic Research' in South Korea	2014	*Science and Public Policy*
107	'We Nicked Stuff from All over the Place': Policy Transfer or Muddling Through?	2009	*Policy and Politics*
108	The Drivers of Regulatory Networking: Policy Learning between Homophily and Convergence	2019	*Journal of Public Policy*
109	Institutional Amnesia and Public Policy	2019	*Journal of European Public Policy*
110	Cluster Governance: A Practical Way Out of a Congested State of Governance Plurality	2016	*Politics and Space C*
111	Overseas and Over Here: Policy Transfer and Evidence-based Policy-making	2012	*Policy Studies*
112	The March toward Marriage Equality: Reexamining the Diffusion of Same-sex Marriage among States	2016	*Public Policy and Administration*
113	Mimicry, Persuasion, or Learning? The Case of Two Transparency and Anti-Corruption Policies in Romania	2015	*Public Administration and Development*
114	Elite, Exclusive and Elusive: Transgovernmental Policy Networks and Iterative Policy Transfer in the Anglosphere	2016	*Policy Studies*
115	Policy Learning and Policy Networks in Theory and Practice: The Role of Policy Brokers in the Indonesian Biodiesel Policy Network	2017	*Policy and Society*
116	Immature Relationships in the New Multi-level United Kingdom: Perspectives from Wales	2015	*Public Money and Management*
117	Evidence Translation: An Exploration of Policy Makers' Use of Evidence	2016	*Policy & Politics*

118	The Legacy of the Northern Way?	2015	*Local Government Studies*
119	Powering over Puzzling? Downsizing the Public Sector during the Greek Sovereign Debt Crisis	2014	*Journal of Comparative Policy Analysis: Research and Practice*
120	Basic Income in Our Time: Improving Political Prospects Through Policy Learning?	2016	*Journal of Social Policy*
121	The Global Financial Crisis in Comparative Perspective: Have Policy Makers "Learnt Their Lessons"?	2015	*Journal of Comparative Policy Analysis: Research and Practice*
122	How Different Forms of Policy Learning Influence Each Other: Case Studies from Austrian innovation Policy-making	2015	*Policy Studies*
123	Moving Context from the Background to the Forefront of Policy Learning: Reflections on a Case in Gipuzkoa, Basque Country	2016	*Government and Policy C*
124	Explaining the Content of Impact Assessment in the United Kingdom: Learning across Time, Sectors, and Departments	2016	*Regulation and Governance*
125	Policy Failures, Policy Learning and Institutional Change: The Case of Australian Health Insurance Policy Change	2017	*Policy & Politics*
126	Institutional Change Through Policy Learning: The Case of the European Commission and Research Policy	2016	*Review of Policy Research*
127	Governance Change and Governance Learning in Europe: Stakeholder Participation in Environmental Policy Implementation	2017	*Policy and Society*
128	Crisis, Learning and Policy Change in the European Union	2016	*Journal of European Public Policy*
129	Regional Competitiveness Policy Evaluation as a Transformative Process: From Theory to Practice	2016	*Government and Policy C*
130	Pathologies of Policy Learning: What Are They and How Do They Contribute to Policy Failure?	2017	*Policy & Politics*
131	Policy Failure and Policy Learning: Examining the Conditions of Learning after Disaster	2017	*Review of Policy Research*
132	Explaining Science-led Policy-making: Pandemic Deaths, Epistemic Deliberation and Ideational Trajectories	2016	*Policy Sciences*

133	Policy Learning and Smart Specialization: Balancing Policy Change and Continuity for New Regional Industrial Paths	2016	*Science and Public Policy*
134	The Irony of epistemic Learning: Epistemic Communities, Policy Learning and the Case of Europe's Hormones Saga	2017	*Policy and Society*
135	Youth-oriented Active Labour Market Policies: Explaining Policy Effort in the Nordic and the Baltic States	2017	*Social Policy & Administration*
136	Government Purchase of Services in China: Similar Intentions, Different Policy Designs	2017	*Public Administration and Development*
137	Policy Transfer: The Case of European Union–China Cooperation in Public Administration Reform	2019	*International Review of Administrative Sciences*
138	Target Groups on the Mainline: A Theoretical Framework of Policy Layering and Learning Disparity	2020	*Administration & Society*
139	Policy Learning and Information Processing	2020	*Policy Studies Journal*
140	The Past in the Present-The Role of Analogical Reasoning in Epistemic Learning About How to Tackle Complex Policy Problems	2020	*Policy Studies Journal*
141	On the Acoustics of Policy Learning: Can Co-Participation in Policy Forums Break Up Echo Chambers?	2019	*Policy Studies Journal*
142	Policy Processes sans Frontières: Interactions in Transnational Governance of Global Health	2020	*Policy Sciences*
143	Policy Learning and Crisis Policy-making: Quadruple-Loop Learning and COVID-19 Responses in South Korea	2020	*Policy and Society*
144	Lobbying, Learning and Policy Reinvention: An Examination of the American States' Drunk Driving Laws	2018	*Journal of Public Policy*
145	Can Policy Forums Overcome Echo Chamber Effects by Enabling Policy Learning? Evidence from the Irish climate Change Policy Network	2020	*Journal of Public Policy*
146	Disputed Policy Change: The Role of Events, Policy Learning, and Negotiated Agreements	2020	*Policy Studies Journal*
147	Regulatory Indicators in the European Union and the Organization for Economic Cooperation and Development: Performance Assessment, Organizational Processes, and Learning	2018	*Public Policy and Administration*

About the Authors

Bishoy Louis Zaki is a final-year PhD candidate at the Department of Public Governance and Management at Ghent University, Belgium. His main research is in public policy where he also focuses on policy learning, its conceptualization, operationalization, and how it is undertaken across a wide range of contexts. His research also explores the interactions of policy learning with expertise and scientific evidence. Before joining academia, he served as a practitioner for over 12 years in policy and public management positions in various governments and international development agencies, where he was involved in the design and management of policy learning and transfer programs.

Ellen Wayenberg is a professor at the Faculty of Economics and Business Administration at the University of Ghent, Belgium. She specializes in public policy and administration with a specific interest in policy analysis and evaluation, local government, and multi-level governance where she has several publications. Ellen co-organizes and co-chairs several international conferences and research meetings including the annual meeting of the European Group for Public Administration (EGPA) Study Group on Regional and Local Government as well as several other study groups, conferences, and symposia.

Bert George is a professor at the Department of Public Governance and Management at Ghent University, Belgium. His research focuses on strategic planning and management in public administration, public service performance and behavioral public policy using experimental, observational, and meta-analytical research methods. Bert is also a managing editor for *Public Administration Review* (PAR), acts as an expert advisor to a.o. the OECD, and teaches strategy-related courses in several executive programs including at the Hertie School (Berlin).

References

Adcock, Robert, and David Collier. "Measurement Validity: A Shared Standard for Qualitative and Quantitative Research." *American Political Science Review* 95 (3): 529–546. Accessed on November 28, 2021. https://www.jstor.org/stable/3118231

Alvesson, Mats, and Martin Blom. 2021. "The Hegemonic Ambiguity of Big Concepts in Organization Studies." *Human Relations* 75 (1): 58-86. DOI: 10.1177/0018726720986847

Alvesson, Mats, and Jorgen Sandberg. 2020. "The Problematizing Review: A Counterpoint to Elsbach and Van Knippenberg's Argument for Integrative Reviews." *Journal of Management Studies* 57 (6): 1290-1304. DOI: 10.1111/joms.12582

Ansell, Christopher. 2019. "Coping with Conceptual Pluralism: Reflections on Concept Formation." *Public Performance and Management Review* 44 (5): 1118-1139. DOI: 10.1080/15309576.2019.1677254

Badger, D., J. Nursten, P. Williams, and M. Woodward. 2000. "Should All Literature Reviews be Systematic?" *Evaluation and Research in Education* 14 (3-4): 220-230. DOI: 10.1080/09500790008666974

Baekkeskov, Erik. 2016. "Explaining Science-led Policy-making: Pandemic Deaths, Epistemic Deliberation and Ideational Trajectories." *Policy Sciences* 49: 395–419. DOI: 10.1007/s11077-016-9264-y

Baekkeskov, Erik, and PerOla Öberg. 2016. "Freezing Deliberation through Public Expert Advice." *Journal of European Public Policy* 24 (7): 1006-1026. DOI: 10.1080/13501763.2016.1170192

Bakır, Caner. 2017. "Policy Learning and Policy Change: Learning from Research Citations." *Policy Sciences* 50: 585–597. DOI: 10.1007/s11077-017-9299-8

Bandelow, Nils C., Colette Vogeler, Johanna Hornung, Johanna Kuhlmann, and Sebastian Heidrich. 2017. "Learning as a Necessary but Not Sufficient Condition for Major Health Policy Change: A Qualitative Comparative Analysis Combining ACF and MSF." *Journal of Comparative Policy Analysis: Research and Practice* 21 (2): 167-182. DOI: 10.1080/13876988.2017.1393920

Bennett, Colin J., and Michael Howlett. 1992. "The Lessons of Learning: Reconciling Theories of Policy Learning and Policy Change." *Policy Sciences* 25: 275-294. DOI: 10.1007/bf00138786

Biegelbauer, Peter. 2016. "How Different Forms of Policy Learning Influence Each Other: Case Studies from Austrian Innovation Policy-making." *Policy Studies* 37 (2): 129-146. DOI: 10.1080/01442872.2015.1118027

Bomberg, Elizabeth. 2007. "Policy Learning in an Enlarged European Union: Environmental NGOs and New Policy Instruments." *Journal of European Public Policy* 14 (2): 248-268. DOI: 10.1080/13501760601122522

Borrás, Susana. 2011. "Policy Learning and Organizational Capacities in Innovation Policies." *Science and Public Policy* 38 (9): 725-734. DOI: 10.3152/030234211X13070021633323

Bryson, John M., Barbara C. Crosby, and Laura Bloomberg. 2014. "Public Value Governance: Moving Beyond Traditional Public Administration and the New Public Management." *Public Administration Review* 74 (4): 445-456. DOI: 10.1111/pu ar.12238

Callahan, Jamie. 2014. "Constructing a Manuscript: Distinguishing Integrative Literature Reviews and Conceptual and Theory Articles." *Human Resource Development Review* 13: 271–275. DOI: 10.1177/1534484310371492

Casey, Bernard H., and Michael Gold. 2006. "Peer Review of Labour Market Programmes in the European Union: What Can Countries Really Learn from One Another?" *Journal of European Public Policy* 12 (1): 23-43. DOI: 10.1080/13501 76042000311899

Checkel, Jeffrey. 2001. "Why Comply? Social Learning and European Identity Change." *International Organization* 55 (3): 553-588. doi:10.1162/002081801525 07551

Cole, Stephen. 1983. "The Hierarchy of the Sciences?" *American Journal of Sociology* 89: 111-139. DOI: 10.1086/227835

Collins, Christopher S., and Carrie M. Stockton. 2018. "The Central Role of Theory in Qualitative Research." *International Journal of Qualitative Methods* 17: 1-10. DOI: 10.1177/1609406918797475

Corley, Kevin G., and Dennis A. Gioia. 2011. "Building Theory about Theory Building: What Constitutes a Theoritical Contribution?" *Academy of Management Review* 36 (1): 12-32. DOI: 10.5465/amr.2009.0486

Crow, Deserai A., Elizabeth A. Albright, Todd Ely, Elizabeth Koebele, and Lydia Lawhon. 2018. Do Disasters Lead to Learning? Financial Policy Change in Local Government. *Review of Policy Research* 35 (4): 564-589. DOI: 10.1111/ropr.12297

Crozier, Michael. 2008. "Listening, Learning, Steering: New Governance, Communication and interactive Policy Formation." *Policy and Politics* 36 (1): 3-19. DOI: 10.1332/030557308783431616

De Houwer, Jan. 2011. "Why the Cognitive Approach in Psychology Would Profit from a Functional Approach and Vice Versa." *Perspectives on Psychological Science* 6: 202–209. DOI: 10.1177/1745691611400238

De Houwer, Jan, Dermot Barnes-Holmes, and Agnes Moors. 2013. "What Is Learning? On the Nature and Merits of a Functional Definition of Learning." *Psychonomic Bulletin and Review* 20 (4): 631-642. DOI:10.3758/s13423-013-0386-3

De Vries, Hanna, Victor Bekkers, and Lars Tummers. 2015. "Innovation in the Public Sector: A Systematic Review and Future Research Agenda." *Public Administration* 94 (1): 146-166. DOI: 10.1111/padm.12209

Deutsch, Karl W. 1966. *The Nerves of Government: Models of Political Communication and Control.* New York, NY: The Free Press.

Dewey, John. 1938. *Logic: The Theory of Inquiry.* New York, NY: Rinehart and Winston.

Di Mascio, Fabrizio, Davide Galli, Alessandro Natalini, Edoardo Ongaro, and Francesco Stolfi. 2016. "Learning-Shaping Crises: A Longitudinal Comparison of Public Personnel Reforms in Italy, 1992–2014." *Journal of Comparative Policy Analysis: Research and Practice* 19 (2): 119-138. DOI: 10.1080/13876988.2016.1154279

Dolowitz, David P., and David Marsh. 2002. "Learning from Abroad: The Role of Policy Transfer in Contemporary Policy-Making." *Governance* 13 (1): 5-23. DOI: 10.1111/0952-1895.00121

Domjan, Michael. 2010. *Principles of Learning and Behavior.* Belmont, CA: Wadsworth.

Dudley, Geoff. 2007. "Individuals and the Dynamics of Policy Learning: The Case of the Third Battle of Newbury." *Public Administration* 85 (2): 405 - 428. DOI: 10.1111/j.1467-9299.2007.00648.x

Dunleavy, Patrick, Helen Margetts, Simon Bastow, and Jane Tinkler. 2006. "New Public Management Is Dead—Long Live Digital-Era Governance." *Journal of Public Administration Research and Theory* 16 (3): 467-494. DOI: 10.1093/jopart/mui057

Dunlop, Claire A. 2009. "Policy Transfer as Learning: Capturing Variation in What Decision Makers Learn from Epistemic Communities." *Policy Studies* 30 (3): 289-311. DOI: 10.1080/01442870902863869

_____. 2017. "Pathologies of Policy Learning: What Are They and How Do They Contribute to Policy Failure?" *Policy and Politics* 45 (1): 19-37. DOI: 10.1332/030557316X14780920269183

_____. 2015. "Organizational Political Capacity as Learning." *Policy and Society* 34 (3-4): 259-270. DOI: 10.1016/j.polsoc.2015.09.007

Dunlop, Claire A., and Claudio M. Radaelli. 2013. "Systematising Policy Learning: From Monolith to Dimensions." *Political Studies* 61 (3): 599–619. DOI: 10. 1111/j.1467-9248.2012.00982.x

_____. 2016. "Policy Learning in the Eurozone Crisis: Modes, Power and Functionality." *Policy Sciences* 49: 107-124. DOI: 10.1007/s11077-015-9236-7

_____. 2017. "Learning in the Bath-tub: The Micro and Macro Dimensions of the Causal Relationship between Learning and Policy Change." *Policy and Society* 36 (2): 304-319. DOI: 10.1080/14494035.2017.1321232

_____. 2018. "Does Policy Learning Meet the Standards of an Analytical Framework of the Policy Process?" *Policy Studies Journal* 46 (S1): S48-S68. DOI: 10.1111/ psj.12250

_____. 2020. "Policy Learning in Comparative Policy Analysis." *Journal of Comparative Policy Analysis: Research and Practice.* DOI: 10.1080/13876988.2020.1762077

Dunlop, Claire A., Claudio M. Radaelli, and P. Trein. 2018. *Learning in Public Policy: Analysis, Modes and Outcomes*, edited by Claire A. Dunlop, Claudio M. Radaelli, and P. Trein. Basingstoke, UK: Palgrave Macmillan.

Dunlop, Claire, S. James, and Claudio Radaelli. 2019. "Can't Get No Learning: The Brexit Fiasco through the Lens of Policy Learning." *Journal of European Public Policy* 27 (5): 703-722. DOI: 10.1080/13501763.2019.1667415

Easton, David. 1965. *A System Analysis of Political Life.* New York, NY: Wiley.

Elsbach, Kimberley D., and Daan van Knippenberg. 2020. "Creating High-Impact Literature Reviews: An Argument for 'Integrative Reviews.'" *Journal of Management Studies* 57 (6): 1277-1289. DOI: 10.1111/joms.12581

Garcia, Rosanna, and Roger J. Calantone. 2002. "A Critical Look at Technological Innovation Typology and Innovativeness Terminology: A Literature Review." *Journal of Product Innovation Management* 19 (2): 110-32. DOI: 10.1016/S0737-6782(01)00132-1

George, Bert, Bram Verschuere, Ellen Wayenberg, and Bishoy L. Zaki. 2020. "A Guide to Benchmarking COVID-19 Performance Data." *Public Administration Review* 80 (4): 696-700. DOI: 10.1111/puar.13255

Gerlak, Andrea K., Tanya Heikkila, Sharon L. Smolinski, Dave Huitema, and Derek Armitage. 2018. "Learning Our Way Out of Environmental Policy Problems: A Review of the Scholarship." *Policy Sciences* 51: 335–371. DOI: 10.1007/s11077-017-9278-0

Gerring, John. 1999. "What Makes a Concept Good? A Criterial Framework for Understanding Concept Formation in the Social Sciences." *Polity* 31 (3): 357-393. DOI: 10.2307/3235246

Goyal, Nihit, and Michael Howlett. 2018. "Framework or Metaphor? Analysing the Status of Policy Learning in the Policy Sciences." *Journal of Asian Public Policy* 12 (3): 257-273. DOI: 10.1080/17516234.2018.1493768

Haas, Peter M. 1992. "Introduction: Epistemic Communities and International Policy Coordination." *International Organization* 46: 1-35. DOI: 10.1017/S0020818300001442

Hamilton, Malcolm B. 1987. "The Elements of the Concept of Ideology." *Political Studies* 35 (1): 18-38. DOI: 10.1111/j.1467-9248.1987.tb00186.x

Harmancioglu, Nukhet, Cornela Droge, and Roger J. Calantone. 2009. "Theoretical Lenses and Domain Definitions in Innovation Research." *European Journal of Marketing* 43 (1/2): 229-263. DOI: 10.1108/03090560910923319

Heclo, Hugh. 1974. *Modern Social Politics in Britain and Sweden: From Relief to Income Maintenance.* London: Yale University Press.

Heikkila, Tanya, and Krister Andersson. 2018. "Policy Design and the Added-value of the Institutional Analysis Development Framework." *Policy and Politics* 46 (2): 309–324. DOI: 10.1332/030557318X15230060131727

Heikkila, Tanya, and Andrea Gerlak. 2013. "Building a Conceptual Approach to Collective Learning: Lessons for Public Policy Scholars." *Policy Studies Journal* 41 (3): 484–511. DOI: 10.1111/psj.12026

Howlett, Michael, Ishanee Mukherjee, and Joop Koppenjan. 2017. "Policy Learning and Policy Networks in Theory and Practice: The Role of Policy Brokers in the Indonesian Biodiesel Policy Network." *Policy and Society* 36 (2): 233-250. DOI: 10.1080/14494035.2017.1321230

Huijbregts, Rowie, Bert George, and Victor Bekkers. 2021. "Public Values Assessment as a Practice: Integration of Evidence and Research Agenda." *Public Management Review.* Early View. DOI: 10.1080/14719037.2020.1867227

Jenkins-Smith, Hank C. 1988. "Analytical Debates and Policy Learning: Analysis and Change in the Federal Bureaucracy." *Policy Sciences* 21: 169–211. DOI: 10. 1007/BF00136407

Jenkins-Smith, Hank, Julie Krutz, Nina Carlson, and Chris Weible. 2020. "The 2020 Public Policy Yearbook." *Policy Studies Journal* 48 (S1): S6-S13. DOI: 10.1111/ psj.12384

Jones, Michael D., and Claudio Radaelli. 2015. "The Narrative Policy Framework: Child or Monster?" *Critical Policy Studies* 9 (3): 339-355. DOI: 10.1080/19460 171.2015.1053959

Kamkhaji, Jonathan C., and Claudio Radaelli. 2017. "Crisis, Learning and Policy Change in the European Union." *Journal of European Public Policy* 24 (5): 714-734. DOI: 10.1080/13501763.2016.1164744

Kaplan, Andreas M., and Michael Haenlein. 2006. "Toward a Parsimonious Definition of Traditional and Electronic Mass Customization." *Journal of Product Innovation Management* 23 (2): 168-182. DOI: 10.1111/j.1540-5885.2006.00190.x

Karlsen, James, and Miren Larrea. 2016. "Moving Context from the Background to the Forefront of Policy Learning: Reflections on a Case in Gipuzkoa, Basque Country." *Environment and Planning C: Politics and Space* 35 (4): 721-736. DOI: 10.1177/0263774X16642442

Kerber, Wolfgang, and Martina Eckardt. 2007. "Policy Learning in Europe: The Open Method of Co-ordination and Laboratory Federalism." *Journal of European Public Policy* 14 (2): 227-247. DOI: 10.1080/13501760601122480

Kern, Kristine, and Harriet Bulkeley. 2009. "Cities, Europeanization and Multi-level Governance: Governing Climate Change through Transnational Municipal Networks." *Journal of Common Market Studies* 47 (2): 309–332. DOI: 10.1111/j.1468-5965.2009.00806.x

Kingdon, John W. 1984. *Agendas, Alternatives, and Public Policies.* Boston and Toronto: Little, Brown and Company.

Klochikhin, Evgeny A. 2013. "Innovation System in Transition: Opportunities for Policy Learning between China and Russia." *Science and Public Policy* 40 (5): 1-17. DOI: 10.1093/scipol/sct021

Knoepfel, Peter, and Ingrid Kissling-Näf. 1998. "Social Learning in Policy Networks." *Policy and Politics* 26 (3): 343-367. DOI: 10.1332/030557398782213638

Lachman, Sheldon J. 1997. "Learning is a Process: Toward an Improved Definition of Learning." *Journal of Psychology* 131 (5): 477–480. DOI: 10.1080/002239897 09603535

Laffin, Martin, and Christianne Ormston. 2013. "Disconnected Communities? ICT, Policy Learning and the Lessons for Central–local Relations." *Public Money and Management* 33 (3): 185-191. DOI: 10.1080/09540962.2013.785703

Lee, Jusil. 2017. "Why Have Policies Often Remained Symbolic? Understanding the Reasons for Decoupling between Policy and Practice." *Review of Policy Research* 34 (5): 617-635. DOI: 10.1111/ropr.12241

Lee, Sabinne, Changho Hwang, and M. Jae Moon. 2020. "Policy Learning and Crisis Policy-making: Quadruple-loop Learning and COVID-19 Responses in South Korea." *Policy and Society* 39 (3): 363-381. DOI: 10.1080/14494035.2020.1785195

Lee, Taedong, and Susan Van de Meene. 2012. "Who Teaches and Who Learns? Policy Learning through the C40 Cities Climate Network." *Policy Sciences* 45: 199-220. DOI: 10.1007/s11077-012-9159-5

Legrand, Timothy. 2012. "Overseas and Over Here: Policy Transfer and Evidence-based Policy-making." *Policy Studies* 33 (4): 329-348. DOI: 10.1080/01442872.2012. 695945

_____. 2016. "Elite, Exclusive and Elusive: Transgovernmental Policy Networks and Iterative Policy Transfer in the Anglosphere." *Policy Studies* 37 (5): 440-455. DOI: 10.1080/01442872.2016.1188912

Leifeld, Philip. 2013. "Reconceptualizing Major Policy Change in the Advocacy Coalition Framework: A Discourse Network Analysis of German Pension Politics." *Policy Studies Journal* 41 (1): 169-198. DOI: 10.1111/psj.12007

Levy, Jack S. 1994. "Learning and Foreign Policy: Sweeping a Conceptual Minefield." *International Organization* 48 (2): 279-312. Accessed on November 29, 2021. http://www.jstor.org/stable/2706933

Maggetti, Martino, and Fabrizio Gilardi. 2016. "Problems (and Solutions) in the Measurement of Policy Diffusion Mechanisms." *Journal of Public Policy* 36 (1): 87-107. DOI: 10.1017/S0143814X1400035X

Malkamäki, Arttu, Paul M. Wagner, Maria Brockhaus, Anne Toppinen, and Tuomas Ylä-Anttila. 2019. "On the Acoustics of Policy Learning: Can Co-Participation in Policy Forums Break Up Echo Chambers?" *Policy Studies Journal* 49 (2):

431-456. DOI: 10.1111/psj.12378

Marshall, Aasa, and Daniel Béland. 2019. "Street-level Bureaucrats, Policy Learning, and Refugee Resettlement: The Case of Syrian Refugees in Saskatoon, Canada." *Canadian Public Adminstration* 62 (3): 393-412. DOI: 10.1111/capa.12339

McKim, Courtney A. 2015. "The Value of Mixed Methods Research: A Mixed Methods Study." *Journal of Mixed Methods Research* 11 (2): 202-222. DOI: 10.11 77/1558689815607096

Merton, Robert. 1984. "Socio-economic Duration: A Case Study of Concept Formation in Sociology." In *Conflict and Consensus: A Festschrift in Honor of Lewis A. Coser*, edited by W. W. Powel, and R. Robbins, pp. 262-285. New York, NY: Free Press.

Miles, M. B., and Huberman, A. M. 1994. *Qualitative Data Analysis.* Thousand Oaks, CA: Sage.

Moher, David, Alessandro Liberati, Jennifer Tetzlaff, and Douglas G. Altman. 2009. "Preferred Reporting Items for Systematic Reviews and Meta-Analyses: The PRISMA Statement." *Annals of Internal Medicine* 151 (4): 264–69. DOI: 10.1136/ bmj.b2535

Molina-Azorin, Joseph F. 2016. "Mixed Methods Research: An Opportunity to Improve Our Studies and Our Research Skills." *European Journal of Management and Business Economics* 25 (2): 37-38. DOI: 10.1016/j.redeen.2016.05.001

Montpetit, Éric. 2009. "Governance and Policy Learning in the European Union: A Comparison with North America." *Journal of European Public Policy* 16 (8): 1185-1203. DOI: 10.1080/13501760903332720

Montpetit, Éric, and Erick Lachapelle. 2017. "Policy Learning, Motivated Scepticism, and the Politics of Shale Gas Development in British Columbia and Quebec." *Policy and Society* 36 (2): 195-214. DOI: 10.1080/14494035.2017.1320846

Mooney, Christopher Z., and Mei-Hsien Lee. 1999. "The Temporal Diffusion of Morality Policy: The Case of Death Penalty Legislation in the American States." *Policy Studies Journal* 27 (4): 766-780. DOI: 10.1111/j.1541-0072.1999.tb02002.x

Mossberger, Karen, and Kathleen Hale. 2002. "'Polydiffusion' in Intergovernmental Programs: Information Diffusion in the School-to-Work Network." *The American Review of Public Administration* 32 (4): 398-422. DOI: 10.1177/027507402237867

Motta, Michael J. 2018. "Policy Diffusion and Directionality: Tracing Early Adoption of Offshore Wind Policy." *Review of Policy Research* 35 (3): 398-421. DOI: 10.1111/ropr.12281

Moyson, Stéphane, Peter Scholten, and Christopher M. Weible. 2017. "Policy Learning and Policy Change: Theorizing Their Relations from Different Perspectives." *Policy and Society* 36 (2): 161-177. DOI: 10.1080/14494035.2017.1331879

Nedergaard, Peter. 2009. "Policy Learning Processes in International Committees: The Case of the Civil Servant Committees of the Nordic Council of Ministers." *Public Management Review* 11 (1): 23-37. DOI: 10.1080/14719030802490011

Newman, Joshua, and Malcolm G. Bird. 2017. "British Columbia's Fast Ferries and Sydney's Airport Link: Partisan Barriers to Learning from Policy Failure." *Policy and Politics* 15: 71-85. DOI: 10.1332/policypress/9781447352006.003.0005

Nilsson, Mans. 2006. "The Role of Assessments and Institutions for Policy Learning: A Study on Swedish Climate and Nuclear Policy Formation." *Policy Sciences* 38: 225–249. DOI: 10.1007/s11077-006-9006-7

Nowlin, Matthew C. 2020. "Policy Learning and Information Processing." *Policy Studies Journal* 49 (4): 1019-1039. DOI: 10.1111/psj.12397

O'Donovan, Kristin. 2017. "Policy Failure and Policy Learning: Examining the Conditions of Learning after Disaster." *Review of Policy Research* 34 (4): 537-558. DOI: 10.1111/ropr.12239

Ormrod, J. E. 2008. *Human Learning.* New Jersey: Prentice Hall.

Ostrom, Elinor. 2007. "Institutional Rational Choice: An Assessment of the Institutional Analysis and Development Framework." In *Theories of the Policy Process*, edited by Paul A. Sabatier, pp. 21-64. Cambridge, MA: Westview Press.

Pattison, Andrew. 2018. "Factors Shaping Policy Learning: A Study of Policy Actors in Subnational Climate and Energy Issues." *Review of Policy Research* 35 (4): 535-563. DOI: 10.1111/ropr.12303

Peters, B. Guy. 2017. "What Is So Wicked about Wicked Problems? A Conceptual Analysis and a Research Program." *Policy and Society* 36 (3): 385-396. DOI: 10.1080/14494035.2017.1361633

Pickering, Catherine, Julien Grignon, Rochelle Stevena, Daniela Guitarta, and Jason Byrne. 2014. "Publishing not Perishing: How Research Students Transition from

Novice to Knowledgeable Using Systematic Quantitative Literature Reviews." *Studies in Higher Education* 40 (10): 1756-1769. DOI: 10.1080/03075079.2014.914907

Porter, Tony, and Michael Webb. 2008. "Role of the OECD in the Orchestration of Global Knowledge Networks." In *The OECD and Transnational Governance*, edited by R. Mahon, and S. McBride, pp. 43-59. Vancouver, BC: UBC Press.

Post, Corinne, Riikka Sarala, Caroline Gatrell, and John E. Prescott. 2020. "Advancing Theory with Review Articles." *Journal of Management Studies* 57 (2): 351-376. DOI: 10.1111/joms.12549

Radaelli, Claudio M. 2009. "Measuring Policy Learning: Regulatory Impact Assessment in Europe." *Journal of European Public Policy* 16 (8): 1145-1164. DOI: 10.1080/13501760903332647

Raudla, Ringa, Aleksandrs Cepilovs, Vytautas Kuokstis, and Rainer Kattel. 2018. "Fiscal Policy Learning from Crisis: Comparative Analysis of the Baltic Countries." *Journal of Comparative Policy Analysis: Research and Practice* 20 (3): 288-303. DOI: 10.1080/13876988.2016.1244947

Rose, Richard. 1991. "What is Lesson Drawing?" *Journal of Public Policy* 11 (1): 3-30. DOI: 10.1017/S0143814X00004918

Rough, Elizabeth. 2011. "Policy Learning through Public Inquiries? The Case of UK Nuclear Energy Policy 1955–61." *Environment and Planning C: Politics and Space* 29 (1): 24-45. DOI: 10.1068/c09184

Sabatier, Paul A. 1988. "An Advocacy Coalition Framework of Policy Change and the Role of Policy-Oriented Learning Therein." *Policy Sciences* 21: 129-168. DOI: 10.1007/BF00136406

Sanderson, Ian. 2009. "Intelligent Policy Making for a Complex World: Pragmatism, Evidence and Learning." *Political Studies* 57 (4): 699–719. DOI: 10.1111/j.1467-9248.2009.00791.x

Sotarauta, Markku. 2012. "Policy Learning and the 'Cluster-Flavoured Innovation Policy' in Finland." *Environment and Planning C: Politics and Space* 30 (5): 780-795. DOI: 10.1068/c1191

Stark, Alastair. 2019. "Policy Learning and the Public Inquiry." *Policy Sciences* 52: 397–417. DOI: 10.1007/s11077-019-09348-0

Stark, Alastair, and Brian Head. 2019. "Institutional Amnesia and Public Policy."

Journal of European Public Policy 26 (0): 1521-1539. DOI: 10.1080/13501763.20 18.1535612

Tamtik, Merli. 2016. "Institutional Change Through Policy Learning: The Case of the European Commission and Research Policy." *Review of Policy Research* 33 (1): 5-21. DOI: 10.1111/ropr.12156

Tavits, Margit. 2003. "Policy Learning and Uncertainty: The Case of Pension Reform in Estonia and Latvia." *Policy Studies Journal* 31 (4): 643-660. DOI: 10.11 11/1541-0072.00047

Thomann, Eva, and Martino Maggetti. 2017. "Designing Research with Qualitative Comparative Analysis (QCA): Approaches, Challenges, and Tools." *Sociological Methods and Research* 49 (2): 356-386. DOI: 10.1177%2F0049124117729700

Thunus, Sophie, and Frédéric Schoenaers. 2017. "How Does Policy Learning Occur? The Case of Belgian Mental Health Care Reforms." *Policy and Society* 36 (2): 270-287. DOI: 10.1080/14494035.2017.1321221

Toens, Katrin, and Claudioa Landwehr. 2009. "The Uncertain Potential of Policy-learning: A Comparative Assessment of Three Varieties." *Policy Studies* 30: 347-363. DOI: 10.1080/01442870902863927

Torraco, Richard J. 2005. "Writing Integrative Literature Reviews: Guidelines and Examples." *Human Resource Development Review* 4: 356-367. DOI: 10.1177/1534484305278283

Wai Yip So, Bennis. 2012. "Learning as a Key to Citizen-centred Performance Improvement: A Comparison between the Health Service Centre and the Household Registration Office in Taipei City." *Australian Journal of Public Administration* 71 (2): 201-2010. DOI: 10.1111/j.1467-8500.2012.00769.x

Weiss, C. 1986. "Research and Policy-making: A Limited Partnership." In *The Use and Abuse of Social Science*, edited by F. Heller, pp. 214–235. London: Sage.

Weissert, Carol S., and Daniel Scheller. 2008. "Learning from the States? Federalism and National Health Policy." *Public Administration Review* 68 (S1): S162-S174. DOI: 10.1111/j.1540-6210.2008.00986.x

Wilson, Christopher. 2019. "Multi-stakeholder Initiatives, Policy Learning and Institutionalization: The Surprising Failure of Open Government in Norway." *Policy Studies* 42 (2): 173-192. DOI: 10.1080/01442872.2019.1618808

Yackee, Susan W., and Christine K. Palus. 2010. "Learning from Experience? Second-Order Policy Devolution and Government Responsiveness." *Lex Localis* 8 (1): 65-92. DOI: 10.4335/8.1.65-92

Zaki, Bishoy L., and Bert George. 2021. "New Development: Policy Learning and Public Management—A Match Made in Crisis." *Public Money and Management* (in press). DOI: 10.1080/09540962.2021.1956212

Zaki, Bishoy L., and Ellen Wayenberg. 2021. "Shopping in the Scientific Marketplace: COVID-19 through a Policy Learning Lens." *Policy Design and Practice* 4 (1): 15-32. DOI: 10.1080/25741292.2020.1843249

Zhang, Yanzhe, and Xiao Yu. 2019. "Policy Transfer: The Case of European Union–China Cooperation in Public Administration Reform." *International Review of Administrative Sciences* 87 (1): 3-20. DOI: 10.1177/0020852319841427

Zito, Anthony R. 2009. "European Agencies as Agents of Governance and EU Learning." *Journal of European Public Policy* 16 (8): 1224-1243. DOI: 10.1080/13 501760903332795

Expanding the Utility of Cross-Sectoral Collaboration in Policy Studies: Present and Future

Madeleine W. McNamara

Old Dominion University

John C. Morris

Auburn University

Across many disciplines, scholars develop and test theoretical frameworks to describe and explain collaborative processes. Much of the focus in the policy sciences links collaboration to policy implementation. Collaboration theory is not only applicable to other stages of the policy process but could serve to enhance the repertoire of relevant policy theories. This article applies collaboration theory to a common five-stage model of the policy process (agenda setting, formulation, adoption, implementation, and evaluation). We examine the state of the policy model literature and offer opportunities for the inclusion of cross-sectoral collaboration theories to create mutual benefit. While the necessity of time and resources may create fundamental challenges in wholeheartedly linking the collaboration literature to the command-and-control processes of public policy, small but important linkages can be made through the local service network level. The power of cross-sector collaboration can be channeled through the engagement of grassroots collaboratives, street-level bureaucrats, stakeholders, and citizens throughout various stages of the policy process. We present some current examples, including linkages to the COVID-19 pandemic, to highlight how cross-sectoral collaboration relates to policy dilemmas.

Keywords: Public Policy, Policy Process, Mandated Collaboration, Voluntary Collaboration, Agenda Setting, Formulation, Adoption, Policy Implementation, Policy Evaluation, Deliberative Democracy, COVID-19, Collaborative Federalism.

Ampliación de la utilidad de la colaboración intersectorial en Estudios de Políticas: Presente y Futuro

En muchas disciplinas, los académicos desarrollan y prueban marcos teóricos para describir y explicar procesos colaborativos. Gran parte

Policy Studies Yearbook 12.1: 53-70. 10.18278/psy.12.1.3

del enfoque en las ciencias de las políticas vincula la colaboración con la implementación de políticas. La teoría de la colaboración no solo es aplicable a otras etapas del proceso político, sino que podría servir para mejorar el repertorio de teorías políticas relevantes. Este artículo aplica la teoría de la colaboración a un modelo común de cinco etapas del proceso de políticas (establecimiento de la agenda, formulación, adopción, implementación y evaluación). Examinamos el estado de la literatura sobre modelos de políticas y ofrecemos oportunidades para la inclusión de teorías de colaboración intersectorial para generar un beneficio mutuo. Si bien la necesidad de tiempo y recursos puede crear desafíos fundamentales para vincular de todo corazón la literatura de colaboración con los procesos de comando y control de las políticas públicas, se pueden establecer vínculos pequeños pero importantes a través del nivel de la red de servicios local. El poder de la colaboración intersectorial se puede canalizar a través de la participación de colaboradores de base, burócratas a nivel de calle, partes interesadas y ciudadanos a lo largo de las diversas etapas del proceso de políticas. Presentamos algunos ejemplos actuales, incluidos los vínculos con la pandemia de COVID-19, para resaltar cómo la colaboración intersectorial se relaciona con los dilemas de políticas.

Palabras clave: Política pública, Proceso de políticas, Colaboración obligatoria, Colaboración voluntaria, Establecimiento de agenda, Formulación, Adopción, Implementación de políticas, Evaluación de políticas, Democracia deliberativa, COVID-19, Federalismo colaborativo.

擴大跨部門合作的效用在政策研究：現在和未來

在許多學科中，學者開發和測試理論框架來描述和解釋協作過程。政策科學的大部分重點將合作與政策實施聯繫起來。協作理論不僅適用於政策過程的其他階段，而且可以用於增強相關政策理論的全部內容。本文將協作理論應用於政策過程的常見五階段模型（議程設置、制定、採納、實施和評估）。我們研究了政策模型文獻的狀態，並提供了納入跨部門合作理論以創造互惠互利的機會。雖然時間和資源的必要性可能會在全心全意將協作文獻與公共政策的命令和控制過程聯繫起來時產生根本性挑戰，但可以通過本地服務網絡級別建立小而重要的聯繫。跨部門合作的力量可以通過草根合作組織、街頭官僚、利益相關者和公民在政策過程的各個階

段的參與來發揮作用。我們提供了一些當前的例子，包括與
COVID-19　大流行的聯繫，以強調跨部門合作如何與政策困
境相關。

關鍵詞：公共政策、政策過程、授權合作、自願合作、議
程設置、制定、採用、政策實施、政策評估、協商民主、–
COVID-19、合作聯邦制。

The publication of Barbara Gray's 1985 article on collaboration, followed by her book (*Collaborating*) four years later (Gray 1989), spawned a deluge of scholarship the purpose of which was to develop and test theory regarding voluntary relationships in the policy arena. Some 35 years later, scholarship on collaboration may be found across the social sciences, and in other disciplines as well. Collaboration has indeed become an integral concept in the academic literature.

The policy sciences have also seen a growth in the amount of attention paid to collaboration. To date, however, most of this research tends to be focused on policy implementation, but comparatively little has been published regarding collaboration in other stages of the policy process. From the standpoint of scholars of collaboration, much of the literature's empirical work also focuses on implementation processes. Moreover, at least in the policy sciences, the bulk of the empirical studies employing collaboration as an element of interest are focused on the realm of environmental policy and questions of collective action in the natural resources arena.

While this work is certainly interesting and important, it is our contention that collaboration theory is also applicable to other stages of the policy process. Indeed, to make such connections not only enhances our knowledge of the policy process but serves to build our repertoire of relevant policy theories. Gray's (1985, 1989) focus is clearly on the role of voluntary collaboration as a means to enhance policy implementation. By harnessing the resources of volunteers, implementation could be enhanced through a range of mechanisms. Although her attention is on implementation, it is largely left to the reader to make the leap—Gray views collaboration through the lens of organization theory, even if the larger contextual frame is implementation. More recent literature keeps the frame of implementation but shifts collaboration to a focus on network relationships. We contend that a narrow focus on implementation misses an opportunity to enhance theoretical and practical richness by extending our conceptions of collaboration in other stages of the policy process. In developing new possibilities for the application of collaboration, we create potential opportunities to further develop collaboration theory which can then be used to further extend its practical application to the policy sciences.

The present article explores the current state of knowledge (and application) of collaboration theory in the policy sciences. Through the application of a common five-stage model of the policy process (agenda setting, formulation, adoption, implementation, and evaluation), we examine the state of the literature, and identify several opportunities for the inclusion of cross-sectoral collaboration theories across the spectrum of policy studies. We address each policy stage in turn. We then present some examples about how cross-sectoral collaboration might relate to current policy dilemmas, before concluding with some thoughts about the utility of linkages between the literatures on collaboration and the policy sciences.

Agenda Setting

The agenda-setting process represents both opportunities and challenges for collaborative action. The collaboration literature tends to treat collaborative activity as an action-oriented enterprise, with a focus on tangible outputs and outcomes (see Sabatier *et al.* 2005; Morris *et al.* 2013; Reed 2015). Indeed, voluntary collaboration (Gray 1989) relies on a sense of accomplishment of measurable goals to motivate participants. Resource sharing is typically structured around implementation activities in pursuit of outputs and outcomes.

Agenda setting also requires resources, but the outputs and outcomes are not as clear, at least on a macro scale. One area of convergence is between the policy network and collaboration literatures. Following Gray's (1989) initial definition of collaboration as an organizational process, a spate of work in the 1990s and 2000s began to view collaboration through a lens of network theory (see O'Toole 1995; Mandell and Keast 2007; deLeon and Varda 2009). Policy networks are long-established elements of the agenda-setting process and serve to tie policy makers together through common interests and information sharing. In the abstract, policy networks share elements in common with collaboration, and one may reasonably argue that collaborative efforts can include policy networks (or parts of networks). However, we contend that, while collaborations can include policy networks, policy networks are not, in an of themselves, collaborations. Following Gray's (1985) discussion of collaboration, collaborations have clear, agreed-upon goals, forge collective decisions regarding shared resources, and exhibit high levels of social capital—traits that are not prerequisites of policy networks.

Still, collaborations have a role to play in agenda setting. In their study of grassroots environmental groups, Morris and others (2013) note that grassroots environmental collaborations can serve to coalesce interests in the community and help to garner support for policy initiatives. Similarly to an interest group, collaborations can also mobilize their members in support of, or opposition to, policy initiatives and serve as an information source for problem definition and the development of policy alternatives. However, little research to date, either in the policy literature or the collaboration literature, has sought to explore the specific role of collaboration at the agenda-setting stage. Understanding the role of collaborations in agenda setting, and efforts to better define the similarities and differences between policy networks and collaborative groups, can offer an interesting and theoretically fruitful line of inquiry.

Formulation

Hudson, Hunter, and Peckham (2019) suggest that collaboration is lacking in policy making, particularly in terms of policy design. Their argument is constructed around a model of policy making that rejects a "siloed" approach to policy design in favor of interorganizational partnering (Hudson, Hunter, and Peckham 2019, 3) and engagement with a range of stakeholders. They suggest that "policy design requires continuous collaboration with a range of stakeholders at multiple political, policy-making, managerial and administrative levels as well as the engagement of local "downstream" implementation actors" (Hudson, Hunter, and Peckham 2019, 4). Their larger point is well taken, even though their conceptualization of "collaboration" is likely different than that found in the broader collaboration literature.

The implications for governance (see Kekez, Howlett, and Ramesh 2018) in terms of the inclusion of collaborative processes in policy formulation are profound, although the ability to apply the term "collaboration" to this setting depends entirely on the operative definition of the term. Collaboration has been used to describe a wide range of interactions, and the lack of conceptual clarity in the collaboration literature (see McNamara 2012; Morris and Miller-Stevens 2016) is both liberating and constraining. It is liberating in the sense that one can apply the term to a given interaction, and one would not necessarily be wrong to describe that interaction as "collaboration." It is constraining in that if collaboration is everything, it is nothing. When applied to policy formulation, the interactions described generally are not congruent with Gray's (1989) definition; rather, they tend to be cooperative or consultative. This should not suggest that these interactions are pointless, but instead that the lack of conceptual clarity in this space limits our ability to move much beyond atheoretical description.

The lack of conceptual clarity is not as much a limitation within the policy sciences as it is a limitation in the collaboration literature (see Morris and Miller-Stevens 2016). Collaborative policy design may be aspirational, but it is not clear whether collaborative policy design is preferable to cooperative (or coordinative) policy design. Likewise, because policy design occurs in different ways in different settings, it may be the case that collaborative policy design is more likely (or, perhaps, more likely to be successful) in settings with different characteristics. Lacking any theoretical guidance, policy scholars must revert to a form of "barefoot empiricism" when applying collaboration to the formulation stage.

Adoption

Policy adoption is limited in its linkages to collaboration by the democratic process and the interests of elected officials. As adoption focuses on the decision making of government actors, elected officials have significant power to determine the acceptable course of action among policy alternatives (Lindblom and Woodhouse 1993). Therefore, an elected official's individual and political interests influence the trajectory of the remainder of the policy process through their decision making and policy preferences. An emphasis on continuity and stability, supported by incremental decision making and bounded rationality, further supports a rigidity within the process that may stunt opportunities for collaboration.

While collaboration may be an unlikely tool to reduce political constraints, it can be used to improve the state of knowledge for elected officials during the decision-making process. In other words, opportunities for collaboration exist through a desire to balance knowledge and power. Lindblom and Woodhouse (1993) describe this process of discussion and analysis as reasoned persuasion in the determination of a policy choice. Collaboration can help elected officials identify and leverage common ground in their decision-making process. Their abilities to manage these differences in the early stages of the policy process can improve implementation (Hudson, Hunter and Peckham 2019).

Linkages with collaboration may help address inherent inequalities based on access to influence decision makers in the policy process. Establishing linkages between elected officials and street-level professionals with specialized knowledge to inform policy selections could reduce these inequalities through informed discussions. A collaborative manager plays a significant role in establishing the group (McNamara, Leavitt, and Morris 2010; Bryson, Crosby, and Stone 2006) and facilitating interactions to generate stability between organizations (Morris and Burns 1997). The responsibilities of elected officials could be similarly oriented toward legitimizing the collaborative process to enhance understanding prior to making policy decisions.

The engagement of street-level specialists within the decision-making process can help elected officials best understand the complexities of the policy problem while allowing for a more equitable and diverse exchange of ideas. To the extent that street-level bureaucrats have discretion during policy implementation, they can also serve as an important source of information during the adoption phase. Hudson and others (2019, 4) describe these "downstream implementation actors" as service recipients, frontline staff, and service agency employees at the local level. Tapping into this already identified position would increase the flow of information to the politician making the decision. In effect, this creates a continuous feedback loop from service delivery collaborators.

The benefit of linking the collaboration literature with the policy adoption phase has to do with minimizing information gaps. The end state could offer insight into how to draw information not just from traditional policy actors that provide information at the formulation stage but also from bureaucrats and stakeholders involved in service delivery during implementation. Focusing on these vertical and horizontal connections allows policy actors to identify common ground with an emphasis on sufficiency rather than total agreement (Ansell, Sorensen, and Torfing 2017).

Implementation

The importance of partnerships in the achievement of policy and program goals is well documented in the public policy and collaboration literatures. Administrators often rely on cross-sector collaboration to enhance public goods and services as complex problems and resource stresses challenge the abilities of single organizations to address public needs. Discussions regarding this type of relationship are prominent among public administration practitioners and scholars as nuances are explored in areas such as collaborative management, organizational processes, service delivery outcomes, and distinctions from other types of interactions. In other words, the topic of collaboration has expanded within public administration theory and practice. However, this scale and scope of collaboration interest is not mirrored in the implementation literature.

Partnerships within the multiorganizational implementation literature are primarily viewed as formalized interactions based on policy mandate, agency rule making, or organizational procedures. Emphasis is placed on the extent to which policies identify interorganizational partners (Hall and O'Toole 2004), policy characteristics that induce or constrain interdependence (May 1995; O'Toole 1995), or the structures used in multiorganizational implementation (see, e.g., Hall and O'Toole 2004; Mandell 1994). "Structural signatures" for collaboration networks are identified (deLeon and Varda 2009, 661) but maintain a more formal focus on relationships. This emphasis on organized efforts does not address fully the complete picture in which nuanced, or even informal, relationships are used to improve policy implementation. Linkages between policy implementation and collaboration may help expand the range of interactions considered within network settings.

When thinking about implementation action at the level of service delivery, the collaboration literature can be beneficial when considering sustaining horizontal relationships across hierarchical structures through middle level personnel that have the discretion to enter horizontal arrangements and allocate organizational resources to collective efforts (McNamara and Morris 2021). If implementation action occurs at the service delivery level through the discretion of cumulative decision making as Lipsky (1980) suggests, then relationships outside the hierarchical structure play a significant role in developing and sustaining relationships. Connecting the implementation literature's street-level bureaucrats (Lipsky 1980) with the collaboration literature's manager may help facilitate conditions that support the implementation process. Decisions are made constantly at the lower levels of an organization to create public policy in a cumulative way. It is through this discretionary judgment that the policy implementation literature already acknowledges an opportunity to move beyond command-and-control authority inherent in bureaucratic organizations. In collaborative arrangements, stakeholders work together to make program decisions and set collective goals through the development of shared norms and interests (Thomson and Perry 2006). Through this process, organizational boundaries are blurred (Keast, Brown, and Mandell 2007).

As cross-sector arrangements become increasingly prevalent, implementation success may have a lot to do with how well organizations connect across boundaries in addition to policy specificity or the acknowledgement of environmental conditions at the local level (McNamara 2016). The power lies in connecting the people that already have discretionary judgment within their organizations. In collaboration, public managers facilitate connections across organizations to connect people across organizations to improve service delivery networks. Some basic elements of collaboration may not fit easily into the more formal, hierarchical approach of network theory. However, engaging service delivery networks at the street-level creates a "sweet spot" for the intersection of policy implementation and collaboration. The policy literature could better capitalize on the power of connection by engaging street-level bureaucrats in cross-sector collaboration.

If policy implementation can be improved by connecting middle-level actors across different organizations, the position of the person who has legitimacy to support these connections becomes paramount. Certainly, the burden of this responsibility falls on government employees to transcend highly centralized and hierarchical structures to create and sustain horizontal linkages between organizations. Public administrators and policy implementors must understand how to work within and across stovepipe specializations to address complex problems. The demands of managing cross-sector arrangements are addressed empirically in the collaboration literature (McGuire 2006; McNamara and Morris 2021). Linkages between hierarchical and collaborative management are necessary, and part of making those linkages require public managers to understand the nuances of different arrangements (McNamara 2016). Policy implementors within service delivery networks are public administrators, but the nuances and challenges associated with managing these complex network arrangements are not addressed in the policy implementation literature and would be helpful.

Practically speaking, multiorganizational implementation does occur outside the boundaries of operational authority. Therefore, multiorganizational arrangements should not be treated as a mere extension of hierarchical organizations that only abide by specifications in policy mandates. An emphasis on formal interactions assumes that relationships between organizations can be predetermined, centrally controlled, and monitored to meet policy goals by focusing on formally initiated interactions as the sole source for action. This approach fails to consider that legislators are limited in their abilities to foresee and specify the interactions required in complex implementation settings (O'Toole and Montjoy 1984).

The collaboration literature acknowledges the importance of formal and information relationships in cross-sector arrangements (McNamara 2012; 2016). Formalized interactions are often initiated through grant contracts and create important accountability mechanisms for the distribution of financial resources among organizations that operate outside command-and-control authorities. Informal interactions are an important aspect of partnerships working across organizational boundaries to achieve collective goals or align resources. Understanding the missions and interests of partnering organizations helps personnel informally develop and sustain relationships. Linkages to the collaboration literature may help policy theorists apply the different ways in which arrangements are initiated during policy implementation.

Evaluation

There are different ways to think about utilization and the process of evaluation to determine if intended goals are met based on consideration for the importance placed on values, the responsibilities of the evaluator, and the inclusion of stakeholders. When conducting evaluation in the constructivist paradigm through the deliberative democratic view, the values of all actors are considered important in the construction of reality. The role of the evaluator and the process used to engage participants are driven by value choices and a desire to be better informed through the constructions of stakeholders.

The policy evaluation and collaboration literatures most naturally link through the constructivist paradigm and the deliberative democratic view where values are acknowledged in determining effectiveness. The role of values takes on significant importance when considering that evaluation creates opportunity to inject new information into the policy process. Linking themes from the policy evaluation and collaboration literatures may therefore be helpful in better understanding the complexities of the role of the evaluator and the power of stakeholder inclusion.

The facilitation skills of the collaborative manager may help expand the role of the policy evaluator beyond the authoritative expert in the constructivist paradigm. Both positions must find ways to include relevant stakeholders in the process. According to the deliberative democratic view, evaluation is value-laden with emphasis on inclusion, dialogue, and deliberation (House and Howe 1999). Stakeholder inclusion is important and determined by the evaluator based on evaluation context and typical perspective criteria. Complexity arises as conflicting value claims change, evaluators are placed in the role as authoritarian expert to define the parameters for stakeholder legitimacy, the worth of value claims, and the establishment of evaluation criteria. The deliberative democratic view assumes that appropriate decisions among potentially competing democratic values can be made by evaluators who operate outside all channels of political accountability. Through their authoritarian position, the evaluator can limit morally questionable and extreme value claims within the dialectic to control the focus of the evaluation and who is included in the study (House and Howe 1999). Both collaborative managers and policy evaluators require an element of legitimacy. In addition to an appreciation for the potential of mutual exchange, the convener must be seen as a legitimate figure to facilitate trust with and between participants (Gray 1985).

The purposeful way collaborative managers facilitate stakeholder inclusion may help the policy evaluator balance competing values throughout the dialectic process. In the deliberative democratic view, the evaluator attempts to equalize value claims by legitimate stakeholders through neutralizing power imbalances. The representation of all legitimate value claims prevents the most powerful stakeholders from distorting the dialogical process. Therefore, major decisions are based on stakeholders' abilities to persuade the evaluator in the legitimacy of their value claims. In the hermeneutic dialectic, topics are placed on the agenda for negotiation when agreements among stakeholders are not secured. The cyclical nature of the dialectic process creates multiple opportunities for stakeholders to persuade one another (Guba and Lincoln 1989). Stakeholder value claims are not weighted equally, and evaluators use impartial and reflective deliberation to make unbiased judgments to determine legitimate value claims (House and Howe 1999). For this process to work, citizens must be willing and able to articulate their values claims and present evidence (deLeon 1992). As public deliberation explores the problems most pressing for administrators, inquiry improves.

Stakeholder inclusion is also important in collaborative management and policy evaluation. The collaborative manager also encourages the framing of values, norms, and rules to help mold the perceptions of participants (Agranoff and McGuire 2001) while scanning the environment to determine the appropriate sense of timing (Honig 2006). Through the process participants from different organizations with unique missions and cultures build consensus for a shared vision. Group discussions allow opportunities to learn from other participants in order to find common ground and increase knowledge of other perspectives to develop creative solutions and shared agreement on goals and objectives (McNamara and Morris 2012). Notably missing from the literature are efforts to comprehend why collaboration fails. Empirically speaking, not all collaborations are successful, yet there is little in the way of guidance to recognize the underlying causes for failure. Continued exploration of why some collaborative efforts succeed while others fail is needed.

Influence within the group and resources shared with the group may not be equal, but the opportunity to participate freely within the group is shared through a governance structure that provides equality to each participant's voice (Mc-

Namara and Morris 2012). Creating a governance structure that operates outside hierarchical structures promotes inclusivity within the group. The collaborative manager facilitates relationships and provides opportunities for participants to identify solutions in ways that are productive individually and collectively.

In anchoring the themes of stakeholder inclusion and deliberative dialogue to the collaboration literature, the evaluator can move beyond the role of the authoritarian expert toward the role of collaborative evaluator. Collaborative managers bring equal partners together to identify resolutions to complex problems through a participative approach that emphasizes shared power (McNamara 2012). There is a predetermined nature to the arrangement in the sense that collaborative managers match problems with participants who have the resources and expertise to provide solutions for the identified problem (McGuire 2006) while facilitating understanding of the benefits of a mutually beneficial relationship through persuasion and strategic problem solving (McNamara and Morris 2012; McGuire 2006).

Some Examples

The COVID-19 pandemic provides a vivid context for thinking about how cross-sector collaboration may relate to the practice of policy studies. In the U.S. context of federalism, the national, state, and local government share implementation responsibility across a range of policy arenas. Certainly, the national government can be directive (see Kettl 2020), but much of the substance of policy implementation takes place via a form of shared governance in which resources are also shared. During 2020 there were examples of collaborative efforts among U.S. states to address the pandemic, such as the sharing of information, protective equipment, and regional agreements among states to determine when to relax restrictions (see "Seven States to Coordinate" 2020). A similar approach was initiated by several states in the western part of the nation. However, anecdotal evidence suggests that, despite the best intentions of these governors, states ultimately relaxed restrictions based on the conditions within their states, rather than as part of a collective decision process.

At the same time, the relationships between most states and the national government were not only not collaborative, they were often combative. The "transactional federalism" (Bowling, Fisk, and Morris 2020) practiced by the Trump administration valued fealty to the president above all else. Shared goals and shared decision making were largely nonexistent. While the United States has practiced different conceptions of federalism at different points in its history, Wright (2003) notes that the period between the 1980s and the beginning of the twenty-first century was marked by growth in intergovernmental networks and collaborative approaches to policy implementation. The first decade of the new century saw a change in approach in federalism that was market by partisanship (Bulman-Pozen 2014), fragmentation (Bowling and Pickerill 2013), claims of overreach, and opportunism (see Conlan 2006; Burke 2014). This trend turned sharply upward in the four years following the Obama administration, resulting in transactional federalism (Bowling, Fisk, and Morris 2020). In many ways, this new form of federalism was the opposite of collaborative (or even cooperative) approaches to federalism, in that relationships were seen as a competitive exchange. This was especially evident during the COVID-19 pandemic, during which the federal government sought to trade basic medical supplies, testing kits, ventilators, and other necessities for support for the president (see Rupar 2020). Likewise, the president suggested that states that made policy changes on issues such as payroll taxes, sanctuary city status, and other policies might receive more favorable treatment from his administration (Sheth 2020). The president's intergovernmental management style was, in effect, to reward political allies and to punish political foes. The president also made several claims that asserted executive (or federal) control over long-standing areas of state responsibility (see Craig and Dennis 2020).

A second policy arena in which we can detect evidence of collaboration is in efforts to address global warming. International efforts have been focused on participation by large numbers of nations. Participants work together to develop emissions targets (goals), and pledge resources to meet those goals. Information and technical expertise are shared between participants. Not all nations are participants, but collaboration theory does not require that all stakeholders must participate in any collaborative effort. Collaboration may be more successful if all major stakeholders participate (see Morris *et al.* 2013), but collaboration can work without the participation of major stakeholders. At a smaller level, efforts such as The Climate Pledge in the United States can provide tangible benefits by engaging with stakeholders in collaborative efforts to reduce carbon emissions.

Collaboration may be particularly useful at the local level. Morris and others (2013, 2014) conclude that a connection to "place" serves to motivate collaborative participants, even among industries not generally known for collaborative activity. Grassroots environmental collaborative groups exhibit activity in all stages of the policy process: agenda setting (problem definition); policy formulation (goal setting); adoption (decision making); implementation (project work); and evaluation (achievement of outputs and outcomes). Scale may also be an important factor, in that voluntary collaboration efforts are collections of like-minded people who seek to make a difference in their community. Indeed, if Morris and others (2013) are correct, voluntary collaboration may be ideally suited to localized problems, and the application of collaboration to larger (or more geographically dispersed) policy problems may limit the utility of collaboration.

Another challenge to collaboration models in the policy sciences is that voluntary collaboration is often cross-sectoral, but *public* policy infers a governmental process. Many nations have a long history of cross-sectoral implementation, but public policy makers are less sanguine about relinquishing their policy authority to non governmental actors. Leveraging resources from nongovernmental entities at implementation is often regarded as an indicator of "good" public policy; however, allowing unofficial policy participants to engage in adoption decisions, for example, may be a "bridge too far" for many, and raises important questions regarding governance.

We would be remiss if we did not also raise the issue of hyper-partisanship in American policy making. Voluntary collaboration is built on mutual respect, shared decision making, an equal voice in the process, and respect for all participants. These are generally not the first thoughts that come to mind when describing American policy making in the twenty-first century. Indeed, the agenda denial so prevalent in the U.S. Senate in the past decade, coupled with more recent efforts to restrict voter participation in many states, are anathema to collaboration. Successful collaboration requires the ability to agree on a common goal, a feat that seems nearly impossible in our current political environment.

Conclusion

This article explores linkages between cross-sector collaboration and the policy cycle. In general, cross-sector collaboration takes time and resources to develop long-standing relationships based on trust and high levels of commitment as stakeholders make group decisions based on collective goals (Keast, Brown, and Mandell 2007; McNamara 2012). The necessity of time and resources may create fundamental challenges in wholeheartedly linking the collaboration literature to the command-and-control processes in policy and policy making.

However, the collaboration literature acknowledges that resolutions to complex problems can be achieved in small increments that accumulate into something bigger with time (Morris *et al.* 2013). Through small but important linkages, there are ways to couple the two literatures by focusing on the stages of the policy cycle that make the most sense for cross-sector collaboration. The lens for applicability is also impacted by the level of analysis for application. At the local, service network level, the power of cross-sector collaboration can be channeled through the engagement of grassroots collaboratives, street-level bureaucrats, stakeholders, and citizens throughout the various stages of the policy process. While the linkages between collaboration and implementation are the most obvious and best represented in both literatures, small connections in other policy stages may also be valuable.

Much can still be done in the cross-sector collaboration and public policy literatures to create mutual benefit. Conceptual clarity for interaction terms is paramount. The collaboration literature makes important distinctions between interaction terms (see e.g., Keast, Brown, and Mandell 2007; McNamara 2012, 2016). There is continued room for growth and distinction among interaction terms. Distinctions are overwhelmingly ignored in the public policy literature but need to be included in future discussion in order to situate properly a full range of interactions and their potential uses.

About the Authors

Madeleine Wright McNamara is an adjunct assistant professor in the School of Public Service at Old Dominion University. She served previously as a Visiting Assistant Professor in the Department of Political Science at the University of New Orleans and as the Waterways Management Coordinator for the U.S. Coast Guard's Eighth District in New Orleans. Her research interests include collaboration, public policy, and interorganizational theory. Her work appears in journals such as *Public Works Management & Policy, International Journal of Public Administration, Politics & Policy,* and the *Journal for Nonprofit Management,* among others. In addition, she authored chapters in *Speaking Green with a Southern Accent: Environmental Management and Innovation in the South* (2010), and *Advancing Collaboration Theory: Models, Typologies, and Evidence* (2016, Routledge).

John C. Morris is a Professor of Political Science at Auburn University. He is the author/co-author/editor of 12 books and more than 100 journal articles, book chapters, and reports. His work has appeared in journals such as *Policy Studies Journal, Public Administration Review, Politics & Policy, The Journal of Politics,* and the *American Review of Public Administration,* among others. His research interests include state comparative policy, governance and collaboration, and environmental policy.

References

Agranoff, Robert, and Michael McGuire. 2001. "Big Questions in Public Network Management Research." *Journal of Public Administration Research and Theory* 11 (3): 295-326. DOI: 10.1093/oxfordjournals.jpart.a003504

Ansell, Christopher, Eva Sorensen, and Jacob Torfing. 2017. "The COVID-19 Pandemic as a Game Changer for Public Administration and Leadership? The Need for Robust Governance Responses to Turbulent Problems." *Public Management Review* 23 (7): 949-960. DOI: 10.1080/14719037.2020.1820272

Bowling, Cynthia, Jonathan Fisk, and John Morris. 2020. "Seeking Patterns in Chaos: Transactional Federalism in the Trump Administration's Response to the COVID-19 Pandemic." *American Review of Public Administration* 50 (6-7): 512-18. DOI: 10.1177/0275074020941686

Bowling, Cynthia, and J. Mitchell Pickerill. 2013. "Fragmented Federalism: The

State of American Federalism 2012-13." *Publius* (43)3: 315-346. DOI: 10.1093/publius/pjt022

Bryson, John, Barbara C. Crosby, and Melissa Middleton Stone. 2006. "The Design and Implementation of Cross-Sector Collaborations: Propositions from the Literature." *Public Administration Review* 66 (Special Issue): 44-53. DOI: 10.1111/j.1540-6210.2006.00665.x

Bulman-Pozen, Jessica. 2014. "Partisan Federalism." *Harvard Law Review* 127 (4): 1077-1146.

Burke, Brendan. 2014. "Understanding Intergovernmental Relations, Twenty-five Years Hence." *State and Local Government Review* 46 (1): 63-76. DOI: 108.82.132.104

Conlan, Timothy. 2006. "From Cooperative to Opportunistic Federalism: Reflections on the Half-Century Anniversary of the Commission on Intergovernmental Relations." *Public Administration Review* 66 (5): 663-676. DOI: 10.1111/j.1540-6210.2006.00631.x

Craig, Tim, and Brady Dennis. 2020. "Governors Consider Lifting Virus Restrictions; Trump Says He Alone Will Decide." *Washington Post*, April 13. Accessed on October 25. 2021. https://www.washingtonpost.com/politics/governors-form-groups-to-explore-lifting-virus-restrictions-trump-says-he-alone-will-decide/2020/04/13/f04a401e-7d84-11ea-a3ee-13e1ae0a3571_story.html

deLeon, Peter. 1992. "The Democratization of the Policy Sciences." *Public Administration Review* 52 (2): 125-129. DOI: 10.2307/976465

deLeon, Peter, and Danielle Varda. 2009. "Toward a Theory of Collaborative Policy Networks: Identifying Structural Tendencies." *Policy Studies Journal* 37 (1): 59-74. DOI: 10.1111/j.1541-0072.2008.00295.x

Gray, Barbara. 1989. *Collaborating: Finding Common Ground for Multiparty Problems*. San Francisco, CA: Jossey-Bass.

_____. 1985. "Conditions Facilitating Interorganizational Collaboration." *Human Relations* 38: 911-936. DOI: 10.1177/001872678503801001

Guba, Egon, and Yvonna Lincoln. 1989. *Fourth Generation Evaluation*. Thousand Oaks, CA: Sage.

Hall, Thad, and Laurence J. O'Toole, Jr. 2004. "Shaping Formal Networks Through the Regulatory Process." *Administration & Society* 36 (2): 186-207. DOI: 10.1177/00 95399704263476

Honig, Meredith. 2006. "Street-Level Bureaucracy Revisited: Frontline District Central-Office Administrators as Boundary Spanners in Education Policy Implementation." *Educational Evaluation and Policy Analysis* 28 (4): 357-383. DOI: 10.3102/01623737028004357

House, Ernest R., and Kenneth R. Howe. 1999. *Values in Evaluation and Social Research.* Thousand Oaks, CA: Sage Publications.

Hudson, Bob, David Hunter, and Stephen Peckham. 2019. "Policy Failure and the Policy-Implementation Gap: Can Policy Support Programs Help?" *Policy Design and Practice* 2 (1): 1-14. DOI: 10.1080/25741292.2018.1540378

Keast, Robyn, Kerry Brown, and Myrna Mandell. 2007. "Getting the Right Mix: Unpacking Integration Meanings and Strategies." *International Public Management Journal* 10 (1): 9-33. DOI: 10.1080/10967490601185716

Kettl, Donald F. 2020. *The Divided States of America: Why Federalism Doesn't Work.* Princeton, NJ: Princeton University Press.

Kezek, Anka, Michael Howlett, and M. Ramesh. 2018. "Varieties of Collaboration in Public Service Delivery." *Policy Design and Practice* 1 (4): 243-252. DOI: 10.1080/25741292.2018.1532026

Lindblom, Charles E., and Edward Woodhouse. 1993. *The Policy-Making Process.* Upper Saddle River, NJ: Prentice-Hall.

Lipsky, Michael. 1980. *Street-Level Bureaucracy: Dilemmas of the Individual in Public Services.* New York: Crane Russak.

McGuire, Michael. 2006. "Collaborative Public Management: Assessing What we Know and How We Know It." *Public Administration Review* 66 (Supplement): 33-43. DOI: 10.1111/j.1540-6210.2006.00664.x

McNamara, Madeleine W. 2016. "Unraveling the Characteristics of Mandated Collaboration." In *Advancing Collaboration Theory: Models, Typologies, and Evidence,* edited by John C. Morris and Katrina Miller-Stevens, 65-86. New York: Routledge Press.

_____. 2012. "Starting to Untangle the Web of Cooperation, Coordination, and Collaboration: A Framework for Public Managers." *International Journal of Public*

Administration 35 (6): 389-401. DOI: 10.1080/01900692.2012.655527

McNamara, Madeleine W., and John C. Morris. 2012. "More than a One-Trick Pony: Exploring the Contours of a Multi-Sector Convener." *Journal for Nonprofit Management* 15 (1): 84-103.

_____. 2021. *Multiorganizational Arrangements for Watershed Protection: Working Better Together*. New York: Routledge Press.

McNamara, Madeleine W., William M. Leavitt, and John C. Morris. 2010. "Multiple Sector Partnerships and the Engagement of Citizens in Social Marketing Campaigns." *Virginia Social Science Journal* 45: 1-20. DOI: 10.1177/1087724X18803116

Mandell, Myrna. 1994. "Managing Interdependencies through Program Structures: A Revised Paradigm." *American Review of Public Administration* 24 (1): 99-121. DOI: 10.1177/027507409402400106

Mandell, Myrna, and Robyn Keast. 2007. "Evaluating Network Arrangements: Toward Revised Performance Measures." *Public Performance & Management Review* 30 (4): 574-597. DOI: 10.2753/PMR1530-9576300406

May, Peter. 1995. "Can Cooperation be Mandated? Implementing Intergovernmental Environmental Management in New South Wales and New Zealand." *Publius: The Journal of Federalism* 25 (1): 89-113. DOI: 10.2307/3330658

Morris, John C., and Mark Burns. 1997. "Rethinking the Interorganizational Environments of Public Organizations: An Examination of the Role of Referent Organizations." *Southeastern Political Review* 25(1): 3-25. DOI: 10.1111/j.1747-1346.1997.tb00449.x

Morris, John C., and Katrina Miller-Stevens (Eds). 2016. *Advancing collaboration theory: Models, typologies, and evidence*. New York: Routledge Press.

Morris, John C., William Gibson, William M. Leavitt, and Shana C. Jones. 2014. "Collaborative Federalism and the Emerging Role of Local Nonprofits in Water Quality Implementation." *Publius: The Journal of Federalism* 44 (3): 499-519. DOI: 10.1093/publius/pju019

_____. 2013. *The Case for Grassroots Collaboration: Social Capital and Ecosystem Restoration at the Local Level*. Lanham Park, MD: Lexington Press.

O'Toole, Laurence J., Jr. 1995. "Rational Choice and Policy Implementation: Implications for Interorganizational Network Management." *American Review of Public*

Administration 25 (1): 43-57.

O'Toole, Laurence J., Jr., and Robert S. Montjoy. 1984. "Interorganizational Policy Implementation: A Theoretical Perspective." *Public Administration Review* 44 (6): 491-503. DOI: 10.1177/027507409502500103

Reed, Christine. 2015. *Saving the Pryor Mountain Mustang: A Legacy of Local and Federal Cooperation*. Reno, NV: University of Nevada Press.

Rupar, Aaron. 2020. "Trump Commits to Helping Blue States Fight the Coronavirus—If their Governors are Nice to Him." *Vox. Com*, March 25. Accessed October 25, 2021. https://www.vox.com/2020/3/25/21193803/trump-to-governors-coronavirus-help-ventilators-cuomo

Sabatier, Paul, Will Focht, Mark Lubell, Zev Trachtenberg, Arnold Vedlitz, and Marty Matlock. 2005. *Swimming Upstream: Collaborative Approaches to Watershed Management*. MIT Press.

"Seven States to Coordinate on Amassing Medical Equipment to Fight Coronavirus." *New York Times*, May 3. Accessed October 24, 2021. https:// www.nytimes.com/2020/05/03/nyregion/coronavirus-new-york-update.html

Sheth, Sonam. 2020. "Trump Says He Might Give Federal Coronavirus Aid to States if they Comply with his Political Demands." *Business Insider*, May 5. Accessed October 26, 2021.https://www.yahoo.com/news/trump-says-might-condition-federal-201032305.html

Thomson, Ann Marie, and James Perry. 2006. "Collaboration Process: Inside the Black Box." *Public Administration Review* 66 (Special Issue): 20-32. DOI: 10.1111/j.1540-6210.2006.00663.x

Wright, Deil S. 2003. "Federalism and Intergovernmental Relations: Traumas, Tensions, and Trends." *Spectrum: The Journal of State Government* 76 (3): 10-13.

A Decade in Drug Policy and Research: Evaluating Trends from 2010 to 2020 and Presenting Major Policy Developments

Saahir Shafi

Penn State Harrisburg

Daniel J. Mallinson

Penn State Harrisburg

The War on Drugs still structures much of U.S. drug policy, but recent trends toward liberalization indicate a shifting policy landscape and a corresponding shift in drug policy research. Though 2020-21 will forever be remembered for the global COVID-19 pandemic, it has also been a significant time in the development of U.S. drug policy. Some developments are directly tied to the pandemic; others are part of larger trends that have predated it. Using a scoping review and reflexive thematic analysis, this article captures both the trajectory of research on drug policy over the past decade and substantial drug policy developments within the United States in 2020-2021. The results of our analysis indicate four major research areas of interest: drugs and substances, policy advocacy and appraisal, governance and regulation, as well as treatment and interventions. Within each area, emerging subthemes indicate research preferences that closely follow policy developments. The movement of states and countries toward more liberal drug policies is reflected in the growing body of literature on decriminalization and legalization. Scholarly interest in opioids has remained predominant over the decade as the opioid crisis has unfolded in waves, while interest in cannabis was most prominent in the years following its legalization across several states. Recent developments in cannabis, psychedelics, broader decriminalization, opioid overdose deaths, treatment, and the increasing centrality of social equity in drug policy reforms are reviewed with a focus on the issues that continue to plague the drug policy landscape (i.e., restrictions on research, surging overdose deaths, restrictions on evidence-based treatments, and equity concerns in a newly legal cannabis industry).

Keywords: Drug Policy 2020-2021, Cannabis, Opioids, Scoping Review, United States, War on Drugs, Trends in Drug Policy Research, Policy Advocacy, Drug Decriminalization.

Policy Studies Yearbook 12.1: 71-102. 10.18278/psy.12.1.3
©2022 Policy Studies Organization

Una década en políticas e investigación sobre drogas: evaluación de las tendencias de 2010 a 2020 y presentación de los principales avances en materia de políticas

La Guerra contra las Drogas todavía estructura gran parte de la política de drogas de Estados Unidos, pero las tendencias recientes hacia la liberalización indican un panorama político cambiante y un cambio correspondiente en la investigación de políticas de drogas. Aunque 2020-21 será recordado para siempre por la pandemia mundial de COVID-19, también ha sido un momento importante en el desarrollo de la política de drogas de EE. UU. Algunos desarrollos están directamente relacionados con la pandemia, mientras que otros son parte de tendencias más amplias que la han precedido. Utilizando una revisión del alcance y un análisis temático reflexivo, este artículo captura tanto la trayectoria de la investigación sobre políticas de drogas durante la última década como los desarrollos sustanciales de políticas de drogas en los Estados Unidos en 2020-2021. Los resultados de nuestro análisis indican cuatro áreas principales de investigación de interés: drogas y sustancias, promoción y evaluación de políticas, gobernanza y regulación, así como tratamiento e intervenciones. Dentro de cada una de estas áreas, los subtemas emergentes indican preferencias de investigación que siguen de cerca los desarrollos de políticas. El movimiento de los estados y países hacia políticas de drogas más liberales se refleja en el creciente cuerpo de literatura sobre despenalización y legalización. El interés académico en los opioides ha seguido predominando durante la década a medida que la crisis de los opioides se ha desarrollado en oleadas, mientras que el interés en el cannabis ha sido más prominente en los años posteriores a su legalización en varios estados. Los desarrollos recientes en el cannabis, los psicodélicos, la despenalización más amplia, las muertes por sobredosis de opioides, el tratamiento y la creciente centralidad de la equidad social en las reformas de las políticas de drogas se revisan con un enfoque particular en los problemas que continúan plagando el panorama de las políticas de drogas (es decir, las restricciones a la investigación). , el aumento de las muertes por sobredosis, las restricciones a los tratamientos basados en la evidencia y las preocupaciones sobre la equidad en una industria del cannabis recientemente legal).

Palabras clave: Política de drogas 2020-2021, Cannabis, Opioides, Revisión de alcance, Estados Unidos, Guerra contra las drogas, Tendencias en la investigación de políticas de drogas, Promoción de políticas, Despenalización de las drogas.

毒品政策和研究十年：評估 2010 年至 2020 年的趨勢並介紹主要政策發展*

毒品戰爭仍然構成了美國毒品政策的大部分內容，但最近的自由化趨勢表明政策格局正在發生變化，毒品政策研究也相應發生了變化。儘管全球 COVID-19 大流行將永遠銘記 2020-21 年，但它也是美國藥物政策發展的重要時期。一些事態發展與大流行直接相關，而另一些事態發展則是早於大流行的更大趨勢的一部分。本文使用範圍界定和反思性主題分析，捕捉了過去十年毒品政策研究的軌跡和美國 2020-2021 年毒品政策的實質性發展。我們的分析結果表明了四個主要的研究領域：藥物和物質、政策倡導和評估、治理和監管，以及治療和乾預。在這些領域中的每一個領域內，新興的子主題表明密切關注政策發展的研究偏好。越來越多的關於非刑事化和合法化的文獻反映了國家和國家朝著更自由的毒品政策發展的趨勢。十年來，隨著阿片類藥物危機的爆發，學術界對阿片類藥物的興趣仍然占主導地位，而在大麻在多個州合法化後的幾年裡，對大麻的興趣最為突出。審查了大麻、迷幻劑、更廣泛的去罪化、阿片類藥物過量死亡、治療以及社會公平在毒品政策改革中日益重要的最新發展，特別關注繼續困擾毒品政策格局的問題（即對研究的限制、過量用藥死亡人數激增、對循證治療的限制以及新近合法的大麻產業的公平問題）。

關鍵詞：2020-2021 年毒品政策，大麻，阿片類藥物，範圍審查，美國，毒品戰爭，毒品政策研究趨勢，政策倡導，毒品非刑事化。

The landscape for drug policy in the United States has been both shifting and stuck over the last three decades. In many ways, the War on Drugs still structures much of U.S. drug policy. However, its foundation is eroding, especially in the states. Nixon's War turned 50 in 2021, but U.S. drug policy has shifted substantially. In recent decades, decriminalization and legalization of Schedule I controlled substances have proliferated at the state level, in a departure from federal prohibition (Mosher and Akins 2019). California emerged as a pioneer in legalizing medical marijuana in 1996, while Colorado and Washington spearheaded the legalization of recreational marijuana in 2012. Other states have followed suit with a patchwork of drug policy reforms across the United States, presenting a complex and disjointed policy environment.

Globally, drug policy has been informed by the United Nations (UN) drug control conventions of 1961, 1971, and 1988. While most nations, being parties to these conventions, are pledged to prohibitionary stances, the relatively ambiguous nature of such "political compromises" (Bewley-Taylor, Blickman, and Jelsma 2014, 44) offers considerable discretion for nations to pursue their own agendas (Chatwin 2017). Reminiscent of state vs. federal divergence, drug policies vary across UN member states with many favoring a more pragmatic and nonpunitive approach to drug policy rather than the zero-tolerance approach expressly negotiated in international treaties (Bewley-Taylor 2013). Canada and Uruguay were the first to legalize recreational cannabis nationwide. Countries like the Netherlands have been home to decriminalization policies since the 1970s, and still others have adopted various forms of national decriminalization in the past two decades (Rosmarin and Eastwood 2012). Despite the prominent existence of moves toward decriminalization worldwide, critics still abound arguing against progressive drug policy and its potential societal harms.

Considering the increasingly complex and fragmented drug policy environment, we identify the need for a more in-depth understanding of the state of the research on drug policy. This article captures both the trajectory of research on drug policy over the past decade and recent noteworthy changes in U.S. drug policy. In doing so, we highlight and explain the trends in scholarly research over time and relate these trends to recent policy developments. The results of our analysis indicate research preferences that closely follow policy developments. For instance, the movement of states and countries toward more liberal drug policies is reflected in the growing body of literature on decriminalization and legalization. Though prohibition is represented most consistently across all regulatory regimes throughout the decade, research on decriminalization and legalization has shown a steady rise since 2012—corresponding with the legalization of recreational cannabis in Colorado and Washington. Similarly, scholarly interests in opioids and cannabis over the decade parallel the significance of these drugs in the overall policy environment (i.e., the waves of opioid overdose deaths, and states' legalization of recreational and medical cannabis).

Recent developments in cannabis, psychedelics, broader decriminalization, opioid overdose deaths, treatment, and social justice are expanded upon with a focus on the issues that continue to plague the drug policy landscape (e.g., restrictions on research pertaining to the medicinal value of drugs, surging overdose deaths, restrictions on evidence-based treatments, and equity concerns in a newly legal cannabis industry). In this study, we highlight key legislative changes and advancements while emphasizing the work that still needs to be done. This article is structured as follows. First, we describe our approach to a scoping review and reflexive thematic analysis of drug policy research published from 2010 to 2020. Next, we present a review of the trajectory of that research. We then present major policy developments in the United States that were highly visible in 2020-21. Finally, we offer concluding remarks and directions for future research.

Methodological Approach

We conducted a scoping review to evaluate the trends in drug policy research over the past decade. This methodology enabled us to determine the range of the body of literature, the volume of research published on this topic, and an impression of key areas of focus (Munn *et al.* 2018). Figure 1 shows a visual mapping of the process used to find relevant articles.

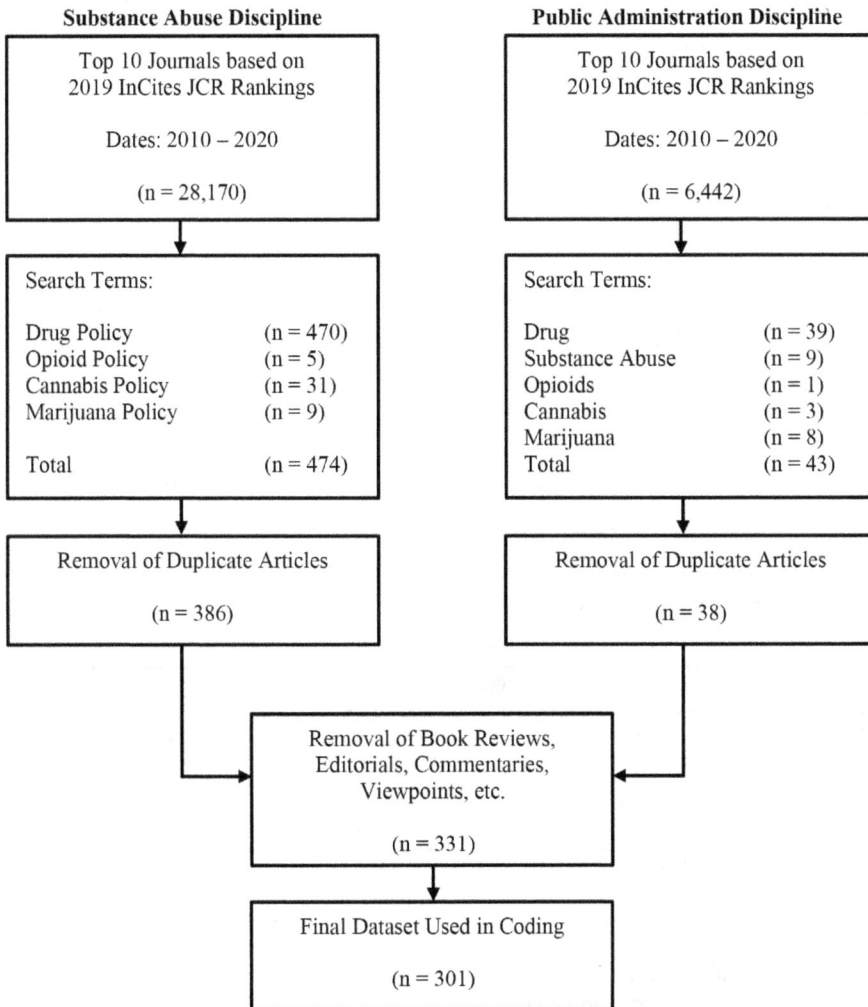

Substance Abuse Discipline   **Public Administration Discipline**

Top 10 Journals based on 2019 InCites JCR Rankings Dates: 2010 – 2020 (n = 28,170)	Top 10 Journals based on 2019 InCites JCR Rankings Dates: 2010 – 2020 (n = 6,442)

| Search Terms:

Drug Policy   (n = 470)
Opioid Policy   (n = 5)
Cannabis Policy   (n = 31)
Marijuana Policy   (n = 9)

Total   (n = 474) | Search Terms:

Drug   (n = 39)
Substance Abuse   (n = 9)
Opioids   (n = 1)
Cannabis   (n = 3)
Marijuana   (n = 8)
Total   (n = 43) |

Removal of Duplicate Articles (n = 386)	Removal of Duplicate Articles (n = 38)

Removal of Book Reviews, Editorials, Commentaries, Viewpoints, etc.

(n = 331)

Final Dataset Used in Coding

(n = 301)

Figure 1. Visual Mapping of Search Protocol Process

We conducted our search using ProQuest (Multiple Databases). Using 2019 InCites Journal Citation Reports (JCR), we determined the top ten journals in the "public administration" and "substance abuse" disciplines (see Table 1). First, we searched for peer-reviewed articles published in these 20 journals between 2010 and 2020. This generated 28,170 and 6,442 articles in the substance abuse and public administration disciplines, respectively. Next, we narrowed the results using distinct search terms for each discipline. For substance abuse journals, we searched "all subjects and indexing" for four key terms: (1) drug policy, (2) opioid policy, (3) cannabis policy, and (4) marijuana policy.[1] For public administration journals, we used five key terms: (1) drug, (2) substance abuse, (3) opioids, (4) cannabis, and (5) marijuana. Then, duplicates were removed yielding 386 substance abuse and 38 public administration articles. Further removal of book reviews, commentaries, etc., resulted in 331 articles. We then read all abstracts to identify any studies that were not relevant to our research and excluded these.[2] Our exclusion and inclusion criteria resulted in a final database of 301 articles.

Table 1. List of Journals in Dataset

Journal Title	2019 Impact Factor	Articles Collected	Total Articles	% of Articles Focused on Drug Policy
Substance Abuse Journals				
Tobacco Control	6.726		2,170	0.0%
Addiction	6.343	50	9,243	0.5%
International Journal of Drug Policy	4.444	182	1,751	10.4%***
Alcohol Research: Current Reviews	4.214		238	0.0%
Nicotine & Tobacco Research	4.079		2,346	0.0%
Drug and Alcohol Dependence	3.951	16	4,976	0.3%
Harm Reduction Journal	3.818	13	639	2.0%
Addictive Behaviors	3.645	6	4,884	0.1%
Addiction Science & Clinical Practice	3.088	2	263	0.8%
Journal of Substance Abuse Treatment	3.083		1,660	0.0%
*European Addiction Research	2.269	6	440	1.4%
*Addiction Research & Theory	2.223	3	685	0.4%
*International Journal of Mental Health and Addiction	1.648	2	1,143	0.2%

---

1   We chose to include specific search terms for opioid, cannabis, and marijuana policy because of the high degree of policy attention paid to these areas over the last decade. We did not search every possible drug name, which may bias the results of the search in favor of these topics, but we argue that this bias is almost imperceptible. As key words are not mutually exclusive (e.g., an article can be indexed as both "drug policy" and "cannabis policy"), the use of other specific drug names expanded the scope of our search by four articles in the substance abuse discipline and one in the public administration discipline—a difference of .9 percent and 2.3 percent, respectively.

2   Articles that focused on alcohol solely—not polysubstance—were excluded from the database.

*Journal of Addiction Medicine	**3.014	1	523	0.2%
Public Policy & Administration Journals				
Journal of Policy Analysis and Management	5.018	13	501	2.6%
Public Management Review	4.221		727	0.0%
Journal of European Public Policy	4.177		938	0.0%
Public Administration Review	4.063		1,566	0.0%
Climate Policy	4.011		782	0.0%
Policy Studies Journal	3.797	4	762	0.5%
Policy Sciences	3.609		267	0.0%
Regulation & Governance	3.375		258	0.0%
Journal of Public Administration Research and Theory	3.289	2	253	0.8%
Policy and Politics	3.069	1	388	0.3%
Total		**301**	**37,403**	**0.8%**

Notes: * Journals that do not rank in the top ten SSCI journal rankings per 2019 InCites JCR, but were captured in our sample by keyword search parameters.

** The Journal of Addiction Medicine is not ranked in the SSCI. The SCIE Ranking is given instead.

*** The International Journal of Drug Policy (IJDP) provides a multidisciplinary forum for research that extends beyond drug policy and includes research on drug use topics in a wide range of disciplines (epidemiology, modelling, economics, criminology and law, psychology, sociology, anthropology, etc.). Consequently, our research topic captures 10.4 percent of the articles published in IJDP from 2010 to 2020.

The journals represented in our dataset are listed in Table 1 along with 2019 journal impact factors, the number of articles captured in our review, and the total number of articles published by each journal from 2010 to 2020. Notably, of the top ten journals in each discipline, four substance abuse journals and six public administration journals did not return any articles focused on drug policy.[3] Further, our search parameters yielded articles from journals outside the top ten SSCI ranking. Thus, the final collection of relevant articles represents ten substance abuse and four public administration journals. The bulk of the articles captured in our review belong to substance abuse journals (93.4 percent), indicating that drug policy research has low representation in top public administration (and policy) journals (6.6 percent).

---

3   The use of specific search terms narrowed our selection of articles, and journals, considerably as the journals included in our analysis are multidisciplinary and feature a broad scope of material that extends beyond our research topic (pharmacological and behavioral addictions, patterns of drug use, epidemiology, psychosocial research, etc.) or are overwhelmingly clinical in nature (Drug and Alcohol Dependence, Addictive Behaviors, Addiction Science & Clinical Practice, etc.).

Reflexive Thematic Analysis

We evaluated the aggregate literature on drug policy using a reflexive thematic analysis.[4] This method includes six recursive phases: familiarization, code generation, theme generation, theme review and development, theme definition, and reporting results. With this approach, themes emerge and are refined, split, or merged as papers are reviewed. Two researchers worked independently to review and code the articles, met to discuss thematic developments, and conducted a cross-party review of coded articles to ensure consensus. This method facilitated an inductive approach whereby reviewers familiarized themselves with the dataset, coded the articles, refined the codes through a recursive process of data engagement and interpretation, developed themes from the codes, and further refined these to develop comprehensive core themes (Braun and Clarke 2021). Results of our scoping review and thematic analysis are reported next.

Trends in Drug Policy Research

In the following section, we discuss the themes emerging from our analysis focusing on three key areas: research themes and subthemes, methodological approaches, and the geospatial distribution of research.

Research Themes

Major Areas of Interest

The research themes emerging from our analysis are listed in Table 2. As each of the articles represented multiple themes, the classifications illustrated in Table 1 are not mutually exclusive. It is fitting that Drugs & Substances emerged as the most dominant theme, represented in 93.7 percent of all articles. Other predominant topics in the literature were Policy Advocacy and Appraisal (82.1 percent), Governance & Regulation (71.8 percent), and Treatment & Interventions (63.5 percent). A clustering of topics focused on the microeconomics of drug policy, including Drug Supply/Cultivation (20.9 percent), Drug Demand/Consumption (20.3 percent), and Drug Markets (11.3 percent). Adverse consequences of drug use were an additional focal area with articles exploring Harms & Risks (20.6 percent), Disease (14.6 percent), Addiction & Substance Abuse (13.3 percent), Crimes & Incarceration (8.3 percent), and Mortality & Overdose (8.0 percent). Another group of topics focused on users (22.6 percent) and user behaviors (5.6 percent). Other represented research themes were attitudes toward drugs (i.e., public opinion, stigma, and consumer attitudes) (20.6 percent), Social Equity Issues (16.3 percent), Research & Education (15.9 percent), and Contextual Factors (5.3 percent).

---

4   Reflexive thematic analysis is a recursive approach to thematic analysis—an analytic method for detecting and extracting meaning-based patterns (or themes) from qualitative data (Braun and Clarke 2006; Braun *et al.* 2019).

Table 2. Research Themes of Published Articles

Key Themes	Frequency	Percentage
Drugs & Substances	282	93.7%
Policy Advocacy & Appraisal	247	82.1%
Governance & Regulation	216	71.8%
Treatment & Interventions	191	63.5%
Drug Users	68	22.6%
Drug Supply/Cultivation	63	20.9%
Attitudes Toward Drugs	62	20.6%
Harms & Risk	62	20.6%
Drug Demand/Consumption	61	20.3%
Social Equity	49	16.3%
Research & Education	48	15.9%
Disease	44	14.6%
Addiction & Substance Abuse	40	13.3%
Drug Markets	34	11.3%
Crimes & Incarceration	25	8.3%
Mortality & Overdose	24	8.0%
User Behavior	17	5.6%
Contextual Factors	16	5.3%

Thematic Trends over Time

Annual trends in major research themes are displayed in Figure 2. We focus on those themes that are represented in over 50 percent of the articles analyzed: (1) Drugs & Substances, (2) Policy Advocacy & Appraisal, (3) Governance & Regulation, and (4) Treatment & Interventions. These four research themes represent over 60 percent of the articles analyzed. Over the decade, Drugs & Substances was generally the most prominent theme, making up the bulk of the research in the early 2010s and continuing to be prominent throughout the latter half of the decade. Policy Advocacy & Appraisal was most prominent in 2014 and 2018, accounting for a third of the research across major themes in both years. Treatment & Interventions was the leading theme in 2013, albeit the least represented in the following years, from 2014 through 2018.

We also evaluate annual research interest in drugs and substances over time, shown in Figure 3. Here, we focus on those drugs that are represented in over 5 percent of articles: (1) cannabis, (2) opioids, (3) stimulants, and (4) psychoactive drugs. Opioids and cannabis make up the bulk of the research on drugs and substances, with research on opioids dominating the beginning (2010-12) and end of the decade (2018-20). Within opioids research, 25 percent of articles focus on heroin, 22 percent on prescription opioids (buprenorphine and oxycodone), and

10 percent on opioid antagonists (methadone and naloxone). Research interest in opioids in the beginning of the decade corresponds with the second wave of opioid overdose deaths in the United States (CDC 2021). This wave is partly attributable to increases in the supply of heroin and the introduction of synthetic opioids like illicitly manufactured fentanyl (IMF) into drug markets in the same year (CDC 2021; O'Donnell, Gladden, and Seth 2017). Research interest in opioids at the end of the decade shows a delayed response to the third wave of opioid overdose deaths in the United States. This wave began in 2013 and continues through the COVID-19 pandemic (CDC 2021, 2020).

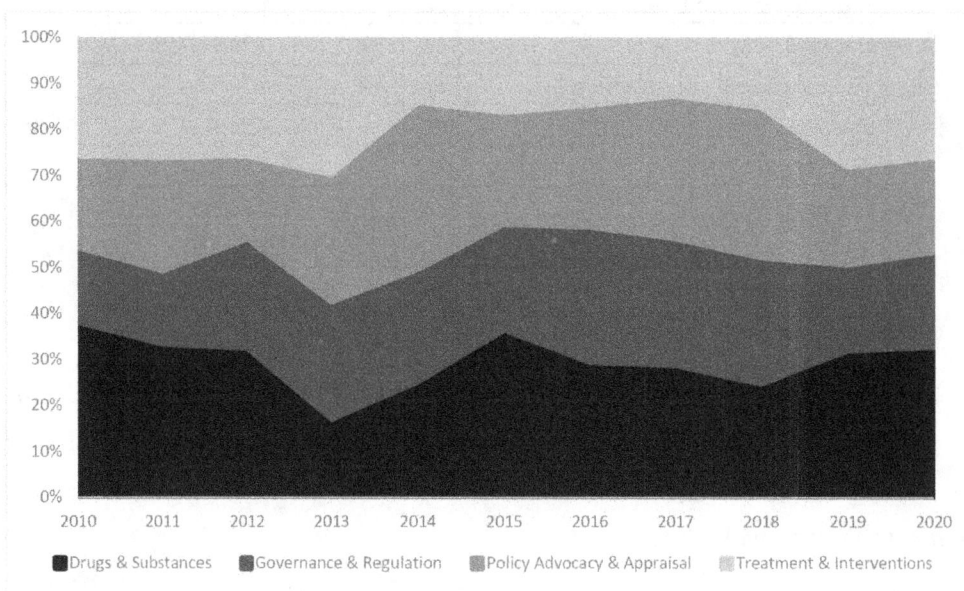

Figure 2. Annual Trends of Major Themes

Research on cannabis was most pronounced during the mid-decade (2014-18), with 21 percent of cannabis studies focusing on medical cannabis and 11 percent on adult-use recreational. The growth in cannabis-specific research from 2014 to 2018 came two years after Colorado and Washington became the first states to legalize recreational cannabis (2012) and two decades after the steady march of states adopting medical cannabis began in California (1996).

Research interest in stimulants was greater in the early half of the decade, highest in 2016, and diminished thereafter as studies on cannabis and opioids dominated the field. Stimulant research focused primarily on cocaine (27 percent), followed by methamphetamines (22 percent), amphetamines (11 percent), benzylpiperazine (11 percent), mephedrone (8 percent), and ecstasy (MDMA) (5 percent). Research on psychoactive drugs[5] was most prominent in the early 2010s

---

5 As the term "psychoactive drugs" refers to a broad range of chemical substances that alter nervous system function (i.e., alcohol, caffeine, nicotine, cannabis, ecstasy, amphetamines, methamphetamines, opioids, heroin, and cocaine), those articles that focused on drugs in general without

and diminished in the second half of the decade, likely attributable to the shift of research from generic drug topics to more targeted studies on specific drugs (e.g., cannabis and opioids.).

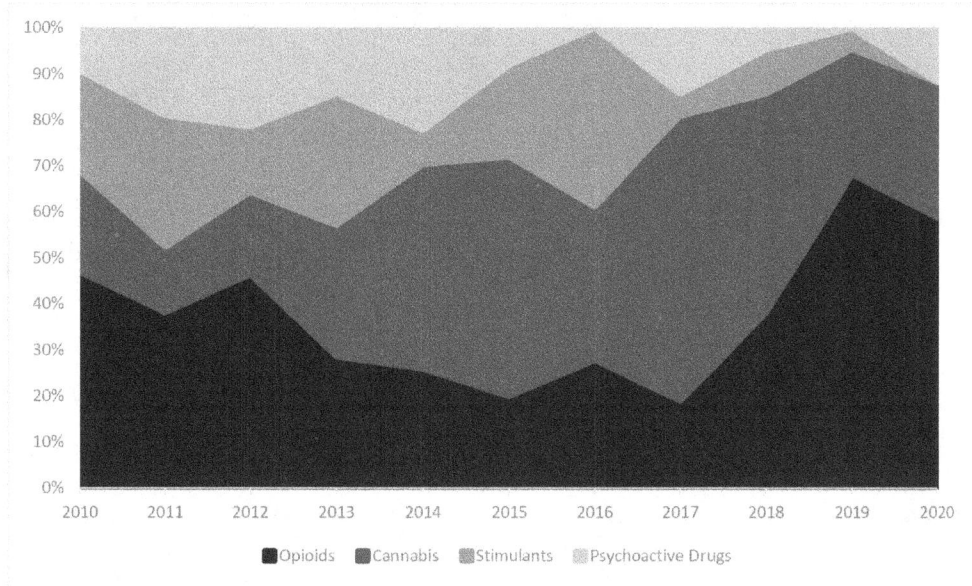

Figure 3. Annual Trends of Drugs and Substances

Subthemes

Next, we disaggregated each broad research theme to determine the scope of research within each major area of interest. Figure 4 illustrates the breakdown of major research themes into subthemes.

Drugs and Substances

Opioids received the greatest attention in the Drugs & Substances theme, accounting for a third of the articles in this category, followed closely by cannabis (29 percent), stimulants (13 percent), and psychoactive drugs (10 percent). Drugs with a lesser research focus were tobacco and nicotine (5 percent), and new psychoactive substances (NPS)[6] (4 percent). Other drugs and substances including alcohol (polysubstance), hallucinogens, and sedatives comprise the remaining 6 percent of research in this area.

---

identifying specific types (i.e., cannabis, opioids) or classes (i.e., stimulants, hallucinogens), were categorized as psychoactive drugs.

6   NPSs are distinct from psychoactive drugs. They are manufactured to mimic the effects of illicit drugs by replacing banned chemicals with new and legal, though unregulated, chemicals (i.e., synthetic cannabis).

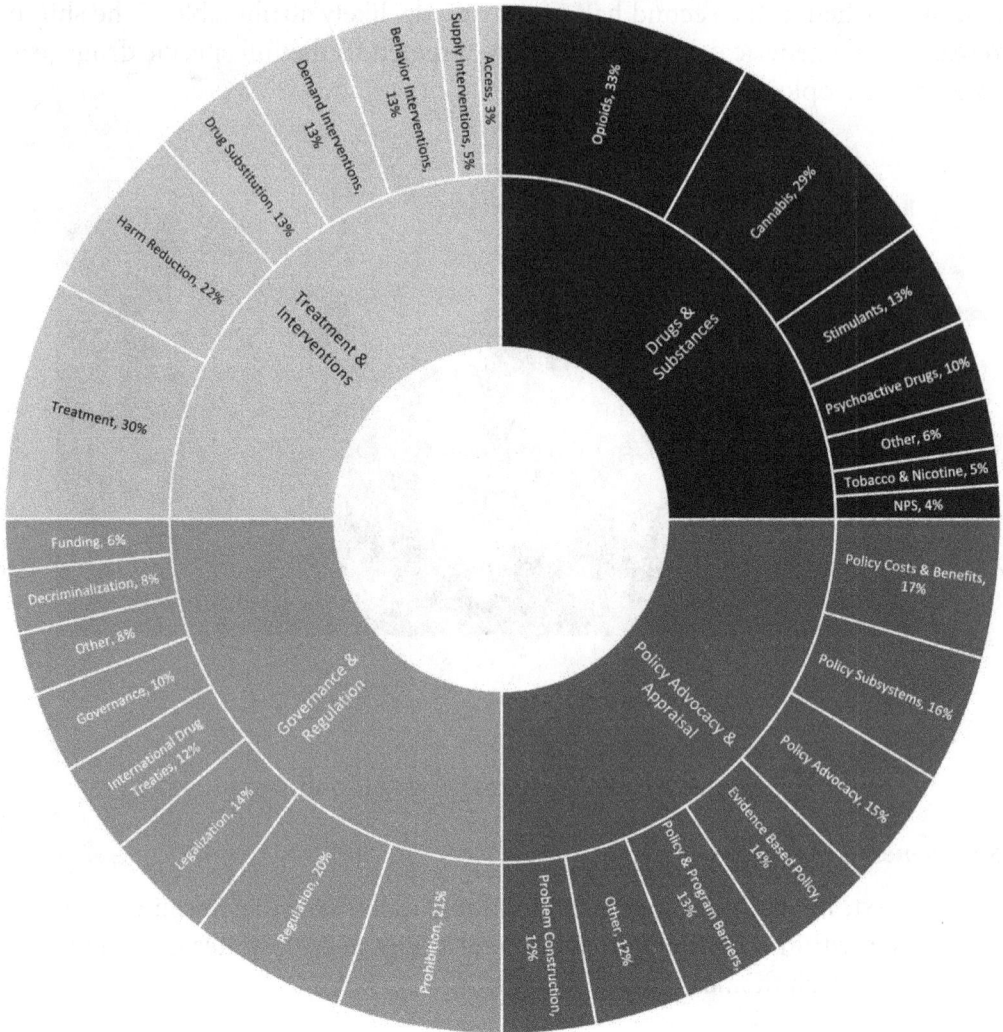

Figure 4. Disaggregation of Research Themes into Subthemes

Policy Advocacy and Appraisal

Articles focusing on policy advocacy and appraisal ran the gamut of policy cycle stages from problem construction to policy evaluation. Policy costs and benefits emerged as the largest subtheme with 17 percent of the articles in this category evaluating the economic costs, health benefits, efficacy, and unintended consequences of drug policy. Policy subsystems were also predominant, the 16 percent of studies in this area focused on advocacy coalitions, policy entrepreneurs, and diverse policy actors (i.e., civil society stakeholders, government officials, etc.). Closely related to policy subsystems, policy advocacy made up 15 percent of articles with topics including drug discourse and policy development. Evidence-based policy was a focal point of 14 percent of articles with many articles identifying the marginal role evidence plays in drug policy formulation (Lancaster 2014; Monaghan 2014) and the need for evidence-based interventions (Guerrero *et al.* 2014; Miclette *et al.* 2018). Policy and program barriers made up 13 percent of articles, followed by problem construction (12 percent). Other topics under this thematic umbrella were policy reform (9 percent) and policy innovation and diffusion (3 percent).

Governance and Regulation

Prohibition was a prominent subtheme within governance and regulation studies, with 21 percent of articles exploring drug control practices (i.e., drug scheduling, repressive policing, etc.). Regulation and legalization were the focus of 20 percent and 14 percent of articles, respectively. Articles exploring regulation with respect to legalization underscored regulating drug markets to ensure drug quality and potency (Manthey 2019). Research on regulation with respect to prohibition stressed supply-side interventions (i.e., restricting medical cannabis prescriptions) (Fischer, Kuganesan, and Room 2015). International drug treaties represented 12 percent of the articles in this thematic group, followed by governance (10 percent), decriminalization (8 percent), and funding (6 percent). Other subthemes were law enforcement (4 percent) and federalism (4 percent).

Treatment and Interventions

While treatment of substance abuse disorders was expected to be the most prominent subtheme within the Treatment & Interventions thematic group, harm reduction was the second most researched topic (22 percent) with articles focusing on methadone maintenance therapies, syringe exchange programs, and HIV/AIDS prevention (Csete and Grob 2012; Järvinen and Miller 2014; Torre, Lucas, and Barros 2010). Drug substitution treatments, demand-side interventions, and behavioral interventions were each represented in 13 percent of articles, followed by supply-side interventions (5 percent) and treatment access (3 percent).

Methodological Approaches

Tables 3 and 4 list the data collection and analysis methodologies used across all articles. Our review indicates that qualitative methods were used more often than quantitative ones, both for data collection and analysis. Over half of drug policy articles used qualitative methods of data collection and analysis while only about a third of the articles employed quantitative methods.

Table 3. Frequency of Data Collection Methodologies

Data Collection Methods	Frequency	Percentage
Conceptual	**8**	**2.7%**
Literature Review	**19**	**6.3%**
Literature Review	9	3.0%
Systematic Literature Review	7	2.3%
Scoping Review	3	1.0%
Mixed Methods	**11**	**3.7%**
Qualitative	**163**	**54.2%**
Discussion	30	10.0%
Interviews	28	9.3%
Document Analysis	22	7.3%
Case Study	21	7.0%
Description	13	4.3%
Multi Method	12	4.0%
Ethnographic Study	10	3.3%
Exploratory Study	6	2.0%
Derived/Compiled Data	5	1.7%
Focus Groups	5	1.7%
Critical Analysis	3	1.0%
Field Study	3	1.0%
Delphi	2	0.7%
Secondary Data	2	0.7%
Phenomenology	1	0.3%
Quantitative	**100**	**33.2%**
Survey	30	10.0%
Secondary Data	19	6.3%
Experiment	17	5.6%
Longitudinal Study	13	4.3%
Derived/Compiled Data	11	3.7%
Simulation	3	1.0%
Document Analysis	2	0.7%
Field Study	2	0.7%
Cost of Illness Study	1	0.3%
Multi Method	1	0.3%
Twins Study	1	0.3%
Total	**301**	**100.0%**

Table 4. Frequency of Data Analysis Methodologies

Data Analysis Methods	Frequency	Percentage
Qualitative	**186**	**60.4%**
Qualitative Analysis (General)	108	35.1%
Content/Thematic/Textual Analysis	36	11.7%
Descriptive Research	11	3.6%
Discourse Analysis	7	2.3%
Critical Analysis	6	1.9%
Inductive Analysis	6	1.9%
Historical Analysis	3	1.0%
Narrative Analysis	2	0.6%
Participatory Evaluation	2	0.6%
Integrative Data Analysis (IDA)	1	0.3%
Interpretive Description	1	0.3%
Multiple Criteria Decision Analysis (MCDA)	1	0.3%
Situational Analysis	1	0.3%
Template Analysis	1	0.3%
Quantitative	**119**	**38.6%**
Regression Analysis & ANOVA	53	17.2%
Non-Regression Statistical Analysis	20	6.5%
Descriptive Analysis	18	5.8%
Event History Analysis	5	1.6%
Time-Series Analysis	4	1.3%
Comparative Analysis	3	1.0%
Mathematical Modelling	2	0.6%
Meta-analysis	2	0.6%
Narrative Analysis	2	0.6%
Sensitivity Analysis	2	0.6%
Area under the Curve (AUC) Analysis	1	0.3%
Attributable Fraction Analysis	1	0.3%
Cost of Illness Analysis	1	0.3%
Herfindahl-Hirschman index (HHI)	1	0.3%
Markov Model	1	0.3%
Spatial Temporal Analysis	1	0.3%
Survival Analysis	1	0.3%
Threshold Analysis	1	0.3%
Mixed Methods Analysis	**3**	**1.0%**

Geospatial Distribution of Research

Figure 5 presents the geospatial distribution of research. For those articles with a global focus or without an identified geographical area of interest, locations were determined by author affiliations. The United States was the most prominent country of focus, represented by 21.4 percent of articles. Other countries with prolific research were the United Kingdom (11.3 percent), Australia (8 percent), and Canada (5.1 percent). Notably, scholars conducting drug policy research in these countries paid relatively more attention to cannabis topics than opioids. This difference was most pronounced in Canada as 52.2 percent of research focused on cannabis compared to 34.8 percent on opioids. A closer look at drug specific research by region indicates that opioids research is most pronounced in North America, Europe, and Asia, while cannabis research is concentrated in Europe, North America, and South America.

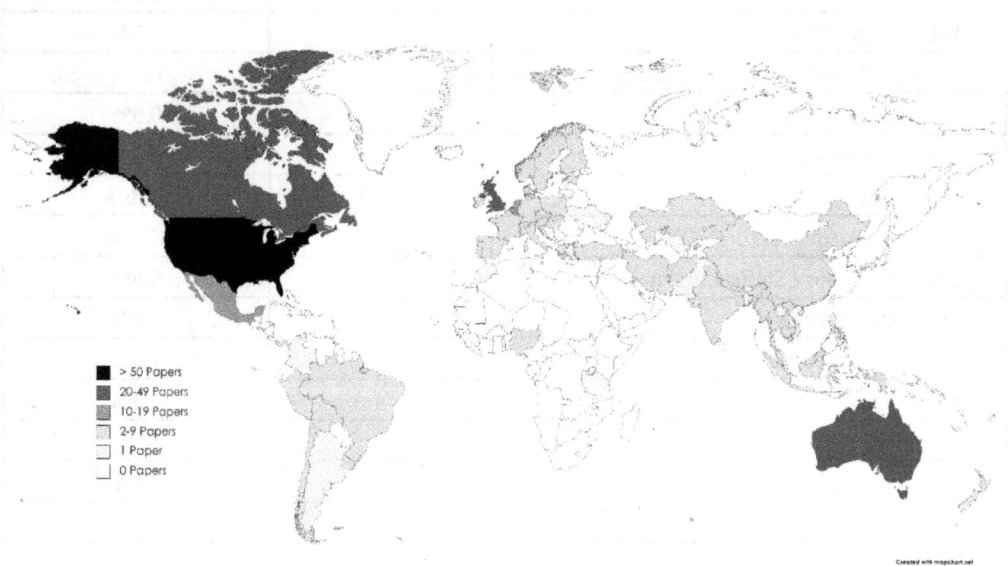

Legend:
- > 50 Papers
- 20-49 Papers
- 10-19 Papers
- 2-9 Papers
- 1 Paper
- 0 Papers

Figure 5. Countries and Regions of Research Focus

Below we discuss the implications of the above trends for the future of drug policy research, but first, we examine major policy developments that occurred in 2020-21. Not only does this provide a sense of how policy is changing, but we can later evaluate how well prevailing research trends match these developments.

Major Policy Developments

While 2020-21 will forever be remembered for the global COVID-19 pandemic, it was also a significant year in the development of U.S. drug policy. Some developments were directly tied to the pandemic, while others were part of larger trends that predated it. This section reviews developments in cannabis, psychedelics, broader decriminalization, overdose deaths, treatment, and the increasing centrality of social equity and justice in drug policy debates and reforms.

From Reefer Madness to Essential Service

Cannabis has a long and fraught history in the United States. It was one of the earliest substances to be demonized and controlled and has a particularly discriminatory history of regulation (Anguelov 2018). The tide in cannabis policy began to shift in 1996 when California adopted the first statewide comprehensive medical marijuana program via a ballot initiative. Medical cannabis has spread widely in defiance of federal prohibition under the Controlled Substances Act of 1970 (Hannah and Mallinson 2018; Mallinson and Hannah 2020). It is being followed by the spread of adult-use recreational cannabis. Recreational cannabis use has been legalized in 18 states and the District of Columbia as of June 2021 and decriminalized in an additional 13 states, where although illegal, violations by first time offenders are met with fines rather than incarceration (Ballotpedia 2021).

Something both practical and profoundly symbolic occurred for cannabis policy during the COVID-19 pandemic. As all U.S. states declared emergencies and many shut down broad swaths of their economies to stem the initial tide of infections, governors had discretionary authority over defining which essential services would remain available. Figure 6 shows that of the U.S. states that had operational recreational and/or medical marijuana programs in spring 2020, all either deemed their programs to be essential services or did not issue blanket closures and left dispensaries open (North Dakota and Arkansas). Many states also relaxed stringent rules for controlling how customers access recreational and medical cannabis. To prevent indoor gatherings in dispensaries, states allowed home delivery and curbside service, in a pronounced shift from the typical regime of purchasing cannabis behind closed doors. States also expanded the number of days' supply that patients could purchase at one time and allowed caregivers to buy medical cannabis for patients. Many of these changes are becoming permanent as states like Pennsylvania reform their cannabis statutes. The decision to deem marijuana an essential service was not completely rooted in epidemiological science. Governors relied on a mixture of scientific, political, and economic factors in making these decisions (Opp and Mosier 2020). Nonetheless, the symbolic importance cannot be denied. With state action, cannabis has transitioned from the status of a stoner subculture to a government-recognized essential service.

The steady march of cannabis liberalization in the states did not halt during the pandemic. South Dakota adopted both medical and recreational cannabis, New Jersey adopted recreational, and Mississippi adopted medical all via the ballot in 2020.[7] Connecticut, New York, Virginia, and New Mexico all adopted recreational cannabis in the first half of 2021. However, the federal government

---

7   South Dakota's recreational and Mississippi's medical laws were subsequently deemed unconstitutional.

remains a fickle partner for states on cannabis liberalization (Mallinson, Hannah, and Cunningham 2020). Significant legislation like the MORE Act, which would address the industry's banking problems, or the STATES Act, which would explicitly leave cannabis regulation to the states, has been introduced, but faces slim hope of passage in the near term. Other bills are circulating that would go much further in decriminalizing many or all drugs, but it is unclear how these will navigate the sharply divided Senate.

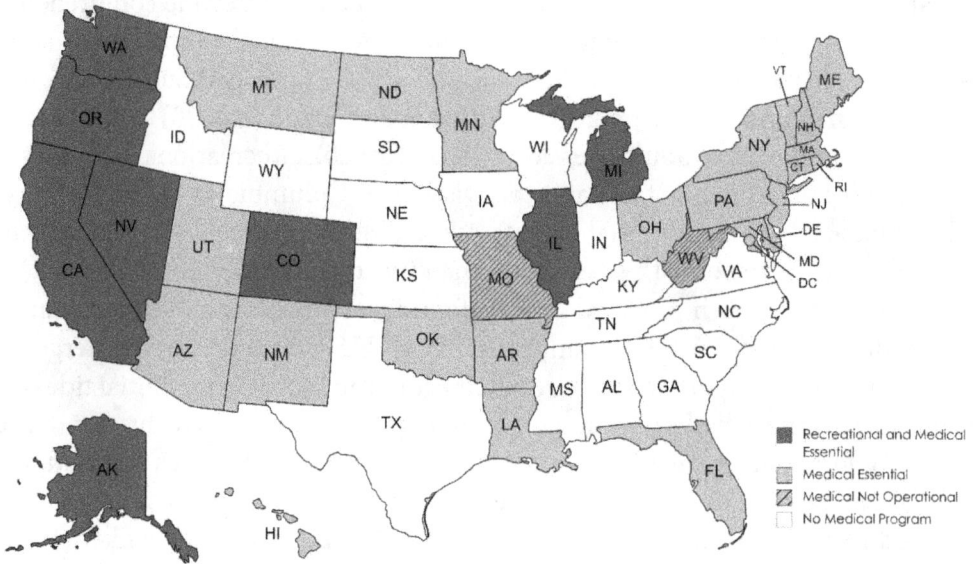

Figure 6. States That Deemed Recreational and/or Medical Marijuana an Essential Service During COVID-19

One significant advancement in federal policy occurred quietly, though not fully willingly, through administrative action. The Drug Enforcement Agency (DEA) announced in 2021 that it was following through on an Obama-era regulatory change that would allow additional growers for cannabis research. Since 1968, the University of Mississippi has been the sole grower for DEA-approved cannabis research. However, there is longstanding criticism that its cannabis is not near the potency or purity of that being sold in state-legal programs (Wadman 2021). Effective research is important for not only better establishing the specific medicinal value of cannabis, but also for overcoming the chicken-and-egg debate over that value. Opponents of medical cannabis argue that the science is not there, but the highly controlled nature of cannabis research, poor quality of research in cannabis, and the fact that most federal research funding related to cannabis goes to addiction—not medical—research (O'Grady 2020), makes assembling such evidence difficult.

Rise of Psychedelics

The paradox of banning substances for having no perceived medicinal value and high potential for abuse while also restricting high quality research on their medicinal value is not limited to cannabis. In a 2014 call to end the ban on psychedelics research, the editors of *Scientific American* stated "these drugs are banned because they have no accepted medical use, but researchers cannot explore their therapeutic potential because they are banned" (Editors 2014).

Psilocybin mushrooms, LSD, and MDMA—like cannabis—are Schedule I drugs, but show potential for treating several psychiatric disorders (Vollenweider and Preller 2020; Carhart-Harris *et al.* 2016; Fuentes *et al.* 2020). Like the early cannabis successes, advocates have scored initial wins in decriminalizing or legalizing mushrooms via local and state ballot initiatives. The city of Denver was the first to decriminalize in 2019, followed by Oakland and Santa Cruz in California. Ann Arbor, MI, followed suit in 2020 and Cambridge and Northampton, MA, joined in 2021. It is notable that these city ordinances do not legalize mushroom possession or sale, they simply prevent local prosecution for possession. Of even greater significance was Oregon's 2020 legalization of psilocybin mushrooms for medical use through Measure 109.

Research on the medical potential for psychedelics is also advancing. There has been a rapid growth in clinical trials for mushrooms, MDMA, and LSD over the past decade (Tullis 2021). Positive results of an FDA-approved Phase 3 clinical trial for MDMA-assisted treatment of PTSD were recently published (Mitchell *et al.* 2021) and another large-scale FDA-approved trial of the combination of MDMA and LSD has begun Phase 1. In 2017, FDA granted MDMA "breakthrough therapy" status for PTSD and assisted psychotherapy, which expedites research, development, and possible approval for treatment. It did the same for psilocybin mushrooms for the treatment of major depression in 2019.

State Decriminalization

Some states are further expanding the front in pushing back on the War on Drugs. In 2020, Oregon became the first state to decriminalize possession of small amounts of *all* drugs via a ballot initiative (Measure 110). Since then, states like Washington, Virginia, California, and Maine have seriously debated and voted on similar measures (Adlin 2021a; Jaeger 2021). One must always bear in mind that decriminalization is not legalization. Drug possession remains illegal in Oregon, but the penalty for it has been reduced to a $100 fine with stiffer penalties for selling. Essentially, decriminalization laws reallocate policing resources by reducing the emphasis on combating drug possession. Expansion of this policy is not guaranteed, however, as evinced by Washington. The state's Supreme Court struck down the state's possession law in February 2021, forcing legislators to fill the gap. Instead of moving decriminalization forward, the Washington Senate amended a decriminalization bill to *add* jail time and a fine to possession (Adlin 2021b).

Increasing Overdose Deaths

Overdoses that were already surging in the United States in 2019 continued to do so during the pandemic (CDC 2020). Evidence suggests the increased rates of overdoses and deaths are due to synthetic opioids (e.g., fentanyl) (Appa *et al.* 2021; CDC 2020). The direct effects of the pandemic, however, are not clear. Emergency department visits for overdose initially fell in March during the first lockdowns, but grew thereafter (Holland *et al.* 2021). Evidence from San Francisco suggests that lockdowns themselves increased overdoses (Appa *et al.* 2021). Further, research from Ontario found that 17,843 more years of life were lost in opioid-related deaths in the first six months of 2020 compared to 2019 (Gomes, Kitchen, and Murray 2021). Based on preliminary estimates, in the United States overdose deaths are predicted to have been as high as 90,000 in 2020, compared to 70,000 in 2019 (Baumgartner and Radley 2021). While COVID-19 dominated the attention of government and public health agencies in 2020, overdoses have surged back to the forefront of their agendas in 2021.

The path forward in the long, grinding opioid epidemic is challenging for governments at all levels. Overdoses continue to rise even in the face of over a decade of increased policy responses. In a positive development, state and local governments are deciding how to appropriate a flood of resources: $4.25 billion in emergency substance abuse and mental health funding from the Consolidated Appropriations Act of 2020 and $3.5 billion more from the American Rescue Plan Act of 2021. A related, and long-demanded, policy advancement came in 2021: the relaxation of buprenorphine prescription rules.

Relaxing Buprenorphine Rules

Buprenorphine and methadone are two effective evidence-based treatments for opioid use disorder (West, O'Neal, and Graham 2000). Methadone must be administered in a clinical setting, but buprenorphine can be prescribed in doctors' offices. Providers are restricted, however, in prescribing it unless they hold an "X-waiver," which requires additional education (an eight-hour course). It has long been noted that doctors are not similarly limited in prescribing opioids for pain in the first place but are restricted in prescribing for medication-assisted treatment. This dissonance, combined with the ongoing opioid epidemic in the United States, has prompted calls for reform.

President Biden included relaxation of the X-waiver rules in his campaign platform[8] and the Department of Health and Human Services (2021) altered the waiver requirement in April 2021. Now, doctors, physician's assistants, and nurses can prescribe buprenorphine to a maximum of 30 patients before requiring an X-waiver. The waiver initially raises the cap to 100, and eventually 275, patients. If a state requires, however, physician's assistants and nurses would still need to work with a DEA-registered physician when prescribing. While there are still questions regarding why the limits are necessary in the first place, the change will undoubtedly lower the barrier to medication-assisted treatment.

---

8   See https://joebiden.com/opioidcrisis/

Social Justice

It is impossible to look back at policy advances in 2020-21 without considering the larger movement for black lives. Drug control in the United States is tightly woven with racial inequity and the growth of mass incarceration (Alexander 2010). Thus, drug policy reform has likewise been linked with larger movements for justice and equity. Social equity has become a key part of the framing of cannabis legalization efforts and debates over the details of legislation. In fact, it was inadequate attention to social equity concerns that held New York and New Jersey back from adopting recreational cannabis prior to the pandemic (Peltz 2019). While later adopters of medical cannabis, like Pennsylvania, started to address equity in their programs, equity concerns were elevated with full legalization for adult use. Essentially, a substance for which possession or sale resulted in fines and prison for many, largely BIPOC, Americans is now being legalized and sold widely, largely by wealthy white Americans (Danquah-Brobby 2016). Strict rules preventing persons with a criminal record from obtaining a dispensary or grower/processor permit, combined with substantial capital requirements, have prevented the very people most harmed by the War on Drugs from benefiting directly from a newly legal cannabis industry.

In response, states have developed programs to increase the social equity of license awarding. Pennsylvania's early approach to addressing social equity was to simply add points to license applications for evidence of diversity in the applicant's leadership. Such approaches have been criticized for inducing token levels of diversity into the industry. After the first round of licenses in Illinois's recreational program (adopted in 2019) went to all white male applicants, the state instituted a special lottery system whose point-based entry included additional points for racial minority applicants.[9] Lawsuits by applicants dogged this second round, leading to its suspension, and the Illinois legislature acted in 2021 to try to fix problems in the process. Of course, ensuring equity and social justice includes more than diversity in the industry. It also includes robust expungement, appropriate sanctions for cannabis-related offenses, providing funding for communities disproportionately harmed by the War on Drugs, and mitigating the downsides of recreational legalization (Adinoff and Reiman 2019). Much work remains in achieving these aims.

Discussion and Future Research Directions

From the above review, several useful insights on the trajectory of drug policy research and the current state of practice can be teased out. While research on drug policy has been prolific and wide-ranging in the past decade, recent trends toward liberalization indicate a shifting drug policy landscape—and a corre-

---

9   See https://www.civicfed.org/blog/what-state-illinois-cannabis-social-equity-program-and-how-will-new-legislation-reform-it

sponding shift in drug policy research. This parallel change can be attributed to the following. First, policy begets research as the information generated by policy discourse (i.e., legislative bills, official statements, press releases, etc.) is publicly accessible and provides data for social science researchers to study. Second, as drugs are a prominent concern, both in domestic and foreign policy, the availability of research funding also provides an added impetus (O'Grady 2020). As policy has shifted, social scientists have followed suit to explore previously unchartered territory in the research domain, shifting their attention from the study of prohibitionary policy to decriminalization and legalization. Our analysis contributes to the body of work on drug policy by developing an improved understanding of the state of the research and evaluating how well prevailing research trends match policy developments.

The results of our analysis indicate four major research areas of interest: Drugs & Substances, Policy Advocacy & Appraisal, Governance & Regulation, and Treatment & Interventions. Within each of these areas, emerging subthemes indicate research preferences that closely follow policy developments. This is most pronounced in the Drugs & Substances policy and research domain. For instance, scholarly interest in opioids and cannabis has corresponded with waves of opioid overdose deaths and shifts in the cannabis policy environment. Each of these drugs differ in their societal impact and both the literature and policy developments reflect these differences. For instance, research on opioids has tended to focus on Treatment & Interventions for drug abuse (Himmich and Madani 2016; Uchtenhagen 2010), Virus Transmission (Andresen and Boyd 2010; Bartholomew et al. 2020), and Prescribing Patterns (Kiang et al. 2020). This research corresponds with recent policy developments, particularly the relaxation of buprenorphine prescription rules. In contrast to opioids research, research on cannabis policy has focused less on use-reduction and more on the effects of legalization (Caulkins and Kilmer 2016) and regulation of drug markets (Caulkins et al. 2018). Policy developments around cannabis resonate with these research interests as an increasing number of states joined the steady march toward cannabis liberalization, state governments relaxed stringent regulations to cannabis access during the pandemic, and the DEA took action to expand cannabis cultivation for research.

Given that prohibition has been the historically preferred regulatory regime, both in the United States and internationally, the predominant research focus on prohibitionary drug policy is expected. However, research on decriminalization and legalization is burgeoning, with more studies highlighting the positive implications of liberalized drug policies (e.g., health benefits, harm reduction, tax revenues, etc.) (Amroussia, Watanabe, and Pearson 2020; Hall and Kozlowski 2018). This is not to say that scholars are largely in support of decriminalization and legalization regimes. As states and countries implement liberal drug policies, the unintended public health or social effects of these policy shifts remain to be seen (Weiss, Howlett, and Baler 2017).

Despite erosion in the prohibitionist policy regime, the drug policy space continues to be sharply divided. Perhaps most surprising is the marginal role played by evidence in policy development (Lancaster 2014; Monaghan 2014). While it is understood that policy making would benefit from a stronger nexus between science and policy, gaps between research and practice remain problematic (Tieberghien 2014) and establishing this linkage is fraught with challenges. For one, policy making is an iterative process involving interactions and relationships between diverse policy actors (Ritter and Lancaster 2013) and a powerful *status quo* bias. Also, the media plays a large role in influencing public opinion, and subsequently, policy decision making—and this influence can work against science when scientific knowledge is misrepresented or selectively utilized (Ritter and Lancaster 2013; Tieberghien 2014). Finally, the academic literature may not always be correctly interpreted or accessible to policy makers (Ritter and Lancaster 2013; Bennett and Holloway 2010).

While scholars agree on the need for evidence-based policy, science and practice continue to operate in silos with drug policy being "articulated through metaphors" (Moore *et al.* 2015, 420) and informed by competing ideologies (Marlatt 1996). Future research would benefit from bridging the gaps between science and practice through evaluating the ways in which evidence-based policy can be brought to bear on policy making. One approach is to conceptualize policy making as a process of social construction, in which participants engage in discourse and vie for influence and, through this influence, evidence is rendered valid and useful in the policy-making process (Lancaster 2014). By critically analyzing policy making through a social construction framework, scholars can better understand how evidence is interpreted and contested in the policy making space, and thereby be better equipped to facilitate evidence-based interventions.

Our study highlights the shifting and complex drug policy landscape. Recent changes in drug policy will undoubtedly bring new opportunities and challenges as policy makers grapple with the immediate and long-term effects of liberalized drug policies. Future studies will benefit from evaluating immediate, medium-term, and long-term policy consequences—both intended and unintended. Further, the coexistence of opposing regulatory regimes (i.e., federal prohibition vs. state liberalization) and the implications for public health and criminal justice are worth exploring.

This study also demonstrates the need for public policy and administration researchers to engage more on drug policy. While some are contributing to niche outlets like the *International Journal of Drug Policy*, drug policy presents myriad policy and governance questions that warrant greater attention within the pages of policy and administration journals. For example, the evolution of U.S. drug policy reveals important complexities about American federalism. Defiant innovation by the states is now not limited to medical marijuana (Hannah and Mallinson 2018), but is expanding to other substances. States are acting in a vacuum produced by the national government that federalism scholars have noted for years (Rose and Bowling 2015), but state drug policy liberalization goes beyond simply resisting federal mandates or filling federal inaction. The national government remains active in prohibitionist policies. This fractured policy landscape is expanding and has implications not only for governance, but also for new industries and individuals.

Public administration scholars can also speak to the ethical and social justice components of drug policy reform. Since the 1970s, social equity has been a pillar of public administration (Frederickson 1990). Scholars have wrestled with the social equity implications of numerous policies and public service delivery mechanisms, but drug policy has received scant attention. A search of *Public Integrity*, a cornerstone journal for topics of ethics and social equity, yields no pieces examining drug policy. This is a substantial missing voice in the debate over drug policy. Beyond ethics, drug policy presents ample opportunities to explore theories of the policy process, advocacy coalitions, networked governance, and more. Not only can policy and administration research contribute to better understanding drug policy, studying drug policy can advance theory and praxis.

Another notable gap in the research evaluated in this study is the scarcer attention to drugs beyond opioids and cannabis. Policy scholars should not limit themselves to the two substances that elicit the greatest attention but should expand their reach into drugs like psylocibin mushrooms and MDMA, which are advancing in clinical trials and at the forefront in emerging efforts to loosen state-level drug prohibitions.

About the Authors

Saahir Shafi is a Doctoral Candidate at Penn State Harrisburg. Her research agenda focuses on comparative public policy and public health topics including the complex dynamics of crisis decision making, disproportionate policy responses, and healthcare policy issues (i.e., COVID-19, drug policy, and smart home technology for assistive living).

Daniel J. Mallinson is an Assistant Professor of Public Policy and Administration at Penn State Harrisburg. His research focuses on policy diffusion, drug policy (primarily cannabis), energy policy, and the science of teaching and learning.

References

Adinoff, Bryon, and Amanda Reiman. 2019. "Implementing Social Justice in the Transition From Illicit to Legal Cannabis." *The American Journal of Drug and Alcohol Abuse* 45 (6): 673-688. DOI: https://doi.org/10.1080/00952990.2019.1674862

Adlin, Ben. 2021a. "Washington Lawmakers Approve Drug Decriminalization Bill In Committee Vote." *Marijuana Moment* No. 15/2021. Accessed on November 2, 2021. https://www.marijuanamoment.net/washington-lawmakers-approve-drug-decriminalization-bill-in-committee-vote/

_____. 2021b. "Washington Senate Replaces Drug Decriminalization Bill With Revised Measure to Reinstate Penalties." *Marijuana Moment* 16/2021. Accessed on November 2, 2021. https://www.marijuanamoment.net/washington-senate-re places-drug-decriminalization-bill-with-revised-measure-to-reinstate-penalties/

Alexander, Michelle. 2010. *The New Jim Crow: Mass Incarceration in the Age of Colorblindness.* New York, NY: The New Press.

Amroussia, Nada, Mika Watanabe, and Jennifer L. Pearson. 2020. "Seeking Safety: A Focus Group Study of Young Adults' Cannabis-Related Attitudes, and Behavior in a State with Legalized Recreational Cannabis." *Harm Reduction Journal* 17 (1): 92. DOI: 10.1186/s12954-020-00442-8

Andresen, Martin A., and Neil Boyd. 2010. "A Cost-Benefit and Cost-Effective-ness Analysis of Vancouver's Supervised Injection Facility." *International Journal of Drug Policy* 21 (1): 70-76. DOI: 10.1016/j.drugpo.2009.03.004

Anguelov, Nikolay. 2018. *From Criminalizing to Decriminalizing Marijuana: The Politics of Social Control.* Lanham, MD: Lexington Books.

Appa, Ayesha, Luke N. Rodda, Caroline Cawley, Barry Zevin, Phillip O. Coffin, Monica Gandhi, and Elizabeth Imbert. 2021. "Drug Overdose Deaths Before and After Shelter-in-Place Orders During the COVID-19 Pandemic in San Francisco." *JAMA Network Open* 4 (5): e2110452-e2110452. DOI: 10.1001/jamanetworko pen.2021.10452

Ballotpedia. 2021. "Marijuana Laws in the United States." Accessed October 1, 2021. https://ballotpedia.org/Marijuana_laws_in_the_United_States

Bartholomew, Tyler S., Hansel E. Tookes, Corinne Bullock, Jason Onugha, David W. Forrest, and Daniel J. Feaster. 2020. "Examining Risk Behavior and Syringe Coverage Among People Who Inject Drugs Accessing a Syringe Services Program: A Latent Class Analysis." *International Journal of Drug Policy* 78: 102716. DOI: 10.1016/j.drugpo.2020.102716

Baumgartner, Jesse C., and David C. Radley. 2021. "The Spike in Drug Overdose Deaths During the COVID-19 Pandemic and Policy Options to Move Forward."

The Commonwealth Fund No. 25/ 2021. Accessed on November 2, 2021. https://www.commonwealthfund.org/blog/2021/spike-drug-overdose-deaths-during-covid-19-pandemic-and-policy-options-move-forward

Bennett, Trevor, and Katy Holloway. 2010. "Is UK Drug Policy Evidence Based?" *International Journal of Drug Policy* 21 (5): 411-417. DOI: 10.1016/j.drugpo.2010.02.004

Bewley-Taylor, David R. 2013. "Toward Revision of the UN Drug Control Conventions: Harnessing Like-Mindedness." *International Journal of Drug Policy* 24 (1): 60-68. DOI: 10.1016/j.drugpo.2012.09.001

Bewley-Taylor, Dave, Tom Blickman, and Martin Jelsma. 2014. *The Rise and Decline of Cannabis Prohibition.* Amsterdam, NL: Transnational Institute.

Braun, Virginia, and Victoria Clarke. 2006. "Using Thematic Analysis in Psychology." *Qualitative Research in Psychology* 3 (2): 77-101. DOI: 10.1191/1478088706qp063oa

_____. 2021. "Can I use TA? Should I use TA? Should I not use TA? Comparing reflexive thematic analysis and other pattern-based qualitative analytic approaches." *Counselling and Psychotherapy Research* 21 (1): 37-47. DOI: 10.1002/capr.12360

Braun, Virginia, Victoria Clarke, Nikki Hayfield, and Gareth Terry. 2019. "Thematic Analysis." In *Handbook of Research Methods in Health Social Sciences*, edited by Pranee Liamputtong. Gateway East, SG: Springer Singapore. 843-860.

Carhart-Harris, Robin L., Mark Bolstridge, James Rucker, Camilla M. J. Day, David Erritzoe, Mendel Kaelen, Michael Bloomfield, James A. Rickard, Ben Forbes, Amanda Feilding, David Taylor, Steve Pilling, Valerie H. Curran, and David J. Nutt. 2016. "Psilocybin with Psychological Support For Treatment-Resistant Depression: An Open-Label Feasibility Study." *The Lancet Psychiatry* 3 (7): 619-627. DOI: 10.1016/S2215-0366(16)30065-7

Caulkins, Jonathan P., and Beau Kilmer. 2016. "Considering Marijuana Legalization Carefully: Insights for Other Jurisdictions from Analysis for Vermont." *Addiction* 111 (12) : 2082-2089. DOI: 10.1111/add.13289

Caulkins, Jonathan P., Yilun Bao, Steve Davenport, Imane Fahli, Yutian Guo, Krista Kinnard, Mary Najewicz, Lauren Renaud, and Beau Kilmer. 2018. "Big Data on a Big New Market: Insights from Washington State's Legal Cannabis Market." *International Journal of Drug Policy* 57: 86-94. DOI: 10.1016/j.drugpo.2018.03.031

CDC. 2020. "Increase in Fatal Drug Overdoses Across the United States Driven by Synthetic Opioids Before and During the COVID-19 Pandemic." *Centers for Disease Control and Prevention* No. 17/2020. Accessed on November 2, 2021. https://emergency.cdc.gov/han/2020/han00438.asp

_____. 2021. "Understanding the Epidemic." *Centers for Disease Control and Prevention* No. 17/2021. Accessed on November 2, 2021. https://www.cdc.gov/opioids/basics/epidemic.html

Chatwin, Caroline. 2017. "UNGASS 2016: Insights from Europe on the Development of Global Cannabis Policy and the Need for Reform of the Global Drug Policy Regime." *International Journal of Drug Policy* 49: 80-85. doi: 10.1016/j.drugpo.2015.12.017

Csete, Joanne, and Peter J. Grob. 2012. "Switzerland, HIV and the Power of Pragmatism: Lessons for Drug Policy Development." *International Journal of Drug Policy* 23 (1): 82-86. DOI: 10.1016/j.drugpo.2011.07.011

Danquah-Brobby, Elizabeth. 2016. "Prison for You: Profit for Me: Systemic Racism Effectively Bars Blacks from Participation in Newly-Legal Marijuana Industry Comments." *University of Baltimore Law Review* 46: 523.

Department of Health and Human Services. 2021. *Practice Guidelines for the Administration of Buprenorphine for Treating Opioid Use Disorder*. Washington, D.C.: Federal Register.

Editors. 2014. "End the Drug War's Reserach Bans." *Scientific American* No. 01/2014. Accessed on November 2, 2021. https://www.scientificamerican.com/article/end-the-ban-on-psychoactive-drug-research/

Fischer, Benedikt, Sharan Kuganesan, and Robin Room. 2015. "Medical Marijuana Programs: Implications for Cannabis Control Policy – Observations from Canada." *International Journal of Drug Policy* 26 (1): 15-19. DOI: 10.1016/j.drugpo.2014.09.007

Frederickson, H. George. 1990. "Public Administration and Social Equity." *Public Administration Review* 50 (2): 228-237. Accessed on November 2, 2021. https://www.jstor.org/stable/976870

Fuentes, Juan José, Francina Fonseca, Matilde Elices, Magí Farré, and Marta Torrens. 2020. "Therapeutic Use of LSD in Psychiatry: A Systematic Review of Randomized-Controlled Clinical Trials." *Frontiers in Psychiatry*. DOI: 10.3389/fps yt.2019.00943

Gomes, Tara, Sophie A. Kitchen, and Regan Murray. 2021. "Measuring the Burden of Opioid-Related Mortality in Ontario, Canada, During the COVID-19 Pandemic." *JAMA Network Open* 4 (5): e2112865-e2112865. DOI: 10.1001/jamanetworkop en.2021.12865

Guerrero, Erick G., Jorge Ameth Villatoro, Yinfei Kong, Marycarmen Bustos Gamiño, William A. Vega, and Maria Elena Medina Mora. 2014. "Mexicans' Use of Illicit Drugs in an Era of Drug Reform: National Comparative Analysis by Migrant Status." *International Journal of Drug Policy* 25 (3): 451-457. DOI: 10.1016/j. drugpo.2014.04.006

Hall, Wayne, and Lynn T. Kozlowski. 2018. "The Diverging Trajectories of Cannabis and Tobacco Policies in the United States: Reasons and Possible Implications." *Addiction* 113 (4): 595-601. DOI: 10.1111/add.13845

Hannah, A. Lee, and Daniel J. Mallinson. 2018. "Defiant Innovation: The Adoption of Medical Marijuana Laws in the American States." *Policy Studies Journal* 46 (2): 402-423. DOI: 10.1111/psj.12211

Himmich, Hakima, and Navid Madani. 2016. "The State of Harm Reduction in the Middle East and North Africa: A Focus on Iran and Morocco." *International Journal of Drug Policy* 31: 184-189. DOI: 10.1016/j.drugpo.2016.02.013

Holland, Kristin M., Christopher Jones, Alana M. Vivolo-Kantor, Nimi Idaikkadar, Marissa Zwald, Brooke Hoots, Ellen Yard, Ashley D'Inverno, Elizabeth Swedo, May S. Chen, Emiko Petrosky, Amy Board, Pedro Martinez, Deborah M. Stone, Royal Law, Michael A. Coletta, Jennifer Adjemian, Craig Thomas, Richard W. Puddy, Georgina Peacock, Nicole F. Dowling, and Debra Houry. 2021. "Trends in US Emergency Department Visits for Mental Health, Overdose, and Violence Outcomes Before and During the COVID-19 Pandemic." *JAMA Psychiatry* 78 (4): 372-379. DOI: 10.1001/jamapsychiatry.2020.4402

Jaeger, Kyle. 2021. "Maine Lawmakers Approve Bill to Decriminalize All Drugs on 50th Anniversary of Nixon's 'War on Drugs.'" *Marijuana Moment* No. 25/2021. Accessed on November 2, 2021. https://www.marijuanamoment.net/maine-lawmak ers-approve-bill-to-decriminalize-all-drugs-on-50th-anniversary-of-nixons-war-on-drugs/

Järvinen, Margaretha, and Gale Miller. 2014. "Selections of Reality: Applying Burke's Dramatism To A Harm Reduction Program." *International Journal of Drug Policy* 25 (5): 879-887. DOI: 10.1016/j.drugpo.2014.02.014

Kiang, Mathew V., Keith Humphreys, Mark R. Cullen, and Sanjay Basu. 2020. "Opioid Prescribing Patterns Among Medical Providers in the United States, 2003-17: Retrospective, Observational Study." *BMJ* 368: l6968. DOI: https://doi.org/10.1136/bmj.l6968

Lancaster, Kari. 2014. "Social Construction and the Evidence-Based Drug Policy Endeavour." *International Journal of Drug Policy* 25 (5): 948-951. DOI: 10.1016/j.drugpo.2014.01.002

Mallinson, Daniel J., and A. Lee Hannah. 2020. "Policy and Political Learning: The Development of Medical Marijuana Policies in the States." *Publius: The Journal of Federalism* 50 (3): 344-369. DOI: 10.1093/publius/pjaa006

Mallinson, Daniel J., A. Lee Hannah, and Gideon Cunningham. 2020. "The Consequences of Fickle Federal Policy: Administrative Hurdles for State Cannabis Policies." *APSA Preprints.* DOI: 10.33774/apsa-2020-jbzvh

Manthey, Jakob. 2019. "Cannabis use in Europe: Current Trends and Public Health Concerns." *International Journal of Drug Policy* 68: 93-96. DOI: 10.1016/j.drugpo.2019.03.006

Marlatt, G. Alan. 1996. "Harm Reduction: Come as you are." *Addictive Behaviors* 21 (6): 779-788. DOI: 10.1016/0306-4603(96)00042-1

Miclette, Matthew A., Jared A. Leff, Isabella Cuan, Jeffrey H. Samet, Brendan Saloner, Gary Mendell, Yuhua Bao, Michael A. Ashburn, Marcus A. Bachhuber, Bruce R. Schackman, Daniel E. Polsky, and Zachary F. Meisel. 2018. "Closing the Gaps in Opioid Use Disorder Research, Policy and Practice: Conference Proceedings." *Addiction Science & Clinical Practice* 13 (1): 22. DOI: 10.1186/s13722-018-0123-3

Mitchell, Jennifer M., Michael Bogenschutz, Alia Lilienstein, Charlotte Harrison, Sarah Kleiman, Kelly Parker-Guilbert, Marcela Ot'alora G, Wael Garas, Casey Paleos, Ingmar Gorman, Christopher Nicholas, Michael Mithoefer, Shannon Carlin, Bruce Poulter, Ann Mithoefer, Sylvestre Quevedo, Gregory Wells, Sukhpreet S. Klaire, Bessel van der Kolk, Keren Tzarfaty, Revital Amiaz, Ray Worthy, Scott Shannon, Joshua D. Woolley, Cole Marta, Yevgeniy Gelfand, Emma Hapke, Simon Amar, Yair Wallach, Randall Brown, Scott Hamilton, Julie B. Wang, Allison Coker, Rebecca Matthews, Alberdina de Boer, Berra Yazar-Klosinski, Amy Emerson, and Rick Doblin. 2021. "MDMA-Assisted Therapy for Severe PTSD: A Randomized, Double-Blind, Placebo-Controlled Phase 3 Study." *Nature Medicine* 27 (6): 1025-1033. DOI: 10.1038/s41591-021-01336-3

Monaghan, Mark. 2014. "Drug Policy Governance in the UK: Lessons from Changes to and Debates Concerning the Classification of Cannabis Under the 1971 Misuse of Drugs Act." *International Journal of Drug Policy* 25 (5): 1025-1030. DOI: 10.1016/j.drugpo.2014.02.001

Moore, David, Suzanne Fraser, Jukka Törrönen, and Mimmi Eriksson Tinghög. 2015. "Sameness and Difference: Metaphor and Politics in the Constitution of Addiction, Social Exclusion and Gender in Australian and Swedish Drug Policy." *International Journal of Drug Policy* 26 (4): 420-428. DOI: 10.1016/j.drugpo.2015.01.011

Mosher, Clayton, and Scott Akins. 2019. *In the Weeds: Demonization, Legalization, and the Evolution of U.S. Marijuana Policy*. Philadelphia, PA: Temple University Press.

Munn, Zachary, Micah D. J. Peters, Cindy Stern, Catalin Tufanaru, Alexa McArthur, and Edoardo Aromataris. 2018. "Systematic Review or Scoping Review? Guidance for Authors When Choosing Between a Systematic or Scoping Review Approach." *BMC Medical Research Methodology* 18 (1): 143. DOI: 10.1186/s12874-018-0611-x

O'Donnell, Julie K., R. Matthew Gladden, and Puja Seth. 2017. "Trends in Deaths Involving Heroin and Synthetic Opioids Excluding Methadone, and Law Enforcement Drug Product Reports, by Census Region - United States, 2006-2015." *MMWR. Morbidity and Mortality Weekly Report* 66 (34): 897-903. DOI: 10.15585/mmwr.mm6634a2.

O'Grady, Cathleen. 2020. "Cannabis Research Database Shows How U.S. Funding Focuses on Harms of the Drug." *Science* No. 27/2020. Accessed on November 2, 2021. https://www.sciencemag.org/news/2020/08/cannabis-research-database-shows-how-us-funding-focuses-harms-drug

Opp, Susan M., and Samantha L. Mosier. 2020. "Liquor, Marijuana, and Guns: Essential Services or Political Tools During the Covid-19 Pandemic?" *Policy Design and Practice* 3 (3): 297-311. DOI: 10.1080/25741292.2020.1810397

Peltz, Jennifer. 2019. "Pot 'Legalization 2.0:' Social Equity Becomes a Key Question." *AP News* No. 19/2019. Accessed on November 2, 2021. https://apnews.com/dcce234afaa7441483f59a190d84c62f

Ritter, Alison, and Kari Lancaster. 2013. "Measuring Research Influence on Drug Policy: A Case Example of Two Epidemiological Monitoring Systems." *Interna-

tional Journal of Drug Policy 24 (1): 30-37. DOI: 10.1016/j.drugpo.2012.02.005

Rose, Shanna, and Cynthia J. Bowling. 2015. "The State of American Federalism 2014–15: Pathways to Policy in an Era of Party Polarization." *Publius: The Journal of Federalism* 45 (3): 351-379. DOI: 10.1093/publius/pjv028

Rosmarin, Ari, and Niamh Eastwood. 2012. *A Quiet Revolution*. London, UK: Release.

Tieberghien, Julie. 2014. "The Role of the Media in the Science-Policy Nexus. Some Critical Reflections Based on an Analysis of the Belgian Drug Policy Debate (1996–2003)." *International Journal of Drug Policy* 25 (2): 276-281. DOI: 10.1016/j.drugpo.2013.05.014

Torre, Carla, Raquel Lucas, and Henrique Barros. 2010. "Syringe Exchange In Community Pharmacies—The Portuguese Experience." *International Journal of Drug Policy* 21 (6): 514-517. DOI: 10.1016/j.drugpo.2010.09.001

Tullis, Paul. 2021. "The Rise of Psychedelic Psychiatry." *Nature* 589: 506-509. DOI: 10.1038/d41586-021-00187-9

Uchtenhagen, Ambros. 2010. "Heroin-Assisted Treatment in Switzerland: A Case Study in Policy Change." *Addiction* 105 (1): 29-37. DOI: 10.1111/j.1360-0443.2009.02741.x

Vollenweider, Franz X., and Katrin H. Preller. 2020. "Psychedelic Drugs: Neurobiology and Potential for Treatment of Psychiatric Disorders." *Nature Reviews Neuroscience* 21 (11): 611-624. DOI: 10.1038/s41583-020-0367-2

Wadman, Meredith. 2021. "United States Set to Allow More Facilities to Produce Marijuana for Research." *Science Magazine* No. 17/2021. Accessed on November 2, 2021. https://www.sciencemag.org/news/2021/05/us-set-allow-more-facilities-produce-marijuana-research

Weiss, Susan R. B., Katia D. Howlett, and Ruben D. Baler. 2017. "Building Smart Cannabis Policy from the Science Up." *International Journal of Drug Policy* 42: 39-49. DOI: 10.1016/j.drugpo.2017.01.007

West, Steven L., Keri K. O'Neal, and Carolyn W. Graham. 2000. "A Meta-Analysis Comparing the Effectiveness of Buprenorphine and Methadone." *Journal of Substance Abuse* 12 (4): 405-414. DOI: 10.1016/S0899-3289(01)00054-2

Seeing the Visual: A Literature Review on Why and How Policy Scholars Would Do Well to Study Influential Visualizations

Eduardo Rojas-Padilla

Tamara Metze

Katrien Termeer

Public Administration and Policy Group,
Wageningen University & Research, Netherlands

Visualizations are important for policy debates. In a single image, visuals convey information, values, and emotions. Think of the shocking image of Alan Kurdi's drowning and the abrupt shift in immigration policy debates in Europe. Visualizations influence policy and politics, but how? This article presents a detailed and analytic overview of the state-of-the-art research on visualizations from the policy and political sciences and suggests a research agenda. We identified five explanatory roles for how visualizations influence policy and policy debates as: 1) sense-making devices for interpreting complex information; 2) emotional triggers to strategically manipulate the viewers' sentiments for political gains; 3) objects of political meaning making; 4) icons that convey social and cultural norms; and 5) portrayals of the underlying values that matter when representing situations in society. We applied our findings to a visualization of the controversial gene-editing technology CRISPR-Cas applied to food. We claim that these five roles need to be combined to better understand how visualizations are influential over time and for different policy actors. We argue for studying visualizations as boundary objects whose meaning is negotiated between (groups of) policy actors and that can change over time.

Keywords: Visualizations, Policy Diffusion, Policy Influence, Political Behavior, Framing, Meaning in Policy Making, Social Network Analysis, Media and Policy, Embracing the Visual Turn in Policy Research.

Policy Studies Yearbook 12.1: 103-136. 10.18278/psy.12.1.5
©2022 Policy Studies Organization

Ver lo visual: una revisión de la literatura sobre por qué y cómo los académicos de políticas harían bien en estudiar visualizaciones influyentes

Las visualizaciones son importantes para los debates sobre políticas. En una sola imagen, las imágenes transmiten información, valores y emociones. Piense en la impactante imagen del ahogamiento de Alan Kurdi y el cambio abrupto en los debates sobre políticas de inmigración en Europa. Las visualizaciones influyen en la política y la política, pero ¿cómo? Este artículo presenta una descripción detallada y analítica de la investigación de vanguardia sobre visualizaciones de las ciencias políticas y políticas y sugiere una agenda de investigación. Identificamos cinco roles explicativos de cómo las visualizaciones influyen en las políticas y los debates de políticas como: 1) dispositivos de creación de sentido para interpretar información compleja; 2) disparadores emocionales para manipular estratégicamente los sentimientos de los espectadores en busca de ganancias políticas; 3) objetos de creación de significado político: 4) iconos que transmiten normas sociales y culturales, y 5) representaciones de los valores subyacentes que importan al representar situaciones en la sociedad. Aplicamos nuestros hallazgos a una visualización de la controvertida tecnología de edición de genes CRISPR-Cas aplicada a los alimentos. Afirmamos que estos cinco roles deben combinarse para comprender mejor cómo las visualizaciones son influyentes a lo largo del tiempo y para los diferentes actores políticos. Abogamos por estudiar las visualizaciones como objetos de frontera cuyo significado se negocia entre (grupos de) actores políticos y que pueden cambiar con el tiempo.

Palabras Clave: Visualizaciones, Políticas, Comportamiento político, Encuadre, Significado en la formulación De Políticas, Análisis de redes sociales.

看到視覺：關於政策學者為什麼以及如何做好研究有影響力的視覺效果的文獻綜述

可視化對於政策辯論很重要。在單個圖像中，視覺傳達信息、價值觀和情感。想想艾倫·庫爾迪（Alan Kurdi）溺水的令人震驚的畫面以及歐洲移民政策辯論的突然轉變。可視化影響政策和政治，但如何影響？本文對來自政策和政治科學的可視化的最新研究進行了詳細和分析性的概述，並提出

了研究議程。我們確定了可視化如何影響政策和政策辯論的
五個解釋性角色：1）解釋複雜信息的意義製造設備；2）為
了政治利益，戰略性地操縱觀眾情緒的情緒觸發器；3）產
生政治意義的對象：4）傳達社會和文化規範的圖標，以及
5）描繪在代表社會情況時重要的潛在價值。我們將我們的
發現應用於有爭議的基因編輯技術 CRISPR-Cas 應用於食品
的可視化。我們聲稱需要將這五個角色結合起來，以更好地
了解可視化如何隨著時間的推移以及對不同政策參與者的影
響。我們主張將可視化研究為邊界對象，其含義是在（組）
政策參與者之間協商的，並且會隨著時間而改變。

關鍵詞：可視化、政策、政治行為、框架、決策意義、社會
網絡分析。

The use of visuals in policy and political issues is omnipresent in public debates: a flaming faucet in the shale gas controversy (Gommeh, Dijstelbloem, and Metze 2020; Metze 2018b); a toddler's body on the seashore in the immigrant crisis (Adler-Nissen, Andersen, and Hansen 2020; Prøitz 2018; Farida and Olga 2015); polar bears adrift on a tiny ice sheet in the Arctic; the burning embers in the climate change debates (Born 2019; see also Metze 2020 on Schellnhuber's diagram); the visual campaign against GMOs (Clancy and Clancy 2016; Clancy 2016); or the pair of scissors precisely cutting out a fragment of DNA, visualizing the potential genome editing capabilities of CRISPR-Cas technology (Hurtley 2013).

We define visualizations as condensed graphical elements depicting realities, knowledge, ideas, or messages capable of packaging cognitive, normative, and emotional information in non-necessarily verbal form. All sorts of actors in policies and politics use visualizations to represent particular views on policy issues, spread (framed) information, and influence the general public and decision makers (Adams and Albin 1980; Jenner 2012). Visualizations are studied increasingly in policy and political studies. For example, in studies on framing in political campaigns (Grabe and Bucy 2009; Rosenberg, Kahn, and Tran 1991), or studies into discourse coalitions and policy learning (Gommeh, Dijstelbloem, and Metze 2020; Metze 2018b). Additionally, there is influential work on the role of visualizations on culture and democracy—for instance, Hariman and Lucaites (2007), and Zelizer (2010) take a cultural perspective to study visual icons. Moreover, the works of Morseletto (2017), Mendonça, Ercan, and Asenbaum (2020), Metze (2018b, 2020), Moody and Bekkers (2018), Hill and Helmers (2012), Stocchetti (2014), Gommeh, Dijstelbloem, and Metze (2020), and van Beek and others (2020) point out an undertheorized, intricate, and nuanced role of visualizations in policy and political sciences.

Across the policy and political sciences, much is to gain by embracing the visual turn that Mitchell (1994) argued for and focusing on understanding how the visual influences social and political life in modern societies (Green 2010; Mendonça, Ercan, and Asenbaum 2020). In the context of a fast-changing online media landscape, the role of visualization takes a different dimension for political and policy research. For example, Kasra (2017) described how digital-networked images facilitated a new means for underrepresented minorities to reappropriate the political and cultural construction of (Egyptian) women as political agents, both in the Arab world and beyond, from studying female nude selfies as personal acts of political expression during the 2011 uprisings in Egypt. In comparison, Doerr (2017) exposed how far-right groups used visualizations strategically to forge cross-linguistic transnational alliances against immigration to Europe. These examples illustrate an understudied dimension of nonverbal forms of communication, political participation, and framing in and through the use of visualizations in modern networked societies.

Although there exist theoretical limitations surrounding the systematic research of visualizations in policy science, there is empirical literature highlighting the influence of visuals in framing and reframing policies (van Beek *et al.* 2020), fueling controversies online (Rabello *et al.* 2021), unifying debates (Born 2019), or giving gravitas to environmental governance (Morseletto 2017).

Empirical evidence indicates an intricate role for visualizations across the policy sciences. For example, in the interplay between science, policy, and society, Clancy (2016) dissects the role of visualizations in the Genetically Modified Organisms (GMO) controversy in Europe and the United States at multiple levels. The central point is that visualizations function as a resistance mechanism, expanding on different ways their influence reached policy framing and decisions. The research further explains how an international coalition of actors used visuals to contest dominant views about agrobiotechnology. By visualizing GMO crops as "Frankenfoods," GMO technology became visible to the public and *different* from regular crops, sedimenting a debate that would shape and reframe public and regulatory policy on GMO technology on both sides of the Atlantic (Clancy 2016).

Additionally, anti-GMO campaigners' use of "visual events" proved to be an instrumental strategy for constructing visual rhetorics through digital media that hindered policy framing and influenced policy decisions in the UK. The most iconic was the image of a Greenpeace truck in 1999, dumping four tons of soybeans outside No. 10, Downing Street with a sign that read "Tony, don't swallow Bill's seed." Weeks later, Prime Minister Tony Blair backtracked standing public policy on agrobiotechnology, electing to implement a five-year moratorium on GM crops in the UK instead (Clancy and Clancy 2016; Durant and Lindsey 1999).

Academic attention toward visualizations also showcases recent examples of how a better understanding of visualizations can help policies. Wardekker and Lorenz (2019) analyzed the visualizations of an Intergovernmental Panel on Climate Change (IPCC) report to show that the IPPC's visual framing focused on the (science-oriented) existence of climate impacts, hindering attention to adaptation policies to climate change. Their research suggests that IPCC reports pay more attention to adopting a visual framing from a solution-oriented perspective while researching better ways to visualize adaptation. Metze (2018b) makes a similar call for analyzing visual framing for policy learning and policy making. Notably, the urge to theorize better the role of visualizations also comes from those natural scientists who are increasingly aware of the relevance of visuals in communicating information for science and policy (McInerny *et al.* 2014).

Overall, these points indicate that scholarship in the policy sciences would therefore benefit greatly from a better understanding of visualizations as influential elements in negotiating and framing policy in modern society. This article aims to give a systematic overview of the current state of the research into influential visualizations and use that as a starting point for a research agenda and conceptual framework that better take into account the challenges of studying influential visualizations in a networked, globalized, and mediatized world.

We innovatively combined a quantitative and qualitative Social Network Analysis (SNA) to study the most referred literature about visualizations within a selection of policy studies and political science journals. We analyzed the concepts, methods, and explanations they use to study influential visualizations. We then argue that visuals should be studied as boundary objects whose meaning is negotiated between (groups of) policy actors. This meaning differs between groups of actors and changes over time. Moreover, visual boundary objects travel easily, and their traveling and influence on policy and politics should be further conceptualized. The article is structured as follows: we first explain our methods, then the results, and develop a research agenda in the discussion and conclusion. Since our analysis concerns the theoretical starting points, methods, and empirics of a broad range of literature on visualizations, we will not develop a theoretical framework at this point.

Methods

We created a dataset of relevant papers and conducted a two-step social network analysis. In the first, we performed a social network analysis based on co-citations. Co-citation analyses map the connection of ideas in academic knowledge evolution in literature clusters (Boyack and Klavans 2010; Baker 1990). This approach allowed clustering of the literature by affinity. In the second step, we analyzed those clusters manually to understand their ontological, epistemological, methodological, and empirical similarities and differences.

Dataset

To retrieve our raw data, we conducted a Boolean search of the Web of Science (WoS) repository comprised of the terms Poli* AND Visual,* followed by a refined inclusion/seclusion criteria of research topics using indexation topics. The inclusion criteria focused on political sciences and multidisciplinary sciences, including communication, social sciences, or experimental psychology. We excluded areas like ophthalmology or engineering (see Appendix 1).

A raw dataset of 1,500 papers was collected from WoS on June 25, 2020, spanning from 1945 to the collection date. Equivalent searches were run on Scopus. We compared both datasets for indexation of accessions and journals to prevent overlapping data. The comparison showed that WoS had 2.7 times more relevant journals than Scopus; Scopus also had a 49.4-percent overlap data with WoS. We thus chose to work with the WoS dataset.

The raw data consisted of 1,500 accessions of peer-reviewed papers and academic books. We ran a first co-citation analysis (see below) and decided to include only papers and books that were co-cited at least ten times in order to be able to identify the most important papers and clusters. The final dataset consisted of 77 accessions, of which 43 were articles and 34 books.

Step 1: Quantitative Social Network Analysis

In the first step, we applied a quantitative SNA and established networks between publications based on bibliometrics—more specifically, the number of co-citation incidences (Aria and Cuccurullo (2017); Cowhitt, Butler, and Wilson (2020). We ran co-citation network analyses to our corpus data using the R-package bibliometrix (Aria and Cuccurullo 2017) and used VOSViewer and Gephi to map the network and analyze statistics (Van Eck and Waltman 2010; Bastian Mathieu 2009) (see Appendix 2).

We then organized our corpus data by degree centrality and betweenness centrality of each network node[1] based on co-citations[2] parameters. Degree centrality analysis identifies the principal works of reference spearheading academic literature on visualizations in the political and policy sciences. The betweenness centrality analysis allowed us to identify references bridging literature clusters but not as co-cited as the literature analyzed by degree centrality is. However, they are not mutually exclusive, and some works can have a high degree and high betweenness centrality values. Our next step was to identify the conceptual characteristics that gave each cluster their affinity in our qualitative social network analysis.

Step 2: Qualitative Social Network Analysis

In this step, we analyzed the conceptual, methodological, and empirical similarities and differences in the literature in each of the five clusters. Based on

---

1   We set the threshold for the minimal node size at ten co-citations for degree centrality and four co-citations for betweenness centrality. These thresholds were identified in a sequence of try-outs to find a point of workable clustering in the network.

2   We used fractional counting to account for the differences in number of total citations between articles, and between articles and books.

a 10-percent sample from each cluster (about ten papers in total), we inductively built a codebook to analyze which concepts, methods, and objects of study were applied in the literature. The codebook was tested and refined by applying it to a manual selection of the ten papers that varied from older books, papers, and more recent publications.

We coded publications at (1) a *conceptual* level: 1a. What are visualizations (definition)? 1b. What is the nature of visualizations (ontology)? 1c. What is the subject matter studied in visualizations (epistemology)? and 1d. Theoretical relationships between visualizations and text. At (2) an empirical level, we coded for 2a. the type of visualizations (inter alia, photos, data visualizations, or cartoons), and 2b. methods used. We also coded (3) *explanatory level*: What roles are addressed to visualizations in policy or political processes (see Appendix 3)? We coded the five clusters separately until extracting no new data from the literature. We reached this saturation point at around 2/3s of the entries per cluster.

Results: Seeing the Visual in Policy and Politics

Quantitative Review: Mapping Research on Visualizations in the Political and Policy Sciences

The quantitative SNA resulted in 95 nodes, of which 49 were articles and 46 books. We identified five clusters of literature in the network structure (Figure 1). We labeled them as visual framing as sense making *(VAS)* (in red), visual framing as politics *(VAP)* (in green), discourse as visual language *(VAD)* (in yellow), cultural imagery as representation *(CIR)* (in blue), and aesthetics as representation *(AR)* (in purple). Below we describe each cluster more extensively, but we first present each cluster's makeup: the crucial authors, books, and papers. When presenting the qualitative analysis results, we will describe how visualizations and their role in policy and politics are studied in each cluster.

Composition of Clusters: Primary References and Affinities

VAS is the cluster with the highest number of publications in the network, with 27 entries, of which 19 are articles, and eight are books. The most co-cited works within this cluster are Entman (1993), Griffin (2004), and Messaris and Abraham (2001) (Table 1). Publications, such as Geise and Baden (2015), Gitlin (1980), Coleman (2010), and Graber (1990), suggest that the literature found in this cluster shares a similar theoretical and methodological research approach from a framing perspective. Research in this cluster is oriented to study visualizations in processes of sense making of policy or political issues. In other words, how the use of (passive or active) visual framing enables individuals and groups to process and make sense of the issues at hand.

The next larger cluster in the network is *VAP*, consisting of 16 articles and four books. The most co-cited publications are Grabe (2009), Schill (2012), and

Nagel, Maurer, and Reinemann (2012) (Table 1). These works and the work of authors like Shawn Rosenberg (1986, 1987, 1991), Alexander Todorov and others (2005), or Rein Vliegenthart (2012) suggest this cluster conglomerates research on visualizations and framing for persuasion in political events, campaigns, and electoral purposes. Quantitatively, the cluster *VAP* is the closest to the cluster *VAS*.[3] The two distinct clusters suggest differences in approaches to research visualizations between those intended for political and electoral purposes and framing as a sense-making process in general. In the *VAP* cluster, researchers consider visual framing to be intentional. Visual framing is used strategically to persuade and attract viewers/voters, whereas, in *VAS*, visual framing could be passive, not necessarily strategic.

The *VAD* cluster consists of 18 books and one journal article. The most relevant works are Kress and van Leeuwen (1996), Barthes (1977), and Kress (2001) (Table 1), who suggest that visualizations—just like text—are forms of semiology that function to communicate explicit and implicit messages. However, culture and history are essential to decoding those messages. The authors argue that the meaning of visualizations is embedded in history, culture, and "rhetoric threads" from specific social groups, and as such, there are multiple ways to interpret visualizations. Additionally, the authors in this cluster expand the notion of visualization beyond the mere image, and they draw from works by, for example, Anderson (1983), Lakoff (1980), and Foucault (1977) to include discursive imaginaries, metaphors, or visions, as part of their study of discourses. The use of visual language influences forms of thinking and how actors negotiate policy and political issues. Authors in this cluster understand visualizations as discursive, meaning as part of the language used in political and policy interactions—hence as part of larger discourses.

The *CIR* cluster contains 15 books and five articles, and Hariman and Lucaites (2007), Rose (2018), and Mitchell (1994) are its principal works (Table 1). These authors approach visualizations as devices that convey meanings through visual elements and symbols, and these visuals are of cultural importance in political and policy sciences. Other relevant authors are Sontag (1977, 2003), Zelizer (2010), and Ahmed (2004). They emphasize the use of (iconic) visualizations as communicational resources in the (re)production of culture and social practices, ideology, power of representations, and the shaping of collective memories and identities through the media.

AR is the smallest cluster and consists of eight articles and one book. Its main works are Hansen (2015), Campbell (2007), and Williams (2003) (Table 1). They all write about visuals' essential role (particularly photojournalism) in representing conflicts in international relations and their influence in subsequent foreign policy decisions. Moreover, Bleiker (2001, 2015) and Heck and Schlag

---

3   This differentiation is visible in our network due to the threshold established as the minimum node size. With node size parameters higher than ten, these two clusters tend to aggregate.

(2013) focus on power dynamics in representing people and issues through photojournalism. Authors in this cluster emphasize aesthetic values' power to underpin people's representations and understandings of (international) issues through visualizations. Table 1 gives an overview of the top three most cited works per cluster.

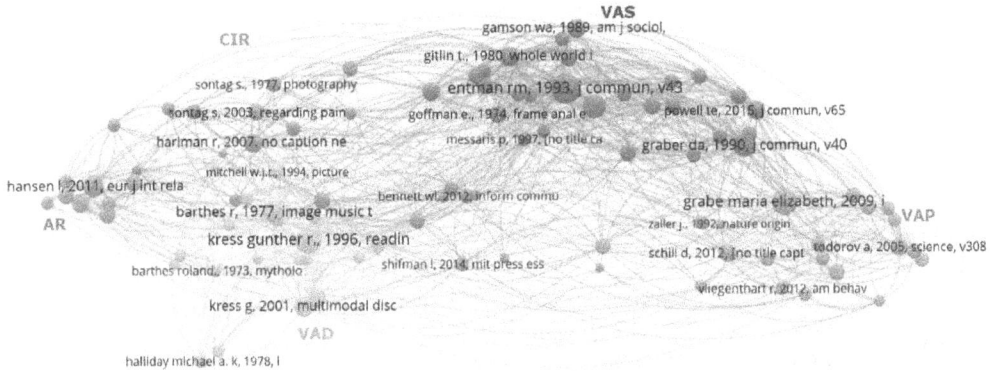

Figure 1. Five Clusters on the Study of Visualizations in the
Political and Policy Science Literature

Table 1. Top Three Literature Works per Cluster

Authors	Title	Year	Literature Cluster	Degree centrality value	Total links weight
Entman	Framing: Toward Clarification of a Fractured Paradigm	1993	VAS	53	46
Griffin	Picturing America's War on Terrorism in Afghanistan and Iraq	2004	VAS	53	17
Messaris & Abraham	The Role of Images in Framing News Stories	2001	VAS	52	31
Grabe	Image Bite Politics: News and the Visual Framing of Elections	2009	VAP	51	37
Schill	The Visual Image and the Political Image: A Review of Visual Communication Research in the Field of Political Communication	2012	VAP	40	18
Nagel	Is There a Visual Dominance in Political Communication? How Verbal, Visual, and Vocal Communication Shape Viewers' Impressions of Political Candidates	2012	VAP	38	11

Kress & van Leeuwen	Reading Images: The Grammar of Visual Design	1996	VAD	60	38
Barthes	Image, Music Text	1997	VAD	53	25
Kress	Multimodal Discourse Analysis	2001	VAD	39	22
Hariman	No Caption Needed	2007	CIR	41	19
Rose	Visual Methodologies	2012	CIR	41	16
Mitchell	Picture Theory	1994	CIR	36	7
Hansen	How Images Make World Politics: International Icons and the Case of Abu Ghraib	2011	AR	38	27
Campbell	Geopolitics and Visuality: Sighting the Darfur Conflict	2007	AR	26	15
Williams	Words, Images, Enemies: Securitization and International Politics	2003	AR	26	14

Qualitative Analysis: An In-depth Look into Visualizations in the Political and Policy Sciences

This section describes the (1) theoretical starting points, (2) empirical focus, (3) the role in policy and politics for each cluster, and we illustrate the differences and similarities between the five clusters with the empirical example of a visualization of CRISPR-Cas applications in foods, which is known as "This not a GMO." "This is not a GMO" is a visualization featuring corn (see Figure 2) and was circulated online, for example, by European Greens (the coalition of green parties in the European Parliament) and the Synbiowatch Initiative.

Visual Framing as Sense Making (VAS)

Overall, *VAS* cluster literature understands visuals as framing devices that evoke and reinforce social and cultural schemata in an audience, leading to priming audiences to understand textual messages in a particular way. Authors in this cluster describe their approaches to visualizations on political issues as framing effects (Arpan *et al.* 2006; Fahmy 2004; Zillmann, Knobloch, and Yu 2001), news framing (Entman 1993, 2004; Gamson and Modigliani 1989), visual framing (Powell *et al.* 2015; Rodriguez and Dimitrova 2011; Messaris and Abraham 2001), and visual framing effects (Druckman 2003; Brantner, Lobinger, and Wetzstein 2011).

Theoretical Starting Point

Most authors in the cluster describe their ontological position as social constructivists, in which visualizations are constructed understandings of reality (Entman 1993; Arpan *et al.* 2006; Gamson and Modigliani 1989; Rodriguez and

This is not a gmo.

Figure 2. Example of a Visualization Used in the Debate about CRISPR Technology in Europe to Oppose the Technology

Dimitrova 2011; Messaris and Abraham 2001; Powell *et al.* 2015; Griffin 2004). We identified three epistemic approaches based on the relation between text and visual. 1) Reinforcing: text leads the visual (Entman 1993; Arpan *et al.* 2006; Fahmy 2004); 2) Priming: visual leads the text (Griffin 2004; Gamson and Modigliani 1989; Zillmann, Knobloch, and Yu 2001; Domke, Perlmutter, and Spratt 2002); and 3) Multimodal: text and visuals as a single package (Brantner, Lobinger, and Wetzstein 2011; Gibson and Zillmann 2000; Powell *et al.* 2015; Rodriguez and Dimitrova 2011; Messaris and Abraham 2001; Entman 2004).

a) *The text leads the visual (reinforcing):* visualizations are framing devices competing for the reader's attention. Visual framing focuses on the visual itself as a selected fragment illustrating a reality. Authors such as Arpan and others (2006), Griffin (2004), Brantner, Lobinger, and Wetzstein (2011), and Gibson and Zillmann (2000) emphasize the role of journalists and media outlets in constructing part of the interpretive schemata of the public by selecting and repeating particular textual framings, and the visualizations used to illustrate them.

b) *Visual leads the text (priming):* visualizations evoke previous social and cultural schemata and set the context for processing new textual information. In this way, visualizations become the easiest route to process and interpret frames from a cultural reference framework. Visualizations then "set a frame" (Brantner, Lobinger, and Wetzstein 2011) for meaning-making of the textual frames. In framing effects, visualizations are the most effective way to associate information to previous knowledge (Griffin 2004; Domke, Perlmutter, and Spratt 2002; Gamson and Modigliani 1989; Zillmann,

Knobloch, and Yu 2001). Hence, visualizations can be used as references to make sense of new issues by framing emotions, values, and political positions associated with previous events to process the new information and attract members of the public (Gamson and Modigliani 1989; Zillmann, Knobloch, and Yu 2001).

c) *Visual and the text as a single package (Multimodal)*: visual framing is an analytical differentiation of the textual framing process. In practice, their framing effects cannot be disentangled (Geise and Baden 2015; Powell *et al.* 2015; Rodriguez and Dimitrova 2011). The bimodal (textual and visual) framing message triggers a cognitive and emotional response that influences public opinion formation. Over time, these influences create a public schema to process new issues and controversies in which visualizations have denotative meanings, framing capacity, connotative potential, and ideological representation (Rodriguez and Dimitrova 2011). Authors like Fahmy (2004), Gamson and Modigliani (1989), Powell and others (2015), and Rodriguez and Dimitrova (2011) suggest that the fusion of visualizations and storytelling, discourses, and congruence between text and visuals leads to passive stereotyping, cultural resonance, and ideological representation that can confer visualizations symbol status which, in turn, can trigger political mobilization.

In the *VAS* cluster, authors adopt a cognitive approach and consider frames to be schemata: a pre-existing set of experiences, emotions, values, and ideas that work as general cognitive mental plans, as abstract structures for interpreting information that serves as guides for action (Griffin 2004; Gamson and Modigliani 1989; Geise and Baden 2015). The authors focus on different aspects from schema theory to describe how visuals frame policy issues. For example, the relevance of emotions (Gamson and Modigliani 1989; Fahmy 2004; Brantner, Lobinger, and Wetzstein 2011); previous experiences (Domke, Perlmutter, and Spratt 2002; Gamson and Modigliani 1989; Rodriguez and Dimitrova 2011); or priming audiences (Domke, Perlmutter, and Spratt (2002). In our CRISPR-Cas example, the visualization would prime the viewer to make sense of CRISPR-Cas technology in terms of the GMO debate, emphasizing the (negative) emotions triggered by CRISPR-Cas food applications and drawing on previous experiences with genomic technologies in food crops like GMO crops.

Empirical Focus

The type of empirical visual most studied in the cluster is news photographs and TV images (Arpan *et al.* 2006; Griffin 2004; Fahmy 2004; Gibson and Zillmann 2000; Powell *et al.* 2015; Zillmann, Knobloch, and Yu 2001; Messaris and Abraham 2001). The type of visualization is relevant because photographs are associated with closer representations of reality (Rodriguez and Dimitrova 2011; Powell *et al.* 2015; Gibson and Zillmann 2000; Gamson and Modigliani 1989). Most authors relied on quantitative content analysis and experimental methods settings to implement their methods. However, authors like Griffin (2004), Gamson and Modigliani (1989), Rodriguez and Dimitrova, and Messaris and Abraham (2001) advocate adopting qualitative and interpretive methods to research visualizations. Lastly, Entman (2004) suggests a mixed-method (quantitative and qualitative) approach to visualizations in framing research.

Explanatory: Role of Visuals in Policy and Politics

The *VAS* cluster contributes in two ways to analyzing visualizations in the political and policy sciences.

1) Visuals are attention-grabber symbols (Arpan *et al.* 2006; Zillmann, Knobloch, and Yu 2001; Gibson and Zillmann 2000) associated with an individual's or social schemas and are used to prime readers/watchers of visualizations (Entman 1993; Barthes 1977; Fahmy 2004; Gamson and Modigliani 1989; Rodriguez and Dimitrova 2011; Messaris and Abraham 2001). In our example, this means CRISPR-Cas technology is framed in the context of the debate as indistinguishable from GMO technology. The reference primes viewers to make sense of novel CRISPR-Cas applications in terms of the older GMO technology, drawing from the highly contested topic of producing and consuming GMO crops in Europe.

2) Visuals are devices for influencing public opinion and gathering support on a policy issue (Brantner, Lobinger, and Wetzstein 2011; Domke, Perlmutter, and Spratt 2002; Powell *et al.* 2015; Entman 2004). For the CRISPR-Cas example, the corn cob and the referencing to the GMO technology draws from the highly effective campaign to mobilize the public opinion against GMO crops' approval in Europe during the 1990s and early 2000s. This campaign made the GMO technology visible in the public debate by using corn as a symbol in different visualizations intended to frame GMO technology as undesirable, dangerous, or unnatural (see Clancy and Clancy 2016; Clancy 2016).

Visual Framing as Politics (VAP)

The fundamental ideas behind the *VAP* cluster are similar to the concepts of *VAS*. The main difference is that authors in this cluster understand actors to deploy framing strategies in intentionally strategic ways. Policy actors visually select elements of a policy or political issue to seduce others to support a particular political stance.

Theoretical Starting Point

Grabe and Bucy (2009), whose groundbreaking research describes the process of visual communication in the viewer's brain, is the most central work in the cluster. Visuals first trigger the more primitive brain areas associated with emotional responses before activating the more recent cognitive areas in the frontal lobe. The cluster's central tenet is that emotions mediate visual communication, and emotional responses influence cognitive political behavior (Grabe and Bucy 2009; Valentino *et al.* 2011). Similarly, political communication and political psychology research indicate that visualizations also work for emotional communication to persuade voters, build the candidate's impression, or picture abstract scenarios like climate change impacts (Caprara *et al.* 2006; Nagel, Maurer, and Reinemann 2012; Nicholson-Cole 2005; Rosenberg, Kahn, and Tran 1991; Rosenberg *et al.* 1986; Schill 2012; Todorov *et al.* 2005; Vliegenthart 2012). In our CRISPR-Cas case, this cluster suggests the strategic use of corn and GMO to visualize CRISPR-Cas technology as a persuasive communication strategy to stock rejection to CRISPR-Cas amongst the public based on fears or negative emotions associated with GMOs, drawing on the 20-year-long controversy about that technology.

Empirical Focus

Most authors in this cluster focus on the effect of images on the public when used in political communication and campaigning. Images in these studies are considered in their literal form as TV images or images in campaign posters. Moreover, the effect of those images is studied in the construction of networks of politically engaged people.

Visualizations research in this cluster pays attention to online images that connect people and promote political engagement. Researchers like Bennett and Segerberg (2012) and Loader, Vromen, and Xenos (2014) apply digital research methods and engagement metrics to explore the construction of political imaginaries (Prior 2014), political identities, engagement in political action, and the dissemination of visual political information in social media and epistemic networks.

Explanatory: Role of Visuals in Policy and Politics

The role—and deliberate manipulation—of emotions in visualizations is a strategy for political actors to influence the public's cognitive behavior. The dissemination of visuals in new media like social networks allows for personalized information and networks of engaged people in organized political actions. These strategic uses have implications for research on political and policy issues. In the CRISPR-Cas visualization case, the strategic use of corn and GMO references plays to the emotions elicited by the visualization to mobilize viewers in actively opposing CRISPR-Cas technology in food crops applications.

Discourse as Visual Language (VAD)

In this cluster, visualizations are understood and researched to study social problems through visual language. Visualizations—as in language—are structures of symbols and signifiers. They are (incomplete) representations, materializations, or constructions of (social) phenomena, such as nationalism, identity, migration, class relations, culture, knowledge, and gender. Authors in this cluster share semiology as a common ground to study the role of visualizations in political and policy issues (Kress 2001, 2010; Kress and Van Leeuwen 1996; Blair 2004; Billig 1995). Most authors distinguish between denotation and connotation (following Barthes 1977) in which denotation is the technical process of production of the image and the description of what is on the image, its literal meaning. Moreover, the connotation is the encoded second meaning of the image, its figurative meaning.

Theoretical Starting Point

In the *VAD* cluster, authors introduce their approach as (poststructuralist) semiotics: the study of signs and symbols. In this cluster, most authors aim to understand what (political) messages are conveyed using visuals and how these visuals resonate with broader social and cultural discourses. A distinction in this cluster's evolution is made between: 1) semiotics, and 2) social semiotics.

1. *Semiotics:* The main contributors are Kress and Van Leeuwen (1996) with Reading Images: The Grammar of Visual Design. In this book, Kress introduces the baseline for a standard grammar in designing images in Western-like cultures.

2. *Social semiotics:* the critical difference between social semiotics and semiotics lies in the use of cultural resources (icons, symbols, stories, mythologies, popular culture, among others.) rather than structuralist "codes" (color, framing, zooming) for producing and taking up visualizations in communication (Kress 2001, 135-6). Visual language is not considered universally understood; but rather culturally specific.

The CRISPR-Cas visualization case, depicting CRISPR-Cas using GMO and corn in allusion to Magritte's painting *The Treachery of Images*, is culturally specific for European and Westernized cultures. The corn symbol used to illustrate CRISPR-Cas as a GMO reinforces broader discourses against genomic biotechnologies in food crops (e.g., health risks, cultural and environmental threats, unnatural scientific interventions, or corporate overreach). Ultimately, the visual language used in the visualization draws from the negative GMO rhetoric to portray CRISPR-Cas technology as an extension of the same issue.

Empirical Focus

In this cluster, authors adopt a broad scope to approach the empirics of visualizations. Kress and Van Leeuwen (1996) take photographs in the media, textbook illustrations, art photographs, and technical schematics as the basis for their "visual grammar." They propose a way to study visualizations based on their formal elements and design structures—color, perspective, framing, and image composition. Barthes (1977) uses press photographs to add additional layers of meaning to the visual: it is the structure of the image (what is in it, color, among other components) as well as their interactions with written text which allows for a visual syntax that can be studied. Authors like Anderson (1983), Billig (1995), Hill and Helmers (2012), and Lakoff and Johnson (1980) take the interactions between socially relevant images and image objects (like flags, banners, artisan crafts, works of art, among others) and political behaviors (such as revolutions, uprisings, protest movements, wars, nationalism) to develop a discursive understanding of visual narratives, visual metaphors, and visual rhetoric.

Finally, Kress (2001, 2010) studies pictures of parking instructions at British supermarkets, children's drawings at Museum visits, textbook images, art photos, and commercial products' photographs to develop his social semiotics epistemology and multimodality in discourse analysis, implying that the visual and the textual are social and cultural meaning structures.

Explanatory: Role of Visuals in Policy and Politics

Visualizations in this cluster are considered objects of political meaning making and thus intrinsic parts of larger discourses. A vital aspect of the evolution of discourse literature on visualizations is power relations in and through the structural components of visualizations, namely connotative messages, culturally dependent signs and signifiers, and other graphic features (colors, forms, text) that function as rhetorical visual resources. These visual resources are part of the struggle of groups of (policy and political) actors to establish them as dominant discourses in public debates. In our CRISPR-Cas example, the symbolic use of corn and the text's connotative use create a visual rhetoric that CRISPR-Cas technology is indistinguishable from GMO technology; hence, it should be treated as a GMO. Moreover, a differentiation between the two is artificial and deceptive (like in *The Treachery of Images*). This use of "visual language" provides a plasticity to the visualization that allows connection with other groups opposed to GMO and/ or CRISPR-Cas technology in non-European contexts.

Cultural Imagery as Representation (CIR)

In this cluster, visuals are icons that convey social norms. Exposure to those icons shapes the sentiments of groups of people. Overall, this cluster's studies understand and research visuals to comprehend how emotions encoded in visualizations become salient sociological phenomena. And, how this may lead to action by individuals or groups. The studies explore the persuasive effects of sentiment-laden visualizations of the media in society. They also analyze representation in visualizations and social order construction, for example, the representation of power relations and discourses about race in media visualizations.

Theoretical Starting Point

Researchers in this cluster consider highly recognizable visualizations (mostly photographs and film) as constructed icons and symbols that become cultural resources that represent social and political life (i.e., protests photographs, coverage of asylum seekers, or political ads (see Hariman and Lucaites 2007; Thompson 2005; Zelizer 2010; Hariman and Lucaites 2002). In these studies, the authors understand visualizations from a constructivist perspective.

Culture is shaped over time in this cluster by visualizations conveying norms and values considered acceptable for society. Those representations of values (family, obedience, sacrifice, gender roles, and so on) shape how society interprets and responds to other media's visual inputs. In turn, individuals' responses may reproduce or contest a dominant culture, a relation of power, or influence political actions. In the CRISPR-Cas example, corn is an iconic resource used to protest against biotechnological applications in food crops (Clancy and Clancy 2016). The corn represents "traditional" knowledge and values involved in food production. The corn cob is a historic cultural icon for diverse cultures. The use of corn as a symbol of genetic manipulation in Europe triggers identity and defense responses of non-biotechnological food production systems.

Empirical Focus

Hariman and Lucaites (2007) use content analysis, critical discourse analysis, or interpretivist approaches to study issues of power, culture, and political behavior in iconic visualizations. Their focus is on the connotative message of visualizations and their effect on viewers. The literature in this cluster also takes a critical approach to analyze visualizations' cultural connotations. Authors like Hariman and Lucaites (2007), Rose (2012), Thompson (2005), and Mitchell (1994) describe the role of visualizations as a vehicle to establish relations of power. For Hariman and Lucaites (2007) and Mitchell (1994), politics in and around visualizations connect deeply with issues of representation and construction of cultural icons. These icons reflect social norms and relations of power in society.

Explanatory: Role of Visuals in Policy and Politics

The communication of sentiments in the visualizations' connotative message is a common characteristic across the cluster. Ahmed (2004) proposes that emotions are relational responses and, through their repetition, shape cultural norms that are followed collectively. The role of visualizations in this process is one of repetition and mobilization of emotions in the public. Sentiments can become a way for actors to get people invested in political or policy issues by appealing to social norms and enticing a particular behavior. Connotative emotions in iconic visualizations are an essential part of the schemata used by individuals and groups for the meaning-making of visuals and processing new information. In this way, political actors can stoke sentiments of rejection or approval toward a particular political or policy issue by strategically deploying and mobilizing iconic visualizations. Our CRISPR-Cas visualization is an example of negative sentiments towards novel genomic technologies applied to food crops, drawing on two icons: one referencing an iconic art piece by Magritte and the other referencing the corn, an iconic image to protest against GMO foods. Through both iconic pieces, the visualization conveys a connotative emotional appeal to see and beware of novel biotechnologies such CRISPR-Cas, because they are GMOs.

Aesthetics as Representation (AR)

This cluster focuses on the role of aesthetic values underpinning what is worth representing in a visualization. These aesthetic values influence the representation of issues and people, conferring agenda-setting power to the actors producing and reproducing visuals in the media.

Theoretical Starting Point

Authors in this cluster understand visualizations (especially photographs and video) to represent reality revealing (international) issues or conflicts. However, this reality is also socially constructed as the meaning of those visualizations is negotiated between nations' leaders and institutions. The central point shared by authors like Campbell (2007) and Hansen (2015, 2011) is the issue of who is represented, how, and by whom as presented in the media coverage of (international) issues. However, Bleiker's work (Bleiker 2001) brings attention to the aesthetic power of representation in (international) policy and politics. Aesthetic values underpin photojournalism, TV footage, images, narratives, visual arts, and caricatures. The producer(s) of visualizations decides what elements of a political event matter to be portraited and broadcasted. The aesthetics of representations brings out power relations issues as Westernized media values dominate global affairs' coverage (and framing). In our example, the visualization is deeply rooted in the context (and values) of actors representing the European CRISPR-Cas technology debate as equal to the GMO debate.

Empirical Focus

At the empirical level, analyses in the cluster draw from diverse methods. Hansen (2015, 2011) advances multi-level methods combining visual, textual, and contextual analysis (i.e., discourses, policies, or intertextual contexts). Alternatively, authors such as Williams (2003) and Campbell (2007) opt for heuristic methods. However, Bleiker (2001, 2015) acknowledges the methodological challenges of implementing an empirical aesthetic approach to study visuals in (international) politics and policy and hence advocates for the development, validation, and adoption of pluralist methods to visualizations research in politics and policy.

Explanatory: Role of Visuals in Politics and Policy

Here, international politics considers the production and transmission of visual images complementary to how a nation perceives an issue and decides its international policy (Williams 2003). In Bleiker's proposed aesthetic turn, he calls for researchers to be acutely aware of which actors are engaging in the representation of political and policy issues and what values underpin the visualizations used as data because those decisions have implications over how a particular issue is represented and understood, also influencing policy decisions. In our CRIS-PR-Cas example, the values represented in the visualization are about the types of technologies acceptable in food crops to the actors that produced the visualization in the European context.

Table 2. Summary and Contribution Per Cluster to the Study of Visualizations in Political and Policy Sciences

Cluster	What are visualizations?	How are visualizations studied?	What do visualizations do?	How do they do it?
VAS	Frames of reference	Content analysis and experiments with media photographs and footage	Prime and convince audiences passively (use is not necessarily strategic)	Visuals work as sensemaking devices by evoking references to previous information
VAP	Emotional triggers	Engagement analysis and digital methods on candidates' image projections, pictures, and videos	Strategic appeal to emotions to influence viewers' behavior.	Visuals trigger emotional responses that influence cognitive (political) behavior
VAD	Objects of political meaning-making	Semiotics and multimodality in a mixture of visuals (photographs, cartoons) and text	Produce, reproduce (dominant) discourses	Visuals work as a sphere for meaning-making of social problems by combining signs and text in (visual) discourses
CIR	Symbolic icons	CDA and interpretivist approach to famous photographs and videos	Provide cultural references to audiences	Famous visuals resonate with culture, societal norms, identity, and historical references to audiences
AR	Aesthetical representations	Pluralist methods to portraits of conflicts in photographs and footage	Represent a situation according to what the maker of the visual considered valuable	Visuals define what values matter when representing a situation in society

Discussion and Conclusions

The systematic review of the literature identified five explanatory roles for the influence of visualizations on policy and politics:

1. *VAS*: Visualizations work as visual framing by passive (cognitive) priming or active visual rhetorical framing. Visuals work as sense-making devices by evoking references to previous information, emotions, or experiences at individual or group levels. They help to interpret complex information and (actively or passively) inform opinion formation on policy issues.

2. *VAP*: Visualizations work as emotional triggers to strategically manipulate the viewers' sentiments and emotions for political gains. Actors use *VAP* as a strategy to influence the public's cognitive (political) behavior.

3. *VAD*: Visualizations are objects of political meaning-making and intrinsic parts of larger discourses. Visualizations work as language: structures of symbols and signifiers that different knowledge groups use, produce, and reproduce in their rhetoric over time. However, influential visualizations' visual language is flexible enough to converge shared discourses across (groups of) actors as different knowledge groups use visualizations. Over time, successful groups of actors manage to ascertain specific symbols as discursive resources.

4. *CIR*: Visualizations work as icons that convey social and cultural norms. Visuals directly influence political dynamics by constructing iconic imagery widely known and used to reference popular culture. These icons become referential by intensive reproduction in the media. At the societal level, iconic imagery provides cultural context to (re)produce visual frames reinterpreting over time the social and cultural norms associated with those icons.

5. *AR*: Visualizations work as objects to define what values matter when representing a situation in society. Production and circulation of visualizations underlie what a valuable representation of, by, in, and for a particular society is. Decisions about what is worth representing in visual framing are inherently relations of power. The aesthetics of representation can influence a policy issue's framing, how it is valued and assessed.

The limitations of this study include a low probability of recent works to meet our quantitative parameters in the co-occurrence analysis. Recent works tend to have lower incidences of co-occurrence, which is also a measure of their influence. Interestingly, there were not many studies in our dataset focusing on data visualizations, whereas in environmental studies and studies on climate change—the role of data visualization is increasingly studied (Metze 2020). Finally, information stored in a different repository than WoS is a limitation in our data; however, our co-occurrence parameters offset the impacts of our repository selection.

Our five clusters offer valuable concepts to explain the multiple ways in which visualizations influence policy and politics. These clusters reject the understanding of influential visualizations as static events; they see visualizations as constructed by their makers and (constructed and reconstructed) by the audience. However, their methods collect and study empirical data as snapshots in time and space of public debates. They research how a particular visual can prime and convince audiences; how selected visuals influence their viewers' political behavior by appealing to emotions; how dominant visuals produce and reproduce discourses; how iconic visuals provide cultural references to audiences, or how normative influences from visualizations' makers underpin representations of societal issues. Notwithstanding, visualizations can simultaneously do all of these things—for different groups of actors—across platforms (in newspapers, online, in social media), shifting the way they influence policy and politics over time.

In our example, the "This is not a GMO" visualization (Figure 2) was produced as a strategic device for the European Greens to position their policy in the European Parliament. However, the Confédération Paysanne in France repurposed the visual reference to frame their CRISPR as GMO campaign in the public debate. Simultaneously, similar visualizations of CRISPR as GMO travelled as discursive objects across a coalition of local and international actors who successfully replicated their discourse, influencing the ruling of the CJEU to regulate CRISPR techniques in food as GMOs (Confédération Paysanne and Others *v.* Premier Ministre and Ministre de l'Agriculture 2018). An alternative visualization of CRISPR-Cas9 is as molecular scissors (Science 2013). This visualization has been used as a framing device to make sense of the CRISPR technology in online and traditional media. The scissors visualization is also part of alternative discourses like the precision of the technology, novelty of the technology, or differentiation from GMO. In their interactive setting, the meaning of these contesting visualizations of the technology would be negotiated over time by groups of actors in the debate about CRISPR in different policy scenarios—these negotiated shifts in meaning change over time the way visualizations influence local policy and politics.

Hence, there are at least two reasons to further combine elements of the five clusters in studying shifts in meaning and influence of visualizations over time and the ways these shape policies, political behavior, and public debates:

1. In a globalized and mediatized world, multiple policy actors (at local and global levels) use visualizations differently in their struggles to frame issues, set agendas, position discourses, shape contexts, and set values in public debates to influence policy decisions. Policy making takes place in a complex network of actors. These actors in different settings use visualizations to

convince others—but they also form coalitions around visualizations that may compete over problem definitions of policy issues.

2. The public is no longer a passive receiver of visualizations: they reproduce and produce their own. New media technology landscapes change the dynamics of (visualizations in) public debates. The online sphere has opened new avenues of participation in modern democracies' political life, challenging traditional understandings in political sciences about the emergence and dynamics of policy and politics in society (Green 2010; Castells 2008, 2011). Visualizations online on policy and political issues are an increasingly common form of political participation. The dynamics of visualizations in online debates raise questions such as how a particular visual becomes iconic/symbolic. Do actors with similar discourses also use similar visualizations, and if so, how? What discourses have been used with different visualizations? By which actors? What actors and positions are represented in the visualizations of an emerging controversy? And equally importantly, which are not? How has the use of visualizations evolved? How do controversies emerge and evolve along with the use of visualizations? These are all relevant questions to understand better the dynamics of visualizations in the emergence and evolution of online policy and political debates.

When we want to trace better the different roles that visualizations play in policy making and politics over time and for different groups of actors, we propose conceptualizing and empirically studying the traveling of visualizations over different (internet) regions, different policy settings, and across platforms. This will give better insights into their shifts in meanings for different actors, shifts in meaning and influence through time, and their shifts in ways of influencing policy and politics at local levels. This (digital) approach can be implemented by adopting an encompassing analysis of textual and visual framing, including the online network dimension in the research.

The focus on the visual as a boundary object (Metze 2020; Star and Griesemer 1989; Carlile 2002) that can be traced through policy-making processes enables for the study of their (online) traveling, the different meanings it can have for different policy actors—and the shift in meanings and influence it can have over time. Understanding these dynamics of visualizations in online policy issues offers an untapped source of information on the interplay between the role(s) of visualizations, the dynamics of (globalized) online debates, and their link to local policy decisions.

About the Authors

Eduardo Rojas-Padilla is a PhD candidate in the Public Administration and Policy group at Wageningen University & Research, Netherlands. His interests are in the intersection between innovation, society, and public policy. He studies the political role of visualizations online in the international governance of agrobiotechnology developments. His background combines biotechnology and innovation sciences with policy advisory.

Dr. Tamara Metze is an Associate Professor (*ius promovendi*) in the Public Administration and Policy group at Wageningen University & Research. Her research focuses on the governance of sustainability transformation in energy and food. She specializes in studying the role of conflict in—and design of democratic deliberations for—these transitions. Metze is Principal Investigator of the Amsterdam Institute for Advanced Metropolitan Solutions, co-editor of the *Journal of Environmental Policy and Planning*, and member of the advisory board of the international conference on Interpretive Policy Analysis. Recent publications include "Visualization in Environmental Policy and Planning: A Systematic Review and Research Agenda," in *Journal of Environmental Policy & Planning* (2020): doi: 10.1080/1523908X.2020.1798751

Prof. Katrien Termeer is Professor and Chair of public administration at Wageningen University & Research. She is a Crown-appointed member of the Social and Economic Council of the Netherlands; a member of the Council of Public Governance, and the Continental Supervisory Board *Solidaridad Europe*. Her research focuses on modes of governance of wicked problems in climate change and sustainable agro-food chains. Recent publications include, co-authored with A. Dewulf, "A Small Wins Framework to Overcome the Evaluation Paradox of Governing Wicked Problems," in *Policy and Society* (2018): doi: 10.1080/14494035.2018.1497933

APPENDIX 1.

Search Criteria for Raw Data Download from Web of Science Repository

To retrieve our raw data, we conducted a Boolean search of the Web of Science (WoS) repository comprised of the terms on the June 25, 2020, followed by a refined inclusion criteria and exclusions of research topics using the following string:

TS= (Poli* AND Visual*) [including]: web of science categories: (communication or social sciences interdisciplinary or political science or psychology applied or psychology multidisciplinary or multidisciplinary sciences or psychology or social issues or psychology experimental) AND [excluding]: research areas: (area studies or psychiatry or development studies or literature or environmental sciences ecology or sport sciences or education educational research or geriatrics gerontology or ophthalmology or engineering or computer science or art or rehabilitation or biotechnology applied microbiology or criminology penology or family studies or transportation or biomedical social sciences or medical ethics or film radio television or health care sciences services or nursing or business economics or mathematics or respiratory system or history philosophy of science or telecommunications or information science library science or philosophy or audiology speech language pathology or public environmental occupational health or social work or genetics heredity or anthropology or life sciences biomedicine other topics or physiology or zoology or neurosciences neurology or substance abuse).

Timespan: All years (1945-2020) Indexes: SCI-EXPANDED, SSCI, A & HCI, ESCI

The resulting entries were manually curated by relevance of title (or abstracts in case of doubt) and the raw retrieved data consisted of 1,500 entries. Entries were downloaded with all 28 fields of records selected in .txt file format to be processed and analyzed with R package *bibliometrix* and mapped in a network on VOSviewer.

APPENDIX 2.

Additional Information on the Quantitative Method of Social Network Analysis

All txt. files containing the co-citation data of 1,500 papers (for a total amount of 63,442 cited references) were uploaded in the R package *bibliometrix*. First, the raw data was filtered to avoid duplicates. Then, the data was analyzed for fundamental bibliometrics analysis and creating a co-citation matrix.

The co-citation of bibliographic data was visualized in the extension VOSviewer for bibliographic mapping. First, two distance-based maps of co-citations were configured in VOSviewer. The first map was intended for a degree centrality analysis of the co-citation matrix. The second map was intended for a betweenness centrality analysis of the co-citation matrix.

The parameters of both maps were configured based on fractional counting of links to account for differences in the number of references between journal articles and between journal articles and books. For the degree centrality map, the minimum amount of co-cited references was set at 10, as lower numbers resulted in unmanageable numbers of nodes and higher numbers resulting in low numbers of nodes. Afterward, the data were manually filtered to remove references to research methods and statistics literature identified in the bibliometric analysis but not relevant to the research. The number of resulting nodes in the degree centrality map was 102 (before the manual filtering of references unrelated to the study). Similarly, the minimum amount of co-cited references for the betweenness centrality map was set at 4, resulting in 885 nodes.

The data for both maps were normalized by fractionalization of the strength of the links in the network. The layout of the VOS mapping algorithm was set to default values for co-citation mapping; 2 for attraction and 1 for repulsion, with a random start for the optimization of the algorithm and a maximum iteration of 10,000 times. Clustering of the maps Several node sizes were performed with the VOS technique, and minimum node sizes were set to 10 and 4 for degree centrality and betweenness centrality maps, respectively.

GML files for the betweenness centrality network were exported from VosViewer to run SNA statistics in Gephi, as the software supports estimation and display of statistical values per node instead of by the network. The data was organized from the highest centrality values to the lowest. Most of the degree centrality was found as top values of betweenness centrality, indicating a considerable overlap. Therefore, the focus of the manual search was on the top 20% of the highest value in betweenness centrality. From that top 20% of betweenness entries, six papers were manually included to achieve the final 95 nodes network used for the qualitative step.

APPENDIX 3.

Coding Book

A. ID	B. Title	C. Authors	D. Type of publication	E. Key words	F. Cluster	G. Field of study	H. Definition of visualization	I. Ontology of visualization research
			D1 Book		E1 VAS			
			D2 Article		E2 VAP			
					E3 VAD			
					E4 CIR			
					E5 AR			

J. Epistemology of visualization research	K. Category of visualizations	L. Issues researched (policy issue, topic)	M. What methods are used to study visualizations?	N. What is the link between visuals and text?	O. What roles do visuals have in policy processes?
	H1. Pictures				
	H2. Photographs				
	H3. Cartoons				
	H4. Infographs				
	H...i. etc				

References

Adams, William, and Suzanne Albin. 1980. "Public Information on Social Change: TV Coverage of Women in the Workforce." *Policy Studies Journal* 8 (5): 717-734. DOI: 10.1111/j.1541-0072.1980.tb01276.x

Adler-Nissen, Rebecca, Katrine Emilie Andersen, and Lene Hansen. 2020. "Images, Emotions, and International Politics: The Death of Alan Kurdi." *Review of International Studies* 46 (1): 75-95. DOI: 10.1017/S0260210519000317

Ahmed, Sara. 2004. *Cultural Politics of Emotion*. Edinburgh: Edinburgh University Press.

Anderson, Benedict. 1983. *Imagined Communities: Reflections on the Origin and Spread of Nationalism*. London: Verso Books.

Aria, Massimo, and Corrado. Cuccurullo. 2017. "*Bibliometrix*: An R-tool for Comprehensive Science Mapping Analysis." *Journal of Informetrics* 11 (4): 959-975. DOI: 10.1016/j.joi.2017.08.007

Arpan, Laura M, Kaysee Baker, Youngwon Lee, Taejin Jung, Lori Lorusso, and Jason Smith. 2006. "News Coverage of Social Protests and the Effects of Photographs and Prior Attitudes." *Mass Communication & Society* 9 (1): 1-20.

Baker, Donald R. 1990. "Citation Analysis: A Methodological Review." Social Work Research and Abstracts.

Barthes, Roland. 1977. *Image-music-text*. London: Macmillan.

Bastian, Mathieu, Heymann Sebastien, Jacomy Mathieu. 2009. "Gephi: An Open-Source Software for Exploring and Manipulating Networks." International AAAI Conference on Weblogs and Social Media.

Bennett, W. Lance, and Alexandra Segerberg. 2012. "The Logic of Connective Action: Digital Media and the Personalization of Contentious Politics." *Information, Communication & Society* 15 (5): 739-768. DOI: 10.1080/1369118X.2012.670661

Billig, Michael. 1995. *Banal Nationalism*. London and New York: Sage.

Blair, J. Anthony. 2004. "The Rhetoric of Visual Arguments." In *Defining Visual Rhetoric*, edited by Charles A. Hill and Marguerite Helmers. Mahwah, NJ: Lawrence Erlbaum Associates, 41-61. DOI: 10.1007/978-94-007-2363-4_19

Bleiker, Roland. 2001. "The Aesthetic Turn in International Political Theory." *Millennium* 30 (3): 509-533. DOI: 10.1177/03058298010300031001

_____. 2015. "Pluralist Methods for Visual Global Politics." *Millennium* 43 (3): 872-890. DOI: 10.1177/0305829815583084

Born, Dorothea. 2019. "Bearing Witness? Polar Bears as Icons for Climate Change Communication in *National Geographic*." *Environmental Communication* 13 (5): 649-663. DOI: 10.1080/17524032.2018.1435557

Boyack, Kevin W., and Richard Klavans. 2010. "Co-citation Analysis, Bibliographic Coupling, and Direct Citation: Which Citation Approach Represents the Research Front most Accurately?" *Journal of the American Society for information Science and Technology* 61 (12): 2389-2404. DOI: 10.1002/asi.21419

Brantner, Cornelia, Katharina Lobinger, and Irmgard Wetzstein. 2011. "Effects of Visual Framing on Emotional Responses and Evaluations of News Stories about the Gaza Conflict 2009." *Journalism & Mass Communication Quarterly* 88 (3): 523-540. DOI: 10.1177/107769901108800304

Campbell, David. 2007. "Geopolitics and Visuality: Sighting the Darfur Conflict." *Political Geography* 26 (4): 357-382. DOI: 10.1016/j.polgeo.2006.11.005

Caprara, Gian Vittorio, Shalom Schwartz, Cristina Capanna, Michele Vecchione, and Claudio Barbaranelli. 2006. "Personality and Politics: Values, Traits, and Political Choice." *Political Psychology* 27 (1): 1-28. DOI: 10.1111/j.1467-9221.2006.00457.x

Carlile, Paul R. 2002. "A Pragmatic View of Knowledge and Boundaries: Boundary Objects in New Product Development." *Organization Science* 13 (4): 442-455. DOI: 10.1287/orsc.13.4.442.2953

Castells, Manuel. 2008. "The New Public Sphere: Global Civil Society, Communication Networks, and Global Governance." *The Annals of the American Academy of Political and Social Science* 616 (1): 78-93. DOI: 10.1177/0002716207311877

_____. 2011. *The Rise of the Network Society*. Vol. 12. London: John Wiley & Sons.

Clancy, Kelly A. 2016. *The Politics of Genetically Modified Organisms in the United States and Europe*. Springer.

Clancy, Kelly A., and Benjamin Clancy. 2016. "Growing Monstrous Organisms: The Construction of Anti-GMO Visual Rhetoric Through Digital Media." *Critical Studies in Media Communication* 33 (3): 279-292. DOI: 10.1080/15295036.2016.1193670

Coleman, Renita. 2010. "Framing the Pictures in Our Heads." *Doing News Framing Analysis: Empirical and Theoretical Perspectives.* London: Routledge.

Confédération Paysanne and Others *v.* Premier Ministre and Ministre de l'Agriculture, de l'Agroalimentaire et de la Forêt. 2018. "Organisms *obtained* by *mutagenesis* are GMOs and are, in Principle, Subject to the Obligations Laid Down by the GMO Directive 2001/18," in *CJEU Case C-528/16 Confédération Paysanne and Others v Premier Ministre and Ministre de l'Agriculture, de l'Agroalimentaire et de la Forêt,* edited by CURIA. Luxemburg: Court of Justice of the European Union.

Cowhitt, Thomas, Timothy Butler, and Elaine Wilson. 2020. "Using Social Network Analysis to Complete Literature Reviews: A New Systematic Approach for Independent Researchers to Detect and Interpret Prominent Research Programs within Large Collections of Relevant Literature." *International Journal of Social Research Methodology* 23 (5): 483-496. DOI: 10.1080/13645579.2019.1704356

Doerr, Nicole. 2017. "Bridging Language Barriers, Bonding Against Immigrants: A Visual Case Study of Transnational Network Publics Created by Far-Right Activists in Europe." *Discourse & Society* 28 (1): 3-23.

Domke, David, David Perlmutter, and Meg Spratt. 2002. "The Primes of Our Times? An Examination of the 'Power' of Visual Images." *Journalism* 3 (2): 131-159. DOI: 10.1177/146488490200300211

Druckman, James N. 2003. "The Power of Television Images: The First Kennedy-Nixon Debate Revisited." *The Journal of Politics* 65 (2): 559-571. DOI: 10.1111/1468-2508.t01-1-00015

Durant, John, and Nicola Lindsey. 1999. *The Great GM Food Debate: A Report to the House of Lords Select Committee on Science and Technology Sub-Committee on Science and Society.* Science Museum.

Entman, Robert. 1993. "Framing: Toward Clarification of a Fractured Paradigm." *Journal of Communication* 43 (4): 51-58. DOI: 10.1111/j.1460-2466.1993.tb01304.x

_____. 2004. *Projections of Power: Framing News, Public Opinion, and U.S. Foreign Policy: Studies in Communication, Media, and Public Opinion.* Chicago, IL: University of Chicago Press.

Fahmy, Shahira. 2004. "Picturing Afghan Women: A content Analysis of AP Wire Photographs During the Taliban Regime and after the Fall of the Taliban Regime." *Gazette* (Leiden, Netherlands) 66 (2): 91-112.

Farida, Vis, and Goriunova Olga. 2015. "The Iconic Image on Social Media: A Rapid Research Response to the Death of Aylan Kurdi."

Foucault, Michel. 1977. *Discipline and Punish: The Birth of the Prison*. New York: Vintage Books.

Gamson, William A., and Andre Modigliani. 1989. "Media Discourse and Public Opinion on Nuclear Power: A Constructionist Approach." *American Journal of Sociology* 95 (1): 1-37. DOI: 10.1086/229213

Geise, Stephanie, and Christian Baden. 2015. "Putting the Image Back into the Frame: Modeling the Linkage between Visual Communication and Frame-processing Theory." *Communication Theory* 25 (1): 46-69. DOI: 10.1111/comt.12048

Gibson, Rhonda, and Dolf Zillmann. 2000. "Reading between the Photographs: The Influence of Incidental Pictorial Information on Issue Perception." *Journalism & Mass Communication Quarterly* 77 (2): 355-366. DOI: 10.1177/107769900007700209

Gitlin, Todd. 1980. *The Whole World Is Watching: Mass Media in the Making and Unmaking of the New Left*. Oakland, CA: University of California Press.

Gommeh, Efrat, Huub Dijstelbloem, and Tamara Metze. 2020. "Visual Discourse Coalitions: Visualization and Discourse Formation in Controversies over Shale Gas Development." *Journal of Environmental Policy & Planning*: 1-18. DOI: 10.1080/1523908X.2020.1823208

Grabe, Maria Elizabeth, and Erik Page Bucy. 2009. *Image Bite Politics: News and the Visual Framing of Elections*. Oxford: Oxford University Press.

Graber, Doris A. 1990. "Seeing is Remembering: How Visuals Contribute to Learning from Television News." *Journal of Communication* 40 (3): 134-155. DOI: 10.1111/j.1460-2466.1990.tb02275.x

Green, Jeffrey Edward. 2010. *The Eyes of the People: Democracy in an Age of Spectatorship*. Oxford: Oxford University Press, on Demand.

Griffin, Michael. 2004. "Picturing America's 'War on Terrorism'in Afghanistan and Iraq: Photographic Motifs as News Frames." *Journalism* 5 (4): 381-402. DOI: 10.1177/1464884904044201

Hansen, Lene. 2011. "Theorizing the Image for Security Studies: Visual Securitization and the Muhammad Cartoon Crisis." *European Journal of International*

Relations 17 (1): 51-74. DOI: 10.1177/1354066110388593

_____. 2015. "How Images Make World Politics: International Icons and the Case of Abu Ghraib." *Review of International Studies* 41 (2): 263-288. DOI: 10.1017/S0260210514000199

Hariman, Robert, and John L. Lucaites. 2007. *No Caption Needed: Iconic Photographs, Public Culture, and Liberal Democracy.* Chicago, IL: University of Chicago Press.

Hariman, Robert, and John Louis Lucaites. 2002. "Performing Civic Identity: The Iconic Photograph of the Flag Raising on Iwo Jima." *Quarterly Journal of Speech* 88 (4): 363-392. DOI: 10.1080/00335630209384385

Heck, Axel, and Gabi Schlag. 2013. "Securitizing Images: The Female Body and the War in Afghanistan." *European Journal of International Relations* 19 (4): 891-913. DOI: 10.1177/1354066111433896

Hill, Charles A., and Marguerite Helmers. 2012. *Defining Visual Rhetorics.* London and New York: Routledge.

Hurtley, Stella. 2013. "Genome Editing." *This Week in Science* 339 (6121): 736. DOI: 10.1126/science.2013.339.6121.twis

Jenner, Eric. 2012. "News Photographs and Environmental Agenda Setting." *Policy Studies Journal* 40 (2): 274-301. DOI: 10.1111/j.1541-0072.2012.00453.x

Kasra, Mona. 2017. "Digital-networked Images as Personal Acts of Political Expression: New Categories for Meaning Formation." *Media and Communication* 5 (4): 51-64. DOI: 10.17645/mac.v5i4.1065

Kress, Gunther R. 2001. "Multimodal Discourse Analysis." In *The Routledge Handbook of Discourse Analysis*, 61-76. London and New York: Routledge.

_____. 2010. *Multimodality: A Social Semiotic Approach to Contemporary Communication.* Abingdon, UK: Taylor & Francis.

Kress, Gunther R., and Theo Van Leeuwen. 1996. *Reading Images: The Grammar of Visual Design.* Psychology Press.

Lakoff, George, and Mark Johnson. 1980. *Metaphors We Live By.* Chicago, IL: University of Chicago Press.

Loader, Brian D., Ariadne Vromen, and Michael A. Xenos. 2014. *The Networked Young Citizen: Social Media, Political Participation and Civic Engagement.* Abingdon, UK: Taylor & Francis.

McInerny, Greg J., Min Chen, Robin Freeman, David Gavaghan, Miriah Meyer, Francis Rowland, David J. Spiegelhalter, Moritz Stefaner, Geizi Tessarolo, and Joaquin Hortal. 2014. "Information Visualisation for Science and Policy: Engaging Users and Avoiding Bias." *Trends in Ecology & Evolution* 29 (3): 148-157. DOI: 10.1016/j.tree.2014.01.003

Mendonça, Ricardo Fabrino, Selen A Ercan, and Hans Asenbaum. 2020. "More Than Words: A Multidimensional Approach to Deliberative Democracy." *Political Studies.* DOI: 10.1177/0032321720950561

Messaris, Paul, and Linus Abraham. 2001. "The Role of Images in Framing News Stories." In *Framing Public Life,* edited by S.D. Reese, O.H. Gandy and A.E. Grant, 231-242. London: Routledge.

Metze, Tamara. 2018b. "Visual Framing for Policy Learning: Internet as the 'Eye of the Public.'" *Knowledge, Policymaking and Learning for European Cities and Regions*: 165. DOI: 10.4337/9781786433640.00024

_____. 2020. "Visualization in Environmental Policy and Planning: A Systematic Review and Research Agenda." *Journal of Environmental Policy & Planning* 22 (5): 745-760. DOI: 10.1080/1523908X.2020.1798751

Mitchell, W. J. Thomas. 1994. *Picture Theory: Essays on Verbal and Visual Representation.* Chicago, IL: University of Chicago Press.

Moody, Rebecca, and Victor Bekkers. 2018. "Visualizations, Technology and the Power to Influence Policy." *Government Information Quarterly* 35 (3): 437-444. DOI: 10.1016/j.giq.2018.06.004

Morseletto, Piero. 2017. "Analysing the Influence of Visualisations in Global Environmental Governance." *Environmental Science & Policy* 78: 40-48. DOI: 10.1016/j.envsci.2017.08.021

Nagel, Friederike, Marcus Maurer, and Carsten Reinemann. 2012. "Is There a Visual Dominance in Political Communication? How Verbal, Visual, and Vocal Communication Shape Viewers' Impressions of Political Candidates." *Journal of Communication* 62 (5): 833-850. DOI: 10.1111/j.1460-2466.2012.01670.x

Nicholson-Cole, Sophie A. 2005. "Representing Climate Change Futures: A Critique on the Use of Images for Visual Communication." *Computers, Environment and Urban Systems* 29 (3): 255-273. DOI: 10.1016/j.compenvurbsys.2004.05.002

Powell, Thomas E., Hajo G. Boomgaarden, Knut De Swert, and Claes H. de Vreese. 2015. "A Clearer Picture: The Contribution of Visuals and Text to Framing Effects." *Journal of Communication* 65 (6): 997-1017. DOI: 10.1111/jcom.12184

Prior, Markus. 2014. "Visual Political Knowledge: A Different Road to Competence?" *The Journal of Politics* 76 (1): 41-57. DOI: 10.1017/S0022381613001096

Prøitz, Lin. 2018. "Visual Social Media and Affectivity: The Impact of the Image of Alan Kurdi and Young People's Response to the Refugee Crisis in Oslo and Sheffield." *Information, Communication & Society* 21 (4): 548-563. DOI: 10.1080/13691 18X.2017.1290129

Rabello, Elaine Teixeira, Efrat Gommeh, Andrea Benedetti, Gabriel Valerio-Ureña, and Tamara Metze. 2021. "Mapping Online Visuals of Shale Gas Controversy: A Digital Methods Approach." *Information, Communication & Society*: 1-18.

Rodriguez, Lulu, and Daniela V. Dimitrova. 2011. "The Levels of Visual Framing." *Journal of Visual Literacy* 30 (1): 48-65. DOI: 10.1080/23796529.2011.11674684

Rose, Gillian. 2012. *Visual Methodologies: AnIintroduction to Researching with Visual Materials*. London: Sage.

Rosenberg, Shawn W., Lisa Bohan, Patrick McCafferty, and Kevin Harris. 1986. "The Image and the Vote: The Effect of Candidate Presentation on Voter Preference." *American Journal of Political Science*: 108-127. DOI: 10.2307/2111296

Rosenberg, Shawn W, Shulamit Kahn, and Thuy Tran. 1991. "Creating a Political Image: Shaping Appearance and Manipulating the Vote." *Political Behavior* 13 (4): 345-367. Accessed on November 10, 2021. https://www.jstor.org/stable/586121

Science. 2013. "This Week in Science: Genome Editing." *Science* 339 (6121): 736-736. DOI:10.1126/science.2013.339.6121

Schill, Dan. 2012. "The Visual Image and the Political Image: A Review of Visual Communication Research in the Field of Political Communication." *Review of Communication* 12 (2): 118-142. DOI: 10.1080/15358593.2011.653504

Sontag, Susan. 1977. *On Photography*. London: Macmillan.

_____. 2003. *Regarding the Pain of Others*. New York: Picador.

Star, Susan Leigh, and James R. Griesemer. 1989. "Institutional Ecology, Transla-tions' and Boundary Objects: Amateurs and Professionals in Berkeley's Museum of Vertebrate Zoology, 1907-39." *Social Studies of Science* 19 (3): 387-420. DOI: 10.1177/030631289019003001

Thompson, John B. 2005. "The New Visibility." *Theory, Culture & Society* 22 (6): 31-51. DOI: 10.1177/0263276405059413

Todorov, Alexander, Anesu N. Mandisodza, Amir Goren, and Crystal C Hall. 2005. "Inferences of Competence from Faces Predict Election Outcomes." *Science* 308 (5728): 1623-1626. DOI: 10.1126/science.1110589

Valentino, Nicholas A., Ted Brader, Eric W. Groenendyk, Krysha Gregorowicz, and Vincent L. Hutchings. 2011. "Election Night's Alright for Fighting: The Role of Emotions in Political Participation." *The Journal of Politics* 73 (1): 156-170. DOI: 10.1017/s0022381610000939

van Beek, Lisette, Tamara Metze, Eva Kunseler, Hiddo Huitzing, Filip de Blois, and Arjan Wardekker. 2020. "Environmental Visualizations: Framing and Reframing between Science, Policy and Society." *Environmental Science & Policy* 114: 497-505. DOI: 10.1016/j.envsci.2020.09.011

Van Eck, Nees Jan, and Ludo Waltman. 2010. "Software Survey: VOSviewer, a Computer Program for Bibliometric Mapping." *Scientometrics* 84 (2): 523-538. DOI: 10.1007/s11192-009-0146-3

Vliegenthart, Rens. 2012. "The Professionalization of Political Communication? A Longitudinal Analysis of Dutch Election Campaign Posters." *American Behavioral Scientist* 56 (2): 135-150. DOI: 10.1177/0002764211419488

Wardekker, Arjan, and Susanne Lorenz. 2019. "The Visual Framing of Climate Change Impacts and Adaptation in the IPCC Assessment Reports." *Climatic Change* 156 (1-2): 273-292. DOI: 10.1007/s10584-019-02522-6

Williams, Michael C. 2003. "Words, Images, Enemies: Securitization and Internat-ional Politics." *International Studies Quarterly* 47 (4): 511-531. DOI: 10.1046/j.00 20-8833.2003.00277.x

Zelizer, Barbie. 2010. *About to Die: How News Images Move the Public.* Oxford: Ox-ford University Press.

Zillmann, Dolf, Silvia Knobloch, and Hong-sik Yu. 2001. "Effects of Photographs on the Selective Reading of News Reports." *Media Psychology* 3 (4): 301-324. DOI: 10.1207/S1532785XMEP0304_01

Women's Political Empowerment in India and Bangladesh: Gender Quotas and Socio-economic Obstructions

Mahbub Alam Prodip

University of Rajshahi

India and Bangladesh have introduced gender quotas to increase women's presence in politics and bring the desired substantive inclusionary effects at the level of emergent policy outcomes. This qualitative study analyzes the socio-economic barriers that quota-elected women representatives encounter in affecting policies regarding their political empowerment at the local council level—in the Gram Panchayat in India and the Union Parishad in Bangladesh. I contribute to the comparative literature on gender quotas and policy outcomes. Results reveal that women members in both countries face serious social and economic impediments to political participation at this local level. Social barriers such as household responsibilities, lack of family support, and lack of social safety and physical mobility, are no longer a major hindrance for women members in offering services to their constituents. However, in Bangladesh, a majority of women members fail to function effectively because of lack of education—more so than the women members in India. Women members in both countries lack sufficient political training, which makes it challenging to claim their rights when offering goods and services to voters, particularly to women. I also find that women members in both countries have failed to perform their political activities due to financial incapability, although in different ways. Indian women members receive a small amount of money per month, whereas Bangladeshi women members cannot meet the demands of three times higher constituents with irregular honoraria. Lack of financial incapability further leads to corruption in the cases of some women members in both countries. To ensure women's political empowerment through reserved seats in both countries, it is vital to make certain that enough government resources are provided for local councils, together with enough training for elected women members.

Keywords: Gender Quotas, Socio-Economic Barriers, Gender and Policy, Women's Political Empowerment, Reserved Seats, Political Participation, Democratic Representation, Developing Countries, India, Bangladesh, Gender Politics, Asia.

Policy Studies Yearbook 12.1: 137-166. 10.18278/psy.12.1.6

Empoderamiento político de las mujeres en India y Bangladesh: Cuotas de género y obstáculos socioeconómicos

India y Bangladesh han introducido cuotas de género para aumentar la presencia de las mujeres en la política, así como para lograr los efectos de inclusión sustantivos deseados al nivel de los resultados de las políticas emergentes. Este estudio comparativo analiza las barreras socioeconómicas que encuentran las representantes de mujeres elegidas por cuotas al afectar las políticas relacionadas con su empoderamiento político a nivel del consejo local, en el Gram Panchayat en India y en la Union Parishad en Bangladesh. El estudio cualitativa contribuye a la literatura comparada sobre cuotas de género y resultados de políticas. Los resultados revelan que las mujeres miembros en ambos países enfrentan serios impedimentos sociales y económicos para la participación política a este nivel local. En ambos países, las barreras sociales como las responsabilidades del hogar y la falta de apoyo familiar, así como la falta de seguridad social y movilidad física, ya no son un obstáculo importante para las mujeres miembros a la hora de ofrecer servicios a sus electores. Sin embargo, en Bangladesh, la mayoría de las mujeres miembros no funcionan de manera eficaz debido a la falta de educación, más que las mujeres miembros en la India. Las mujeres miembros de ambos países carecen de suficiente formación política, lo que dificulta la reivindicación de sus derechos al ofrecer bienes y servicios a los votantes, y en particular a las mujeres. También encuentro que las mujeres miembros en ambos países no han podido realizar sus actividades políticas debido a la incapacidad financiera. Sin embargo, la dimensión de la incapacidad es diferente en India y Bangladesh. Las mujeres indias reciben una pequeña cantidad de dinero al mes, mientras que las mujeres bangladesíes no pueden satisfacer las demandas de electores tres veces más altos con honorarios irregulares. La falta de incapacidad financiera conduce además a la corrupción de algunas mujeres miembros en ambos países. Para garantizar el empoderamiento político de la mujer mediante la reserva de escaños en ambos países, es fundamental asegurarse de que se proporcionen suficientes recursos gubernamentales para los consejos locales, junto con suficiente capacitación para las mujeres elegidas.

Palabras clave: Cuotas de género, Barreras socioeconómicas, Género y políticas, Empoderamiento político de la mujer, India, Bangladesh, Política de género, Asia.

印度和孟加拉國的婦女政治賦權：
性別配額和社會經濟障礙

印度和孟加拉國引入了性別配額，以增加女性在政治中的參與度，並在緊急政策結果層面帶來預期的實質性包容性影響。這項比較研究分析了配額選舉產生的女性代表在影響地方議會層面的政治賦權政策時遇到的社會經濟障礙——在印度的 Gram Panchayat 和孟加拉國的 Union Parishad。深入的定性研究有助於關於性別配額和政策結果的比較文獻。結果表明，這兩個國家的女性成員在地方一級的政治參與方面面臨嚴重的社會和經濟障礙。在這兩個國家，家庭責任和缺乏家庭支持等社會障礙，以及缺乏社會安全和身體流動性，不再是女性成員為其選民提供服務的主要障礙。然而，在孟加拉國，由於缺乏教育，大多數女性成員無法有效運作——比印度的女性成員更是如此。兩國的女性成員都缺乏足夠的政治培訓，這使得在向選民，尤其是向女性提供商品和服務時主張自己的權利具有挑戰性。我還發現兩國的女性成員都因經濟能力不足而未能開展政治活動。然而，印度和孟加拉國的無能力程度是不同的。印度女性成員每月只能收到少量的錢，而孟加拉國女性成員無法通過不定期的酬金滿足高出三倍的選民的要求。缺乏經濟能力進一步導致兩國一些女性成員腐敗。為確保通過兩國保留席位賦予婦女政治權力，必須確保為地方議會提供足夠的政府資源，並為當選的女性成員提供足夠的培訓。

關鍵詞：性別配額、社會經濟障礙、性別和政策、婦女的政治賦權、印度、孟加拉國、性別政治、亞洲。

Women have a democratic right to participate in politics; this is an essential part of human rights, inclusive growth, and sustainable development which, in turn, are fundamental features of the structure of democracies (OECD 2018; Panday 2010, 25-6). In fact, democracy is presumed to be genuine and effective when political parties and the national assembly take decisions collectively and impartially, involving both men and women regarding their interests and abilities (Dahlerup 2006, 15-16). Women's full and active involvement in all levels of political decision making, including giving equal voice to their views and practices alongside those of men, is therefore a vitally important matter (Mlambo, Kapingura, and Meissner 2019, 2) concerning policy and institutions. However, women's participation in both family decision making and formal political power structures remains low globally (Ara 2017; IPU 2018). Although women's representation in parliament has continued to increase in many places across the world, women continue to lag behind in the formal political power structures (IPU 2018; Jahan 2017, 74).

To enhance women's political participation, more than 130 countries have implemented policies involving gender quotas at the national and local levels (Hughes *et al.* 2019).[1] Gender quotas ensure that a certain number of women appear in candidate lists, in parliament itself, in committees, or in the government (Dahlerup 2006). The aim of the policies is to increase the number of women who participate in legislative activities—which is of primary, if not increasing, democratic policy relevance today. Scholars often argue that gender quotas are not merely about escalating women's numbers; rather, quotas—negatively or positively—can change the quality of elected representative bodies and offer opportunities to advocate group well-being in policy making and participation in politics (see e.g., Franceschet, Krook, and Piscopo 2012). Gender quotas do not, however, have equal positive effects on women, and some studies find cases where quotas have led to inadequate policy changes or even to further/increased gender-inegalitarian outcomes. This is because some factors—especially underexplored dimensions of quota design—actually restrict quota-elected women in their ability to introduce, influence, or change policy (Clayton 2021). Prodip (2021a, 2021b), for instance, found that variations in the institutional design of gender quotas and patriarchy often limit the ability of quota women to introduce durable women-friendly policies in political legislatures. This is particularly so in some parts of the developing world. What is lacking is a detailed understanding, especially in developing countries, of the socio-economic barriers that quota-elected women continue to encounter regarding their full and effective participation in affecting policies. To take some initial steps toward an answer here, I compare the cases of India and Bangladesh with a particular focus on the lowest tier of rural local governments—in the *Gram Panchayat* in India and the *Union Parishad* in Bangladesh.

The number of members of the *Gram Panchayat* is not fixed but varies from five to 30 members including a *Pradhan* (chairperson) and *Upa-Pradhan* (vice-chairperson) depending on the population in the district.[2] The Constitution guarantees the reservation for women of not less than 33 percent of the total number of seats to be filled by direct election in the *Gram Panchayat* (Kasturi 1999, 125; Priebe 2017; Rai *et al.* 2006, 230). The *Union Parishad* in Bangladesh comprises 13 members including the chairperson, three seats reserved for women, and nine general members elected by the direct vote of local inhabitants (Khan and Ara 2006).[3] India and Bangladesh each adopted a system of reserved seats in politics

---

1   For updated information, see https://www.idea.int/data-tools/data/gender-quotas/about

2   The *Gram Panchayat* consists of eight-to-ten villages, although, since the population number is the criteria, this may be just one village. The average is 12,000 to 15,000 inhabitants, leading to variations across the country.

3   All *Union Parishads* in Bangladesh are divided into nine wards/constituencies regardless the size of the population and district magnitude.

during the 1990s. India adopted reserved seats for women at the local level only, but Bangladesh introduced reserved seats for women at both the national and local levels (Rai *et al.* 2006). The expected aims of this electoral quota policy design were to increase women's presence in local politics as well as to bring the desired substantive inclusionary effects at the level of emergent policy outcomes of various kinds. With some exceptions, however, the expected policy outcomes of gender quotas have been limited in both countries. Several studies have identified that institutional factors (Pande and Ford 2011; Jayal 2006; Panday 2010, 2013; Rai *et al.* 2006), socio-economic factors (Baviskar 2002; Bryld 2001; Chathukulam and John 2001; Chowdhury 2013; Panday 2013; Rai *et al.* 2006), and cultural impediments (Bann and Rao 2008; Prodip 2015; Rahman and Khan 2018) have barred women members in both countries from participation in local decision-making processes, particularly in Asia. Less effort has been devoted to exploring the relationship between gender quotas and policy influence in local councils in Asia, especially in India and Bangladesh, from a comparative perspective. In earlier work I have argued that women members in reserved seats in local councils in India and Bangladesh have failed to affect political decisions due to institutional and cultural constraints (Prodip 2021a, 2021b). Yet the relationship between gender quotas and affecting policies understood via a socio-economic lens has been somewhat neglected in the literature. To address this lacuna and update the literature with reference to more recent policy developments, the present article aims to examine and explore to what extent and how socio-economic factors hold back quota-elected women in their ability to influence policies in the political decision-making process in local councils in India and Bangladesh. Both countries are similar in enough respects to conduct a valid and useful comparison. Gender quotas have notably increased women's numbers in local councils in India and Bangladesh. The women this study draws from nevertheless face similar challenges in politics, primarily because both countries are dominated by patriarchal cultures and philosophies. The patriarchal philosophy that molds the political system in the two countries has long presented women as unfit for political activities (Chowdhury 2013).

I hope to contribute to the literature through a qualitative research strategy comparing women's policy influence in the political decision-making process in local councils in India and Bangladesh. I argue that, if the socio-economic barriers identified can be removed through some key policy developments in the near future, women members in reserved seats would have better opportunities and a stronger voice in the decision-making process to secure rights and resources for their voters—and especially women.

The article begins with a review of the literature on the conceptualization of women's political empowerment, women's numbers and policy influence, concepts of socio-economic barriers to women's political participation, and research focusing on India and Bangladesh. This assists in providing a theoretical framework to guide the subsequent analysis. An outline of the research design and methodology follows, then the findings of the study are presented. The final section discusses the findings and provides a conclusion with possible solutions.

Literature Review and Key Concepts

Women's Political Empowerment

Before the 1980s, academics argued that "women are not where the power is" (Nowtony 1980, 147). However, researchers, development and women's organizations, and policy makers changed this view after the UN Beijing Platform for Action in 1995[4] (see e.g., Sheikh 2012). Scholars often amalgamate elements of the concepts of 'gender equality,' 'gender equity,' 'female autonomy,' 'women's status,' and 'women's empowerment' (Malhotra and Schuler 2005, 72; Sheikh 2012, 70). However, the idea of women's empowerment can be differentiated from other concepts by two essential features: 'process' (Kabeer 1999; Rowlands 1997) and 'agency' (Malhotra and Schuler 2005). Kabeer (1999, 436) defines empowerment as an "ability to make choices." To be disempowered, therefore, implies to be denied choice; "the notion of empowerment is that it is inescapably bound up with the condition of disempowerment and refers to the process by which those who have been denied the ability to make a choice acquire such an ability" (Kabeer 1999, 436-7). Kabeer's definition of empowerment is crucial as it contains the two important elements of process and agency and discreetly differentiates 'empowerment' from the general concept of 'power' as exercised by dominant individuals or groups (Malhotra and Schuler 2005, 72).

Political empowerment is a necessary part of the overall empowerment of women (Sheikh 2012, 74). Several scholars have asserted that social freedom leads to women's empowerment and, finally, this empowerment leads to economic and political empowerment (Lopez-Claros and Zahidi 2005; Shroff 2010). However, questions remain as to the necessary ordering of elements of empowerment in a causal chain. For example, women's participation in electoral processes such as national parliaments and local government institutions is a precondition for their political empowerment (Sheikh 2012, 74). Further, Hannan (2003) contends that empowerment is more than promoting the participation of women in politics. It also encompasses procedures that lead women to recognize their rights, to sound their voice to secure political demands, and to have greater access to decision-making processes (cited in Sheikh 2012, 74-5). Lopez-Claros and Zahidi (2005, 4) argue that women's political empowerment is the "equitable representation of women in decision-making structures and their voice in the formulation of policies affecting their societies." This adds nuance to an understanding of wom-

---

4   The Fourth World Conference on Women: Action for Equity, Development, and Peace is known as the Beijing Platform for Action, an agenda for women's empowerment. This platform is important as it aims to advance women's empowerment and remove all barriers to women's active participation in economic, social, cultural, and political decision making.

en's political empowerment in terms of both their participation and their agency, especially their ability to raise their voices to influence decision making to provide resources (public goods and services) to their people (particularly women).

Women's Presence in Political Decision Making and Policy Influence

Women representatives are likely to articulate diverse desires and priorities from their male counterparts worldwide (Clayton 2021; Schwindt-Bayer 2006; Tremblay 1998; Wängnerud 2000). Thomas and Welch (1991) found that women in U.S. state legislatures were different from men, especially in the priority women give to dealing with health and welfare issues for children, women, and families. Thomas (1991, 1994) found that women's numbers have a positive impact on sponsoring and passing bills regarding women, children, and families in 12 U.S. state legislatures. Wangnerud (2000) found that the greater presence of women in Swedish political life has affected policy priorities involving gender equality, family policy, and social policy. Bratton and Ray (2002) found that size has an impact on municipal childcare policy in Norway. Schwindt-Bayer (2006) showed that women legislators place a much higher preference on policies related to women's issues and family/child issues. Kittilson (2008) suggested that women's descriptive representation in national parliaments had a persistent and noteworthy impact on maternity and childcare leave policies in 19 OECD democratic countries. Swiss, Fallon, and Burgos (2012) argued that an increasing number of women in legislatures have an influence on improving child health outcomes in developing countries worldwide.

However, some scholars also argue that an increase in women's numbers alone does not have a significant effect on women's policies and outcomes. Caiazza (2004) contended that, rather than admitting an increased number of women into formal political life, the *right political culture*—party dominance and attitudes toward women politicians—plays a significant role both in promoting women-friendly policy. Chaney (2006) argued that focusing on increasing the overall number of women legislators is not enough to bring substantive representation because a range of other institutional factors—both in party-political and parliamentary contexts—frame the behavior and magnitude to which policy makers act to advance equality in political debate. Dauti (2018) found in several legislatures that, women representatives do not, in fact, wield greater voice and power in decision making even if they constitute significant numbers. Moving to Africa, Wang (2013) claimed that several factors, including the women's caucus in legislatures, their relationships with male colleagues, and the depth of their ties with civil society and the aid community makes a significant contribution to pro-women legislation in the Ugandan Parliament.

Socio-economic Barriers to Women's Political Participation

Several studies have found strong evidence that gender quota policies have produced positive impacts in promoting women's empowerment politically and socially within, as well as outside, developed countries. These include: challenged existing social inequalities (Dahlerup and Freidenvall 2005, in Scandinavia); enhanced equity and efficiency in significant political bodies (Kittilson 2005; Pande and Ford 2011); reduced gender discrimination (Hawkesworth 2012; Dahlerup 2006); influenced government expenditures of social welfare such as education (Chen 2010); changed perceptions of women regarding their roles in legislative accomplishments and politics (Bauer 2008, in East and Southern Africa); and brought changes in government agendas (Franceschet and Piscopo 2008). However, within and beyond the developed nations, quota elected women face many socio-economic barriers to their effective participation in politics.

Scholars have observed that lack of education and training, plus gendered household responsibilities, together with insufficient financial resources, are the principal factors that hinder women's political representation (see e.g., Sawer and Simms 1993; Shvedova 2005). Some have also found that, although there is no explicit correlation between literacy rates and women's participation in politics, a minimum level of education is often needed to obtain candidate selection/nominations in politics (Goetz 2003, 2; Shvedova 2005). Lack of education may therefore exclude women from entering political decision-making bodies or influencing policy from inside them. Indeed, studies have shown that many women lack sufficient political training essential to ensure effective political participation (see e.g., Shvedova 2005). Phillips (1991, 199) argues that the burden of women's private lives is an obstacle to taking part in public matters. In most countries, women carry out the largest portion of household work (Kassa 2015; Phillips 1991) which can make it difficult to become immersed in political activities (Sawer and Simms 1993). Financial resources are likewise needed for sustained political participation, but women often have limited access to, and control over, economic assets as Tolley (2011) shows in her multi-level government study in Canada.

In India, some positive impacts from reserved seats policy include: increased women's interest in contributing to public goods and to offer social benefits (Deininger, Nagarajan, and Xia 2015); reduced discrimination and enhanced voice (Duflo 2005; Duflo and Topalova 2004; Priebe 2017), and addressing practical gender needs (Jayal 2006). Yet many studies have identified some socio-economic problems that hinder women's effective participation in local politics in India and some have found that a lack of education hinders women's effective participation. Illiterate women members, for instance, have limited understanding of training and legal literacy (Bryld 2001; Jayal 2006). Further studies suggest that domestic work creates an extra burden for women members, as women are the primary household workers in rural India (Chathukulam and John 2001, 92; Vissandjee *et al.* 2006). In a study into the potentials and pitfalls of increasing participation through decentralization, Bryld (2001, 160) found that, after maintaining all domestic activities, women members could hardly manage to find time to attend regular *Panchayats'* meetings. Scholars have found that some women members ask for permission from their family members prior to attending meetings in *Panchayats* (Bryld 2001, 158; Vissandjee *et al.* 2006, 443) and scarce resources limit women's effectiveness in offering services to their electorates in India (Baviskar 2002; Rai *et al.* 2006). The most mystifying aspect of *Panchayat* functioning, for women representatives, is that of finance and many women have confessed to being very diffident about financial matters (Baviskar 2002; Jayal 2006). Although the situation of women in local politics has gradually improved due to the policy of reserved seats since the 1990s, women members are still confronted with some crucial socio-economic barriers in local politics in India.

In Bangladesh, positive impacts from reserved seats policy include: the adoption of reserved seats brought a qualitative change in perception of women's roles in politics (Chowdhury 2002); enhanced visibility in different committees and expanded voice and social legitimacy in contributing to specific women's issues (Nazneen and Tasneen 2010), and women members being able to use formal and informal strategies to cope with male dominated political office (Rahman and Khan 2018). However, studies have identified some key socio-economic barriers that bound the effectiveness of reservation policy toward women's political participation. Some underline that women members are deprived of rights and privileges due to their level of understanding of the roles and functions of the *Union Parishads*, caused by limited education and political training (Democracy Watch 2015; Panday 2008, 2013; Prodip 2015; Sogra 2008), household activities, and the lack of spousal support restricts women's engagement in the public sphere (Ahmed 2008; Khan and Ara 2006; Prodip 2016; Zaman 2012). This lack of income and discrimination in resource distribution among male and female members has played a confining part in women's effective roles in local politics (Chowdhury 2013; Sultan *et al.* 2016; Prodip 2014). A lack of safety and security also confines women's mobility to attend meetings and represent their people (Panday 2010; Prodip 2018; Sultan *et al.* 2016). Other scholars agree that violence and fear of sexual harassment reduces women's performance in political matters (Ara 2017; Chowdhury 2013). Even though women's quota reservations were implemented in 1997, certain socio-economic impediments have made women members ineffective in their participation in local politics in Bangladesh.

Although several studies on women's quotas in local governments in India and Bangladesh have been carried out, few comparative studies exist of the two countries (Chowdhury 2013; Panday 2008; Rai *et al.* 2006 are exceptions). None of these studies have explored the relationship of gender quotas and women's political empowerment through a comparative perspective. Rai and others (2006) stand out for their examination of the impact of gender quotas on women's empowerment in three South Asian countries: India, Pakistan, and Bangladesh. That, now fairly dated, study compared the performance of elected women members of the first legislature in the *Union Parishad* in Bangladesh, but this is not enough for us to fully understand the actual outcomes of quota policy in the two countries.

The other two studies (Chowdhury 2001; Panday 2008) were based on secondary resources only. Recently, Prodip (2021a, 2021b) found that quota-elected women in India and Bangladesh have failed to exercise their voice in the decision-making process in a more egalitarian manner due to clear institutional and cultural challenges. Hence the present study contributes to filling the gap in our understanding of women's political participation in the two countries by identifying the socio-economic barriers that the women in reserved seats face with regards to their political empowerment.

Research Design and Methodology

This study is based on a qualitative research strategy (Creswell 2009, 173). Miles, Huberman, and Saldana (2014) argue that qualitative research provides researchers well-grounded sources of rich data (cited in Austin and Sutton 2014)—in this case, women's insight and commentary through in-depth interviews.

Selection of Respondents

The *Nadia* district in West Bengal in India and the *Rajshahi* district in the *Rajshahi* division of Bangladesh were chosen as the study areas—both have analogous cultures and languages, similar administrative evolutions, and contiguity. They can, therefore, contribute toward representing the familiar features of Indian and Bangladesh society. In total, there were 84 respondents to the interviews used for this research. Three elected women members from reserved seats of each *Gram Panchayat* and three *Gram Panchayats* from each of the two *Panchayat Samiti*[5] of Nadia were approached for interviews totaling 18 elected women members. Likewise, three elected women members of each *Union Parishad* and three *Union Parishads* from each of the two *Upazilas*[6] of *Rajshahi* district, totaling 18 elected women, were designated for interviews. Forty-eight key informant respondents were also selected for interviews to explore their perception concerning women members' capabilities in the activities of local councils. The sample sizes and study sites are presented in Table 1:

Table 1: Sample Size and Study Sites[7]

Types of respondents	Data collection method	Number of respondents	Study sites
Elected women members	Semi-structured interviews	18	Nadia, West Bengal, India

---

5   *Panchayat Samiti* are rural local governments at the intermediate level in *Panchayat* Raj Institutions (PRIs) in India.

6   *Upazila* is the intermediate level of rural local government in Bangladesh.

7   5 × 2 means each of five from *Gram Panchayat* and *Union Parishad*.

Elected women members	Semi-structured interviews	18	Rajshahi, Bangladesh
Elected male chairperson	Key informant interviews	5×2= 10	Nadia, West Bengal, India & Rajshahi, Bangladesh
Elected female chairperson	Key informant interviews	5×2= 10	Nadia, West Bengal, India & Rajshahi, Bangladesh
Elected male members	Key informant interviews	5×2= 10	Nadia, West Bengal, India & Rajshahi, Bangladesh
Local women politicians	Key informant interviews	3×2= 06	Nadia, West Bengal, India & Rajshahi, Bangladesh
Local government officers	Key informant interviews	2×2= 04	Nadia, West Bengal, India & Rajshahi, Bangladesh
Officials of women's organizations	Key informant interviews	2×2= 04	India and Bangladesh
Academics	Key informant interviews	2×2= 04	India and Bangladesh

Data Collection and Analysis

Primary data were collected through semi-structured and key informant interviews. Semi-structured interviews were conducted with 33 elected women members (India 16, Bangladesh 17) in the *Gram Panchayat* and the *Union Parishad*. Forty-one key informant interviews were conducted with various respondents (see Table 1). Informed consent was obtained from respondents and pseudonyms were used to respect anonymity and confidentiality. Interviews were conducted in the Bengali language in both countries and for the 74 interviews, recordings were translated into English.[8] Participants' answers were coded and themes then developed. Data analysis was performed through conversation analysis (Damico, Oelschlaeger, and Simmons-Mackie 1999). The study's application for research ethics was granted on July 1, 2018, by the UNE Human Research Ethics Committee.

Findings from the Field

Key findings of this study are organized into two broad categories: social and economic barriers. Social barriers include lack of education, training, and knowledge; household responsibilities; lack of family support; and lack of social security and physical mobility. Economic barriers encompass financial incapacity, corruption, and lack of coalition among women members.

---

8   Ten respondents (7 in India and 3 in Bangladesh) could not be reached due to unavailability and time constraints.

Social Barriers

Lack of Education, Training, and Knowledge

In India, this study corroborates the findings of previous studies that found a lack of expertise in reading and writing confines women's effective participation. Of the 16 interviewed, three women members completed their secondary-level education, five accomplished higher secondary education, and only two women members completed their Bachelor of Arts (BA). The lack of education was noted by all interviewees. Six women members said that less educated women cannot read the acts, circulars, and guidelines of the *Gram Panchayat* because they find them difficult to understand. As a result, they do whatever their *Pradhans* say. They do not know how the *Upa-Samiti*[9] is formed and how projects are distributed among the members. They are also ignorant as to whether they have the signatory power to pass a bill for development projects. As noted by one woman member: "I have never read the acts, circulars and guidelines of the *Gram Panchayat*. I am totally dependent on (the) *Pradhan's* word. I also do not know whether I have a signatory power or not." Another woman member said: "I do not have any idea about the project distribution policy. Party leaders and *Pradhan* distribute all projects among male and female members." Four other women members mentioned that a lack of training made them more vulnerable in the decision-making process. For example: "I did not receive any training over the last five years. I do not also know who provides training to women members."

In Bangladesh, 13 women members did not complete grade-nine education, and they exhibit a limited understanding of the forms, procedures, and functions of projects and standing committees. A woman member remarked:

> The politics of *Union Parishad* is very complex where education plays a crucial role to strengthen someone's position. Without sufficient education, someone cannot influence decision-making process rather saying yes or no almost in all meetings. As I am not educated, I do not know how projects and standing committees are formed and function.

This study also finds that 14 women members have not received any training from NGOs or the National Institute of Local Government (NILG) in Bangladesh. This is in line with Democracy Watch (2015) which found that only 31 percent of women members received training on political capacity building in their study on the constraints of women's political participation in local government in Bangladesh. Among these 14 women members, three of them are working as members for their second terms. One woman member reported: "Although I have passed seven years as member, I am yet to receive training on any issue. As I could not

---

9   Each *Gram Panchayat* in West Bengal has five committees, called *Upa-Samiti*.

complete Grade Five, I failed to claim my rights for my local citizens." An NGO official who works with a women's empowerment project in local government said:

> NILG and NGOs do not provide trainings to women members on time. As I know, women members that were elected in 2016 did not receive any training. A few of them received training at the end of their tenure. Finally, these trainings did not work for them at all.

It was observed that few women members in Bangladesh assume that their positions, powers, and authorities are higher than those of male members. They do not have clear ideas about the power and functions of the chairperson. A woman member pointed out: "I heard that the power and authority of the male and women members are equal. I perceived that the status of women in reserved seats are almost nearest to the chairperson." This variant of lack of knowledge has created confusion and tension between women members and chairpersons. A male chairperson further explained: "As women members represent three times bigger constituencies than male members, they assume their positions are nearest to the chairpersons. Thus, they often blame chairpersons without proper understanding."

Household Responsibilities and Lack of Family Support

In India, the majority of women members do not consider household responsibilities and lack of family support as threats to their work in the *Gram Panchayat*. Only three women members revealed that they could not attend meetings regularly, as their first task was to maintain household activities. A woman member noted, "I need to take care of my children, husband, and family members first. If meetings are called in the morning, I could not attend in most cases." Male members of the family often do not support women domestically, as is noted by a male *Pradhan*: "Usually, males do not want to help them in their household's activities. As women have to give priority to their family affairs first, they sometime miss important meetings." A woman member added: "My husband often quarrels with me if I go to the *Panchayat* without completing household tasks. It is hard to maintain family and office together."

In Bangladesh, a majority of women interviewed said that they can manage and balance house and office work well. Only two women noted that they consider household activities as their leading role. One of these women explained: "I have a poultry farm and I look after this, as my husband is very busy with his business. Sometimes, I cannot attend village court and local *shalish*."[10] A female chairperson remarked: "One of the woman members of my *Union Parishad* is busy with taking care of her grandchild. She comes to *Union Parishad* after completing her household activities."

---

10 *Shalish* is a community-based traditional institution for conflict resolution through mediation, which passes informal judgements over property, family, marriage, divorce, or inheritance matters in Bangladesh (see Hossian 2012).

The majority of women studied in Bangladesh were also free to attend *Union Parishad* activities with only one female member reporting that: "My husband reminds me to finish household works first before going to the *Union Parishad*. I do not have any option as nobody helps me to complete my work."

Lack of Social Security and Physical Mobility

In India, most of the women members interviewed said that they are able to move around, attend meetings, and feel safe in public places. Only two women members noted having limited participation in *Panchayat* meetings due to lack of physical mobility. Previous researchers have noted that some women members needed the permission of their family member(s) prior to attending meetings in *Panchayats* (Bryld 2001, 158; Vissandjee *et al.* 2006, 443). However, the reason for a lack of physical mobility here is quite different from the previous studies. Women are not prevented from attending meetings, but they do not feel safe to attend, especially when these are organized in the evening, as reported by a woman member: "Although my family do not restrict me, I have never attended any local disputes meeting. Male members often go to the police station to deal with various issues even at night. However, I never went to police station at night."

In Bangladesh, the majority of women members reported that they could move around freely, go to meetings, and feel safe at outside. Only two women said that they avoid attending local *Salish* due to lack of security, which is similar to cases in India. Previous studies also suggested that lack of safety and security, meetings at inconvenient times and places, and the scarcity of male companions are barriers to women representatives attending meetings in the *Union Parishad* (Panday 2010). Women members said that *Shalish* is usually called in the afternoon and continues up until midnight. To avoid criticism of the senior male citizens of society, women members often refrained from attending local *Shalish*. One-woman member who has had a 28-year political career in the *Union Parishad* pointed out:

> I attended only two local *Shalish* over the last 28 years. In most cases, *Shalish* was called in the afternoon and it took more time to finish. Sometimes, my husband was busy, and he could not escort me. It does not look good to come back house alone at late night while people treated me badly and often used slang languages. I personally also feel insecure to return home alone.

Economic Barriers

Financial Incapacity

Financial resources provide scope for women's full and effective involvement in politics (Tolley 2011). In India, this study finds that the financial status of the women members is very low, as on average they receive only Rs.150 (about 2 USD) per month as a sitting allowance. Thirteen women members said that, due to their lower economic status, they could not carry out their political work effectively. They hesitate to participate in social programs in their villages and are dependent on their husbands to meet the cost associated with *Panchayat's* activities. As noted by one: "I feel shame to talk about my financial condition. How can I meet people's demands with Rs. 150? I always request my husband to give me some money to meet the cost related to the *Panchayat*." A male chairperson observed: "Women come from lower economic strata. Without money, it becomes hard to provide services to women and local people." Two women members noted that finances are an issue: "We have not received our honorarium in the last year."

In Bangladesh, the honorarium of the women members of the *Union Parishad* is BDT 8,000 (around 95 USD) per month; nearly 50 times the amount those in India.[11] Out of this BDT 8,000, women members receive BDT 3,600 (about 43 USD) from the *Union Parishad*. However, the portion that they received from the *Union Parishad* is not regular. In comparison, for male members it is. A woman member said: 'It is almost two years since I received a single payment from the *Union Parishad*. Although our *Union Parishad* has a higher income, the chairperson did not give our honorarium. However, the chairperson has provided honoraria to all male members." An interview with the chairperson of the same *Union Parishad* reveals that the chairperson maintains good relations with the male members in order to run activities smoothly and to avoid hostilities. As the chairperson remarked: "If I do not provide honorarium to male members regularly, it becomes hard to run the *Union Parishad* efficiently. Even though women members do not get their honoraria regularly, they do not create any trouble for me." The underlying and continuing discrepancies in persistent gender perceptions here should need no further underlining.

Women members in Bangladesh also face additional financial costs in relation to their position in society. Many people come to women members' homes to ask for help—which customarily in both countries may lead to offering them breakfast and tea. Sometimes, they are also asked to donate a certain amount and attend various social programs, as well as providing transportation costs for poor people if they meet in the bus or other local transports. A woman member noted this extra burden: "Many people, especially women, come to me to request support for various issues including girl's education costs. Moreover, when people come to my house, I need to offer biscuits and tea. However, I rarely can meet their necessities."

The major source of income of the *Union Parishad* is taxes. Yet most *Union Parishads* do not receive regular tax payments, and, therefore, fail to provide honoraria to women members regularly. The common views of three women members are: "The income of our *Union Parishads* in very limited as majority of the people

---

11   The average monthly labor wages in Bangladesh is around BDT 12,000 (almost 142 USD).

do not pay tax regularly. Thus, the chairpersons do not provide us honorarium regularly." Finally, women members become more vulnerable when they cannot spend their earnings without their husband's permission, with husbands deciding where and how the honorarium should be spent. One woman member said: "I am accountable to my husband for each case regarding use of money that I have received from the *Union Parishad*. My husband manages, uses, and controls my salary."

Corruption

In India, this study found that the low honoraria tied some female (as well as male) members of the *Pradhan* and *Upa-Pradhan* in the *Gram Panchayat* to be open to (or have been open to) corruption. They have earned some money illegally from the development projects and social safety net funds. A male member said:

> Members (male and female) of the *Gram Panchayat* receive only Rs. 150 (2 USD) per month as sitting allowance. A member has to spend much money to do the works of the council. To manage the cost associated with services, I see a few elected representatives earn extra money from development projects. How can we expect women's empowerment if they do corruption?

Further, party leaders often distribute resources such as social welfare programs (e.g., ration cards, maternity cards, disability cards etc.) among their relatives—as noted by a woman member: "I see our party leaders often allocate resources to their relatives. When government resources are distributed among the relatives, women members are automatically excluded from those project's shares."

In Bangladesh, in recent years the majority of women members have found themselves near destitute due to the corruption and/or malpractice of the chairperson and male members (Rahman and Khan 2018). In this study, four women members revealed that the chairpersons managed, distributed, and implemented development projects and social safety net cards without consulting with female members. To pay for development projects, the chairperson needs the signature of women members on the cheque and sometimes the chairperson forced women members to provide signatures. As one woman member noted, if any of them refused to provide a signature, the chairperson changed the signatory in the following year:

> No sooner had we come to the *Union Parishad* than the chairperson called a general meeting. He requested us to provide signatures on an empty resolution book. We (male and female members) trusted him and gave signature without any doubt. The chairperson has done everything by his own way as we have signature on resolution book. He did all of development projects and grabbed all of money.

It was observed that a number of women members provide their signatures on the cheques without receiving an equal share of projects they are signing for. One woman member stated: "I am also responsible for not securing women's rights in my electorates. I agreed to be chair of a project committee to get some economic benefits." A limited number of woman members and the majority of male members distributed resources (such as social safety net cards) to their kin instead of distributing them among the needy people and poor women they were supposed to reach. A woman member said: "male members always care about their families and relatives. If they get projects or social safety net cards, they always wish to distribute those resources to their lineages rather than other poor people in the village." She further added: "I also distributed one widow card and one disability card to my sister-in-law and one of my nephews. If my relatives are eligible to get social safety net cards, why I will not offer them? If somebody calls me a corrupt woman, what I can do for that?"

Lack of Coalition among Women Members

If women become sizable in legislatures, in theory they have an opportunity to form strong coalitions to promote women's issues in the decision-making process (Franceschet, Krook, and Piscopo 2012, 8). This study asked women members whether they engage in coalition building to strengthen their voice and ability to promote women's issues in policy making in local councils in both countries. Strikingly, all women members in India reported that they do not need to form a coalition to argue for or promote their rights in the meetings. In Bangladesh, nine women members of three *Parishad* reported that they maintain strong unity among themselves to argue for an equal share of projects. However, six women members of three *Union Parishads* said that they always maintain good relations with the chairpersons and male members. Concomitantly, they do not cooperate and support other women members to claim their rights for fear of losing the few benefits that support of male members brings. The chairperson and male members offered them gifts, a little money, or transportation services, as noted by one woman reflecting the voices of another two women members:

> Three women members have never come to same platform to claim their rights. The chairperson managed an other two women members by offering BDT 2,000 to 5,000 (around 24-60 USD 24) during distribution of development projects. It is impossible to fight alone against the chairperson and nine male members to secure my rights.

Again, this evidence from interviews highlights the long way that gender quotas still have to go, particularly in Bangladesh, to be able to even approach the kind of equality or gender parity these policies were specifically designed to create—or at least support. On their own, gender quota policies do not, in practice, always advance gender equalization or women's empowerment. Without the appropriate changes in perceptions, and the political and social cultural norms that continue to drive them, women's quotas may not amount to more than a highly visible, but substantively thin, band aid that, in the end, fails to support women's political empowerment or undergird policies to institutionalize equality politically in these countries.

Discussion and Conclusion

This study has discussed the socio-economic barriers that women members in reserved seats face in affecting policies with regards to their political empowerment at the local council level in India and Bangladesh. The findings are important as they reveal the personal insights of women members in reserved seats who are currently encountering rather significant socio-economic barriers to their political empowerment. This study contributes comparatively to the literature on gender quotas by applying a socio-economic lens, which—in addition to the other barriers identified and focused on strongly in the literature to date—is vital for identifying issues, developing solutions, and assisting women to work effectively in political decision-making.

Gender quotas aim to increase women's presence in the political decision-making as well as to bring expected substantive inclusionary effects at the level of emergent policy outcomes. Feminist political scholars have argued that women's presence in all levels of government makes a difference in political decision making as they bring a diverse set of experiences and perspectives to bear on the political and administrative issues discussed and decided upon at the grassroots level in local government fora (Philipps 1995, 65). I find that gender quotas have formally and demonstrably increased the number of women in local political councils; additionally, I found that quota-elected women indeed are very vocal in articulating their desire to influence the policy-making process to open up more resources for their constituents, and women in particular. However, they have encountered grave socio-economic challenges in attempting to influence decisions in local councils.

Lack of education and political training may debar women representatives from fuller and more effective participation in the policy-making process (Shvedova 2005). This study finds that more women members in Bangladesh than in India fail to perform their activities effectively as a result of a lack of education—both political and more generally. These findings are corroborated by previous studies (Democracy Watch 2015; Panday 2008, 2013; Sogra 2008). This study does suggest that fewer women members in India faced challenges due to a low level of education than expected—or at least fewer self-reported educational gaps as a major encumbrance. What is more important to note is that women members from both countries continue to face a serious lack of training in politics—such as leadership qualities, assertiveness, and capacity building—which makes it difficult to claim their rights as council members or rights for their constituents and is corroborated by earlier studies in India (Bryld 2001; Jayal 2006) and Bangladesh (Panday 2013; Sogra 2008). Lack of education and training further leads to a scarcity of knowledge among women members in Bangladesh, which is not the case in India.

Women devote much time to fulfilling the basic demands of their family members, which limits their involvement in political structures (Kassa 2015; Philipps 1995). Previous studies in India (Bryld 2001; Chathukulam and John 2001; Vissandjee et al. 2006) and Bangladesh (Ahmed 2008; Khan and Ara 2006; Zaman 2012) have found that household responsibilities seriously hindered women members' roles in local councils. However, this study suggests that in recent years (excepting those affected by the pandemic—which is likely only to exacerbate the issue and the lack of functional equality in the near future), only a few women members in both countries fail to attend council meetings due to the burden of household responsibilities. The possible explanation might be that women members in both countries can and have managed work at home and in the office effectively. But again, their ability to do so is not always an autonomous individual choice and needs to take into account more external factors than their male counterparts generally face. Women members are often restricted to venture outside of their homes to offer services to citizens in India due to the lack of permission from husbands and family members (Bryld 2001; Vissandjee et al. 2006), and in Bangladesh for lack of overall safety and security (Panday 2010). What this study does suggest is that, in the last decade, fewer women members in both countries remain restricted from leaving home to offer services to local people as in Panday's (2010) study. These restrictions now mainly come from a lack of social safety and security, not from husbands or family members, on which the pandemic has again had a serious effect. However, male members in India indicated an awareness that some women members faced barriers from their family members, which suggests a possible wider perception shift may be possible in the future. It is also promising to see that lack of physical security and mobility appear to have been less serious obstacles to women members in their ability to perform their activities in local councils in India and Bangladesh, at least until early 2020. One plausible interpretation of this worth noting is that patriarchal behaviors and norms in the families might be changing for women in relation to their participation in local politics. However, further in-depth studies, particularly as the pandemic subsides, are required to understand the role played by familial support in promoting women's participation in the local councils.

Financial resources are significant requirements for both men and women to ensure their participation in politics. Women, in particular, continue to have minimal access to economic resources compared to men in many developing countries (Tolley 2011). This study updates Tolley's findings with respect to India and Bangladesh and shows how women remain perceived, in some places, as secondary when it comes to timely financial remuneration or funding for their public duties. Importantly, in relation to this research, limited resources confine women's effective roles in local politics in India (Baviskar 2002; Jayal 2006; Rai *et al.* 2006) and Bangladesh (Chowdhury 2013; Democracy Watch 2015; Sultan *et al.* 2016). The situation has not yet sufficiently changed to deliver the egalitarian aims of gender quotas. Indeed, lack of financial ability continues to keep women members alienated from, or unable to adequately perform their duties in, many social and political activities in both countries. The study found, though, that the dimension of financial inability is quite different from country to country.

Women members in India are provided a small amount of money per month, whereas women members in Bangladesh, despite receiving a relatively high payment, are not regularly provided with their honoraria from the *Union Parishad*. Although the honoraria of Bangladeshi women members is almost 50 times higher than that for Indian women members, Bangladeshi women members cannot meet the demands of three times more numerous constituents compared to their male counterparts. Financial incapacity has, in some cases noted by the interviewees, further led to corruption of the *Pradhans*/chairpersons and male members in both countries. This undermines women members. Also, a few women members in both countries have sought illegal incomes from development projects rather than offering services to their voters because of their financial condition. Some women members in Bangladesh maintain good relations with the chairpersons and male members to secure any economic benefits from the projects. The study also found a tendency for women members to opine that they do *not* consider supporting and cooperating with other women members to claim their rights and privileges in a legal way because they were unlikely to lead to effective lobbying positions, and/or might undermine the support of male members that secures what little financial or other benefits women members can or do receive and use.

This study also uncovered some new factors that are important to discuss more deeply in future research. These revolve around corruption, shifts in cultural norms or circumstances regarding general security and personal autonomy, and coalition building based on group advocacy for gendered issues. First, some women members have used corrupt practices due to lack of enough financial resources in both countries. They justified this by claiming that they earned extra money illegally from the development projects to provide services to their citizens that they would not otherwise have been able to give. Second, a few women members in India do not often attend meetings due to lack of safety and security, which suggest some advances have indeed been made that specifically assist the aims of gender quota policy. Previously, in line with cultural norms, many women had to ask permission from their family members before attending meetings in the *Panchayat,* which I found is less of an issue now, especially in India. Third, and perhaps most significantly, some women members in Bangladesh have been open in reporting that they have chosen *not* to form coalitions with other women members to secure their political rights or increase the strength of their voice or lobbying power the at local government level. Other negotiation tactics have been used to support women members' bargaining positions: several reported that they entered into informal negotiation with council chairpersons to acquire an equal (or more equal) share of projects. They rationalized this alternative by stating that, if they do not maintain good relations with the chairperson, they would be deprived of projects and funds and would fail to provide services to their voters. The implications of this for the efficacy of gender quotas in achieving their substantive goals are serious. Without concomitant shifts in both broader cultural perceptions (concerning political equality and women's empowerment), and women's educational preparedness to function as equal bargaining partners in local government administration, gender quotas are indeed unlikely to fulfil their aims substantively. The point concerning formal versus substantive gains in gender equality and/or parity, and its implications, is well known and well discussed in developed polities. It is more marked and certainly recognized, yet less discussed, in developing ones.

Overall, women's political empowerment may be formally enhanced by inclusive policies like electoral quotas but, as the findings show, if these do not function alongside additional inclusive policies promoting effective political training, rhetorical, and public speaking/bargaining skills, legal and rights knowledge, etc., any leverage or inclusory advantages formal quotas may be expected to give cannot actually filter into mainstream politics and mainstream gender equalization. Women members in reserved seats in both countries are faced with economic hurdles that seriously affect their ability to influence policy. To ensure that gender quotas/reserved seats offer more than just a formal recognition of women's political empowerment, more government resources for local councils need to be made available to women. Sufficient training to elected women members in both countries, as well as more encouragement for educated women to participate actively, will be paramount in this endeavor.

Acknowledgements

I am truly grateful to Professor Helen Ware and Dr. Johanna Garnett at the University of New England, Australia, for their suggestions and comments in preparing this article.

Declaration of Conflicting Interests

The author declared no potential conflicts of interest with respect to the research, authorship, and/or publication of this article.

Funding

The author received no financial support for the authorship and/or publication of this article.

About the Author

Mahbub Alam Prodip is an Associate Professor in Public Administration at the University of Rajshahi in Bangladesh. He is currently pursuing doctoral studies in Peace Studies at the University of New England, Australia. His research interests are gender and politics, gender and violence, and Rohingya refugee issues in Bangladesh.

References

Ahmed, Kamal U. 2008. "Women and Politics in Bangladesh." In *Women's Political Participation and Representation in Asia*, edited by K. Iwanaga, 276-296. Copenhagen, Denmark: NIAS Press.

Ara, Fardaus. 2017. *Women's Political Participation in the Context of Modernisation: A Comparative Study of Australia and Bangladesh.* Unpublished Doctoral Dissertation, Murdoch University, Australia.

Austin, Zubin, and Jane Sutton. 2014. "Qualitative Research: Getting Started." *The Canadian Journal of Hospital Pharmacy* 67 (6): 436. DOI: 10.4212/cjhp.v67i6.1406

Ban, Radu, and Vijayendra. Rao. 2008. "Tokenism or Agency? The Impact of Women's Reservations on Village Democracies in South India." *Economic Development and Cultural Change* 56 (3): 501-530. DOI: 10.1086/533551

Bauer, Gretchen. 2008. "Fifty/fifty by 2020: Electoral Gender Quotas for Parliament in East and Southern Africa." *International Feminist Journal of Politics* 10 (3): 348-368. DOI: 10.1080/14616740802185668

Baviskar, B. S. 2002. "Including the Excluded: Empowering the Powerless." *Sociological Bulletin* 51 (2): 168-174. Accessed November 18, 2021. https://www.jstor.org/stable/23619968

Bratton, Kathleen A., and Leonard P. Ray. 2002. "Descriptive Representation and Policy Outcomes: Evidence from Municipal Day Care Coverage." *American Journal of Political Science* 46 (2): 428-437. DOI: 10.2307/3088386

Bryld, E. 2001. "Increasing Participation in Democratic Institutions through Decentralization: Empowering Women and Scheduled Castes and Tribes through Panchayat Raj in Rural India." *Democratization* 8 (3): 149-172. DOI: 10.1080/714000213

Caiazza, Amy. 2004. "Does Women's Representation in Elected Office Lead to

Women-Friendly Policy? Analysis of State-level Data." *Women & Politics* 26 (1): 35-70. DOI: 10.1300/J014v26n01_03

Chaney, Paul. 2006. "Critical Mass, Deliberation and the Substantive Representation of Women: Evidence from the UK's Devolution Programme." *Political Studies* 54 (4). 691-714. DOI: 10.1111/j.1467-9248.2006.00633.x

Chathukulam, Jos, and M.S. John. 2001. "Empowerment of Women Panchayat Members: Learningfrom Kerala (India)." *Asian Journal of Women's Studies* 6 (4): 66-101. DOI: 10.1080/12259276.2000.11665894

Chen, Li-Ju. 2010. "Do Gender Quotas Influence Women's Representation and Policies?" *The European Journal of Comparative Economics* 7 (1): 13-60. DOI: 10.1086/708336

Chowdhury, F. Deba. 2013. "Women's Participation in Local Governments in Bangladesh and India. In Commonwealth." In *The Impact of Women's Political Leadership on Democracy and Development: Case Studies from the Commonwealth*, 64-85. United Kingdom: Commonwealth Secretariat.

Chowdhury, Najma. 2002. "The Implementation of Quotas: Bangladesh Experience–Dependence and Marginality in Politics." In *International IDEA Workshop "The Implementation of Quotas: Asian Experiences,"* Jakarta, Indonesia, September 25.

Clayton, Amanda. 2021. "How Do Electoral Gender Quotas Affect Policy?" *Annual Review of Political Science* 24: 235-252. DOI: 10.1146/annurev-polisci-041719-102019

Creswell, J. W. 2009. *Research Design: Qualitative, Quantitative, and Mixed Methods Approaches*. London: Sage Publications.

Dahlerup, Drude. 2006. *Women, Quotas and Politics*. New York: Routledge.

Dahlerup, Drude, and L. Freidenvall. 2005. "Quotas as a 'Fast Track' to Equal Representation for Women: Why Scandinavia is No Longer the Model." *International Feminist Journal of Politics* 7 (1): 26–48. DOI: 10.1080/1461674042000324673

Damico, Jack S., Mary Oelschlaeger, and Nina Simmons-Mackie. 1999. "Qualitative Methods in Aphasia Research: Conversation Analysis." *Aphasiology* 13 (9-11): 667-679. DOI: 10.1080/026870399401777

Dauti, Marsela. 2018. "Women's Decision-Making Power in the Local Councils of

Albania: Do Numbers Make a Difference?" *Global Social Welfare* 5 (4): 253-263. DOI: 10.1007/s40609-017-0105-5

Deininger, Klaus, Songqing Jin, Hari K. Nagarajan, and Xia Fang. 2011. *Does Female Reservation Affect Long-term Political Outcomes? Evidence from Rural India.* The World Bank.

Democracy Watch. 2015. *Constraints of Women's Political Participation in the Local Government and Political Parties at Grassroots of Bangladesh.* Dhaka: Swiss Agency for Development and Cooperation.

Duflo, Esther. 2005. "Why Political Reservations?" *Journal of the European Economic Association* 3 (3): 668-678. DOI: 10.1162/jeea.2005.3.2-3.668

Duflo, Esther, and Petia Topalova. 2004. "Unappreciated Service: Performance, Perceptions, and Women Leaders in India." *Manuscript, Department of Economics, Massachusetts Institute of Technology.*

Franceschet, Susan, and Jennifer M. Piscopo. 2008. "Gender Quotas and Women's Substantive Representation: Lessons from Argentina." *Politics & Gender* 4 (3): 393-425. DOI: 10.1017/S1743923X08000342

Franceschet, Susan, Mona Lena Krook, and Jennifer M. Piscopo. 2012. *The Impact of Gender Quotas.* New York: Oxford University Press.

Goetz, A. M. 2003. *Women's Education and Political Participation.* Background paper prepared for the Education for All Global Monitoring Report 2003/4 Gender and Education for All: The Leap to Equality. UNESCO.

Hannan, Carolyn. 2003. *Policy Dialogue on Empowering Women in Autonomy and Decentralisation Processes,* organized by Permanent Mission of the Republic of Indonesia, May 29, 2003, New York.

Hawkesworth, M. E. 2012. *Political Worlds of Women: Activism, Advocacy, and Governance in the Twenty-First Century.* Boulder, CO: Westview Press.

Hossain, Md. Anwar. 2012. "Influence of Social Norms and Values of Rural Bangladesh on Women's Participation in the *Union Parishad.*" *Indian Journal of Gender Studies* 19 (3): 393–412. DOI: 10.1177/097152151201900303

Hughes, Melanie M., Pamela Paxton, Amanda B. Clayton, and Par Zetterberg, P. 2019. "Global Gender Quota Adoption, Implementation, and Reform." *Comparative Politics* 5 (1): 219-238. DOI: 10.5129/001041519X15647434969795

IPU. 2018. *Women in Parliament in 2018. The Year in Review.* Courand.

Jahan, Selim. 2017. *Human Development Report 2016-Human Development for Everyone.* New York: UNDP.

Jayal, Niraja Gopal. 2006. "Engendering Local Democracy: The Impact of Quotas for Women in India's Panchayats." *Democratisation* 13 (1): 15-35. DOI: 10.1080 /13510340500378225

Kabeer, Naila. 1999. "Resources, Agency, Achievements: Reflections on The Measurement of Women's Empowerment." *Development and Change* 30 (3): 435-464. DOI: 10.1111/1467-7660.00125

Kassa, Shimelis. 2015. "Challenges and Opportunities of Women Political Participation in Ethiopia." *Journal of Global Economics* 3 (4): 1-7. DOI: 10.4172/2375-4389.1000162

Kasturi, Leela. 1999. "Pernicious or Necessary?" *Indian Journal of Gender Studies* 6 (1): 123-128. DOI: 10.1177/097152159900600108

Khan, Mostafizur R., and Fardaus Ara. 2006. "Women, Participation and Empowerment in Local Government: Bangladesh Union Parishad Perspective." *Asian Affairs* 29 (1): 73-92. Accessed November 17, 2021. http://cdrb.org/journal/current/1/3.pdf

Kittilson, Miki C. 2005. "In Support of Gender Quotas: Setting New Standards, Bringing Visible Gains." *Politics & Gender* 1 (4): 638-645. DOI: x 10.1017/S1 743923X05230192

Kittilson, Miki C. 2008. "Representing Women: The Adoption of Family Leave in Comparative Perspective." *The Journal of Politics* 70 (2): 323-334. DOI: 10.1017/ S002238160808033X

Krook, M. L. 2009. *Quotas for Women in Politics: Gender and Candidate Selection Reform Worldwide.* New York: Oxford University Press.

Lopez-Claros, A., and S. Zahidi. 2005. *Women's Empowerment: Measuring the Global Gender Gap.* World Economic Forum.

Malhotra, Anju, and Sidney R. Schuler. 2005. "Women's Empowerment as a Variable in International Development." In *Measuring Empowerment: Cross-disciplinary Perspectives,* edited by D. Narayan, 71-88. Washington, D.C.: The World Bank.

Miles, M. B., A.M. Huberman, and J. Saldana. (3rd Ed.) 2014. *Qualitative Data Analysis: A Methods Sourcebook*. London: Sage Publications.

Mlambo, Courage, Forget Kapingura, and Richard Meissner. 2019. "Factors Influencing Women Political Participation: The Case of the SADC Region." *Cogent Social Sciences* 5 (1): 1681048. DOI: 10.1080/23311886.2019.1681048

Nazneen, Sohela, and Sakiba Tasneem. 2010. "A Silver Lining: Women in Reserved Seats in Local Government in Bangladesh." *IDS Bulletin* 41 (5): 35-42. DOI: 10.1111/j.1 759-5436.2010.00164.x

Nowtony, H. 2018. "Women in Public Life in Austria." In *Access to Power: Cross National Studies of Women and* Elite, edited by C. F. Epstein and R. L. Coser. London: Routledge.

OECD. 2018. *Women's Political Participation in Egypt: Barriers, Opportunities, and Gender Sensitivity of Select Political Institutions*. Accessed June 15, 2021. https://www.oecd.org/mena/governance/womens-political-participation-in-egypt.pdf

Panday, Pranab Kumar. 2008. "Representation without Participation: Quotas for Women in Bangladesh." *International Political Science Review* 29 (4): 489-512. DOI:10.1177/0192512108095724

Panday, Pranab Kumar. 2010. "Women's Political Participation in Bangladesh and India: Symbolic or Real?" *Women in Patriarchal Society* 37 (11): 26-44. DOI: 10.1080/01900692.2014.90327211

_____. 2013. *Women's Political Participation in Bangladesh*: India: Springer.

Pande, R., and D. Ford. 2011. *Gender Quotas and Female Leadership: A Review of Background Paper*. Accessed May 10, 2021. https://www.hks.harvard.edu/publica tions/gender-quotas-and-female-leadership-review

Phillips Anne. 1995. *The Politics of Presence*. Oxford, UK: Clarendon.

Phillips, Anne. 1991. *Engendering Democracy*. Cambridge, UK: Polity Press.

Priebe, Jan. 2017. "Political Reservation and Female Empowerment: Evidence from Maharashtra, India." *Oxford Development Studies* 45 (4): 499-521. DOI: 10. 1080/13600818.2017.1298740

Prodip, Mahbub A. 2014. "Decentralization and Women Empowerment in Bangladesh: Union Parishad Perspectives." *International Journal of Scientific & Tech-*

nology Research 3 (12): 215-223.

Prodip, Mahbub A. 2015. *Women's Participation and Decision-Making Power after the Local Government Act of 2009: A Study of Local Government (Union Parishad) in* Bangladesh, *Unpublished Master's Dissertation.* Bangkok: Asian Institute of Technology.

Prodip, Mahbub A. 2016. "Gender Quotas in Politics and Empowerment of Women in Bangladesh: Symbolic or Real?" *Jahangirnagar Journal of Administrative Studies* (July): 53-68.

Prodip, Mahbub A. 2018. "Barriers to Women's Participation in the Decision-Making Process: Evidence from Rural Local Government (Union Parishad) In Bangladesh." *Journal Of Socialand Economic Studies* 17: 70-89. DOI: 10.1007/978-3-319-57475-2_14

Prodip, Mahbub A. 2021a. "Exclusion through Inclusion: Institutional Constraints on Women's Political Empowerment in India and Bangladesh." *World Affairs 184* (2): 213-244. DOI: 10.1177/00438200211013017

Prodip, Mahbub A. 2021b. "Cultural Obstacles to Women's Political Empowerment in India and Bangladesh: A Comparative Perspective." *Asian Journal of Comparative Politics* (Online First, February 2021). DOI: 10.1177/2057891121990742

Rahman, Md. Mizanur, and Ainsur Khan. 2018. "Challenges and Coping Strategies of Women Leaders at the Local Level in Bangladesh." *Italian Sociological Review* 8 (1): 43-63. DOI: 10.13136/isr.v8i1.155

Rai, S. M., F. Bari, N. Mahtab, and B. Mohanty. 2006. "South Asia: Gender Quotas and the Politics of Empowerment–A Comparative Study." In *Women, Quotas and Politics*, edited by Drude Dahlerup. 222-246. London: Routledge.

Rowlands, Jo. 1997. *Questioning Empowerment: Working with Women in Honduras.* London: Oxfam.

Sawer, M., and M. Simms. 1993. *A Woman's Place: Women and Politics in Australia.* North Sydney: Allen & Unwin.

Schwindt-Bayer, Leslie A. 2010. *Political Power and Women's Representation in Latin America.* New York, NY: Oxford University Press.

_____. 2006. "Still Supermadres? Gender and the Policy Priorities of Latin American Legislators." *American Journal of Political Science* 50 (3): 570-585. DOI:

10.1111/j.1540-5907.2006.00202.x

Sheikh, S. A. 2012. *Women's Political Empowerment at National and Local Levels through Quotas: A Case Study of Pakistan and Bangladesh.* Unpublished Doctoral Dissertation. Canberra: University of Canberra.

Shroff, G. 2010. *Towards a Design Model for Women's Empowerment in the Developing World* Unpublished Master's Dissertation. Pittsburg: Carnegie Mellon University.

Shvedova, N. 2005. "Obstacles to Women's Participation in Parliament." In *Women in Parliament: Beyond Numbers*, edited by J. Ballington and A. Karam, 33-50). Stockholm: IDEA.

Sogra, Khair Jahan. 2008. "Mainstreaming Women in Local Government System: The Case of Bangladesh." *Pakistan Journal of Women's Studies* 15 (2): 117-127.

Sultan, M., B. M., Hasan, I. S., Khondaker, A. A., Enam, I. T. Mahmood, and S. Nazneen. 2016. *Women's Representation in Union Parishad.* Local Governance Programme Sharique-III, BIGD, BRAC University.

Swiss, Liam, Kathleen M., Fallon, and Giovani Burgos. 2012. "Does Critical Mass Matter? Women's Political Representation and Child Health in Developing Countries." *Social Forces* 91 (2): 531-558. DOI: 10.1093/sf/sos169

Thomas, Sue. 1991. "The Impact of Women on State Legislative Policies." *Journal of Politics* 53 (4): 958-976. DOI: 10.2307/2131862

Thomas, Sue. 1994. *How Women Legislate.* New York, NY: Oxford University Press.

Thomas, Sue, and Susan Welch. 1991. "The Impact of Gender on Activities and Priorities of State Legislators." *Western Political Quarterly* 44 (2): 445–456. DOI: 10.2307/448788

Tolley, Erin. 2011. "Do Women 'Do Better' in Municipal Politics? Electoral Representation across Three Levels of Government." *Canadian Journal of Political Science* 44 (3): 573-594. DOI: 10.1017/S0008423911000503

Tremblay, Manon. 1998. "Do Female MPs Substantively Represent Women? A Study of Legislative Behaviour in Canada's 35th Parliament." *Canadian Journal of Political Science/Revue canadienne de science politique* 31 (3): 435-465. DOI: 10.S000 8423900009082

Vissandjée, B., S. Abdool, A. Apale, and S. Dupére. 2006. "Women's Political Participation in Rural India: Discerning Discrepancies through a Gender Lens." *Indian Journal of Gender Studies* 13 (3): 425-450. DOI: 10.1177/097152150601300305

Wang, Vibeke. 2013. "Women Changing Policy Outcomes: Learning from Pro-women Legislation in the Ugandan Parliament." In *Women's Studies International Forum* 41: 113-121. Pergamon. DOI: 10.1016/j.wsif.2013.05.008

Wängnerud, Lena. 2000. "Testing the Politics of Presence: Women's Representation in the Swedish Riksdag." *Scandinavian Political Studies* 23 (1): 67-91. DOI: 10.1111/1467-9477.00031

Zaman, Farhana. 2012. "Bangladeshi Women's Political Empowerment in Urban Local Governance." *South Asia Research* 32 (2): 81-101. DOI: 10.1177/02627280 12453488

An Arctic Promised Land: Greenlandic Independence and Security

John Ash[*]

Scott Polar Research Institute,
University of Cambridge

The Arctic is exempt neither from the global process of decolonialization, nor the geopolitical effects of climate change. In the case of Greenland (Kalaallit Nunaat), the desire on the part of the Greenlandic people for full political autonomy from Denmark is driving a secessionist process that stands on the threshold of conclusion. This movement has deep roots in a growing sense of Greenlandic cultural identity and confidence in the population and is strongly represented in the current political discourse. Despite its physical extent, Greenland has a small population. Independence would transform it into a microstate, sharing many of the economic and other problems common to such polities, but in a strategic location. However, the political drive toward independence is gathering momentum. The time is at hand for definitive policy decisions to be made regarding the security aspects of Greenlandic nationhood. Practical policy questions will have to be addressed, both for the protection of sovereign rights and as a new states party actor in the security of the Arctic region. Absent sound security policy, independence will be compromised—or worse, may lead to open conflict. To better inform these choices, this article considers five principal defense policy options open to a newly independent Greenlandic state, including indicative costs. The analysis explores themes of more general policy application, including microstate independence and sovereignty, neutrality, and non-alignment, aspects of climate change, and the influence of microstates on regional stability.

Keywords: Security Policy, Defense Policy, Geopolitics, Greenland, Arctic Region, Independence, Conflict, Sovereignty, Microstates, Climate Change, Regional Stability.

---

[*] Acknowledgements: The author gratefully acknowledges the comments and suggestions made by Hans Peder Kirkegaard, Brigadier (AF) Jan K. Toft, and two anonymous respondents. This article represents the opinions of the author. No connection with the views of Her Majesty's Government is implied or should be inferred.

Policy Studies Yearbook 12.1: 167-213. 10.18278/psy.12.1.7
©2022 Policy Studies Organization

Una tierra ártica prometida: independencia y seguridad de Groenlandia

El Ártico no está exento ni del proceso global de descolonialización ni de los efectos geopolíticos del cambio climático. En el caso de Groenlandia (Kalaallit Nunaat), el deseo del pueblo groenlandés de una autonomía política plena de Dinamarca está impulsando un proceso secesionista que se encuentra en el umbral de la conclusión. Este movimiento tiene profundas raíces en un creciente sentido de identidad cultural groenlandesa y de confianza en la población y está fuertemente representado en el discurso político actual. A pesar de su extensión física, Groenlandia tiene una población pequeña. La independencia lo transformaría en un microestado, compartiendo muchos de los problemas económicos y de otro tipo comunes a tales organizaciones políticas, pero en una ubicación estratégica. Sin embargo, el impulso político hacia la independencia está cobrando impulso. Ha llegado el momento de que se tomen decisiones políticas definitivas con respecto a los aspectos de seguridad de la nacionalidad groenlandesa. Deberán abordarse cuestiones de política práctica, tanto para la protección de los derechos soberanos como como nuevo actor de los Estados parte en la seguridad de la región ártica. Sin una política de seguridad sólida, la independencia se verá comprometida o, lo que es peor, puede conducir a un conflicto abierto. Para informar mejor estas opciones, este artículo considera cinco opciones principales de política de defensa abiertas a un estado groenlandés recién independizado, incluidos los costos indicativos. El análisis explora temas de aplicación de políticas más generales, incluida la independencia y soberanía de los microestados, la neutralidad y la no alineación, los aspectos del cambio climático y la influencia de los microestados en la estabilidad regional.

Palabras clave: Política de seguridad, Política de defensa, Geopolítica, Groenlandia, Región Ártica, Independencia, Conflicto, Soberanía, Cambio climático, Estabilidad regional.

北極應許之地：格陵蘭的獨立與安全

北極既不受全球非殖民化進程的影響，也不受氣候變化的地緣政治影響。就格陵蘭（Kalaallit Nunaat）而言，格陵蘭人民對丹麥完全政治自治的渴望正在推動一個即將結束的分離主義進程。這一運動深深植根於人們對格陵蘭文化認同感和信心日益增強的意識，並在當前的政治話語中得到了強有力的體現。格陵蘭島雖然地域遼闊，但人口很少。獨立會將其轉變為一個微觀國家，共享此類政體共有的許多經濟和其他問題，但處於戰略位置。然而，爭取獨立的政治動力正在積聚。現在是就格陵蘭國家的安全方面做出明確政策決定的時候了。無論是為了保護主權權利還是作為北極地區安全的新締約國，都必須解決實際的政策問題。如果沒有健全的安全政策，獨立性就會受到損害——或者更糟的是，可能會導致公開衝突。為了更好地告知這些選擇，本文考慮了對新獨立的格陵蘭國家開放的五種主要國防政策選擇，包括指示性成本。該分析探討了更普遍的政策應用主題，包括微觀國家的獨立和主權、中立和不結盟、氣候變化的各個方面以及微觀國家對區域穩定的影響。

關鍵詞：安全政策、國防政策、地緣政治、格陵蘭、北極地區、獨立、衝突、主權、氣候變化、區域穩定。

This article is concerned with military security in the Arctic region and the policy options surrounding it. The knowledge gap it addresses is in two parts: first, how Greenland as a nascent Arctic state could properly discharge the responsibility of defending itself and its population. Second, the prospective effects of Greenlandic independence on Arctic geopolitical stability. It is not directed at any specific stakeholder group and has no comment to make regarding the moral rights to self-determination of a population—indigenous or otherwise—that identifies itself as a distinct community. Nor does it address any aspect of perceived or actual historical wrongdoing by any state party. Inevitably defense issues, and how they are to be addressed, will form a part of the governmental considerations of any new nation state, including the likely response by other nations.

Despite the formal cessation of the Cold War, the balance of geopolitical forces that exercise sovereignty over the Arctic remains extant.[1] In effect, the Arctic is a mediterranean ocean across which Russia confronts four NATO nations. Due to its geographical location, Greenland forms a key element in that balance—a wedge in one of the power blocs—which makes it an excellent case, pertinent to *Policy Studies Yearbook* readers, for studying the intersection of several recent and current policy issues well beyond defense and security concerns. Climate change has brought the prospect of increased availability of Arctic natural resources, and with it, concerns that these might provide focal points for conflict (Ash 2016).

---

1   For a discussion of the historic strategic tensions in the Arctic, see Huebert (2019).

To date, these fears have proven groundless and the latest assessment by the U.S. National Intelligence Council (U.S. NIC 2021, 8) anticipates a regional increase in competition, largely economic in nature, with a modest increase in the risk of miscalculation by 2040. What has not abated is the sensitivity in Russia concerning the nuclear second-strike capability of its Northern Fleet submarines based on the Kola Peninsula (Boulègue 2019, 6-8). In a future major armed conflict, air, maritime, and land assets would contest control of critical circum-Arctic regions. If the situation escalated, nuclear missiles from both sides would cross the Arctic on ballistic trajectories. Consequently, close attention is paid to any increment or reduction in regional military capability (see e.g., Poulin 2016), and the continued presence, or future absence of Greenland as a sovereign polity from the balance of power would influence the political symmetry that underpins current stability.

Shi (2019 and citations therein) identifies four principal incentives behind the demand for Greenlandic independence. First, a long-term growth in the confidence of Greenlandic people with respect to the management of domestic and foreign affairs. Citing Beukel, Jensen, and Rytter (2010 30), Shi notes the Second World War (WWII) as a turning point in this regard, as it brought contact with external actors other than Danes. Second, increased prosperity in a more diversified and efficient economy. Third, a long-term dissatisfaction with Denmark at an emotional level, relating to the colonial past. And finally, the sense of identity among indigenous Greenlandic people and a related growing national identity. However, the desire for independence is nuanced. While a poll in 2016 indicated a 64-percent majority among the Greenlandic people for full autonomy (Skydsbjerg and Turnowsky 2016), a 2017 survey revealed a 78-percent opposition if it entailed a fall in living standards (Bjerregaard 2017).

The political process leading toward independence has been protracted. A 1953 change to the Danish constitution incorporated Greenland into Denmark as a province, conferring parliamentary representation (constituteproject.org 2021). Home rule was granted in 1979 with defense, together with foreign affairs, currency, and the legal system remaining under the jurisdiction of Denmark.[2] Following a 2008 referendum (Göcke 2009), a 2009 self-rule law granted the Greenlandic government (*Naalakkersuisut*) extensive rights, including autonomy with respect to the legal system, law enforcement, the Coast Guard, and foreign affairs in matters relating exclusively to Greenland and those responsibilities transferred under the Act.[3] The powers granted to *Naalakkersuisut* did not limit the Danish authorities' constitutional responsibility and powers in foreign and security policy. However, the Act authorized Greenland to declare full independence, subject to approval by a referendum of the Greenlandic people.

Despite reservations among the Greenlandic population, the drive toward

---

2   Act No. 577 of November 29, 1978: The Greenland Home Rule Act.

3   Act No. 473 of June 12, 2009: Act on Greenland Self-Government.

independence has momentum, and the question of how the Greenland government would exercise sovereign authority with respect to defense is now becoming urgent. Greenland, together with the Faroe Islands, is assuming greater authority in foreign affairs and defense, having recently signed terms of reference with Denmark for the creation of a special contact committee to discuss matters of national and common interests (Danilov 2021). This agreement comes against the backdrop of a cabinet reshuffle in the Greenland government, in which the premier took personal charge of foreign affairs, relieving the foreign minister of those responsibilities (McGwin 2021). The action follows publication of a news article in which the minister was reported as questioning whether non-Inuit individuals should be permitted to participate in a vote on Greenland's independence (McGwin 2021). While the minister regarded the article as misinterpreting his comments (McGwin 2021), the premier's response underlines the sensitivity and currency of the independence question. At the same time, a general increase in international tension is reflected in perceptions of the Arctic as a potential future battlespace. As Faroe Islands' Prime Minister Bárður á Steig Nielsen observed: "The North Atlantic and the Arctic are increasingly in the spotlight of security policy, and therefore the active participation of the Faroe Islands and Greenland is also of growing importance" (cited in Danilov 2021).

The Defense of a New Arctic State: Key Questions

The problem of defending an independent Greenland has many conflicting elements. These may be summed up under four general headings: strategic geography, limited revenue, practical military necessity, and the prospective reaction of other states to a newly independent nation (see Figure 1). These will be examined in greater detail shortly, but in elementary terms, the cost of becoming independent entails the protection of an island whose size renders conventional defense very expensive, but whose position confers military advantage to leading powers currently in political dispute, and potentially in future military conflict. While Greenland has an areal extent of 2,166,086km,[2] the population numbers only some 56,000 (Statistics Greenland 2020). Quite apart from the many other funding demands that will be made against whatever revenue streams are available, the island stands at the frontline of climate change, and there may be significant costs in preserving extant civil infrastructure. Creating a sustainable Greenlandic economy that can support adequate public services is a task fraught with problems. Factors including the island's geography, small population, demographics, education standards, and related language issues frustrate efforts to diversify and attract investment (Andersen 2015; Einarsdóttir 2006; Tomala 2014). Thus, an autonomous Greenlandic government will need to consider the question: *What are the defense options for a newly independent Greenland?*

STRATEGIC GEOGRAPHY	REVENUE	PRACTICAL MILITARY NECESSITY
1. Critical to the defence of other nations. 2. Presents an opportunity for other nations to improve their strategic position.	1. May be challenged even to afford a sufficient capability to assert elementary sovereignty. 2. Alliance membership may require a minimum financial commitment.	1. Greenland currently lacks the expertise to establish autonomous defence capabilities. 2. Effective defence against conventional threats entails the protection of a vast battlespace.

SECURITY POLICY
1. Needs to protect minimal aspects of sovereignty.
2. Needs to be based on an analysis of plausible threats.
3. May have to rely at least in part on alliance.
4. Needs to consider the reactions of other nations, and the destabilising effects of independence.

REACTIONS OF OTHER STATES
1. US and NATO will not wish to lose strategic sensors and staging facilities on Greenland.
2. US and NATO will wish to preclude Russian and Chinese facilities and staging opportunities from Greenland.
3. Russia will view an independent Greenland as an opportunity to disrupt and disadvantage the US and NATO.

MILITARY CAPABILITIES
1. Driven by security policy.
2. Feedback to policy.

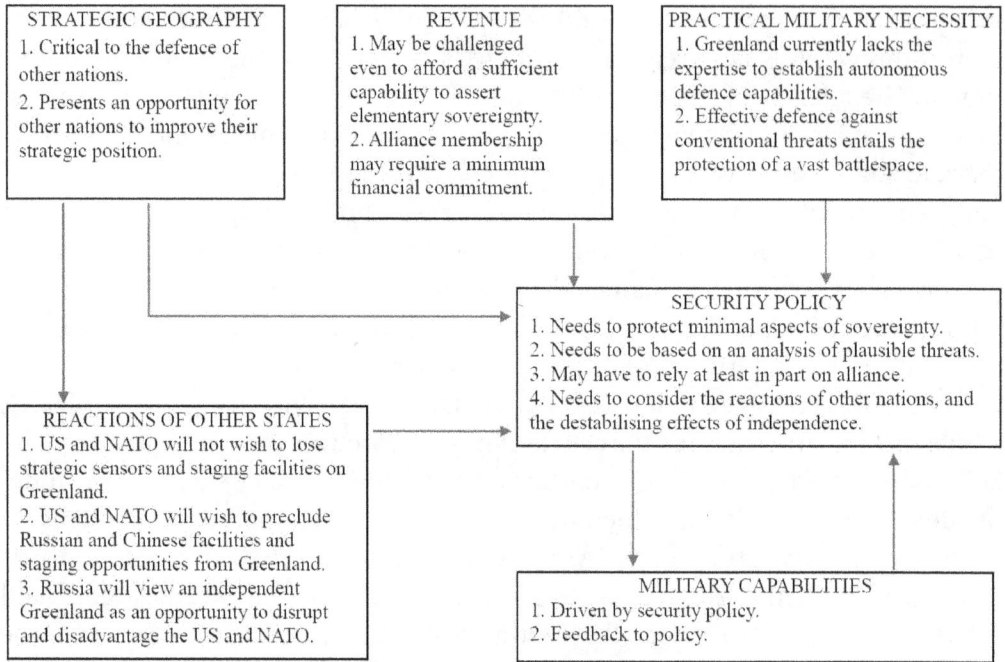

Figure 1: Key Aspects of the Greenlandic Defense Problem

The aim of this article is to explore that problem from an academically independent perspective. It does this by considering five principal defense options that may not be mutually exclusive, but in some cases are impractical for a variety of reasons. While exposing the comparative strengths and weaknesses of the options, this research is not intended as a policy proposal. Rather, it is a document for informing the creation of policy. Indeed, it may be that, on reflection, the options for a comprehensive defense policy are all so undesirable that full independence *per se* is judged by the Greenlandic people as impractical. At the same time, other nations presently contemplating full independence may consider the case of Greenland and the issues entailed in exercising sovereignty and defense useful in their own policy deliberations.

Greenland as a Scene of Historic Conflict

It is erroneous to consider Greenland as a remote Arctic island previously untouched by conflict. Records of violent clashes between the Norse and Inuit can be traced to the fourteenth century (Birket-Smith 1928, 12; Arneborg 2015, 268). WWII saw violence at the interstate level when Germany attempted to operate weather stations on Greenland's east coast (Schuster 1991). Although Denmark had capitulated, residents on the island, both Danish and Inuit, established a light raiding force using dog sledges to confront the German incursion (Howarth 1957). It was the smallest army to fight in WWII (Schuster 1991). Following a skirmish between the Greenlandic force and German personnel in 1943, one member of the patrol travelled 600 miles to warn allied forces (Schuster 1991). The United States sent aircraft to attack the weather station and the Germans withdrew (Schuster 1991). During the Cold War, Denmark established a sledge-based reconnaissance unit under Operation Resolut (Jensen, Bisgaard, and Heinrich 2013). The legacy of that organization exists today in the form of the Sirius Patrol (Jensen, Bisgaard, and Heinrich 2013); a unit of the Danish Special Operations Command that monitors the littoral to the north-east of the island—part of the largest national park in the world. The Cold War also witnessed the creation by the United States of two facilities in the north of the island: a major airfield capable of accommodating heavy bombers, and a radar station, part of the Ballistic Missile Early Warning System (BMEWS), an integrated network of sensors[4] designed to detect a nuclear attack by the Soviet Union. Relevant also to this study are the waters adjacent to Greenland. During WWII, the Denmark Strait was accessed from the north by German warships *en route* to intercept allied convoys in the Atlantic. In early 1941, the battleships *Scharnhorst* and *Gneisnau* transited the Denmark Strait as part of a mission that resulted in the capture or destruction of 22 merchant vessels (Knowles 2020). In May 1941, the battleship *Bismark*, accompanied by the heavy cruiser *Prinz Eugen* sailed south through the Strait, also intent on convoy interception (Bennett 1975, 136-149). Encountering British forces, they sank HMS Hood in an exchange of fire. British retaliation soon followed and *Bismark*, pursued into the Atlantic, was destroyed (Bennett 1975). During the Cold War the Denmark Strait formed part of the Greenland-Iceland-UK (GIUK) 'Gap' and was planted with SOSUS fixed underwater acoustic sensors to detect Soviet submarines (Østreng 1977; Rhode 2019).

The Military Significance of Greenland

The military significance of Greenland resides primarily in its location in the Arctic. Due to its massive size and flanking position to the west of both Svalbard and Iceland, Greenland forms half of the maritime choke points at the Denmark Strait in the south, and the Fram Strait to the north. Thus, it provides an opportunity to exert control over access between the Atlantic and the Greenland Sea, and from the Greenland Sea to the central Arctic Ocean. The importance of the Denmark Strait in particular was recognized during the Cold War, as it formed part of the maritime geography by which NATO hoped to preclude Soviet Russian access to the North Atlantic. In addition to the SOSUS acoustic arrays for detecting submarines, the GIUK gap would have been sown with mines.[5] With the an-

---

4   BMEWS consisted of three sites, one at Clear in Alaska, the Greenland installation, plus another radar complex at Fylingdales Moor in the UK. For a comprehensive description of the system in its initial format see Cocroft and Thomas (2003/2004, 124-133).

5   These would have been U.S. enCAPsulated TORpedo (CapTor) mines, capable of emplacement at depths of at least 1,000ft and designed to release a torpedo on receiving the acoustic signature of a target (Friedman 1989, 444-5, 456; Hartshorn 2009; Truver 2016).

ticipated increase in shipping traffic as the Arctic climate changes, this significance is likely to increase.

The geography of Greenland has military significance in two other respects. First, its position, almost equidistant between the United States and Russia, makes it an ideal location for early warning radar installations—hence its use for BMEWS and former air defense radars directed at the detection and tracking of lower altitude threats. With the introduction of hypersonic missiles by Russia, the value of Greenland as a site for warning sensors is also likely to increase (Breum 2019). Second, its location and geography offer a staging point for aircraft and ships—either for projection of U.S. or NATO power into the Arctic, or potentially, from which a non-NATO entity could direct military activity into the Arctic, North Atlantic, or indeed, against Canada or America.

Related to Greenland's military value is its strategic hard ore potential. In particular, the deposits of Uranium (see Thrane, Kalvig, and Keulen 2014, and citations therein) and rare earths (Andersen 2015; Tomala 2014).

Defense and Sovereignty

The relationship between sovereignty and defense is a complex one. In this article, full independence is considered as the *de facto* capacity by a Greenlandic government to exercise all sovereign rights in respect to state activities. This includes ultimate control and responsibility for the constitution, foreign relations, and defense. While this study is not primarily an examination of sovereignty as a theoretical political subject, it is recognized that it is not a simple phenomenon to define. While Philpott's (2001) definition, "supreme authority within a territory," represents a useful starting point, Krasner (1999) is probably more accurate in recognizing that the term 'sovereignty' has different meanings in different contexts. Krasner notes what has come to be recognized as Westphalian sovereignty—the right to act without interference from other polities—as one of the meanings commonly ascribed to sovereignty.

Defense is one of the principal responsibilities of a sovereign[6] (Smith 1776). While the method by which a sovereign entity undertakes the defense of the nation is its own business, an effective defense forms part of the ability to exercise other sovereign authority, including the sole right to enforce laws over a nation's citizens, control its natural resources, environment, and economy, and the means to exclude non-citizens from its territory, territorial waters, and airspace. At the same time, defense is a demonstration of sovereignty in itself—a function of government that acts as an underpinning to a nation's diplomatic standing. Thus, an inadequate defense risks not only loss of exclusive control over its citizenry and territory, but an affront to its stature as a state party.

---

6   According to Adam Smith (1776), the first duty.

State parties that are internationally recognized as such have two basic methods by which they undertake national defense: first, they can fund the recruitment, training, and equipping of their own armed forces. Second, as internationally recognized polities, they can enter into defense agreements with other nations. Such agreements might take many forms, from simple treaties under which intelligence is shared, through joint training exercises, to mutual defense pacts and, in some cases, the delegation of military defense in its entirety to another nation. In practice, many nations adopt aspects of both the self-defense and treaty approaches.

Cost: How Much Defense Can an Independent Greenland Afford?

Having outlined the key issues underlying any choice the government of a newly independent Greenland may wish to make (Figure 1) and explained both the history of conflict on the island and the manner in which defense relates to sovereignty, it is necessary to introduce the problem of cost. It is not inappropriate to ask: *How independent can Greenland afford to be?*

Defense economics is a complex subject. However, despite the many variables involved in making procurement judgements, it remains essential to provide at least an indication of what Greenland could *not* afford. The first point to make is that legally, Greenland could proceed to full independence without revenue streams to replace the annual grant currently made by the Danish government. The loss of that income would certainly inflict serious shortfalls in the amenities available to the Greenlandic people but, ultimately, the choice is more political than economic. As Wilson (2017) notes with reference to Chapter 8 of the 2009 Self-Government Act,[7] it requires the agreement of both the Greenlandic and Danish governments to conclude full independence, and the endorsement of a referendum in Greenland. She makes special reference to section (4) of that chapter: "Independence for Greenland shall imply that Greenland assumes sovereignty over the Greenland territory" (Wilson 2017). Wilson emphasizes that this part of the agreement is an acknowledgement by both sides that independence presupposes Greenland's willingness and ability to take sovereign responsibility for the territory. This is significant because it places *sovereignty* and the capacity to exercise that authority at the center of the independence debate.

Second, for the purpose of this analysis, Greenland will be regarded as a microstate, having a population of less than a million persons.[8] As such, it shares the problems of most other microstates in terms of its capacity to generate revenue. Aspects of defense spending and indicative costs are introduced as the analysis now

---

7   Act No. 473 of June 12, 2009: *Act on Greenland Self-Government.*

8   This classification is not in any respect intended as pejorative. As Gubb (2000, and citations therein) indicates, attempts to classify nation states by size, either of land area, population, or GDP, have not proven straightforward. Several commentators appear to agree that 'microstate' may be used to refer to a nation state of less than one million persons without misleading complexity (Gubb 2000).

considers the various defense options from which a Greenlandic government may wish to choose. Example costs for specific security capabilities appear in Table 3.

Option 1: The 'Do Nothing' Approach:
The Demilitarised Arctic State Model

> The guarantees of protection of their sovereignty embodied in the UN Charter are, at least in the present state of the world, sadly illusory so far as small states are concerned.
>
> (Diggines 1985)

Rasmussen (2019) notes a tendency for Greenlandic politicians to play down or 'de-securitize' defense issues, and this has been attributed to a desire to prioritize independence as a political goal, rather than facing an objective consideration of the defense issues that such a state of sovereignty would entail. Given the island's strategic geography and the challenging defense problem it constitutes, a government that could not defend a newly independent Greenland would expose its population to unreasonable risk. Should it be confronted with any one of many potential security emergencies, it might also find itself rapidly bleeding political credibility.

Of course, there are nations that have no military forces as such. These may be territories that have been demilitarized by a victorious power following a conflict, or that are simply unable to afford defense forces, in which case a more powerful state provides military security. Costa Rica is an example, having formally disbanded its military in 1948 (see Adams 2018). Yet its police are legally empowered to protect territorial integrity (Adams 2018, 5), it operates a Special Forces unit, the *Unidad Especial de Intervencion*, an air unit and a coastguard (Adams 2018; Kassebaum 1990). Macias (2018/2019) notes no fewer than 36 states that have no regular military force. She bases her report on the CIA World Factbook, and some of the entries in the list are open to question.[9] While it is striking that such a high percentage of the world's nation states and dependencies—15 percent—should have no military organization and resources of their own, they represent only 0.2 percent of the global population. Moreover, having no military is not the same as being undefended. In fact, defense agreements with militarily stronger entities, whether formalized as treaties or otherwise, have mutual benefit. A pertinent example is that of Iceland. A NATO member with no armed forces *per se*, its strategic position is such that other nations provide defense support, partic-

---

9   For example, while the UK certainly defends the Falkland Islands, the CIA make no mention of the Falkland Islands Defence Force, a local volunteer unit funded by the Falkland Islands Government (Bound 2012, 145-153; Tossini 2021). Another curious inclusion is Svalbard, which is part of Norway and not a dependency. Norway received sovereignty of Svalbard by the Treaty of 1920, under the terms of which, the archipelago may not be militarised. However, that does not mean that it may not be defended should it be subject to invasion or any other foreign military action.

ularly deployments of interceptor aircraft for air defense.[10] The advantage to NATO is access to strategic geography and its denial to a potential adversary. At the same time, Iceland's NATO membership—or rather, the threat to leave the alliance—has enabled it to exert political pressure to change maritime law to protect the fisheries on which it depends (Jónsson 1982).

A policy of pacifism in its strictest interpretation is difficult to identify among modern nation states. Some states, for example, Japan, have had a constitutional disbarment from choosing warfare as a political option[11]: a situation imposed by the Allied powers at the end of WWII. Yet Japan today has modern and capable armed forces. Perhaps the clearest example of the fate of polities that practice pacifism in a true sense is that of Moriori, inhabitants of the Chatham Islands, who were almost annihilated in 1835 by invading Māori, who killed, enslaved, and cannibalized them (Brett 2015; Miah 2020; Waitangi Tribunal 2001/2016).

Option 2: Neutrality

We have always been a peaceful nation, and our role in the world community should be to spread the message of peace. We must not participate in wars.

(Ane Hansen, reported in Turnowsky, 2017)

Neutrality and demilitarization are distinct political positions. The first implies a deliberate policy of non-involvement in a dispute between other nations. It does not of itself imply that a nation has no military capability, while the latter certainly does. Political neutrality guarantees neither peace nor freedom from invasion. History is littered with examples of states that claimed neutrality in order to avoid war and were simply engulfed or taken over by the belligerents. A claim to political neutrality did not prevent Britain and the United States from occupying Iceland during WWII, enabling allied aircraft to provide support to convoys *en route* to Europe, and preventing Germany from gaining a foothold.[12] Considering more recent examples, the United States has intervened militarily in a number of nations which, as Chomsky (1992) notes, pose neither a significant military threat nor a source of important economic resources, including Grenada, Guatemala, Laos, and Nicaragua.

---

10 See for example Allied Air Command Public Affairs Office (2020), Einarsdóttir (2021), and Vandiver (2020).

11 See Article 9 of the Constitution of Japan of 1946 (see also Prime Minister of Japan and his Cabinet n.d.).

12 Following the imposition of a defensive British military presence in May 1940, Canadian reinforcements arrived in Iceland in June (Walling 2012, 29-30). The Icelandic government attempted to persuade the United States to declare Iceland part of the Western hemisphere, and therefore subject to the protection of the Monroe doctrine (Fairchild 1990). They were persuaded to invite the United States to garrison the island, relieving the British personnel in spring 1942 (Walling 2012, 29-30).

History suggests that effective neutrality appears to have a number of elements. First, a strong defense, or at least a defense that is too militarily inconvenient for major belligerent powers to expend effort in defeating. Second, the vested political or economic interests of the major belligerents. Thus Switzerland—a former supplier of mercenary soldiers from the fifteenth to the seventeenth centuries to other nations in the form of the Landsknechts—has extensive armed forces, including hard-skinned vehicles and combat aircraft, and a mountainous geography lending itself to defense (ArmedForces.eu 2019; McPhee 1983/1984). Switzerland also extended its political neutrality to accommodating the finances of Nazi Germany, providing the sole source of much needed foreign exchange toward the end of WWII (McComas 2016). Had the outcome of the war not favored the Allies, such economic convenience would probably not have prevented its invasion—German plans for events following the defeat of the Allies included Operation Tannenbaum, an invasion of Switzerland with some territories to be allocated to fascist Italy (Weinberg 1999).

Sweden declared an official policy of non-belligerency during WWII and provided assistance to both Germany and the Allies (Rai 2017; Wahlbäck 1998). Nonetheless, fearing an Allied invasion of Norway, Hitler had his military consider a preventive strike against Sweden (Wahlbäck 1998). During the Cold War, secret preparations were made to receive NATO aid in the event of a Soviet attack, but there were concerns that such support would arrive too late to influence a ground war (Åselius 2005). Substantial defense forces were developed, including the procurement of combat aircraft, although these forces were allowed to diminish following the collapse of the Soviet Union (Åselius 2005). More recently, the Swedish government has agreed a defense pact with Denmark, Estonia, Finland, Iceland, Latvia, Lithuania, the Netherlands, Norway, and the UK, under which it will contribute to the Joint Expeditionary Force (JEF) (JEF 2021). The JEF is designed to be able to respond to aggression including sub-threshold[13] incidents (JEF 2021), and its establishment indicates a renewed concern with recent Russian behavior on the international stage.

Since Greenland is unlikely to be able to afford a strong self-defense—or indeed even a defense against most conventional threats—neutrality does not appear to be a viable strategy. This leads naturally to consideration of the next option.

Option 3: Self-Defense

In the following discussion, it has been assumed as a starting point that the government of a newly independent Greenland will not wish to spend much more

---

13 "Sub-threshold activity does not seek decisive conflict, but is a way that adversaries alter the balance of advantage in order to achieve their objectives without the material, financial and social cost of armed conflict. It is orchestrated by hostile state and non-state adversaries to undermine security, the integrity of democracies, public safety, reputation or economic prosperity" (JEF 2021).

than the average indicated by the global military burden—2.4 percent of GDP[14] (Da Silva *et al.* 2021). This suggests an annual budget of approximately USD 71.6m (2019 figures). With many calls on its income, the government may wish to spend substantially less, but the figure serves as a tool for analysis. In this context, it is worth noting that Iceland, a state that formally eschews a military of its own, has pledged to adhere to the minimum baseline defense budget of 2 percent of GDP enjoined by NATO.[15] Iceland's defense budget for 2019 was USD 17.7m, of which the largest proportion was allocated to the Coast Guard and Keflavik Airport (see Ćirić 2019, and citations therein).

Greenland is potentially vulnerable to air and sea attack against its key economic assets. There are two deep water ports, one at Thule and the other at Nuuk. An air defense capability, at least to protect the ports, would be desirable. In the case of Thule, it may be expected that the United States would provide the appropriate protection for both the port and the other military facilities located there. To safeguard Nuuk, a specimen cost for a single air defense missile battery is some $US 800m - 950m[16] and, while such a cost might be spread over a number of years, such an asset would appear to be simply unaffordable.

Similarly, if a potential enemy wished to ruin the Greenlandic economy, or bring crushing political pressure on the government, it might do so by mining port approaches, thereby crippling the movement of heavy freight. Such an attack might be conducted in a relatively covert fashion, by using a vessel of opportunity to sow the mines, a form of attack exemplified by actions taken by Iraq during the second Gulf War (O'Flaherty 2019). Defense against such an attack would entail the deployment of a mine sweeping or mine hunting capability.[17] Mine sweeping aims to clear weapons by severing the tethers of buoyant mines, or safely triggering bottom-laid mines by mimicking the acoustic or magnetic signatures of ships. Sweeping platforms include surface vessels, drones, and helicopter-towed buoyant sledges. Some mines have sophisticated triggers that react to combinations of acoustic and magnetic stimuli, rendering them resistant to basic sweeping techniques. Others may lie buried in the seabed and require sonar detection before a demolition charge can be set to destroy them. A specimen cost for a mine-hunting sonar may be gleaned from the Type 2093, developed for the British *Sandown* class

---

14 This figure might have been assessed in many ways, and merely represents a point of departure. For comparative information on island nations defence spending, see SIPRI fact sheet in Da Silva and others (2021).

15 For the history and other aspects of the 2-percent guideline, see Dowdy (2017) and NATO (2014/ 2018). In addition to committing capabilities, NATO membership requires a contribution for alliance budgets and programmes (NATO 2021).

16 This is a specimen cost for a single MIM-104 Patriot missile battery, derived from two reports of sales to Poland and Sweden (i24 2017; Trevithick 2018). In the case of the Polish transaction, the missiles were of Israeli manufacture, and 10 percent of the cost of the American versions (i24 2017).

17 For a comprehensive account of mine technology and countermeasures see Friedman (1989, 444-6, 478) and Hartmann and Truver (1991).

minehunter at a reported (1989) cost of £83m.[18] This suggests a notional unit price of USD 22.1m (2019), which would not include operating platform, maintenance, or training. Friedman (1989) notes the development of relatively cheap improvised systems provided by the United States to Vietnam. However, these were simple noise-making and magnetic field-generating systems designed by personnel who knew the type of mines they were attempting to defeat.

Military and Security Capabilities Exercised by Small Nations

> "The Danish defense today is not the actual defense of Greenland. Should there arise a real threat to our country from hostile powers, it is defended by the United States. It is the reality all know but nobody discusses."
>
> (Breum 2018, cited in Rasmussen 2019)

The basis for a capability-based national defense plan is an estimate of the threat (Singer 1958). The population of any state, including those with a relatively small GDP, will expect its government to protect them against terrorist attacks. An anti-terrorist capability implies the availability of some form of armed unit within the *Kalaallit Nunaanni Politiit* trained in the tactical application of firearms in terrorist situations. A state fails in its duty if it cannot address an incident such as the 2019 attack on mosques in Christchurch, New Zealand, in which a gunman killed 51 people (Battersby and Ball 2019). In addition to dealing with the gunman, an improvised explosive device (IED) also had to be disarmed and suspected IEDs dealt with (Ashford, Heron, and Kaldas 2020, 12).

A government will wish also to be able to exert sovereign control over its Exclusive Economic Zone (EEZ). In the case of Greenland, those waters represent not only the asset of a sovereign entity whose authority and status would be affronted by Illegal, Unreported, and Unregulated (IUU) fishing, but also a valuable revenue stream. That implies at least some maritime intervention vessels, since fisheries laws cannot be enforced without boarding for the inspection of fishing gear and documentation. Remote sensing measures, by satellite tracking or drones, may assist in covering the large areas involved, but cannot on their own provide sufficient information. Moreover, the technology is expensive. A specimen cost for an Israeli drone in which the Canadian government showed interest, that was capable of monitoring large areas of the high north, was $CDN 36.16m (Baerson 2021).

These are measures against sub-state level threats. However, both terrorism and access to fishing grounds unauthorized by a coastal state may be state supported activities. Regarding the latter, it should not be forgotten that nations on occasion send military vessels to support fishing vessels flagged to their jurisdiction operating in the waters of other coastal states. In the past this has resulted

---

18 This included development and the delivery if two preprototypes and 10 production units (Friedman 1989, 470).

in violent confrontations, including clashes between NATO allies. In the so-called Turbot War of 1994-6, Spain sent patrol vessels to protect its fishing vessels, which Canada claimed were fishing illegally. The Canadian prime minister authorized Canadian forces to fire if the Spanish vessels uncovered their guns (Gough 2009, 70). Britain sent military vessels to protect fishing vessels in disputed waters adjacent to Iceland on no less than three occasions: the so-called Cod Wars. Icelandic patrol vessels towed trawl cutting gear to impede fishing operations and were in collision with Royal Navy vessels (Ingimundarson 2003).

One devastating—and relatively deniable—form of attack would be to use cyber warfare against state government and economic institutions. A recent case involved a ransomware attack on the government of Nunavut (George 2020). The Nunavut government elected not to pay, and the incident took over five months to resolve (George 2020). A cyber defense capability would appear to be fundamental for any nation state.

In addition to these elementary constabulary functions, governments of small states often find benefit in sending government personnel in support of UN and NATO operations. In addition to the political recognition such commitments garner among the community of nations, there are other benefits including: the sharing of professional skills and up-to-date practice; the establishment of desk-level contacts; and the exchange of intelligence information. For UN operations, the cost of the equipment owned and brought by a state to an operation (Contingent Owned Equipment) and some other expenses are reimbursed by the UN (United Nations Peacekeeping, undated). Once again, Iceland is an example of an Arctic nation that has been one nation sending government personnel to NATO operations, despite having no established military *per se* (Icelandic Government 2018).

Cyber Defense

Consideration of cyber defense follows naturally from discussion of the elementary protection a population will expect from a polity, but the nature and threat posed by the problem merits a separate section. Much of the cyber threat is criminal activity directed against private individuals and organizations. Greenland is increasingly dependent on digital infrastructure and, to a great extent, the first-line protection of critical economic infrastructure may be undertaken by the various private sector companies and organizations of which it is comprised, particularly banking and telecommunications vendors. For example, the Bank of Greenland (2021, 67) reports a capability to restore customer-oriented temporary service following an IT outage within one day. However, an autonomous Greenland government will have to protect itself and legislative plans are already being drawn up for that purpose (Turnowsky 2019).

In the military security context, cyber assaults may be launched by nation states, including third parties acting on a state's behalf in order to provide deniability, or by terrorists or criminals whose motives include avarice, revenge, or hubris. Assaults may be designed to steal data and/or overwhelm or otherwise incapacitate computer systems. A classic example of a cyber attack launched against an Arctic government entity was the ransomware attack that paralyzed Nunavut government activity recently (George 2020).

Key functions of any cyber defense system include provisions for continuity of service, data protection, and the denial of external control. This implies not only the possession of a functional strategy, but the availability of a 24/7 incident response capability and secure data replication. An example of the latter may be found in the Estonian 'data embassy' project—data repositories set up in friendly nations, designed to ensure the digital continuity of the state, even if its territorial sovereignty is compromised (Areng 2014, 8). Other benefits accrue from establishing a center of excellence for coordinating cyber security, or at least collaborating with other nations in sharing expertise in this subject.

The relative vulnerability of Greenland to cyber assault is a mixture deriving largely from its geographic circumstances. The underwater cable connections are relatively vulnerable, and their general positions are open-source information (TeleGeography 2021). With appropriate underwater equipment, finding and cutting them would not be particularly challenging for a determined adversary who wished to make a political point, or support a military operation. Although Huawei Marine Systems, which was jointly involved in laying the cables, is reported to have sold its underwater cable business to another Chinese company (Savov 2019), it is conceivable that software vulnerabilities remain in the system. A certain resilience exists in the Greenland telecommunications system in the form of the number of VHF radiotelephones owned by Greenlanders.[19]

One further point that needs to be made is that if an independent Greenland wishes to become a member of NATO, then it will be required to align with coalition standards for cyber defense, including policy and a coordinating agency. As with every other aspect of defense activity, the establishment of such facilities requires expertise, for which Greenland may have to recruit outside its own borders, and investment, which will place an additional burden on scarce resources.

Option 4: Alliance

The coalition parties stand firm, our country as an independent state must be a member of NATO.

(The Coalition Agreement of 2018 between Siumut, Atassut, Partii Naleraq and Nunatta Qitornai, para 341.
Translation in Rasmussen 2019, 10)

---

19   It is difficult to obtain precise subscriber numbers. One open source (Watkins 2021) suggests that 'many' Greenlanders own a radio/telephone.

Should Greenland wish to join NATO, there will be certain reciprocal expectations in addition to the cyber defense arrangements alluded to above. These include minimal funding levels, and overall defense policy alignment with the precepts of the alliance. There may also be other contributions that Greenland could make. For example, by providing a venue for training in cold weather survival, land warfare, aircraft operation including the use of ice runways, and a location for tactical development.

In choosing an alliance with a larger state as part of its defense strategy, a smaller nation is choosing, at least to some extent, to share any future conflict that stronger power engages in. Thus, if the stronger power or alliance places military resources such as fixed installations, troops, aircraft, or vehicles on the territory of the small state, an enemy of the protector force may attack those resources, potentially inflicting collateral casualties on the population and harm to domestic infrastructure.

There may also be political consequences. The protector polity may insist on judicial oversight over its own troops, thereby visibly diminishing the sovereignty of the small nation. Consider, for example, the 1951 defense agreement drawn up between Denmark and the United States.[20] In Article VIII, the issue of jurisdiction is made explicit:

> The Government of the United States of America shall have the right to exercise exclusive jurisdiction over those defense areas in Greenland for which it is responsible under Article II (3), and over any offenses which may be committed in Greenland by the aforesaid military or civilian personnel or by members of their families, as well as over other persons within such defense areas except Danish nationals, it being understood, however, that the Government of the United States of America may turn over to the Danish authorities in Greenland for trial any person committing an offense within such defense areas. (Defense of Greenland 1951)

Such arrangements may lead to discontent in the host nation when the behavior of visiting military personnel falls short of expected standards. Ultimately, however, a small nation is likely to have to choose from whom it accepts a military safeguard and, indeed, may have simultaneous defense agreements with more than one nation or alliance. Thus, a Greenlandic government might elect to join the JEF in addition to NATO, to provide an assurance that it could avail itself of a response to a sub-threshold threat.

A final point in relation to the establishment of defense alliances relates to procedural limitations. To take the example of NATO, its enlargement is gov-

---

20 Defense of Greenland: Agreement Between the United States and the Kingdom of Denmark, April 27, 1951.

erned by a set of rules, as noted in its 'Study on NATO Enlargement' (NATO 1995, chap. 1 para. 6): "States which have ethnic disputes or external territorial disputes, including irredentist claims, or internal jurisdictional disputes must settle those disputes by peaceful means in accordance with OSCE principles. Resolution of such disputes would be a factor in determining whether to invite a state to join the Alliance." Thus, if Russia, consistent with its view concerning NATO and the Arctic (Barbin 2021) chose to foment discord in a newly independent Greenland, such dissent might obstruct the nation's entry into the alliance.

Option 5: Post-Independence Alliance with Denmark

Related to the option of alliance, one strategy not often discussed would be to form a post-independence alliance with Denmark. This approach could provide significant benefits to all parties, alleviating many of the issues confronting a nascent Arctic state, smoothing the transition to the exercise of full sovereignty, and providing a secure foundation for NATO membership—if that is what Greenlanders choose. As Greenland transitioned to full independence, Danish forces would continue to play a role as alliance guests, the conditions of their presence and authority to act defined by a defense agreement between Nuuk and Copenhagen. Greenland would achieve autonomy, without as material a burden on its stretched resources, and there would not be a significant hiatus in defense capability and potential insecurity.

Under a defense agreement with Denmark, the essentials of the sovereignty role would be retained by Greenland, with counterterrorism, fisheries protection, and most search and rescue responsibilities falling under the operational control of Nuuk. The operational control of Danish forces would be exercised by local Danish commanders in accordance with overall procedures agreed in advance with the Greenlandic government. The presence and role of the Danish forces would form part of Denmark's contribution to NATO.

Danish forces would continue to provide defense capabilities, in a location in which they already possess experience. Although these capabilities would have to be the subject of a defense agreement, potential examples include:

1. Home guard training, for an organization broadly similar to the Canadian Rangers, to enable it to undertake sovereignty patrols, early warning, and search and rescue duties.

2. A special forces contingent, able to advise a Greenlandic counter-terrorist unit in cases of state-sponsored terrorism and provide key point defense during heightened periods of tension.

3. Air assets for the protection of Greenlandic airspace, NATO operations, and exercises. These might include combat aircraft such as fighters, reconnaissance aircraft, maritime patrol aircraft, helicopters, drones, and associ-

ated ground support personnel and equipment. Involvement in search and rescue operations would be at the invitation of the Greenland government.

4. Naval assets for defense against maritime threats to Greenland and for NATO operations and exercises. This would not include fisheries protection. Involvement in search and rescue operations would be at the invitation of the Greenland government.

Greenlandic Independence and the Prospective Outcomes for Other Arctic States

Irrespective of the desire of an independent Greenlandic government to live at peace, that peace is contingent on the behavior of other nations. The present political trend is for Arctic nations to follow the rule-based order, and the concerns regarding inter-state conflict arising in the region as a result of climate change have yet to be borne out. Yet there remains the possibility that conflict may spread *to* the Arctic from superpower engagement elsewhere. Moreover, the very process of Greenland becoming independent brings potential political instability to the Arctic. The problem has three key parts (see Figure 1): first, the island of Greenland is almost equidistant between Russia and the United States. It is thus either a buffer or a potential base of operations for one of the belligerents in any future conflict. Second, its geography is critical in the creation of two maritime choke points in such a confrontation. Third, the country is vast, but with a relatively modest GDP. It could not afford armed forces of any scale of its own. A newly independent Greenland represents an opportunity or threat to Arctic superpowers, or indeed, an opportunity for a near-Arctic state, as China regards itself.

The United States has certainly demonstrated a strong wish to influence aspects of Greenlandic affairs—including an offer to purchase the island. While the offer may have caused reactions varying from humor to offence, there are historical precedents. Three of these cases concern Arctic territories. First, the sale of Rupert's Land by the Hudson's Bay Company to Canada in 1870 secured a vast area that drains into Hudson's Bay, including areas to the north of the Arctic Circle (Hudson's Bay Company 2016; Smith 2006). The second case was the 1947 sale of the Jäniskoski-Niskakoski area by Finland to the Soviet Union, which formed part of its war reparations (Finlex n.d.; Katajala 2010, 107). The area was of interest to the Soviet Union due to its potential for hydroelectric power (Katajala 2010). However, the third, and perhaps the most relevant case of an Arctic territorial sale was that of Alaska by Russia to the United States in 1867 (Bolkhovitinov 1996; Mitchell 1976). It had become evident to Russia that it could not defend the territory against potential incursions from either the British Empire or an expanding United States (Bolkhovitinov 1996).

In this history of Arctic territory purchase and occupation, two related factors are predominant in the behavior of state parties: cost and practical military necessity. If a nation cannot afford to defend a territory, or is unable to do so, it may elect to sell it, as Russia did with Alaska. However, if the acquisition of a territory by a hostile party threatens a nation or alliance, it may well respond with the exercise of force in denying the use of the area to the enemy. Thus, the Allied powers occupied Iceland and the Faeroes during WWII (Walling 2012; Fairchild 1990; Miller 2003). The United States would, of course, prefer to retain its facilities at Thule[21] and while, at some expense and inconvenience, these might be repositioned in north-east Canada, it would likely react negatively to the idea of a polity with interests inimical to its own, such as Russia or China, being allowed to position its own military resources in Greenland. Such facilities might range from a capability for collecting intelligence (anything from a ship in harbor to a building housing a company communications station), to a staging base for special forces, or in the worst case, a depot vessel berthed in a deep-water harbor capable of supporting visiting submarines. One of the problems associated with the governance of a newly independent Greenland is that facilities such as runways, docks, and buildings associated with major economic investment, provide potential military assets in time of war. The United States is unlikely to be content with a Chinese or Russian investment in Greenland that provides either nation with a prospective base from which it can conduct operations against either its facilities in Thule (if the government of Greenland consents to their continuance), or indeed in such close proximity to the continental United States. In this regard, it is worth noting the actions of the Danish government to block the acquisition of the abandoned Grønnedal naval base by the Hong Kong-based General Nice Company in 2016, and its funding for Greenland's airports in 2018 in reaction to bids by the China Communications Construction Company to build them (Dams, Van Schaik and Stoetman 2020, 34).

In terms of opportunity, Russia has made no secret of its view that NATO has no place in the Arctic (Barbin 2021). An independent Greenland that withdrew support for NATO operations would drive a physical wedge between the coalition territories that confront its authority across the Arctic. Beyond the cost and inconvenience of relocating the ballistic missile detection radar at Thule, any diminishment of NATO's capacity to close the Denmark Strait to submarines would strengthen Russia's position.

China also has been open in the pursuit of its ambitions to exert influence in the Arctic.[22] China now has observer status on the Arctic Council, and has spent lavishly on polar research, commissioning two icebreakers and establishing a sci-

---

21 The radar at Thule forms part of a system that has an important civil function in monitoring the position and trajectories of space debris (Console 2019, 39; Dickson undated). Objects may damage spacecraft with civil functions or re-enter the Earth's atmosphere without completely burning up before impact. Providing territorial access for the Thule radar facility would be a contribution by the Greenlandic government to the global community.

22 For a comprehensive overview, see Dams, Van Schaik, and Stoetman (2020).

entific station on Svalbard. It has expanded its diplomatic representation, with a large embassy building in Reykjavik, and invested in land purchase and other business ventures in the Arctic. Its wish to use the Northern Sea Route is evident in its dealings with Russia. Augmenting its scientific and political bases in the Arctic with a military base, in particular a port with Arctic access, would provide China with a prospective means of protecting its maritime traffic in the region. An opportunity to position and sustain ballistic missile submarine operations in the Arctic or north Atlantic would bring more targets in the United States into missile range. Additionally, in the case of submarines operating in the Arctic, they could do so from waters that offer the protection of the pack ice.[23] Such a move would counter American presence in the Indo-Pacific, enhancing China's retaliatory capability and splitting U.S. military resources by opening a second front. This would confer not merely an advantage during open conflict, but an enhanced deterrent at a global level.

Greenlandic Independence and Geopolitical Stability

Having considered the potential outcomes of Greenlandic independence for Arctic and 'near' Arctic nations, a key question that follows is whether such a change would influence geopolitical stability. As Niou and others (1989) note, stability has more than one meaning in international relations. For clarity, this article follows the definition of Bragg (2011, 36) in taking geopolitical stability to constitute "a state of relations among nations that is generally consistent with and conducive to change and progress without having to revert to initiating a war with global or regional proportions." Since 'war' is a complex phenomenon to define,[24] this analysis substitutes the concept of 'armed conflict between nation states.' By this definition, stability and war are mutually incompatible circumstances, and the problem becomes one of identifying possible conditions in which Greenlandic independence leads states to risk armed conflict in addressing their grievances and ambitions. But if geopolitical instability is synonymous, or at least correlatable, with causes of war, the problem of reliably identifying such causes appears daunting. As Bueno de Mesquita (1981, 2) observes:

> Despite the attention of such intellectual giants as Spinoza, Rousseau, Kant, and Clausewitz, we know little more about international conflict today than was known to Thucydides four hundred years before Christ. Indeed, the failure to identify a generally accepted theory of war leads some observers to conclude that scientific explanations of such conflicts are not possible.

---

23   For a comprehensive account of the issues associated with Arctic submarine warfare, see Compton-Hall (1988, 173-185).

24   For example, the Correlates of War project adopts a typology of wars based on factors such as number of battle-related fatalities and time (Sarkees n.d.).

Thus, the lack of a general theory of war causation would appear to be a severe impediment in understanding or predicting such instability. Yet Bueno de Mesquita (1981, 2) has a further contribution to make. His endeavor is "to present systematically derived, lawlike statements about war and other serious disputes and to explore the relationship between history and those statements." His solution is to devise an expected utility-based approach that assesses the agency and preferences of key actors in the conflict decision process (Churchman 2005, 153-155; Bueno de Mesquita 1997). Feder (2002) reports remarkable predictive capacity in tests of Bueno de Mesquita's algorithms made in government service.

It is not the purpose of this study to predict future armed conflict in Greenland: merely to identify whether the issues associated with independence are likely to result in a *less stable* geopolitical situation in the Arctic; in other words, if Greenland undertakes the transition to full independence are nation states *more likely* to go to war? To be clear, Bueno de Mesquita's (1981) model considers the specific circumstances of senior and influential decision makers in potentially belligerent nations and the utility of violent conflict as a decision option. Consequently, the potential outcome of the model fluctuates over time with the dynamic interrelation of the key actors. But he is clear also that a critical feature of the analysis is the salience—importance—of the casus belli to each of those actors (Bueno de Mesquita 1997). While the degree of salience may differ with each actor, we may identify themes that have remained of consistently high salience to the collective leaderships of particular nations. We may infer that in the absence of such highly salient factors, stability is more likely.

For the United States, one factor of persistent and high salience is ensuring that a potential belligerent is denied a potential base of operations in close proximity to the continental United States. This priority is satisfied if Greenland hosts no such threat. Referring back to the previous section, China will not wish to surrender any potential monopoly on rare earths and would wish to enjoy the political influence investment in mining would confer. Such an industrial facility could have military potential; that is, it may be 'dual-use.' More directly, China may also favor a base from which to project maritime power into the Arctic, and has shown itself adept at acquiring access to strategically important locations, as it has for example in Sri Lanka (Patrick 2017; Singh 2018). Russia would prefer to see NATO's position in the Arctic fractured and, as in the Ukraine, has shown itself proficient in the use of overt and clandestine military forces in securing its strategic position. Given its modest population size and history, Greenland does not have an extensive pool of expertise from which to recruit its diplomatic corps. This, added to its need to attract investment in order to establish a stable economy, renders it vulnerable to foreign influence—both beneficial and malign. To this may be added the distressing tendency for small nations with poorly developed political and legal systems to be plagued by corruption.

Potential military threats in Greenland are likely to be matters of high salience to any American polity, and thus a source of instability. At the time of writing, commentators in Russia suggest supporting and exploiting independence as a mechanism for diminishing NATO Arctic presence, both within and beyond Greenland (see Goble 2021). In that regard, a post-independence combination of limited Greenlandic diplomatic representation and economic need may give rise to circumstances that undermine stability. However, membership of NATO or other alliance(s) may redress shortfalls not only in defense capability, but in diplomatic presence also.

Balancing Military Options: A Capability-based Approach

Traditionally, nations have founded defense planning largely on the basis of threat, a concept described formally by Singer (1958) as a combination of the Estimated Intent of a foreign power, and that power's Estimated Capability. An alternative is to approach the problem of national security on the basis of risk and view the potential for military and terrorist attack among the many hazards, both natural and anthropogenic, that confront a nation. The UK is one of the nations to draw up a national security risk assessment,[25] and considering the limited resources available to a newly independent Greenlandic state, it might be helpful to take such an overview, particularly since, as an Arctic state, there are likely to be expensive infrastructure costs associated with climate change.

It might be tempting to assume that once such a listing is drawn up, risks associated with national defense can be relegated to a lower order of priority as a matter of political expediency. That view is an error and neglects elementary risk management practice. A risk that is unlikely but catastrophic in eventuation is not ignored. Rather, general management practice for such a risk is by sharing—in military terms, forming an alliance. However, alliance is not cheap defense. It may be an agreement of necessity for a small nation, but as noted earlier, it comes with obligations. Of course, the establishment of such an alliance may in itself signal independence from Denmark, not merely because it is the act of a sovereign, but because it may constitute a pivot from the Nordic to the Anglophone world.

Defense planning has developed in recent years toward a capability-based approach (De Spiegeleire 2011; Stojković et al. 2016). Such a process has been adopted by several NATO nations and incorporates consideration of threat and available resources to devise an appropriate national defense strategy (De Spiegeleire 2011). Following such a method, the remaining discussion is intended as a starting point for an intelligent debate regarding the security aspects of Greenlandic full independence. As such, it is not a comprehensive capability-based analysis per se.

Further to the earlier comments regarding Greenland's military significance, it is possible to devise a set of threat scenarios to form the basis of defense and security planning. For convenience, these have been divided between two ta-

---

25 See, for example, HM Government (2015) Annex A, which is a summary. The source document itself is classified.

bles. Neither table is designed to be exhaustive. Nor is either table a shopping list. Both describe hazards to the people of Greenland that a fully independent polity is responsible for addressing. Given the enormous areal extent of Greenland and its modest population size, attention is focused on defending people, rather than territory. In Table 1, the example threats are those that affront or challenge the basic sovereignty of a Greenland government. They are the types of events from which any population would expect its government to protect them. It has been assumed that for NATO, or other allied installations, the visiting power will assume responsibility for defending their own military facilities.

Table 1: Threat/Option Analysis for an Independent Greenland: Sovereignty Functions

THREAT	EXAMPLE	OPTION	CAPABILITY
ACCIDENTS AT SEA	Fishing vessel on fire in Greenlandic waters	Self-defense	Fixed and rotary wing aircraft and sea vessels to provide assistance
IUU FISHING 1	Increased incidence of illegal fishing associated with climate driven displacement of stocks	Self-defense	Sea vessels for on board inspection and arrest. Aircraft/drones for EEZ surveillance
IUU FISHING 2	EEZ confrontation in which another states party sends vessels into Greenlandic waters to enforce its option to fish the Greenlandic EEZ	Self-defense	Sea vessels/aircraft to confront other state party vessels. Aircraft/drones for EEZ surveillance
TERRORISM	Terrorist attack on a cruise ship in a Greenlandic port	Self-defense / alliance	Armed response unit. Bomb disposal unit. Intelligence collection and sharing.
CYBER ATTACK 1	Ransomware attack against a Greenlandic government	Self-defense / alliance	Cyber defense organization, training, and equipment providing immediate response plus backup data storage.

Table 2 provides a similar threat/option/capability analysis, but for military threats. A stipulation that formed part of the 2018 Greenlandic government coalition agreement was a need to "engage our young people and adults who would like to work for and can participate in our country's defense. E.g. in fishing inspection and in The Sirius sledge patrol (sic)" (The Coalition Agreement of 2018 between Siumut, Atassut, Partii Naleraq, para 344. Translation in Rasmussen 2019, 10). This suggests an intention to establish a patrol force similar to the current Sirius unit operated by the Danish Special Operations Command. It is for consideration also that raising a unit similar to the Canadian Rangers would bring multiple benefits. This is a project that has already received attention, although there is a diversity of opinion regarding the form such a volunteer force should take (Damgaard, Kamp, and Poulsen 2019). The remit of the Canadian Rangers[26] includes the conduct of reconnaissance, sovereignty, and occasional search and rescue operations. While legally a part of the Canadian Armed Forces Reserves, the unit fulfils an important social function, providing training in Arctic field skills for young people, and offering societal engagement and status to people who might otherwise feel disaffected and disenfranchised from the community. Such a force could fulfil a basic set of sovereignty demonstration, enforcement, and defense roles. In the case of conventional attack scenarios 4 and 5 in Table 2, such a force could augment any NATO assets, patrolling the deep field environment surrounding key points. They would not be expected to engage hostile forces as infantry.

To be effective, in addition to appropriate funding, a defending force must also possess the requisite expertise, and morale.[27] Expertise in its broadest sense is key if a military unit is to prevail in operations. Such knowledge may exist in many forms. It may be the recent exercise of operational technique, particularly if the skill set is perishable. This pertains to operations in any part of the battlespace—air, sea, land, or cyber. In the case of the Arctic, physical operations occur in a battlespace characterized by remoteness, extreme seasonality, and often violent weather conditions. Simply surviving in such conditions represents a challenge that requires specialist skills. Thus, a patrol force and/or home guard would benefit from training and exercise collaboration with established overseas forces with Arctic operational experience.

---

26 For an overview of the Canadian Rangers see Lackenbauer (2006, 2013) and Vullierme (2018).

27 Determination of spirit has many manifestations, for example, in the prosecution of search and rescue operations. For a thorough consideration of morale and military success, see Keegan, Holmes, and Gau (1985, 39-56).

Table 2: Threat/Option Analysis for an Independent Greenland: Military Functions

THREAT	EXAMPLE	OPTION	CAPABILITY
CYBER ATTACK 2	Non-NATO forces cut one or more undersea telecommunications cables	Alliance	Cable repair would be the responsibility of the owner. Military units including air and sea assets sufficient to intercept ships or submarines inflicting the damage
CONVENTIONAL ATTACK 1	Non-NATO forces plant sea mines in Greenlandic ports to deny their use to NATO	Alliance	A developed mine-hunting capability
CONVENTIONAL ATTACK 2	Non-NATO forces seize an area of south-east Greenland and establish shore-based missiles to dominate the Denmark Strait	Alliance	Military units sufficient to overmatch a likely invading force. In the case of a fully developed Anti-Access/ Area Denial operation with defended missile batteries established on Greenland, elimination may require a combination of air strike and special forces
CONVENTIONAL ATTACK 3	Non-NATO forces strike key points with air or sea launched weapons to deny their use to NATO	Alliance	A developed air defense capability. A developed capability to interdict non-NATO maritime launching platforms
CONVENTIONAL ATTACK 4	Non-NATO forces strike key points with special forces to deny their use to NATO	Alliance / self-defense	A developed air defense capability plus a developed maritime capability to interdict hostile forces. Ground forces trained in key point defense
CONVENTIONAL ATTACK 5	Non-NATO forces strike NATO facilities and assets in Greenland	Alliance / self-defense	A developed air defense capability plus a developed maritime capability to interdict hostile forces

Capabilities and Cost

While cost is not the sole determining factor in devising an effective defense, it is significant, particularly for a small state. Considering the elementary requirements needed to exercise sovereignty exemplified in Table 1, plus the proposal to establish a home guard, Table 3 offers representative costs, calculated on the basis of analogue units in other parts of the world. Assumptions in deriving costs are described below.

Defense economics is a discipline in itself, and a thorough examination of each of the four capabilities described in Table 3 might consume a paper in its own right. As the purpose here is to indicate what a newly independent Greenland is likely to be able to afford—or more significantly unable to afford—the approach adopted is to evaluate a representative cost for a *minimal* credible capability, that would be consistent with the exercise of national sovereignty. Perhaps other commentators would urge alternative analogues or calculation methods, but in making an objective estimate of an elementary set of capabilities, the analysis is guided by the precept that a polity that does not behave in a sovereign manner, is unlikely to have its sovereignty respected by other states.

The costs in Table 3 have been simplified to:

$$C_{tot} = C_{cap} + C_{opr}$$

where:

C_{tot} = total annual costs expressed in 2019 USD.

C_{cap} = capital costs including buildings, ships, aircraft, and other vehicles. Single-purchase items are amortized over a ten-year period and financed with sovereign debt with an interest rate drawn from historical levels (3.25 percent), after Lindert and Morton (1989).

C_{opr} = operating costs including salaries, maintenance, fuel, and other consumables.

Calculations include currency conversion and inflation, but not insurance. Some aspects of training costs have been included.

Table 3: Representative Annual Costs for Elementary Defense Capabilities

CAPABILITY	ASSETS	REPRESENTATIVE ANNUAL COST
FISHERIES PATROL / SEARCH AND RESCUE / LAW ENFORCEMENT IN GREENLANDIC TERRITORIAL WATERS AND EEZ	Coastguard. 4 offshore patrol vessels, 2 aircraft, associated personnel, ground vehicles, and headquarters. A contracted helicopter service supplying 4 aircraft.	USD 39.78m
COUNTER TERRORISM	Counter terrorism organization of 15 constabulary personnel, to provide armed response, bomb disposal, and intelligence liaison officers.	USD 0.74m
CYBER	Cyber defense organization, including two firewalled servers in secure locations, four personnel to provide a Computer Emergency Response Team, plus advice and education on computer security.	USD 0.40m
TERRESTRIAL SOVEREIGNTY PATROL / SEARCH AND RESCUE / EARLY WARNING	Home guard organization of some 20 local teams with an overall establishment of 735, including 21 officers. A headquarters facility. Communications and basic field equipment for each team. Uniform, a weapon, annual ammunition allowance, and a stipend for each volunteer. One annual training exercise.	USD 6.02m
TOTAL		USD 46.94m

A Greenlandic Coastguard

A Greenlandic coastguard would be essential to exercise the maritime functions of government, including search and rescue, enforcement of law including fisheries law, and response to marine environmental incidents. It should be borne in mind that in becoming fully independent, Greenland would be expected to assume many of the international treaty obligations currently exercised by Denmark.[28] This would include UNCLOS, and the terms of the Arctic Search and Rescue Treaty.[29] The annex to that treaty gives the coordinates delineating the areas for which each Arctic nation has responsibility. In the case of the Greenlandic sector, the area extends from 58°30'00" north, around both sides of the island to the North Pole. It is difficult to see how such an enormous area could be searched

---

28 A listing of primary international relationships pertinent to Greenlandic independence may be found in Taagholt and Hansen (2001, 92-3).

29 Formally, the Agreement on Cooperation on Aeronautical and Maritime Search and Rescue in the Arctic concluded at Nuuk on May 12, 2011.

and intervention enacted effectively without fixed and rotary wing aircraft, plus appropriate vessels. Appendix III to the Search and Rescue Treaty also identifies two rescue coordination centers in Greenland, a Maritime Rescue Coordination Center at Grønnedal and a Rescue Coordination Center at Søndrestrøm/Kangerlussuaq. In this case, the costing assumes a minimum of four patrol vessels to allow for both maintenance cycles and coverage of the large sea areas involved. An airborne patrol would be required for surveillance and search. Future consideration may be given to the use of drones, but an allowance for this technology has not been included. However, a helicopter unit is necessary if loss of life and environmental impacts are to be minimized.

Addressing first the capital costs, Kelleher (2002) provides a detailed analysis of fisheries protection economics. It must be remembered that these vessels must be seaworthy in severe weather conditions, including operation in ice infested waters (DNV classification 1A). A new military ship for Offshore Patrol Vessel (OPV) duties was purchased for USD 25m in 2000 (Kelleher 2002, 12). Darling (2019) reports a €66m 2016 contract for an OPV for the Irish Navy. A 28-year-old vessel of similar type was auctioned for less than USD 75,000 (Kelleher 2002, 12). However, even if suitable vessels were available for purchase, the likely maintenance costs and serviceability of the craft would have to be considered. Vessel hire is an option. The Falklands Island government uses such an arrangement for fisheries protection, with personnel of the Falklands Islands Defence Force providing gun crews. However, such a contract is for a limited period and tends to be directed at fisheries protection only. The fuller range of duties falling to a coastguard requires a 24/7/365 availability. A compromise option would be the purchase and conversion of ocean-going trawlers of suitable hull and machinery classification for polar waters. A vessel of this type was offered recently at DKK 22m (USD 3.52m). Kelleher (2002, 12) suggests some USD 1.5m to convert the vessel.

Two further points should be made. First, the cost of a patrol vessel might vary between USD 1—a notional fee for a secondhand ship provided under a political agreement by a willing ally—to USD 78.3m (2019 values) for a new vessel. A secondhand vessel, suitably refurbished, represents a reasonable investment for a service life of approximately a decade, and might be purchased using sovereign debt. Second, for Greenland to exercise full sovereign authority over its own waters, it cannot depend on a fleet of secondhand trawlers fitted with machine guns. If it is involved in a fisheries dispute with another sovereign nation that sends war vessels of its own, it needs to be represented by vessels with a gun of at least 20mm caliber. This is not to enable them to engage in naval battles, but to reduce the likelihood that Greenlandic government vessels will be rammed or treated with contempt.

A Greenlandic Police Commando Unit

A useful analogue for this would be Iceland's *Sérsveit Ríkislögreglustjórans*, also known as the *Víkingasveitin*. Modelled on the Norwegian Emergency Response Unit, it is a police commando force of only 55 men (Gray 2019). Its duties include counterterrorism and anti-hijack operations, VIP security and key point defense in wartime (Gray 2019). Its specialists include Explosive Ordnance Disposal operatives and personnel trained in diving and boat operations (Gray 2019). While the Greenlandic police have experience in addressing incidents involving firearms, given the widespread ownership of such weapons in the community, this analysis includes an augmentation of capability, albeit with an establishment of 15, relative to the population size.

A Greenlandic Cyber Defense Organization

As a minimum, it is assumed that while many of the government departments may deposit their data in the cloud as a reasonable compromise between security and cost, for the most sensitive data, including aspects of foreign policy and defense, storage and backup will be hosted at locations to which the Greenlandic government has exclusive access. This suggests a dedicated server hosting a firewalled network and associated equipment. There would need to be a second secure server, similarly equipped and located, to provide continuity should the first system be compromised. These facilities should of course be environmentally controlled and provide physical security, which would probably rule out a "data embassy" overseas. Two other elements are required: a Computer Emergency Response Team (CERT), and appropriate policy and law to assert governance over sensitive data. The CERT need only comprise three or four people with appropriate training, experience and security clearance. CERT team members provide a 24/7 response to cyber attacks, restoring service. They may also conduct proactive monitoring, advice, and education on computer security issues. They are not employed to design and build networks, provide routine monitoring, create policy, or audit. One proposal is to source a stand-alone facility from current telecommunications vendors.

A Greenlandic Home Guard[30]

There are several examples of relatively small states with successful citizen armies, including Israel and Switzerland. However, these nations have larger populations and GDPs than Greenland. Moreover, they are not Arctic states. Perhaps the most realistic model for a Greenlandic citizen volunteer patrol is the Canadian Rangers. This force of 5,000 personnel is a sub-component of the Canadian Armed Forces Reserve (Vullierme 2018). Largely centered on their communities, they provide a surveillance ('eyes and ears') role for the government (Lackenbauer 2006). As scouts, their activities constitute an expression of sovereignty as representatives

---

30 The term used to refer to this prospective organization has been chosen with care for readers from the Nordic nations. A general comparison in function may be found with the Danish Home Guard (Fridberg and Larsen 2017). Applying the nomenclature 'militia' is inaccurate, as there is no intention for personnel to fight as soldiers. Similarly, the term 'ranger' would be misleading, as it would normally refer to a person charged with the care of a forest.

of the polity. In that role, they are experts in cold weather and wilderness survival, retaining and transferring indigenous knowledge (Lackenbauer 2006). Canadian Rangers are able to conduct ground search and rescue, medical evacuation and emergency rescue (Lackenbauer 2006). They are not expected to provide aid to the civil power *per se* (Lackenbauer 2006). The equipment with which they are provided is basic: a rifle and yearly ammunition allowance, a uniform, some camping equipment and tools, and fuel for their own vehicles and boats. Lackenbauer (2013, 203) notes an annual program cost for the Canadian Rangers of $CDN 6.5m. The Greenlandic population is largely urbanized, inhabiting towns to the south and west of the island, a Greenlandic home guard might be based on a Headquarters unit at Nuuk, plus 20 patrols to cover the remainder of the country. This suggests an overall force size of approximately 735. To maintain training standards, annual exercises would be needed, these can easily cost between $CDN 150,000-500,000.

The question of a replacement for the Sirius Patrol is complex. One of the tasks of the unit is the demonstration of sovereignty. No serious objections appear to have been raised at the national level against the 1933 judgement of the Permanent Court of International Justice, awarding the whole of Greenland to Denmark (PCIJ 1933). Moreover, as Cavell (2008, and citations therein) notes: "It would be highly unreasonable for international law to apply the criteria for effective occupation as stringently in the polar regions as it does in the temperate zones." Nonetheless, it would be imprudent for a Greenlandic government to act in such a fashion as to evidence an *animus derelinquendi*—an intent to abandon. As Socarras (1984-5) notes, similar behavior by the British in respect to fishing grounds in the south Atlantic led to the Argentinians inferring that Britain had lost interest in the territory and, in turn, promoted the invasion of the Falkland Islands. To date, although eligible, Greenlanders have shown little interest in applying for service with the Sirius Patrol. Interviewees for the present study suggested that adopting responsibility for the patrol might be an iterative process requiring over a decade to complete. For completeness, the financial analysis includes an allowance for an element of a Greenlandic home guard to perform this role, noting that patrol members would almost certainly require the incentive of pay. The patrol would be distinct from a Greenlandic home guard in other respects. They would require certain constabulary powers to enforce the law in the remote areas they monitor. Their weapons would also probably require hunting (expanding) ammunition as protection against polar bears.

The Price of Sovereignty

At an indicative total annual cost of some USD 46.94m, even without the annual block grant, a minimal defense organization with the structure suggested would appear to be affordable.[31] This assumes that a Greenlandic government can

---

31   Values calculated in 2019 USD, using 2019 values for GDP (Statista 2021) and Danish block grant (Statistics Greenland 2020).

obtain NATO membership, avail itself of sovereign debt, and chooses 2 percent of GDP allowance for the defense budget in alignment with alliance expectations. Estimates for the cost of individual capabilities have been provided in Table 3 to enable readers to consider alternatives for themselves. However, the analysis is not intended as a component in an independence transition financial plan. Rather, it is designed to foster intelligent debate on a critical aspect of nationhood.

Conclusions

The problem of how a fully independent Greenland might be defended is one that requires prompt and serious consideration. The Greenland government is acquiring greater authority with respect to foreign affairs, and the political process leading to independence stands on the threshold of completion. Simultaneously, other nations are showing greater interest in Greenland for political or economic reasons. This article has considered the problem: *What are the defense options for a newly independent Greenland?* A nation that gives no thought to defense, and in particular the relationship between sovereignty and defense, is unlikely to remain an independent territory for long. The same may be said for the *option of demilitarization*—true pacifism as a national policy has a sorry history, which is why although some states may have no military *per se*, none are without some constabulary force and many choose alliance as a guarantee against external aggression.

In considering other options, Greenland is caught at the confluence of four related issues: its strategic geography, the reaction of more powerful states to its independence, its modest GDP, and the need to defend a vast battlespace with a population relatively lacking in military skills. These factors place critical limitations on choices for a newly independent Greenlandic government when considering defense and security policy. Constabulary forces able to confront terrorist attacks or to police fisheries; in short, to exercise the elementary functions of a sovereign state, may be possible. Indeed, a patrol force to exercise sovereignty, reconnaissance, and search and rescue duties across Greenland's vast territory would be desirable, and perhaps exercise a valuable social focus for the nation's communities. However, it is difficult to see how as a microstate Greenland could afford, or recruit, all of the appropriately skilled staff from its population to create a capable air defense system, protect its ports against the laying of sea mines, or resist an assault by special forces intent on seizing territory for tactical advantage during a superpower conflict. *The option of self-defense* against significant conventional threats would appear unavailable.

Similarly, the *option of neutrality* is impractical since to be effective, such a policy tends to require a robust self-defense and collusion with stronger states, and while a minimal defense capability consistent with sovereignty would appear to be affordable, that is not the same as a fully capable self-defense. This leaves the *option of alliance*, and in this respect, a newly independent Greenland cannot ignore its own geographical significance in the international order. NATO membership would provide continuity in the balance of Arctic political forces and should address some of the most difficult conventional defense issues. However, it does not come without cost, both financial and political. Membership of the NATO alliance may bring the expectation that it will devote 2 percent of GDP to defense investment, even if that funding is spent on the maintenance of civil projects with potential military utility, such as airports, radar installations, and docks. At the same time, choosing political friends entails the choice of adversaries. In the event of an interstate conflict in the Arctic, Greenland would become part of the contested battlespace. Moreover, in seeking economic opportunities, a Greenlandic government would have to be mindful of NATO, and particularly U.S. security sensitivities. Offering too generous a set of facilities to foreign states for economic development may compromise Greenland's alliance status if the recipient of those facilities is a nation with aims inimical to those of its protector nation or alliance.

In common with other microstates, there is no simple policy option for an autonomous defense of Greenland that is without disadvantage, and this article makes no policy recommendation in that regard. Indeed, given the above discussion, the Greenlandic people may conclude that their best security option is to simply retain their current level of independence as an autonomous territory within the Kingdom of Denmark. The consideration of representative costs included in the analysis suggests that the elementary functions of state sovereignty could be afforded even if the annual block grant from Denmark was not replaced from other sources. Whether that degree of political autonomy is sufficient, and the costs desirable, are matters for the Greenlandic people to decide. Ultimately, Greenlandic independence has the potential to disrupt the peaceful balance of political forces in the Arctic. And that instability is likely to have tragic consequences for Greenland itself, a land that has already known the violent hand of war.

About the Author

Dr. John Ash has extensive operational and scientific experience in the Arctic and subarctic. As a Royal Air Force Fighter Control Officer, he was stationed in the Shetland Islands, and later, serving as an oceanographer and submariner in the Royal Navy, was involved in data collection in the Arctic Ocean to support the study of climate change. Selected to lead a team of Russian researchers at Cambridge University examining radionuclide pollution in the Northern Seas, he was later assigned to undertake the initial design work for the Navy Department's Environmental Management System. He has held a British Safety Council Fellowship at the Judge Institute of Management Studies (now the Judge Business School) at the University of Cambridge, where the focus of his research concerned the management of dynamic risk problems in operational environments. Dr. Ash has lectured on the application of risk management at the Royal Air Force College,

Cranwell, and the Joint Services Command and Staff College. He is an Associate Professor at UiT the Arctic University of Norway, and an Institute Associate of the Scott Polar Research Institute, University of Cambridge.

References

Act on Greenland Self-Government. 2009, June 12 (Act No. 473).

Adams, Matthew. 2018. *Costa Rica: A Peaceful Nation Ready to Fight*. Monterey CA. Naval Postgraduate School.

Allied Air Command Public Affairs Office. 2020. "Italian F-35 Fighters Arrive in Iceland for Second NATO Deployment." June 9. Accessed on October 31, 2021. https://ac.nato.int/archive/2020/ITA_F35_ASIC_IPPN

Andersen, Torben M. 2015. *The Greenlandic Economy: Structure and Prospects*. University of Aarhus, Department of Economics.

Areng, Liina. 2014. *Lilliputian States in Digital Affairs and Cyber Security*. Tallinn Paper No. 4. Tallinn, Estonia: NATO Cooperative Cyber Defense Centre of Excellence. Accessed on October 31, 2021. https://ccdcoe.org/uploads/2018/10/TP_04.pdf

ArmedForces.eu. 2019. "Swiss Armed Forces." Accessed on October 31, 2021. https://armedforces.eu/Switzerland

Arneborg, Jette. 2015. "Norse Greenland–Research into Abandonment." In *Medieval Archaeology in Scandinavia and Beyond: History, Trends and Tomorrow*, edited by Mette Svart Kristiansen, Else Roesdahl, and James Graham-Campbell, 257–271. Aarhus University Press. Accessed on October 31, 2021. https://www.researchgate.net/publication/287645613_Norse_Greenland_-_research_into_abandonment

Ash, John. 2016. "Cold Peace: Arctic Conflict in an Era of Climate Change." *Journal of Intelligence and Terrorism Studies* 1. DOI: DOI: 10.22261/MV5JAC

Ashford Jeff, Michael Heron, and Nick Kaldas. 2020. *Operation Deans - The First 48 Hours: Formal Police Debrief*. New Zealand Police. Accessed on October 31, 2021. https://www.police.govt.nz/about-us/publication/formal-police-debrief-operation-deans-first-48-hours

Åselius, Gunnar. 2005. "Swedish Strategic Culture after 1945." *Cooperation and Conflict* 40 (1): 25-44.

Baerson, Kevin M. 2021. "Canada's New Drone Can Better Surveil Its Challenging Arctic Environment." *Inside Unmanned Systems*, January 4. Accessed on October 31, 2021. https://insideunmannedsystems.com/canadas-new-drone-can-better-surveil-its-challenging-arctic-environment/

Bank of Greenland. 2021. *Annual Report 2020*. CVR no. 80050410. Accessed on October 31, 2021. https://www.banken.gl/media/cm2pqmes/02-%C3%A5rsrapport-2020_eng.pdf

Barbin, Vladimir V. 2021. *The Russian Ambassador Mr V. Barbin's Comment on Questions from the Journalist S. Kruse, which were Partly Reflected in the Publication of the Danish Newspaper "Berlingske" on May 20, 2021*. May 21. Embassy of the Russian Federation in the Kingdom of Denmark. Accessed on October 31, 2021. https://denmark.mid.ru/en/press-centre/the_russian_ambassador_mr_v_barbin_s_comment_on_questions_from_the_journalist_s_kruse_which_were_par/

Battersby, John, and Rhys Ball. 2019. "Christchurch in the Context of New Zealand Terrorism and Right- Wing Extremism." *Journal of Policing, Intelligence and Counter Terrorism* 14 (3): 191-207. DOI: 10.1080/18335330.2019.1662077

Bennett, Geoffrey. 1975. *Naval Battles of World War II*. London and Sydney: B T Batsford.

Beukel, Eric, Frede P. Jensen, and Jens Elo Rytter. 2010. *Phasing Out the Colonial Status of Greenland, 1945-54*. Copenhagen: Museum Tusculanum Press.

Birket-Smith, Kaj. 1928. "The Greenlanders of the Present Day." In *Greenland. Vol. II: The Past and Present Population of Greenland*, edited by Martin Vahl, Georg Carl Amdrup, Louis Alfred Theodor Bobe, and Adolf Severin Jensen, 1–207. Copenhagen: Reitzel. Accessed on October 31, 2021. https://archive.org/details/greenland00vahl_1/page/12

Bjerregaard, Morten. 2017. "Grønlændere Vil Ikke Ofre Levestandard for Selvstændighed." *DR.DK*, July 27. Accessed on October 31, 2021. https://www.dr.dk/nyheder/indland/redaktoer-groenlaendere-vil-ikke-ofre-levestandard-selvstaendighed

Bolkhovitinov, Nikolaï Nikolaevich. 1996. *Russian-American Relations and the Sale of Alaska, 1834-1867*. Fairbanks AK: The Limestone Press

Boulègue, Mathieu. 2019. *Russia's Military Posture in the Arctic*. London: Chatham House.

Bound, Graham. 2012. *Fortress Falklands: Life under Siege in Britain's Last Outpost*. Pen and Sword.

Bragg, Belinda. Ed. 2011. *Concepts & Analysis of Nuclear Strategy (CANS – Theory Team) Framework Report: CANS Integration Meeting September 13-14.* Accessed on October 31, 2021. https://nsiteam.com/social/wp-content/uploads/2016/01/Concepts-Analysis-of-Nuclear-Strategy-Theory-Team-Framework-Report.pdf

Brett, André. 2015. "'The Miserable Remnant of This Ill-used People': Colonial Genocide and the Moriori of New Zealand's Chatham Islands." *Journal of Genocide Research* 17 (2): 133-152. DOI: 10.1080/14623528.2015.1027073

Breum, Martin. 2018. *Hvis Grønland river sig løs -en rejse i kongerigets sprækker* [If Greenland breaks loose - a journey into the fractures of the kingdom]. København: Gyldendal. E-book version.

_____. 2019. "Russia's Hypersonic Missiles Could Be Why Donald Trump Wants to Buy Greenland." *Arctic Today*, December 3. Accessed on October 31, 2021. https://www.arctictoday.com/russias-hypersonic-missiles-could-be-why-donald-trump-wants-to-buy-greenland/

Bueno De Mesquita, Bruce. 1981. *The War Trap*. New Haven, CT: Yale University Press.

_____. 1997. "A Decision-Making Model: Its Structure and Form." *International Interactions* 23 (3-4): 235-266. DOI: 10.1080/03050629708434909

Cavell, Janice. 2008. "Historical Evidence and the Eastern Greenland Case." *Arctic*: 433-441.

Chomsky, Noam. 1992. *What Uncle Sam Really Wants*. Tucson, AZ: Odonian Press.

Churchman, David. 2005. *Why We Fight: Theories of Human Aggression and Conflict*. Lanham, MD: University Press of America Inc.

Ćirić, Jelena. 2019. "Iceland Ups Defense Budget By 37%." *Iceland Review*, June 7. Accessed on October 31, 2021. https://www.icelandreview.com/news/iceland-ups-defense-budget-by-37/

Cocroft, Wayne D and Roger JC Thomas. 2003/2004. *Cold War; Building for Nuclear Confrontation 1946-1989*. Swindon, UK: English Heritage.

Compton-Hall, Richard. 1988. *Submarine Versus Submarine: The Tactics and Technology of Underwater Confrontation*. Newton Abbot, UK: David and Charles Publishers plc.

Console, Andrea. 2019. *Command and Control of a Multinational Space Surveillance and Tracking Network*. Kalkar, Germany: The Joint Air Power Competence Centre. Accessed on October 31, 2021. https://www.japcc.org/wp-content/uplo ads/JAPCC_C2SST_2019_screen.pdf

constituteproject.org. 2021. *Denmark's Constitution of 1953*. Accessed on October 31, 2021. https://www.constituteproject.org/constitution/Denmark_1953.pdf?lan g=en

Constitution of Japan. 1946 (Article 9). Accessed on December 8, 2021. https:// japan.kantei.go.jp/constitution_and_government_of_japan/constitution_e.html #:~:text=Article%209.,means%20of%20settling%20international%20disputes

Da Silva, Diego Lopes, Nan Tian, and Alexandra Marksteiner. 2021. *Trends in World Military Expenditure, 2020*. SIPRI Fact Sheet, April 2021. Accessed on October 31, 2021. https://www.sipri.org/publications/2021/sipri-fact-sheets/trends-world-military-expenditure-2020

Damgaard, Thomas Kamp, and Niels Bo Poulsen. 2020. "The Future Home Guard in Greenland: Its Tasks, Organization and Political Significance." In *the 19th Annual Conference of the Partnership for Peace Consortium Euro-Atlantic Conflict Studies Working Group*, Budapest, Hungary, May 27-31: 171-182. Forsvaret.

Dams, Ties, Louise van Schaik, and Adája Stoetman. 2020. *Presence Before Power: China's Arctic Strategy in Iceland and Greenland*. The Hague, Netherlands: Clingendael Institute.

Danilov, Peter C. 2021. "Greenland and Faroe Islands Take Step Towards More Autonomy on Foreign Affairs and Defense." *High North News*, October 5. Accessed on October 31, 2021. https://www.highnorthnews.com/en/greenland-and-faroe-islands-take-step-towards-more-autonomy-foreign-affairs-and-defense

Darling, Daniel. 2019. "Irish Navy Receives Fourth Offshore Patrol Vessel in Ship Replacement Program." *Defense & Security Monitor*, May 2. Accessed on October 31, 2021. https://dsm.forecastinternational.com/wordpress/2019/05/02/irish-nav y-receives-fourth-offshore-patrol-vessel-in-ship-replacement-program/

Defense of Greenland: Agreement Between the United States and the Kingdom of Denmark. 1951, April 27. The Avalon Project, Yale University. Accessed on December 8, 2021. https://avalon.law.yale.edu/20th_century/den001.asp

De Spiegeleire, Stephan. 2011. "Ten Trends in Capability Planning for Defence and Security." *The RUSI Journal* 156 (5): 20-28. DOI: 10.1080/03071847.2011.626270

Dickson, Patrick. N.d. "Atop the World, a Continuous Eye on Missiles 'Launched in Anger.'" *Stars and Stripes*. Accessed on October 31, 2021. https://media.stripes.com/i/thule/bmews.html#top

Diggines, Christopher E. 1985. "The Problems of Small States." *The Round Table* 74 (295): 191-205. DOI: 10.1080/00358538508453701

Dowdy, John. 2017. "More Tooth, Less Tail: Getting Beyond NATO's 2 Percent Rule." *McKinsey and Company*, November 29. Accessed on October 31, 2021. https://www.mckinsey.com/industries/public-and-social-sector/our-insights/more-tooth-less-tail-getting-beyond-natos-2-percent-rule

Einarsdóttir, Gréta Sigríður, 2021. "Four Norwegian Airforce F-35 Fighter Aircraft Deployed to Iceland." *Iceland Review*, February 19. Accessed on October 31, 2021. https://www.icelandreview.com/politics/four-norwegian-airforce-f-35-fighter-aircraft-deployed-to-iceland/

Einarsdóttir, Elísabet Ingunn. 2006. *Economic Development in Greenland – Towards a More Diversified Economy*. University of Akureyri, Social Science and Law Faculty. Accessed on October 31, 2021. http://vefir.unak.is/samfelag/Ritgerdir/BA-lokaritgerd_El%C3%ADsabet.pd

Fairchild, Byron. 1990. *Command Decisions: Decision to Land United States Forces in Iceland, 1941*. CMH Pub. 70-7-03. 73-97. Washington DC: Center of Military History, United States Army. Accessed on October 31, 2021. https://babel.hathitrust.org/cgi/pt?id=uiug.30112105161027&view=1up&seq=4

Feder, Stanley. 2002. "Forecasting for Policy Making in the Post-Cold War Period." *Annual Review of Political Science* 5: 111-125. DOI: 10.1146/annurev.polisci.5.102601.115116

Finlex. Undated. "Asetus Jäniskosken ja Niskakosken alueen liittämisestä Neuvostoliiton alueeseen sekä Suomessa olevien, Neuvostoliitolle siirtyneiden entisten saksalaisten rahavarojen käytöstä tehtyjen sopimusten voimaansaattamisesta." Finlex. Accessed on October 31, 2021. https://www.finlex.fi/fi/sopimukset/sopsteksti/1947/19470009/19470009_1

Fridberg, Torben, and Mona Larsen. 2017. *Volunteers in the Danish Home Guard 2016*. SFI-The Danish National Centre for Social Research. Accessed on October 31, 2021. https://pure.vive.dk/ws/files/796885/1710_Volunteers_in_the_Danish_Home_Guard_2016.pdf

Friedman, Norman. 1989. *The Naval Institute Guide to World Naval Weapon Sys-*

tems. Annapolis, MD: the United States Naval Institute.

George, Jane. 2020. "Nunavut Government has Spent $5M to Cope with November Ransomware Attack." *Nunatsiaq News*, March 5. Accessed on October 31, 2021. https://nunatsiaq.com/stories/article/nunavut-government-has-spent-5m-to-cope-with-november-ransomware-attack/

Goble, Paul. 2021. "Moscow Ready to Exploit Increasingly Independent-Minded Greenland against West." *Eurasia Daily Monitor*, June 22. Accessed on October 31, 2021. https://jamestown.org/program/moscow-ready-to-exploit-increasingly-independent-minded-greenland-against-west/

Göcke, Katja. 2009. "The 2008 Referendum on Greenland's Autonomy and What it Means for Greenland's Future." *Zeitschrift für ausländisches öffentliches Recht und Völkerrecht* 69 (1): 103-121.

Gough, Adam. 2009. *The Turbot War: The Arrest of the Spanish Vessel Estai and its Implications for Canada-EU relations.*" PhD diss., University of Ottawa.

Gray, Warren. 2019. "Fire and Ice: Iceland's Elite, "Viking Squad" Swat Team." *SOFREP*, February 12. Accessed on October 31, 2021. https://sofrep.com/special operations/fire-and-ice-icelands-elite-viking-squad-swat-team/

Gubb, Matthew. 2000. "Foreign Military Intervention in Response to Microstate Security Crises." Unpublished Doctoral Dissertation, University of Oxford.

Hague Declaration. 1899. *Declaration Concerning Expanding Bullets.* The Hague, July 29. Accessed on October 31, 2021. http://www.weaponslaw.org/assets/downloads/1899_HD_concerning_expanding_bullets.pdf

Hartmann, Gregory K., and Scott C Truver. 1991. *Weapons that Wait; Mine Warfare in the US Navy.* Annapolis, MD: Naval Institute Press.

Hartshorn, Derick. 2009. "Captor." *Mineman Memories.* Accessed on October 31, 2021. https://web.archive.org/web/20120112052835/http://www.hartshorn.us/Navy/navy-mines-10.htm

HM Government. 2015. *National Security Strategy and Strategic Defence and Security Review 2015: A Secure and Prosperous United Kingdom.* Cm 9161. Accessed on October 31, 2021. https://assets.publishing.service.gov.uk/government/uploads/system/uploads/attachment_data/file/478936/52309_Cm_9161_NSS_SD_Review_PRINT_only.pdf

Howarth, David. 1957. *The Sledge Patrol*. London: Collins.

Hudson's Bay Company. 2016. "Deed of Surrender." *Hudson's Bay Company History Foundation*. Accessed on October 31, 2021. https://www.hbcheritage.ca/history/fur-trade/deed-of-surrender

Huebert, Rob. 2019. "A New Cold War in the Arctic?! The Old One Never Ended!" *Arctic Yearbook*: 1-4.

i24 News. 2017. "Poland Agrees to Buy US Patriot Defense System with Israeli Missiles." *i24 News*, July 9. Accessed on October 31, 2021. https://www.i24news.tv/en/news/israel/diplomacy-defense/149944-170709-poland-agrees-to-buy-us-patriot-defense-system-with-israeli-missiles

Icelandic Government. 2018. "FACT SHEET: Iceland's Contributions to NATO." May 2018. Accessed on October 31, 2021. https://www.stjornarradid.is/library/09-Sendirad/NATO/Factsheet%20-%20enska%20-ma%C3%AD%202018.docx

Ingimundarson, Valur. 2003. "Fighting the Cod Wars in the Cold War: Iceland's challenge to the Western Alliance in the 1970s." *The RUSI Journal* 148 (3): 88-94. DOI:10.1080/03071840308446895

International Committee of the Red Cross (ICRC). Undated. *Rule 77. Expanding Bullets*. Customary International humanitarian Law Database. Accessed on October 31, 2021. https://ihl-databases.icrc.org/customary-ihl/eng/docs/v1_rul_rule77

Jensen, Jens Fog, Inge Bisgaard and Jens Heinrich. 2013. *Anlæg fra Den Kolde Krig i Grønland*. Feltrapport 34. Grønlands National Museum og Arkiv / Sila Arktisk Center ved Etnografisk Samling National Museet.

Joint Expeditionary Force (JEF). 2021. *Joint Expeditionary Force – Policy Direction*. Accessed on October 31, 2021. https://assets.publishing.service.gov.uk/government/uploads/system/uploads/attachment_data/file/1001342/Joint_Expeditionary_Force_policy_direction.pdf

Jónsson, Hannes. 1982. *Friends in Conflict: The Anglo-Icelandic Cod Wars and the Law of the Sea*. London: C Hurst and Company.

Katajala, Kimmo. 2010. "Zwischen West und Ost. 800 Jahre an der Ostgrenze Finnlands." *Kirchliche Zeitgeschichte* 23 (1): 81-110. Accessed on October 31, 2021. https://www.jstor.org/stable/pdf/43751879.pdf?refreqid=excelsior%3A2d707d5e3ad414aedd9ec4f00736d12a

Kassebaum, Peter. 1990. "Role of the Police in Costa Rica (Military or Police) the Reality." Paper presented to the Western Society of Criminology Meetings: Las Vegas, Nevada February.

Keegan, John, Richard Holmes, and John Gau. 1985. *Soldiers: A History of Men in Battle*. London: Hamish Hamilton Ltd.

Kelleher, Kieran. 2002. *The Costs of Monitoring, Control and Surveillance of Fisheries in Developing Countries*. FAO Fisheries Circular No. 976. Rome: Food and Agriculture Organization of the United Nations

Knowles, Daniel. 2020. *The Battle of the Denmark Strait: An Analysis of the Battle and the Loss of HMS Hood*. Stroud UK: Fonthill Media.

Krasner, Stephen. 1999. "*Sovereignty: Organized Hypocrisy.*" Princeton, NJ: Princeton University Press.

Lackenbauer, P. Whitney. 2006. "The Canadian Rangers: a "Postmodern" Militia that Works." *Canadian Military Journal*. Winter: 49-60.

_____. 2013. *Canada's Rangers: Selected Stories 1942-2012*. Kingston Ontario: Canadian Defense Academy Press.

Lindert, Peter H., and Peter J. Morton. 1989. "How Sovereign Debt Has Worked." In *Developing Country Debt and Economic Performance, Volume1: The International Financial System,* edited by Jeffrey D Sachs, 39-106. Chicago: University of Chicago Press. Accessed on October 31, 2021. http://www.nber.org/chapters/c8987

Macias, Amanda. 2018/2019. "From Aruba to Iceland, these 36 Nations have no Standing Military." *CNBC*, April 3. February 13. Accessed on October 31, 2021. https://www.cnbc.com/2018/04/03/countries-that-do-not-have-a-standing-army-according-to-cia-world-factbook.html

McComas, Kyra. 2016. "The Neutrality of Switzerland: Deception, Gold, and the Holocaust." *Historical Perspectives: Santa Clara University Undergraduate Journal of History, Series II*: Vol. 21, Article 12. Accessed on October 31, 2021. http://scholarcommons.scu.edu/historical-perspectives/vol21/iss1/12

McGwin, Kevin. 2021. "Greenland Premier Takes on Foreign Policy Portfolio ahead of Arctic Talks with Danish PM." *Arctic Today*, September 30. Accessed on October 31, 2021. https://www.arctictoday.com/greenland-premier-takes-on-foreign-policy-portfolio-ahead-of-arctic-talks-with-danish-pm/

McPhee, John. 1983/1984. *The Swiss Army: La place de la Concorde Suisse*. London: Faber and Faber Limited.

Miah, Tahmida. 2020. "The Loss and Revival of Moriori Culture and Identity." *MUNDI* 1 (1).

Miller, James. 2003. The North Atlantic Front: Orkney, Shetland, Faroe and Iceland at War. Edinburgh UK: Birlinn Ltd.

Mitchell, David Joseph. 1976. "The American Purchase of Alaska and Canadian Expansion to the Pacific." Unpublished Doctoral Dissertation, Simon Fraser University.

Naalakkersuisut. 2018. T*he Coalition Agreement of 2018 between Siumut, Atassut, Partii Naleraq.*

North Atlantic Treaty Organisation (NATO). 1995. *Study on NATO Enlargement*, September 3 (updated November 5). Accessed on October 31, 2021. https://www.nato.int/cps/en/natohq/official_texts_24733.htm

North Atlantic Treaty Organisation (NATO). 2014/2018. *Wales Summit Declaration: Issued by the Heads of State and Government participating in the meeting of the North Atlantic Council in Wales*. Press release issued September 5 2014, last updated August 30 2018. https://www.nato.int/cps/en/natohq/official_texts_112964.htm

_____. 2021. "Funding NATO." Accessed on October 31, 2021. https://www.nato.int/cps/en/natohq/topics_67655.htm

Niou, Emerson MS, Peter C Ordeshook, and Gregory F. Rose. 1989. *The Balance of Power: Stability in International Systems*. Cambridge University Press.

O'Flaherty, Chris. 2019. *Naval Minewarfare: Politics to Practicalities*. Gloucester UK: The Choir Press. Online extract. Accessed on October 31, 2021. https://www.vernonlink.uk/the-gulf-wars

Østreng, Willy. 1977. "The Strategic Balance and the Arctic Ocean: Soviet Options." *Cooperation and Conflict*, 12 no. 1: 41-62. DOI: 10.1177/001083677701200103

Patrick, Anjelina. 2017. "China - Sri Lanka Strategic Hambantota Port Deal." *National Maritime Foundation*, 13 April 2017. Accessed on October 31, 2021. https://www.maritimeindia.org/View%20Profile/636276610966827339.pdf

Permanent Court of International Justice (PCIJ). 1933. *Legal Status of Eastern Greenland.* Judgement: April 5. Accessed on October 31, 2021. https://jusmundi .com/en/document/decision/en-legal-status-of-eastern-greenland-judgment- wednesday-5th-april-1933

Philpott, Daniel. 2001. *Revolutions in Sovereignty: How Ideas Shaped Modern International Relations.* Princeton, NJ: Princeton University Press.

Poulin, Andrew. 2016. "5 Ways Russia is Positioning to Dominate the Arctic." *International Policy Digest*, January 24. Accessed on October 31, 2021. https://intpol icydigest.org/5-ways-russia-is-positioning-to-dominate-the-arctic/

Prime Minister of Japan and his Cabinet. N.d. *The Constitution of Japan.* Accessed on October 31, 2021. https://japan.kantei.go.jp/constitution_and_government_ of_japan/constitution_e.html

Rai, Kaiya. 2017. "Was Sweden Really Neutral in World War Two?" *History is Now Magazine*, December 18. Accessed on October 31, 2021. https://www.historyisno wmagazine.com/blog/2017/12/18/was-sweden-really-neutral-in-world-war-two

Rasmussen, Rasmus Kjærgaard. 2019. "The Desecuritization of Greenland's Security? How the Greenlandic Self-Government Envision Post-Independence National Defense and Security Policy." *Arctic Yearbook*: 287-304. Accessed on October 31, 2021. https://arcticyearbook.com/images/yearbook/2019/Scholarly-Papers/15_A Y2019_Rasmussen.pdf

Rhode, Benjamin, ed. 2019. "The GIUK Gap's Strategic Significance." *Strategic Comments* 25 (Comment 29): October 2019. Accessed on October 31, 2021. https://www.tandfonline.com/doi/abs/10.1080/13567888.2019.1684626

Rogoway, Tyler. 2015. "The Pope Has A Small But Deadly Army Of Elite Warriors Protecting Him." *Jalopnik*, September 28. Accessed on October 31, 2021. https://jalopnik.com/the-pope-has-a-small-but-deadly-army-of-elite-warrio rs-1733268646

Sarkees, Meredith Reid. Undated. *The COW Typology of War: Defining and Categorizing Wars (Version 4 of the Data) by Sarkees.* Accessed on October 31, 2021. https://correlatesofwar.org/data-sets/COW-war/the-cow-typology-of-war-defini ng-and-categorizing-wars/view

Savov, Vlad. 2019. "Huawei is Selling Off Its Undersea Cable Business: and Shrinking Its Smartphone Production, According to a Report." *The Verge*, Jun 3. Accessed on October 31, 2021. https://www.theverge.com/2019/6/3/18650220/huawei-und

ersea-cable-business-sale-trump-ban-smartphone-production

Schuster, Carl O. 1991. "Weather War." *Command Magazine* 13: 70–73.

Shi, Mingming. 2019. "The Role of China in the Questions of Greenlandic Independence." PhD dissertation, University of Iceland. https://skemman.is/bitstre am/1946/34379/1/MA%20thesis%20Mingming%20shi%20West%20Nordic %20Studies.pdf

Singer, J. David. 1958. "Threat-perception and the Armament-tension Dilemma." *Journal of Conflict Resolution* 2 (1): 90-105. DOI: 10.1177/002200275800200110

Singh, Abhijit. 2018. "China's Strategic Ambitions Seen in the Hambantota Port in Sri Lanka." *Observer Research Foundation*, July 27. Accessed on October 31, 2021. https://www.orfonline.org/research/chinas-strategic-ambitions-seen-in-the-ham bantota-port-in-sri-lanka/

Skydsbjerg, Henrik, and Walter Turnowsky 2016. "Massivt Flertal for Selvstæn-dighed." *Sermitsiaq AG*, December 1. Accessed on October 31, 2021. https://ser mitsiaq.ag/massivt-flertal-selvstaendighed

Smith, Adam. 1776. *An Inquiry into the Nature and Causes of the Wealth of Nations*. London: W Strahan and T Cadell.

Smith, Shirlee Anne. 2006. "Rupert's Land." *The Canadian Encyclopedia*. February 7, revised October 8, 2019. Accessed on October 31, 2021. https://www.thecanad ianencyclopedia.ca/en/article/ruperts-land

Socarras, Michael. 1984-5. "The Argentine Invasion of the Falklands and International Norms of Signalling." *Yale Journal of International Law* 10: 356-383. Accessed on October 31, 2021. https://digitalcommons.law.yale.edu/yjil/vol10iss2/9

Statista. 2021. "GDP of Greenland." Accessed on October 31, 2021. https://www.statista.com/statistics/805932/gdp-of-greenland/

Statistics Greenland. 2020. *Greenland in Figures 2020*. Accessed on October 31, 2021. https://stat.gl/publ/en/GF/2020/pdf/Greenland%20in%20Figures%202020. pdf

Stockholm International Peace Research Institute (SIPRI). 2021. *Data for all Countries from 1988–2020 as a share of GDP* (pdf). Accessed on October 31, 2021. https://www.sipri.org/databases/milex

Stojković, Dejan S., Milan S. Kankaraš, and Vlada M. Mitić. 2016. "Determination of Defence Capability Requirements." *Vojno delo* 68 (8): 76-88.

Taagholt, Jørgen, and Jens Claus Hansen. 2001. *Greenland: Security Perspectives.* Fairbanks, Alaska: Arctic Research Consortium of the United States.

TeleGeography. 2021. "Submarine Cable Map." Accessed on October 31, 2021. https://www.submarinecablemap.com/#/

The Greenland Home Rule Act. 1978, November 29 (Act No. 577).

Thrane, Kristine, Per Kalvig, and Nynke Keulen. 2014. "Uranium Potential in Greenland." Paper presented at *Proceedings of the International Symposium on Uranium Raw Material for the Nuclear Fuel Cycle: Exploration, Mining, Production, Supply and Demand, Economics and Environmental Issues (Uram)*, 22-33. Vienna, June 23-27. Accessed on October 31, 2021. https://www.researchgate.net/profile/Harikrishnan-Tulsidas-2/publication335160001_Proceedings_of_the_Internatio nal_Symposium_on_Uranium_Raw_Material_for_the_Nuclear_Fuel_Cycle_Ex ploration_Mining_Production_Supply_and_Demand_Economics_and_En vironmental_Issues_URAM_2014/links5d53ca8d299bf16f0736af3a/Proceed ngs-of-the-International-Symposium-on-Uranium-Raw-Material-for-the-Nuc lear-Fuel-Cycle-Exploration-Mining-Production-Supply-and-Demand-Economi cs-and-Environmental-Issues-URAM-2014.pdf#page=28

Tomala, Magdalena. 2014. "Economic Development of Greenland in the Context of its Way to Independence." *Studia i Materiały. "Miscellanea Oeconomicae"* 18 (2): 67-79. Accessed on October 31, 2021. https://depot.ceon.pl/bitstream/hand le/123456789/6077/424_5-M.Tomala.pdf?sequence=1

Tossini, J. Vitor. 2021. "The Falkland Islands Defense Force – The Oldest Land unit of the British Overseas Territories." *UK Defense Journal*, March 4. Accessed on October 31, 2021. https://ukdefensejournal.org.uk/the-falkland-islands-defense-force-the-oldest-land-unit-of-the-british-overseas-territories/

Trevithick, Joseph. 2018. "Ukraine Requests to Buy Patriot Missiles as it Delivers a Mobile Radar to the U.S. Army." *The Drive*, September 4. Accessed on October 31, 2021. https://www.thedrive.com/the-war-zone/23351/ukraine-requests-to-buy-p atriot-missiles-as-it-delivers-a-mobile-radar-to-the-u-s-army

Truver, Scott. 2016. "Naval Mines and Mining: Innovating in the Face of Benign Neglect." *Center for International Maritime Security (CIMSEC)*, December 20. Accessed on October 31, 2021. https://cimsec.org/naval-mines-mining-innovati ng-face-benign-neglect/

Turnowsky, Walter. 2017. "Debat: Skal grønlandske soldater i krig?" [Debate: Must Greenlandic soldiers be allowed to go to war?]. *Sermitsiaq*, June 2. Accessed on October 31, 2021. https://sermitsiaq.ag/node/197411

_____. 2019. "Grønland vil selv styre cyberforsvar" [Greenland Will Govern Cyber Defense Itself]. *Sermitsiaq*, February 14. Accessed on October 31, 2021. https://sermitsiaq.ag/groenland-styre-cyberforsvar

United Nations Peacekeeping. N, d. "Deployment and Reimbursement." Accessed on October 31, 2021. https://peacekeeping.un.org/en/deployment-and-reimburse ment

United States and Kingdom of Greenland. 1951. *Defense of Greenland: Agreement Between the United States and the Kingdom of Denmark, April 27, 1951.* Accessed on October 31, 2021. https://avalon.law.yale.edu/20th_century/den001.asp#1

U.S. National Intelligence Council (US NIC). 2021. National Intelligence Estimate: Climate Change and International Responses Increasing Challenges to US National Security Through 2040 Accessed on October 31, 2021. NIC-NIE-2021-10030-A. Office of the director of National Intelligence. https://www.dni.gov/files/ODNI/documents/assessments/NIE_Climate_Change_and_National_Security.pdf

Vandiver, John. 2020. "F-15s Out of Lakenheath Patrol the Skies Above Iceland." *Stars and Stripes*. October 13. Accessed on October 31, 2021. https://www.stripes.com/news/f-15s-out-of-lakenheath-patrol-the-skies-above-iceland-1.648384

Vullierme, Magali. 2018. "The Social Contribution of the Canadian Rangers: A Tool of Assimilation or Means of Agency?" *Journal of Military and Strategic Studies* 19 (2).

Wahlbäck, Krister. 1998. "Neutrality and Morality: The Swedish Experience." *American University International Law. Review* 14 (1): 103-121.

Waitangi Tribunal. 2001/2016. *Rekohu: A Report on Moriori and Ngati Mutunga Claims in the Chatham Islands.* Wellington, New Zealand: Legislation Direct.

Walling, Michael G. 2012/2016. *Forgotten Sacrifice: The Arctic Convoys of World War II.* Oxford, UK: Bloomsbury Publishing plc.

Watkins, Claire. 2021. "Greenland Travel Advice." *Red Savannah.* Accessed on October 31, 2021. https://www.redsavannah.com/europe/greenland/greenland-travel-advice

Weinberg, Gerhard L. 1999. "German Plans and Policies regarding Neutral Nations in World War II with Special Reference to Switzerland." *German Studies Review* 22 (1): 99-103. DOI: 10.2307/1431584

Wilson, Page. 2017. "An Arctic 'Cold Rush'? Understanding Greenland's (In)dependence Question." *Polar Record* 53 (5): 512-519. DOI: 10.1017/S003224741700047X

COMMENTARY: Ukrainian Domestic and U.S. Foreign Affairs—Regarding a 2021 Washington Debate and the Nuclear Non-Proliferation Regime

ANDREAS UMLAND[1]

Department of Political Science
National University of Kyiv-Mohyla Academy
ORCID: 0000-0001-7916-4646

A think-tank debate in the United States that emerged in the summer of 2021 illustrates challenges to Western policy toward Eastern Europe in general, and to U.S. policy toward Ukraine in particular. Stereotypes of a post-Soviet Ukraine characterized by ultra-nationalism and authoritarianism spread by Russian propaganda resonate not only in leftist but also in other political circles. This commentary responds to two recent contributions by Ted Galen Carpenter calling for an end to U.S. support for Ukraine.

Keywords: Ukraine, U.S. Foreign Policy, Eastern Europe, Propaganda, Russia, Non-proliferation, Nuclear Nonproliferation, Geopolitics, Post-communist Politics, Ultra-nationalism, Authoritarianism, Ted Carpenter.

Comentario: Los asuntos internos de Ucrania y los asuntos exteriores de Estados Unidos: A propósito de un debate en Washington en 2021 y el régimen de no proliferación nuclear

Un debate de un grupo de expertos en los Estados Unidos que surgió en el verano de 2021 ilustra los desafíos a la política occidental hacia Europa del Este en general y la política estadounidense hacia Ucrania en particular. Los estereotipos de una Ucrania postsoviética caracterizada por el ultranacionalismo y el autoritarismo difundidos por la propaganda rusa resuenan no solo en los círculos de izquierda

1   **Acknowledgements:** A shorter version of this text was first published electronically in the *Forum for Ukrainian Studies* of the Contemporary Ukraine Studies Program at the Canadian Institute of Ukrainian Studies, University of Alberta, Canada. A German translation is forthcoming in the *Zeitschrift für Aussen- und Sicherheitspolitik* (Journal for Foreign and Security Policy) at the University of Cologne.

sino también en otros círculos políticos. Este ensayo examina crítica-mente una contribución reciente de Ted Galen Carpenter que pide el fin del apoyo de Estados Unidos a Ucrania.

Palabras clave: Ucrania, Política exterior de Estados Unidos, Europa del Este, Propaganda, Rusia, No proliferación nuclear.

评论文章。乌克兰国内和美国外交事务--关于2021 年华盛顿辩论和核不扩散制度的 关于2021年的华盛顿辩论和核不扩散制度

2021　年夏天在美國出現的一場智庫辯論說明了西方對東歐政策的總體挑戰，特別是美國對烏克蘭的政策。俄羅斯宣傳所傳播的以極端民族主義和威權主義為特徵的後蘇聯烏克蘭的刻板印像不僅在左翼而且在其他政界引起了共鳴。這篇文章批判性地考察了泰德·蓋倫·卡彭特（Ted Galen Carpenter）最近的一篇呼籲美國停止對烏克蘭的支持的文章。

關鍵詞：烏克蘭，美國外交政策，東歐，宣傳，俄羅斯，核不擴散。

Over the last eight years, Ukraine has—in connection with its pro-Western Euromaidan Revolution of 2013-14, as well as following territorial conflicts with Russia—become a major issue in recent U.S. and European Union foreign policies. Today, Ukraine's domestic and foreign affairs are having geopolitical repercussions that reach well beyond Eastern Europe, especially regarding its confrontation with Moscow and ongoing Europeanization. These repercussions affect the recent tensions between Russia and the West, transatlantic relations, European integration, the work of the UN Security Council, international energy affairs, and other issues. Given this, it is unsurprising that the temperature of controversies about Western policies toward Ukraine had risen already before the major escalation in Russia's war against Ukraine on February 24, 2022. This concerns not least the debate about which approach Washington should take toward Kyiv.

The Start of an Odd Discussion

On May 30, 2021, *The National Interest* (TNI) published a harsh critique of U.S. support for Ukraine, by Ted Galen Carpenter (2021a), under the title

"Ukraine's Accelerating Slide into Authoritarianism." Carpenter's text not only disarranged a number of facts about Ukraine. It is a strange statement in view of the author's listed affiliation—Washington, D.C.'s famous right-libertarian Cato Institute. The attack that Carpenter presented on the (certainly imperfect) Ukrainian state is typical of many left-wing writers rather than of conservative authors, and of Kremlin-linked rather than independent U.S. commentators. The author alleged that Ukrainian politics is beset by deeply anti-democratic and ultra-nationalist tendencies. These putative features, Carpenter (2021a) argued, make this post-Soviet state unfit for U.S. support. Why the Cato Institute's fellow, who seems to have neither much interest in nor ever published any research on Ukraine, came out with a categorical judgement on this country remains a mystery.

Left-wingers and pro-Putin observers around the world dislike post-Soviet Ukraine because its recent revolutions and subsequent governments have been too pro-Western and too pro-American. Moreover, many leftists are confused that the manifestly anti-imperial nationalism of the Orange Revolution of 2004 and Euromaidan Uprising of 2013-14 was *not* rejecting U.S. or/and Western hegemony.[2] Instead, Ukraine's fierce resistance against foreign domination was, and is, entirely focused on the imperialism of Moscow, and sees the United States as an ally rather than threat in defending Ukrainian independence. Today, Putin's Russia is one of the Northern hemisphere's few remaining places that has continued successfully to withstand the promotion of liberal democracy by Washington and its allies across the world.

Above all, for over eight years, Ukraine has been fighting a multi-faceted war for survival against the world's largest nuclear-weapon country and second-largest conventional military power. Putin's Russia is attempting to bring down the Ukrainian state with a shrewd combination of military, paramilitary, and nonmilitary means. Curiously, this aspect is entirely missing from Carpenter's depiction of Ukraine—an omission also customarily found in the Kremlin media's portrayal of Ukraine. The Cato Institute's TNI author instead made accusations against post-Soviet Ukraine that repeat arguments proposed by numerous leftist and pro-Putinist commentators across the world since 2014, if not before. Carpenter (2021a) painted a dark picture of allegedly rising Ukrainian authoritarianism, oppression, and ultra-nationalism. The same kind of caricatures have been spread via the Kremlin's massive propaganda campaign against Ukraine for many years (see Heinemann-Grüder 2015).

Carpenter (2021a) was especially unhappy about two former U.S. ambassadors to Ukraine, Geoffrey Pyatt and William Taylor, who have supported Ukraine's assertion of national sovereignty and demonstrative turn to the West. What needs to be added to Carpenter's critique is that all other U.S. ambassadors to Ukraine over the last 30 years—from the first envoy, Roman Popadiuk, to the most recent

---

2 For an indepth analysis, see Marples and Mills (2015).

and now most famous American diplomat representing Washington in Kyiv, Marie Yovanovitch—could be accused of similarly "biased" attitudes toward Ukraine. A main reason behind the U.S. ambassadors' differences with Carpenter seems to be that, by virtue of their professional specialization, they know a great deal about Eastern Europe. Carpenter, in contrast, has seemingly scant sustained interest in the post-Soviet region—at least not one demonstrated by his previous publications. He reproduces, in his TNI article, distorted images the exact origins of which one can only speculate about. This commentary endeavors to dispel those distortions on a number of fronts.

Ukraine's Imperfect Democratic State

Ukraine is no ideal liberal democracy. In Freedom House's (2021) latest rating of the world's countries according to their political and civil liberties, Ukraine received only 60 out of 100 possible points. It thus lags far behind Norway, Finland, and Sweden, the only three countries assigned 100 points in this democracy ranking. Carpenter (2021a) indicates some possible reasons for Ukraine's unsatisfactory result correctly.

Yet within the peculiar regional and historical context of the post-Soviet space, Ukraine is rather more democratic than one would expect in view of its location and past. By comparison, in 2020, the equally post-Soviet, Eastern Slavic, and Christian Orthodox Republic of Belarus and Russian Federation received, respectively, only 11 and 20 out of 100 points in the Freedom House (2021) ranking. In the Freedom House (2021) table, with 60 points Ukraine is designated as relatively free and democratic. Its mass media and political landscape are distorted by oligarchic influence, yet not dominated by a national autocrat, as in other post-Soviet states (Umland 2009). Ukraine's electoral campaigns suffer from distortions and manipulations (Fedorenko, Rybiy, and Umland 2016), but Ukraine's citizens have a real choice, and their votes are not rigged on a significant scale. Ukraine has a number of far-right parties, but they are weaker than in many other European countries and not represented in the national parliament, as I discuss in more detail shortly. Ukraine is infamous for its corruption, but has, in recent years, introduced a number of new laws and institutions designed to prevent graft. Ukraine is not a member of NATO and the EU, but wants to enter them and is working toward accession (Vereshchuk and Umland 2019; Klimkin and Umland 2020).

Good reasons exist to criticize, for instance, Ukraine's dysfunctional presidentialism, underdeveloped party-system, or incomplete cooperation with the International Criminal Court—a topic dealt with in TNI (Polunina and Umland 2016). Yet these are neither prominent themes in Russian propaganda nor issues that Carpenter raises. The Kremlin rarely speaks about such problems as they often also or even more apply to Russia. Carpenter does not mention these and similar topics, perhaps, because he does not read Ukrainian. Given the contents of his articles on Ukraine (Carpenter 2021a, 2021b, 2021c), he may not have even read much of the widely available English-language scholarly literature on post-Euromaidan Ukraine (e.g., in chronological order, Matsusato 2005; Likhachev 2013a; Grant 2015; Marples and Mills 2015; Bertelsen 2016; Grigas 2016; Kowal, Mink, and Reichardt 2019; Pifer 2017; Wynnyckij 2019; Averre and Wolczuk 2019; Hauter 2021).

Responses to Carpenter in Moscow, Washington, and Elsewhere

Carpenter's Ukraine article in TNI (2021a) triggered multiple reactions within the U.S. and beyond. The first came from Moscow, although Russia was only mentioned *en passant* in Carpenter's text. A day after the text had appeared in the United States, on May 31, 2021, the influential Russian state-owned online resource *inoSMI* (Foreign Mass Media) published a Russian translation of Carpenter's article. The *inoSMI* editor introduced Carpenter's article, stating:

> U.S. officials love to portray Ukraine as 'a courageous democracy that reflects the threat of aggression from an authoritarian Russia'. However, the idealized picture created by Washington has never really matched the darker reality, and the gap between the two, with Ukraine sliding increasingly toward authoritarianism, has now become a real chasm, the article notes. (Karpenter 2021a)

During June 2021, an interactive debate regarding Carpenter's (2021a) attack on Ukraine developed. In TNI, a response to Carpenter's initial article was published by Doug Klain (2021) of the Atlantic Council. A fortnight later, my rebuttal to Carpenter appeared in the Atlantic Council's *Ukraine Alert* (Umland 2021a). In Ukraine, this text was translated into Russian (Umland 2021b) and Ukrainian and republished by the Kyiv website *Gazeta.ua*. Further responses to Carpenter appeared on the Kyiv resource *Khvylia* (Wave) in Russian (Umland 2021c), and on Berlin's Center for Liberal Modernity website *Ukraine verstehen* (Understanding Ukraine) in German (Umland 2021d). On June 28, 2021, Carpenter (2021b) responded to Klain's and my critique of his initial text with a second article entitled "Why Ukraine Is a Dangerous and Unworthy Ally," again published in the web version of TNI, and subsequently reposted on the Cato Institute's website (Carpenter 2021c).

While none of the responses to Carpenter were re-published in Russia, his rebuttal to them was again translated by the Kremlin-controlled *inoSMI* (Foreign Mass Media) website within one day. Carpenter's (2021b) new article was reposted in Russian on June 29, 2021 (Karpenter 2021b), and introduced by an *inoSMI* editor, who wrote:

> In May [2021], an author of *The National Interest* took the liberty of criticizing the Zelensky regime for its authoritarian tendencies.

In response, the German "Ukrainianist" Andreas Umland and similar 'Maidanists' [a term referring to Kyiv's Independence Square] criticized Carpenter so much that he decided to get even with them in this article "One Cannot Remain Silent: Accusations of 'Russian disinformation' are reminiscent of McCarthyism." The defenders of the Kyiv regime have a powerful lobbying organization behind them, the Atlantic Council.

Also on June 29, 2021, a number of Russian-language outlets published sympathetic reviews of Carpenter's (2021a) article.[3] Among other Kremlin-controlled outlets, the website of the Crimean TV channel *Pervyi sevastopol'skii* (2021b) ("Sevastopol's First") briefly reviewed Carpenter's June article. It had already earlier introduced Carpenter's (2021a) initial May attack (*Pervyj sevastopol'skij* 2021a). Among other Russian-language video resources, the YouTube channels "Oleg Kalugin" and "Kognitive Dissonanz" published Russian audio reviews of Carpenter under the titles "On Ukraine's Lobbyists in the US" (June 29, 2021)[4] and "Senior Research Fellow of the Cato Institute [...] Ted Carpenter on Ukraine..." July 1, 2021).[5] Carpenter's two TNI articles on Ukraine were thereafter discussed and commented on by numerous Russian outlets.[6]

Jon Lerner (2021) of the Hudson Institute reviewed the debate surrounding Ukraine in English on June 28, 2021, in TNI. The English versions of the Russian websites *TopWar.ru* (2021) and *Oreanda.ru*, published brief reviews of Carpenter's arguments under the titles "Strategically, Ukraine is a 'trap' for the United States" and "American Political Scientist Called Ukraine a Dangerous and Unworthy Ally" (Oreanda-News 2021). *Oreanda.ru* remarked that, in Ukraine,

> [A] coup in 2014 was carried out with the help of ultra-nationalist and neo-Nazi groups. Carpenter noted that these organizations with their 'ugly values,' continue to influence Kiev's [sic] politics. Supporters of an alliance with Ukraine try not to notice these facts, the article says. The author of the material noted the deplorable situation with human rights and freedoms in this country. (Oreanda-News 2021)

---

3   See for instance, the major daily *Izvestiia* (2021) (Messages) as well as the popular internet resources *Lenta.ru* (2021) and *Gazeta.ru* (Demidov 2021).

4   See https://www.youtube.com/watch?v=grnsAlb302A

5   See https://www.youtube.com/watch?v=XBYZhM7nsK8

6   Including *Yandex.ru, RIA.ru, MK.ru, Sputniknews.ru, Regnum.ru, News.ru, Tsargrad.TV, KP.ru, PolitRos.com, Life.ru, Argumenti.ru, Actualcomment.ru, RUnews24.ru, PolitExpert.net, Versia.ru, Ridus.ru, 360TV.ru, Riasev.com, Inforeactor.ru, Glas.ru, Riafan.ru, Newinform.com, SMI2.ru, Iarex.ru, TopCor.ru, InfoRuss.info, Profinews.ru, Rusevik.ru, Alternatio.org, News2.ru, News22.ru,* and others.

The Ukrainian news agencies *UAzmi.org* and *UAinfo.org* quoted, on July 1, 2021, the prominent Odesa blogger Oleksandr Kovalenko, who had written on June 30, 2021 about Carpenter's articles on Ukraine. Kovalenko's post noted that:

> Interestingly, he used as arguments what we have regularly heard from Russian propagandists since 2014, namely that neo-Nazism is rampant in Ukraine, rights and freedoms of citizens are trampled in Ukraine, there is no freedom of speech in Ukraine, wild monkeys and crocodiles are in Ukraine . . . In fact, a full set of Kremlin fakes about Ukraine is heard from the mouth of an American expert on the pages of a respected and influential publication in the midst of the international exercise SeaBreeze-2021. (Zloy-Odessit 2021)

Ukraine's leading English-language newspaper *Kyiv Post* declared Carpenter—with reference to his articles in TNI—Ukraine's "Foe of the Week" on July 2, 2021 (Ponomarenko 2021).

The varying responses in Russia, the United States, Ukraine, and elsewhere indicate the main issue that many commentators have with Carpenter's (2021a) arguments. What raises eyebrows about his statements on Ukraine is less their critical tone. Rather, it is surprising that Carpenter chose to remark on certain sensitive political topics that have been popular in Russia's state-controlled mass media during the last eight years, if not before. The Cato Institute's researcher makes far-reaching claims about an alleged prevalence of ultra-nationalism and putative slide to authoritarianism in today's Ukraine—claims also pushed daily in Moscow's propaganda channels and by pro-Kremlin public figures for many years. Kremlin-guided newspapers, TV channels, and websites have therefore, and unsurprisingly, eagerly quoted and reviewed Carpenter's two articles. Here comes a senior American commentator working at a leading Washington think-tank publishing in an influential U.S. political magazine and repeating exactly those talking points that the Kremlin has been spreading to justify its thinly veiled hybrid war against Ukraine since 2014 (see Hauter 2021). Carpenter unapologetically calls for an end of Washington's support for Kyiv, with clear reference to the Kremlin's favorite narratives about Ukraine (cf. Bertelsen 2016, 2021). What more could Moscow hope for?

The Problems with Carpenter's Portrayal of Ukraine

Carpenter's insistence on the large role of party-political ultra-nationalism in Ukraine is plainly wrong. Unlike various other European parliaments elected via a proportional representation system, the Ukrainian *Verkhovna Rada* (Supreme Council) has not housed a far-right faction since late 2014 (Umland 2020). It briefly did harbor such a faction for two years only, from 2012 to 2014 (Likhachev

2013a, 2013b, 2013c; Shekhovtsov 2014; Shekhovtsov and Umland 2014).

In 2019, Ukraine's far right—for the first time in its history and unlike many other nationalists around the world—ventured into parliamentary elections with a united list. As Table 1 shows, despite such rare harmony, the list of the right-wing Freedom Party (which also included representatives of the other two major ultra-nationalist groups, the Right Sector and National Corps) received 2.15 percent of the vote—a result roughly equal to, or even below, what many single far-right parties in European countries receive in national elections (Umland 2020; see also Polyakova 2015, 2014). In the 2019 presidential election, the candidate of the united far right gained 1.62 percent. Those who have followed European elections in recent years may note that radical nationalists, in a number of NATO member countries including some older democracies, have received larger or significantly larger support than the Ukrainian united far right.

During its entire post-Soviet history, Ukraine has indeed—as Carpenter (2021a) indicates—been exceptional in terms of support for ultra-nationalism (Likhachev 2015; Polyakova 2014; Umland 2020). However, Ukraine's distinction here lies not in the political *strength* of the far right, but in its electoral *weakness*, as demonstrated in Table 1's list of results of various far-right presidential candidates and parties since the introduction of proportional representation in 1998. The only period during which the far right was able to gain notable nationwide support was during the notorious presidency of Viktor Yanukovych in 2010-14 (Polyakova 2015). Yanukovych both triggered nationalist mobilization with his pro-Russian policies and directly promoted Ukraine's extreme right, as a convenient sparring partner during elections (Likhachev 2015).

Table 1: Vote Shares of Major Ukrainian Far-right Parties in Presidential Elections (shaded rows) and the Proportional-representation Parts of Parliamentary Elections, 1998–2019 (in percentages)

Party or alliance	Bloc "*Natsionalnyy front*" [National Front] (KUN, UKRP & URP) / URP / KUN	UNA / *Pravyi sektor* [Right Sector]	Bloc "*Menshe sliv*" [Fewer Words] (VPO-DSU & SNPU) / VOS
National election			
1998 (parliamentary)	2.71 (NF)	0.39 (UNA)	0.16 (MS)
1999 (presidential)			
2002 (parliamentary)		0.04 (UNA)	
2004 (presidential)	0.02 (Kozak, OUN)	0.17 (Korchyns'kyy)	
2006 (parliamentary)		0.06 (UNA)	0.36 (VOS)
2007 (parliamentary)			0.76 (VOS)
2010 (presidential)			1.43 (Tiahnybok)

2012 (parliamentary)		0.08 (UNA-UNSO)	10.44 (VOS)
2014 (presidential)		0.70 (Iarosh)*	1.16 (Tiahnybok)
2014 (parliamentary)	0.05 (KUN)	1.81 (PS)	4.71 (VOS)
2019 (presidential)			1.62 (Koshulyns'kyy)
2019 (parliamentary)			2.15 (VOS)**

Source: Umland (2020).

Notes: * In the 2014 presidential election, Dmytro Iarosh formally ran as an independent candidate but was publicly known as the leader of Pravyy sector (PS).

** The 2019 Svoboda list was a unified bloc of most of the relevant Ukrainian far-right political parties, but was officially registered only as a VOS list.

Abbreviations: KUN: *Konhres ukrains'kykh natsionalistiv* (Congress of Ukrainian Nationalists); UKRP: *Ukrains'ka konservatyvna republikans'ka partiia* (Ukrainian Conservative Republican Party); URP: *Ukrains'ka respublikans'ka partiia* (Ukrainian Republican Party); VPO-DSU: *Vseukrainske politychne ob'ednannia "Derzhavna samostiynist' Ukrainy"* (All-Ukrainian Political Union "State Independence of Ukraine"); SNPU: *Sotsial-natsionalna partiia Ukrainy* (Social-National Party of Ukraine); OUN: *Orhanizatsiia ukrainskykh natsionalistiv* (Organization of Ukrainian Nationalists); UNA: *Ukrains'ka natsionalna asambleia* (Ukrainian National Assembly); UNSO: *Ukrains'ka narodna samooborona* (Ukrainian National Self-Defense); VOS: *Vseukrains'ke ob'ednannia "Svoboda"* (All-Ukrainian Union Svoboda).

In 2014, something close to panic among many anti-fascists around the world concerning Ukraine's far right generated tension and debate. The Ukrainian ultra-nationalists still had their faction in parliament. They had also been highly visible during the Euromaidan revolution and had entered the first post-Euromaidan government for several months with four ministers (Umland 2020). Above all, the Russian propaganda machine and its various Western branches were, on a daily basis, hammering into worldwide public opinion the idea that former President Yanukovych had been thrown out of power by a "fascist coup" in Kyiv. In fact, Yanukovych only left Kyiv after violence had already ended, and was officially deposed by the same parliament that had earlier supported him. Few non-Russian observers bought the Kremlin's horror story in full. Yet a widespread approach among Western politicians and commentators has since been that there can be no smoke without fire. If Russia is so concerned, ultra-nationalism must be a major problem in Ukraine.

The few academic experts who had researched Ukraine's far right before it became a popular theme and studied it from a cross-cultural perspective warned already in 2014 that the media hype around this topic was misplaced. The Russian historian Viacheslav Likhachev (2015) (Zmina Human Rights Center, Kyiv), Ukrainian political scientist Anton Shekhovtsov (2014) (Center for Democratic Integrity, Vienna), and American sociologist Alina Polyakova (2014, 2015) (Center for European Policy Analysis, Washington, D.C.) had researched pre-Euromaidan and non-Ukrainian permutations of the far right before 2014. From their historical and comparative points of view, they and others warned early on that alarmism is inappropriate. They spoke out against an emerging mainstream Western opinion that ultra-nationalism is a major issue in Ukraine (Polyakova 2015). Some of these researchers explicitly predicted in 2014 that the prospects of Ukraine's far right are limited. Since then, it has indeed turned out to be again only a tertiary national political force, as it had been before its only notable electoral success (10.44 percent) in 2012 (Umland 2020).

Today, the overall domestic political impact of Ukrainian right-wing extremists is lower than in many far richer and securer countries of Europe. Even the highly publicized participation of many radical nationalists in Ukraine's defense against Russia's hybrid war since 2014 has not had much effect on their electoral fortunes. In 2019, Volodymyr Zelensky with his openly Jewish family background won, against a powerful incumbent, in Ukraine's presidential elections with a result of 73 percent.

This leads to the second main point in Carpenter's (2021a; 2021b) portrayals of Ukraine—allegedly authoritarian tendencies disqualifying Ukraine to receive U.S. support. Here again, Carpenter's argument is questionable. Ukraine has indeed been exceptional, within the post-Soviet context, yet in the opposite sense in which it has been presented in TNI. Already early in its post-Soviet history, Ukraine passed, after its emergence as an independent state in 1991, one of the crucial tests that political scientists use to determine the democratic potential of a nation: is an electorate able to evict a country's top official and most powerful politician via popular vote? In 1994, the Ukrainians deposed their incumbent regent in a presidential election. As a result, Ukraine's first president, Leonid Kravchuk (1991-94), was replaced by its second head of state, Leonid Kuchma (1994-2005). The much older and richer Federal Republic of Germany, founded in 1949, passed this particular democracy test only four years *after* Ukraine. In 1998, the Germans, for the first time in history, deposed a sitting Federal Chancellor, the CDU's Helmut Kohl (1982-98), via parliamentary elections that were won by the SPD. The Social Democrat's then-leader, Gerhard Schroeder (today an employee of the Russian state), became the new head of government until 2005 when he too was deposed via popular vote.[7] In the 2010 and 2019 national elections, Ukrainian voters again evicted their sitting heads of state with embarrassing results for the two moderately nationalist incumbents. Outgoing Presidents Viktor Yushchenko and Petro Poroshenko manifestly wanted second terms in Ukraine's highest political office. Yet the one-term presidents were spectacularly beaten by opposition candidates, and duly stepped down after their crushing defeats.

---

7   In 1969, then incumbent CDU/CSU Federal Chancellor Kurt Georg Kiesinger (from 1933 until 1945 a member of Hitler's NSDAP) had been replaced by the SPD's Willi Brandt. Yet, this was the result of a change of Germany's governing coalition and not of that year's parliamentary elections that had been won by Kiesinger's CDU/CSU.

Over the last 30 years, Ukraine has conducted dozens of highly competitive rounds of presidential, parliamentary, and local elections, most of which fulfilled basic democratic standards (Fedorenko, Rybiy, and Umland 2016). This experience is in sharp contrast to almost all other post-Soviet states that had been part of the USSR when it was founded in 1922. What is special about Ukraine, as a successor country of the original Soviet Union, is the opposite of what Carpenter (2021a) asserts: it is not the relative authoritarianism, but the relative *democratism* of Ukraine that is remarkable, and that makes this state more worthy of general Western (not only U.S.) support than other founding republics of the USSR.

Carpenter's (2021b) confusion about these issues became especially visible in his second TNI article of June 28, 2021. He compared various post-Soviet states and concluded that:

> Umland stresses that other countries emerging from the former Soviet Union are noticeably more autocratic than Ukraine, noting that [in a recent Freedom House democracy ranking in which Ukraine had received 60 out of 100 points] Russia received a rating of twenty points and Belarus received eleven points [out of 100 possible 'Global Freedom Scores']. He could have added that Kazakhstan was in the same dismal category with twenty-three points. But no one expects the United States to defend such countries militarily or praise them as vibrant democracies. Umland, Klain, and other fans of Kiev [sic] expect Washington to do both.

However, that is exactly the point: if Russia, Belarus, and Kazakhstan had achieved the same Global Freedom Scores as Ukraine in the quoted Freedom House table, they should be treated like Ukraine. If they were partially free rather than unfree, the three countries would be worth Western support—including assistance by the United States, which received 83 points in the Freedom House (2021) ranking.

What Carpenter Did Not Say

What is most surprising in Carpenter's (2021a; 2021b) articles is not what he writes about, but the preeminent security issue he is entirely silent about: the narrowly understood national interest of the United States in Ukraine's fate as a former atomic power and today a non-nuclear-weapon state. As detailed elsewhere, the United States played a major role in the nuclear disarmament of Ukraine in the early 1990s (Umland 2021d). Together with Moscow, Washington pressured Kyiv at the time to give up a major part of the huge arsenal of weapons of mass destruction that Ukraine had inherited from the USSR when achieving independence in 1991. Russia and the United States also made sure that Ukraine would be deprived of *all* its strategic and tactical nuclear warheads and ammunition (Umland 2021d). Today, Moscow's and Washington's concerted efforts from a quarter of a century ago look like direct preparations for Russia's annexation of Crimea and for the start of a covert war in Eastern Ukraine in 2014 (see also Vereshchuk and Umland 2019).

The only relevant political concession that Washington made in the 1990s to Kyiv was that it agreed to supplement Ukraine's accession to the Nuclear Non-Proliferation Treaty (NPT) as a non-nuclear-weapon state with the—now infamous—1994 Budapest Memorandum on Security Assurances signed by Ukraine, Russia, the United States, and the United Kingdom.[8] The latter country also underwrote this fateful document, although Great Britain had not taken part in the trilateral negotiations about Ukraine's nuclear disarmament with the United States and Russia. London supported this deal, however, with its official signature because the UK had, in 1968, been one of the three founding countries of the world-wide non-proliferation regime, together with United States and the USSR (for the history, see Kohler 1972). It has since been, together with Washington and Moscow, a so-called "Depositary Government" of the NPT. At a CSCE summit at Budapest in December 1994, Washington, Moscow, and London assured Kyiv, in connection with its signing of the NPT, of their respect of Ukrainian sovereignty, integrity and borders (see Budjeryn and Umland 2021).

With its attack on Ukraine since 2014, and especially with its overt annexation of Crimea and escalation in 2022 (as well as also with some earlier and other actions), Moscow has for several years been undermining the logic of the non-proliferation regime (see e.g., Grant 2015). It is no longer clear that countries that refrain from possessing, building, or acquiring nuclear weapons would be secure, and especially be protected from countries that do hold atomic arms. Russia's officially permitted possession of nuclear weapons not only gave it a key military advantage *vis-à-vis* Ukraine. It was also the major reason the West—unlike in Yugoslavia, Iraq, or Libya—has not militarily intervened in the Russian-Ukrainian war.

A June 2021 incident with a British war ship near the port of Sevastopol in the Black Sea thus had a more than symbolic meaning.[9] On a trip from Odesa to Batumi, the UK's destroyer '*HMS Defender*' passed by Crimea without making a detour to avoid Black Sea waters claimed by Russia. This behavior of the UK was a peculiar form of validation of the 1994 Budapest Memorandum and 1968 NPT. Having received Kyiv's permission to pass Ukrainian waters, the '*Defender*' lived up to its name by defending not merely general international law by taking the shortest path from the shores of Southern mainland Ukraine to its destination at Georgia's Black Sea coast. The British vessel also upheld the logic of the non-proliferation regime built on the premise that the borders of non-nuclear-weapon states are as respected as those of the official nuclear-weapon states, under the NPT.

With his explicit demand to end U.S. support for Ukraine, Carpenter (2021a,

---

8   For further reading on the Budapest Memorandum's conditions, see Galaka (2015) and Budjeryn (2014a). On its breach, see Budjeryn and Umland (2021).

9   For a synopsis of the incident and its implications for maritime and international law, see Serdy (2021).

2021b) calls not only for a betrayal of a beacon of democracy in the post-Soviet space. He also proposes to sweep under the carpet the normative and psychological foundations of humanity's non-proliferation regime. If, after Russia as the legal successor of the USSR, the United States, as a second founding country of the 1968 NPT, signaled to the world that Ukraine's territorial integrity and political sovereignty are of secondary importance, this could have far-reaching consequences for the international order. This is especially so as Kyiv once possessed an atomic arsenal that was significantly larger than those of Great Britain, France, and China combined (Budjeryn and Umland 2017).

The Kremlin's manifest violation of the logic of the non-proliferation regime since 2014 can be seen as a temporary and singular aberration of one guarantor of the NPT from a key international norm (see Budjeryn 2015). A U.S. withdrawal from support of the Ukrainian state, which Carpenter (2021b) proposes, would, however, create a pattern in the behavior of the non-proliferation regime's founders. It could signal to political leaders around the world that international law in general, and the NPT in particular, provide no protection for non-nuclear weapons states. Reliable national security can only be achieved through the production or acquisition of weapons of mass destruction. As the ultimate instruments of deterrence, nuclear warheads may also come in handy, if a government decides—as the Kremlin did in 2014—to annex to its state a neighboring territory and wants to scare away third parties from getting involved.

That Carpenter (2021a, 2021b) does not even mention these issues in his two TNI articles is curious. Insofar as Carpenter presents himself in his articles as concerned about core national interests of the United States, one would think that preventing nuclear proliferation is on his agenda. Yet he did not even take an interest in this topic after it had been explicitly mentioned in the first rebuttals to his initial May 2021 article. In fact, the discussion about the grave repercussions of Moscow's violation of the 1994 Budapest nuclear deal and the resulting implications for U.S. foreign policy has been ongoing for more than eight years. The debate has been taking place not the least on the websites of various Washington, D.C. institutions—from the influential Wilson Center for International Scholars to the oldest U.S. journal of its kind, *World Affairs* (founded in 1837) (see e.g., Budjeryn 2014a, 2016, 2019; Sinovets and Budjeryn 2017; Klimkin and Umland 2020; Umland 2016).

Carpenter departs from these debates in his proposal that the United States joins Russia in this signal to national leaders across the globe that international law will not protect their states. For that would be the conclusion for many politicians: if you want your country's national borders and sovereignty secured, you cannot rely on the NPT. What you rather need is "the bomb" (if you have no reliable ally with such a bomb). Is an encouragement of future nuclear proliferation so irrelevant to American national interests, as the Cato Institute's author, seems to imply?

About the Author

Andreas Umland is an Analyst with the Stockholm Center for Eastern European Studies at the Swedish Institute of International Affairs, Associate Professor of Political Science at the Kyiv-Mohyla Academy, and General Editor of the book series "Soviet and Post-Soviet Politics and Society," as well as "Ukrainian Voices" both published by *ibidem* Press in Stuttgart.

References

Averre, Derek, and Kataryna Wolczuk (Eds.). 2019. *The Ukraine Conflict: Security, Identity and Politics in the Wider Europe.* Abingdon, UK: Routledge.

Bertelsen, Olga (Ed.). 2016. *Revolution and War in Contemporary Ukraine: The Challenge of Change.* Stuttgart: *ibidem*-Verlag.

Bertelsen, Olga (Ed.). 2021. *Russian Active Measures: Yesterday, Today, Tomorrow.* Stuttgart: *ibidem*-Verlag.

Budjeryn, M. 2014a. "The Breach: Ukraine's Territorial Integrity and the Budapest Memorandum." *NPIHP Issues Brief* 3. Accessed November 21, 2021. www.wilsoncenter.org/publication/issue-brief-3-the-breach-ukraines-territorial-integrity-and-the-budapest-memorandum

_____. 2014b. "Looking Back: Ukraine's Nuclear Predicament and the Nonproliferation Regime. *ArmsControl Today* 44 (12). Accessed November 21, 2021. www.armscontrol.org/act/2014-12/features/looking-back-ukraine's-nuclear-predicament-nonproliferation-regime

_____. 2015. "The Power of the NPT: International Norms and Ukraine's Nuclear Disarmament." *The Nonproliferation Review* 22 (2): 203-237. DOI: 10.1080/10736700.2015.1119968

_____. 2016. "Was Ukraine's Nuclear Disarmament a Blunder?" *World Affairs* 179 (2): 9-20. DOI:10.1177/0043820016673777

_____. 2019. "Impeachment Backstory: The Nuclear Dimension of US Security Assistance to Ukraine." *Bulletin of the Atomic Scientist*, November 13. Accessed November 21, 2021. https://thebulletin.org/2019/11/impeachment-backstory-the-nuclear-dimension-of-us-security-assistance-to-ukraine/

Budjeryn, Mariana, and Andreas Umland. 2017. "Amerikanische Russlandpolitik, die Souveränität der Ukraine und der Atomwaffensperrvertrag: Ein Dreiecksverhältnis mit weitreichenden Konsequenzen [American policy towards Russia, the sovereignty of Ukraine and the Nuclear Non-Proliferation Treaty: A triangular relationship with far-reaching consequences]." *Sirius: Zeitschrift für Strategische Analysen* 1 (2), 133-142.

_____. 2021. "Damage Control: The Breach of the Budapest Memorandum and the Nuclear Non-Proliferation Regime." In *NATO's Enlargement and Russia: A Strategic Challenge in the Past and Future*, edited by Oxana Schmies, 177-190. Stuttgart: *ibidem*-Verlag.

Carpenter, Ted Galen. 2021a. "Ukraine's Accelerating Slide into Authoritarianism." *The National Interest*, May 30. Accessed November 21, 2021. nationalinterest.org/blog/skeptics/ukraine's-accelerating-slide-authoritarianism-186368

Carpenter, Ted Galen. 2021b. "Why Ukraine Is a Dangerous and Unworthy Ally." *The National Interest*, June 28. Accessed November 21, 2021. nationalinterest.org/blog/skeptics/why-ukraine-dangerous-and-unworthy-ally-188742

Carpenter, Ted Galen. 2021c. "Why Ukraine Is a Dangerous and Unworthy Ally." *Cato Institute*, June 28. Accessed November 21, 2021. www.cato.org/commentary/why-ukraine-dangerous-unworthy-ally

Demidov, A. 2021. "V SShA sochli Ukrainu opasnym i nedostoinym soiuznikom [Why Ukraine Is a Dangerous and Unworthy Ally]." *Gazeta.ru,* 29 June. Accessed November 21, 2021. www.gazeta.ru/politics/news/2021/06/29/n_16173032.shtml

Fedorenko, Kostyantyn, Rybiy, Olena, and Andreas Umland. 2016. "The Ukrainian Party System before and after the 2013–2014 Euromaidan." *Europe-Asia Studies* 68 (4): 609-630. DOI: 10.1080/09668136.2016.1174981

Freedom House. 2021. "Countries and Territories." *Freedom House.* Accessed August 15, 2021. https://freedomhouse.org/countries/freedom-world/scores

Galaka, Serhiy 2015. "Ukrainian Crisis and Budapest Memorandum: Consequences for the European and Global Security Structures." *Ukraine Analytica* 1 (1): 45-51.

Grant, Tom D. 2015. *Aggression against Ukraine: Territory, Responsibility, and International Law.* London, UK: Palgrave Macmillan.

_____. 2019. *International Law and the Post-Soviet Space II: Essays on Ukraine, Intervention, and Non-Proliferation.* Stuttgart: *ibidem*-Verlag.

Grigas, Agnia. 2016. *Beyond Crimea. The New Russian Empire.* New Haven, CT: Yale University Press.

Hauter, Jakob (Ed.). 2021. *Civil War? Interstate War? Hybrid War? Dimensions and Interpretations of the Donbas Conflict in 2014–2020.* Stuttgart: *ibidem*-Verlag.

Heinemann-Grüder, Andreas. 2015. "Lehren aus dem Ukrainekonflikt: Das Stockholm-Syndrom der Putin-Versteher [Lessons from the Ukraine conflict: The Stockholm Syndrome of Putin Understanders]." *Osteuropa* [Eastern Europe] 65 (4): 3-24. Accessed November 21, 2021. https://www.jstor.org/stable/44937292

_____. 2018. "Was lehrt der Ukraine-Konflikt? [What does the Ukraine conflict teach us?]." *Zeitschrift für Außen- und Sicherheitspolitik* [Journal for Foreign and Security Policy] 11 (4): 521–531.

Izvestiia. 2021. "V SShA poshchitali Ukrainu opasnym i nedostoinym soiuznikom [Why Ukraine Is a Dangerous and Unworthy Ally]." *Izvestiia*, June 29. Accessed November 21, 2021. https://iz.ru/1185920/2021-06-29/v-ssha-poschitali-ukrainu-opasnym-i-nedostoinym-soiuznikom

Karpenter [Carpenter], T. 2021a. "The National Interest (SShA): Ukraina vse bystree skatyvaetsia k avtoritarizmu [Ukraine's Accelerating Slide into Authoritarianism]." *inoSMI*, May 31. Accessed November 21, 2021. https://inosmi.ru/politic/20210531/249831592.html

_____2021b. The National Interest (SShA): pochemu Ukraina – opasnyi i nedostoinyi soiuznik dlia SShA. [USA Considered Ukraine a Dangerous and Unworthy Ally]. *inoSMI*, June 29. Accessed November 21, 2021. inosmi.ru/politic/20210629/250003969.html

Klain, Doug. 2021. "Countering the Myth of Ukrainian Authoritarianism." *The National Interest*, June 7. Accessed November 21, 2021. https://nationalinterest.org/feature/countering-myth-ukrainian-authoritarianism-187094

Klimkin, Pavlo, and Andreas Umland. 2020. "Geopolitical Implications and Challenges of the Coronavirus Crisis for Ukraine." *World Affairs* 183 (3): 256-269. DOI: 10.1177/0043820020942493

Kohler, Beate. 1972. *Der Vertrag* über *die Nichtverbreitung von Kernwaffen und das Problem der Sicherheitsgarantien* [The Treaty on the Non-Proliferation of Nuclear Weapons and the Problem of Security Guarantees]. Frankfurt a. M.: Alfred Metzner Verlag.

Kowal, Pavel, Georges Mink, and Iwona Reichardt (Eds.). 2019. *Three Revolutions: Mobilization and Change* Stuttgart: *ibidem*-Verlag.

Kunz, Barbara. 2017. *Kind Words, Cruise Missiles, and Everything in Between: The Use of Power Resources in U.S. Policies towards Poland, Ukraine, and Belarus 1989– 2008.* Stuttgart: *ibidem*-Verlag.

Lenta.ru. 2021. "Ukrainu nazvali nedostoinym i nebezopasnym soiuznikom dlia SShA [Ukraine called an unworthy and unsafe ally for US]." Accessed November 21, 2021. *Lenta.ru-News*, June 29. lenta.ru/news/2021/06/29/usa_ukr/

Lerner, Jon. 2021. "Does Ukraine Matter to America?" *The National Interest*, June 28. Accessed November 21, 2021. nationalinterest.org/feature/does-ukraine-mat-ter-america-188741

Likhachev, Viacheslav. 2013a. *Right-Wing Extremism in Ukraine: The Phenomenon of "Svoboda."* Kyjiv: EAJC.

_____. 2013b. "Right-Wing Extremism on the Rise in Ukraine." *Russian Politics and Law* 51 (5): 59-74. DOI: 10.2753/RUP1061-1940510503

_____. 2013c. "Social-Nationalists in the Ukrainian Parliament: How They Got There and What We Can Expect of Them." *Russian Politics and Law* 51 (5): 75-85. DOI: 10.2753/RUP1061-1940510504

_____. 2015. "The 'Right Sector' and Others: The Behavior and Role of Radical Nationalists in the Ukrainian Political Crisis of Late 2013 – Early 2014." *Communist and Post-Communist Studies* 48 (2): 257-271. DOI: 10.1016/j.postcomst ud.2015.07.003

Manaeva Rice, Natalie, Dean P. Rice, and Howard L. Hall. 2015. "Ukraine at the Fulcrum: A Nuclear House of Cards." *International Journal of Nuclear Security* 1 (1): Art. 7. DOI: 10.7290/v73r0qr9

Marples, David R., and Fredrik V. Mills (Eds.). 2015. *Ukraine's Euromaidan: Analyses of a Civil Revolution.* Stuttgart: *ibidem*-Verlag.

Matsusato, Kimitaka. 2005. "Semipresidentialism in Ukraine: Institutionalist Centrism in Rampant Clan Politics." *Demokratizatsiya* 13 (1): 45-60.

Oreanda-News. 2021. "American Political Scientist Called Ukraine a Dangerous and Unworthy Ally." *Oreanda-News*, June 29. Accessed November 21, 2021. www.

oreanda.ru/en/it_media/american-political-scientist-called-ukraine-a-danger ous-and-unworthy-ally/article1378860/

Pervyi sevastopol'skii. 2021a. "'Naikhudshii vid tsinizma': amerikanskii ekspert prizval Vashington zaniat' storonu Rossii v 'ukrainskom voprose' ['Worst kind of cynicism: An American expert called on Washington to take Russia's side regarding the 'Ukrainian question']." May 31. Accessed November 21, 2021. sev.tv/news/43821.html

Pervyo sevastopol'skii. 2021b. "Ekspert nazval Ukrainu nebezopasnym soiuznikom dlia SShA [Expert calls Ukraine an unsafe ally of the U.S.]." June 21. sev.tv/news/46307.html

Pifer, Steven. 2017. *The Eagle and the Trident: U.S. Ukraine Relations in Turbulent Times.* Washington, DC: Brookings Institution Press.

Polunina, Valentyna, and Andreas Umland. 2016. "If Ukraine Wants the ICC's Help, It Must Play by the ICC's Rules." *The National Interest*, July 24. Accessed November 21, 2021. nationalinterest.org/feature/if-ukraine-wants-the-iccs-help-it-must-play-by-its-rules-17089

Polyakova, Alina. 2014. "From the Provinces to the Parliament: How the Ukrainian Radical Right Mobilized in Galicia." *Communist and Post-Communist Studies* 47 (2): 211-225. DOI: 10.1016/j.postcomstud.2014.04.012

_____. 2015. *The Dark Side of European Integration: Social Foundations and Cultural Determinants of the Rise of Radical Right Movements in Contemporary Europe.* Stuttgart: *ibidem*-Verlag.

Ponomarenko, Ilya. 2021. "Ukraine's Friend & Foe of the Week." *Kyiv Post*, July 2. Accessed November 21, 2021. www.kyivpost.com/article/opinion/op-ed/lllia-ponomarenko-ukraines-friend-foe-of-the-week.html.

Serdy, Andrew. 2021. "HMS Defender Incident: What the Law of the Sea Says." *The Conversation*, June 24. Accessed November 21, 2021. https://theconversation.com/hms-defender-incident-what-the-law-of-the-sea-says-163389

Shekhovtsov, Anton. 2011. *Novye radikal'nye partii v evropeiskikh demokratiiakh: prichiny elektoral'noi podderzhki* [New radical parties in European democracies: Causes for their electoral support]. Stuttgart: *ibidem*-Verlag.

Shekhovtsov, Anton. 2014. "From Electoral Success to Revolutionary Failure:

The Ukrainian Svoboda Party."*Eurozine*, March 5. Accessed November 21, 2021. https://www.eurozine.com/from-electoral-success-to-revolutionary-failure/

Shekhovtsov, Anton, and Andreas Umland. 2014. "Ukraine's Radical Right." *Journal of Democracy* 25 (3): 58-63. DOI: 10.1353/jod.2014.0051

Sinovets, Polina, and Mariana Budjeryn. 2017. "Interpreting the Bomb. Ownership and Deterrence in Ukraine's Nuclear Discourse." *NPIHP Working Paper* 12. Accessed November 21, 2021. www.wilsoncenter.org/publication/interpreting-the-bomb-ownership-and-deterrence-ukraines-nuclear-discourse

_____. 2018. "Denuclearization Again? Lessons from Ukraine's Decision to Disarm." *War on the Rocks*, April 19. Accessed November 21, 2021. warontherocks.com/2018/04/denuclearization-again-lessons-from-ukraines-decision-to-disarm/

TopWar. 2021. "NI: Strategically, Ukraine is a 'trap' for the United States." June 29. Accessed November 21, 2021. en.topwar.ru/184527-ni-ukraina-dlja-ssha-opasnyj-sojuznik.html

Umland, Andreas. 2009. "Averting a Post-Orange Disaster: Constitutional Reforms and Political Stability in Ukraine." *Harvard International Review*, June. Accessed November 21, 2021. https://www.researchgate.net/profile/Andreas-Umland/publication/255918342_Averting_a_Post-Orange_Disaster_Constitutional_Reforms_and_Political_Stability_in_Ukraine/

_____. 2016. "The Ukraine Example: Nuclear Disarmament Doesn't Pay." *World Affairs* 178 (4): 45-49. Accessed November 21, 2021. https://www.jstor.org/stable/24888130

_____. 2020. "The Far Right in Pre- and Post-Euromaidan Ukraine: From Ultra-Nationalist Party Politics to Ethno-Centric Uncivil Society." *Demokratizatsiya* 28 (2): 247-268.

_____. 2021a. "The Dangers of Echoing Russian Disinformation on Ukraine." *Ukraine Alert*, June 19. Accessed November 21, 2021. www.atlanticcouncil.org/blogs/ukrainealert/the-dangers-of-echoing-russian-disinformation-on-ukraine/

_____. 2021b. "Zapadnye deiateli povtoriaiut rossiiskuiu dezinformatsiiu ob Ukraine [The Dangers of Echoing Russian Disinformation on Ukraine]." *Gazeta.ua*, June 24. Accessed November 21, 2021. gazeta.ua/ru/blog/55294/zahidni-diyachi-povtoryuyut-rosijsku-dezinformaciyu-pro-ukrayinu-ce-nebezpechna-gra. Zugegriffen: 15. August, 2021.

_____. 2021c. "'Dalekaia strana, o kotoroi my znaem malo...': o zabluzhdeni-iakh amerikanskikh analitikov ob Ukraine ['A distant country, about which we know little...': About the delusions of American analysts about Ukraine]." *Khvylja*, June 26. Accessed November 21, 2021. analytics.hvylya.net/232611-dalekaya-strana-o-kotoroy-my-znaem-malo-o-zabluzhdeniyah-amerikan skih-analitikov-ob-ukraine

_____. 2021d. "Die Ukraine, USA und Nichtverbreitung von Atomwaffen [Ukraine, USA and nuclear non-proliferation]." *Ukraine verstehen*, June 25. Accessed November 21, 2021. ukraineverstehen.de/umland-ukraine-usa-nichtverb reitung-von-atomwaffen/

_____. 2021e. "Die Ukraine, USA und Nichtverbreitung von Atomwaffen: Replik auf einen Artikel zur amerikanischen Ukrainepolitik [Ukraine, USA and nuclear non-proliferation: Reply to an article on American policy on Ukraine]." *Portal für Politikwissenschaft*, July 30. Accessed November 21, 2021. pw-portal.de/schlaglichter/41275-die-ukraine-usa-und-nichtverbreitung-von-atomwaffen

Vereshchuk, Iryna, and Andreas Umland. 2019. "How to Make Eastern Europe's Gray Zone Less Gray." *Harvard International Review* 40 (1): 38-41. Accessed November 21, 2021. https://hir.harvard.edu/how-to-make-eastern-europes-gray-zone-less-gray/

Wynnyckij, Mychailo. 2019. *Ukraine's Maidan, Russia's War: A Chronicle and Analysis of the Revolution of Dignity*, Stuttgart: *ibidem*-Verlag.

Zloy-Odessit. 2021. "Rossiia cherez The National Interest pytaetsia v ocherednoi raz diskreditirovat' otnosheniia Ukrainy i SShA [Russia tries via The National Interest again to discredit the relations between Ukraine and the U.S.]." June 30. Accessed November 21, 2021. zloy-odessit.livejournal.com/3547087.html

COMMENTARY: The Cultural Determinants of Party System Change

RICCARDO PELIZZO

Graduate School of Public Policy, Nazarbayev University

ZIM NWOKORA

Deakin University

The purpose of this commentary piece is to uncover some of the key the cultural determinants of party systems change. Our basic claim is that the 1960s witnessed what we call the rise of the fluid self, of an individual who had complex, conflicting, and inconsistent preferences. We ground the pervasiveness of fluidity in this notion of the individual in key elements of popular culture (theater, popular music, Western film characters etc.) to show that cultural expressions reflect, but also shape, the culture of a society and transformation in its party system and public policy. We then link this to the crisis of parties, understood in diverse ways, that has faced European party systems and the success of their conocomitant electoral policy offers for decades. We advance three related claims: first, that the rise of the fluid self created a conflict between structures and the individual; second, that this conflict made the previous/existing structures obsolete; and, third, that the obsolescence of such structures led to the unfreezing of Western European party systems and higher levels of party system fluidity, both of which have a bearing on policy making and policy studies.

Keywords: Cultural Determinants, Cultural Approach, Cultural Change, Explaining Party System Change, Political Parties, Political Science, Party Crisis, Democracy, Individuals, Structures, Western European Party Systems, Democratization, Party System Fluidity, Cleavage Structure, Cultural Studies.

Los determinantes culturales del cambio del sistema de partidos

El propósito de este artículo es descubrir los determinantes culturales del cambio en los sistemas de partidos. Nuestra afirmación básica a

Policy Studies Yearbook 12.1: 235-255. 10.18278/psy.12.1.8

este respecto es que la década de 1960 fue testigo de lo que llamamos el surgimiento del yo fluido, de un individuo que tenía preferencias complejas, conflictivas e inconsistentes. Fundamentamos la omnipresencia de la fluidez en elementos clave de la cultura popular (que incluyen teatro, música popular y personajes de películas occidentales) para mostrar que las expresiones culturales reflejan, pero también dan forma, a la cultura de una sociedad y la transformación en su sistema de partidos y política pública. Luego vinculamos esto con la crisis de los partidos, entendida de diversas maneras, que ha enfrentado los sistemas de partidos europeos y el éxito de las ofertas de política electoral durante décadas. Presentamos tres afirmaciones relacionadas: primero, que el surgimiento del yo fluido creó un conflicto entre las estructuras y el individuo; segundo, que este conflicto volvió obsoletas las estructuras anteriores/existentes y, tercero, que la obsolescencia de tales estructuras condujo al descongelamiento de los sistemas de partidos de Europa occidental y niveles más altos de fluidez del sistema de partidos, los cuales tienen relación con la formulación de políticas y estudios de política.

Palabras clave: Determinantes culturales, Enfoque cultural, Cambio cultural, Explicación del cambio del sistema de partidos, Partidos políticos, Ciencias políticas, Crisis de partidos, Democracia, Individuos, Estructuras, Teoría política, Sistemas de partidos de Europa occidental, Democratización, Fluidez del sistema de partidos, Estudios culturales.

黨制變革的文化決定因素

本文的目的是揭示政黨制度變革的文化決定因素。我們在這方面的基本主張是，1960 年代見證了我們所說的流動自我的興起，即具有復雜、衝突和不一致偏好的個人的興起。我們將流動性普遍存在於流行文化的關鍵要素（包括戲劇、流行音樂和西方電影人物）中，以表明文化表現形式反映並塑造了社會文化以及政黨制度和公共政策的轉變。然後，我們將其與政黨危機聯繫起來，以多種方式理解，幾十年來，歐洲政黨體系和選舉政策提議的成功都面臨著政黨危機。我們提出了三個相關的主張：第一，流動自我的興起在結構和個人之間造成了衝突；第二，這場衝突使以前/現有的結構過時，第三，這種結構的過時導致西歐政黨制度解凍，政黨制度流動性更高，這兩者都對政策制定和政策研究。

關鍵詞：文化決定因素、文化途徑、文化變革、解釋政黨制度變革、政黨、政治學、政黨危機、民主、個人、結構、政治理論、西歐政黨制度、民主化、政黨制度流動性、文化研究。

The cultural approach is one of the best-known approaches in the study of political science and, by extension, has a strong bearing on policy making and policy studies. Culture has been used to explain the rise of capitalism (Weber 2002), economic backwardness (Banfield 1965), the functioning of democratic regimes (Almond and Verba 1963), the consolidation and survival of democracy (Lipset 1959), and institutional performance (Putnam, Leonardi, and Nanetti 1993).

Little attention, however, has been paid to whether cultural conditions or factors were in some way responsible for the transformation of party systems or party system change. From Duverger (1954) onward, party systems were believed to be the product of history. Lipset and Rokkan (1967), building on Duverger, went on to say that the structure or the format of West European party systems reflected the number of cleavages that had emerged at various points in history and that were still salient when universal suffrage was granted in the first wave of democratization. The party system reflected what Lipset and Rokkan (1967) called the cleavage structure and, according to this line of inquiry, party system change would occur only as a result of the transformation of the cleavage structure.

Efforts to explain party system change, as evidenced by the emergence of new parties, in cultural terms was limited. Only the rise of the parties of the so-called New Left and, later, the rise of the new radical right parties were explained as a result of a cultural change. The appearance of post-materialist values created an electoral niche that parties of the New Left could exploit and the parties of the radical right could be regarded as a reaction against the New Left. As Ignazi (1992, 6) pointed out, the programs, the platforms, and the policy proposals of the new extreme right are inconsistent with, but not unrelated to, the post-material value system, because they represent "a reaction to it, a sort of 'silent counterrevolution'"—a point further elaborated by Kitschelt and McGann (1997). Hence, a cultural explanation was invoked or adopted only to explain party system change in terms of the appearance of new parties (and, subordinately, the emergence of new cleavages and the transformation of the cleavage structure). However, to the best of our knowledge, it was never—or not consistently—employed to shed light on the transformation of the patterns of inter-party competition, which is how Sartori (1976) understood party system change, or on what Mair (1996) called party system closure.

The purpose of the present work is to uncover the cultural determinants of party systems change. Our basic claim is that the 1960s witnessed what we call the 'rise of the fluid self'—a notion of an individual who had complex, conflicting, and inconsistent preferences. We extend this to argue that the rise of such an individual created a conflict between structures and the individual, that this conflict made the previous/existing structures obsolete, and the obsolescence of such structures led to the unfreezing of Western European party systems and higher levels of party system fluidity. The rest of this commentary article is organized as follows.

The first section deals with the notion of the fluid self. The rise of the fluid self is documented by analyzing the changes that popular (pop/mass) culture experienced in the period under consideration. A brief review of a seminal play of the theater of Absurd, of new vanguards such as Fluxus, of new comic heroes such as Corto Maltese, of the transformation of Western movie characters, of the role that pop music played in bringing down structures, such as racial barriers, and in promoting new, more fluid, gender roles reveals that the notion of fluidity pervaded all types of cultural manifestations. Insofar as cultural expressions reflect, but also shape, the culture of a society, the pervasiveness of fluidity in so many different forms of cultural expression testifies to the fact that the 1960s witnessed the rise of the fluid self. There are two reasons why we decided to explore cultural conditions in this way instead of solely relying, as most political cultural studies tend to do, on survey data. The first is that, in our view, most of the studies produced in the political culture tradition reduce culture to values and attitudes but neglect the extent to which the culture of a given polity is reflected but also shaped by its cultural manifestations; that is, by the products of mass and high culture. The second reason is that, with survey data, survey questions either provide the respondent with binary oppositions (unemployment v. inflation) or with an opportunity of indicating a fixed preference—yet the expression of fixed preferences as well as the supply of binary oppositions structure the respondent's responses, thus preventing her from manifesting the fluidity of her preferences and stances. In order to avoid the twin trappings of neglect (of cultural products and manifestations) and structuring, we decided to adopt an approach closer to what is being used in cultural studies so that we could not only bring culture back in, but also and more importantly show the growing pervasiveness of fluidity in the culture of West European polities. Building on this discussion in the second section, we explore the relationship between the rise of the fluid self and the so-called party crisis. The notion of a party crisis can be understood in two different, though possibly related, ways. In one sense, the party crisis may refer to the crisis of a specific model of party organization; that is, the mass party of social integration (Katz and Mair 1995). With the advent of catch-all parties, the mass party entered a critical phase, and lost members and votes. The notion of a party crisis, however, can be understood in a second way. In this case, the notion of party crisis refers to the crisis of a party as an organization or institution. The evidence presented in this section shows that Western European parties lost members and votes. Parties, as structures, could no longer provide voters with a political offer or with policy offers that could satisfy the demands of new, fluid, voters. The crisis of political parties is then the inevitable consequence of the tension/conflict between the fluidity of voters' demands and the structurally induced rigidity of the policy offers that political parties could provide. The mismatch between voters' demands and parties' policy/political offers has been documented by the literature on the so-called cartel party and it has generally been explained on the basis of parties' alleged unwillingness to satisfy voters' demands. This line of work attempted to find an explanation of such a mismatch by focusing on the supply side. The evidence we discuss here, however, suggests that the demands of a fluid electorate have changed in ways that could not possibly be satisfied by the political offer that political parties could supply. Building on this discussion, in the third section we show how the rise of the fluid self and the ensuing party crisis eventually translated into party system change. We show how, in the end, the emergence of a fluid self was responsible for rising levels of fluidity at the party-system level. In the final section we formulate, as is customary, some tentative conclusions.

The Rise of the Fluid Self

The Fluid Self in Popular Culture

Theater

In 2009 or 2010 Sir Ian McKellen came to Sydney to perform Samuel Beckett's *Waiting for Godot*. McKellen played the part of an Estragon who was, for the first part of the play, acting as a man affected by dementia. One of the authors of the present work recalls watching McKellen from a third-row seat, wondering whether McKellen had become a senile or whether that is how he felt he should characterize the character he was playing on stage—a doubt that was cleared up by the time the play came to an end. McKellen's performance was remarkable. Yet, that spectacular performance of *Waiting for Godot* in some, not insignificant, ways betrayed Beckett's text. There is a rich literature discussing tradition and betrayal, not to mention the tradition of betrayal. But each and every tradition is also always a betrayal in itself. In keeping up with a long tradition of the performance of *Waiting of Godot*, Beckett's script had been, once again, betrayed.

Possibly the single most important play in twentieth-century theater, *Waiting for Godot* is not just a story of two clochards waiting for someone who does not actually show up. The play is not just about the waiting. Neither is it merely about the power relations between Pozzo and Lucky. Likewise, it is not only an almost Nietzschean eternal return of the same as evidenced by the nearly perfect structural resemblance of the two acts. The play is, of course, all these things but it is more. *Waiting for Godot* is the first staging of fluidity.[1] That quasi-phenome-

---

1 As it will soon be clear, our discussion of the fluidity in *Waiting for Godot* has nothing to do with the kind of fluidity that Gupta (2005) thought was associated with this text. For Gupta (2005, 216) the fluidity of the text has to do with the fact that "the act of authorship appears to be an-ongoing pro-

nological infinite web of relations that Vladimir and Estragon enter into is insufficient to capture what is the true and truly innovative contribution of this play: the characters of Vladimir and Estragon are fluid and morph into one another and, as the play unfolds, take on each other's role.

Literature

Waiting for Godot is the first effort, to the best of our knowledge, to put on stage and give representation to the fluidity of roles, characters, and relationships. Seventeen years after the first representation, in Paris, of *Waiting for Godot*, Umberto Eco (1968) published *La Struttura Assente*. While Eco (1962) had already achieved a certain level of fame in cultural circles with the publication of *Opera Aperta* that documented the linguistic techniques and the ideological role of the artistic vanguards, *La Struttura Assente* represented an even more important contribution as it foreshadowed the crisis of structuralism that had been, up to the point, a quasi-hegemonic paradigm in the social sciences and humanities. Eco (1968) was not simply challenging the structuralist approach or paradigm or advocating the virtues of semiotics. Several pages in the book are actually devoted to the crisis, the absence, and eventually the self-destruction of the 'structure.'

Since the publication of Claude Lévi-Strauss's (1955) structural study of the myth, structuralists had focused on what Lévi-Strauss (1955, 431) called bundles of relations. These bundles juxtapose each other, as Eco (1965) noted in his analysis of Ian Fleming's narrative structures, characters, and values. In the Bond novels, relations between characters, values, and situations (and the novels themselves) are structured by the repetition of a formula which is well known to the reader. The role that the characters played in the myth(s) analyzed by Lévi-Strauss or in the novels of the mass/pop culture were structurally determined and, hence, fixed. They had the same juxtaposition of characters, values, and situations that one can detect in the John Ford/John Wayne movies (Wright 1977; Coëgnarts and Kravanja 2014; Yacavone 2018).

Film

By the mid-1960s, the structurally induced fixity of the characters—so clear in the Western movies directed by John Ford—came to be replaced by a new set of more fluid, morally ambiguous, Western movie characters. Sergio Leone's famous

---

cess over an extended period of time." For us, the fluidity of *Waiting for Godot* results from the fact that the two main characters, Vladimir and Estragon, engage not only in a wide phenomenology of relationships but appears in the ongoing inversion, conversion, and subversion of roles. Shahid (2018, 113) claimed that "The silence vigorously discerns the creative hushed revelation of postmodern aspiration for the unsayable and unspoken to proclaim the dissolution of meanings and its subsequent persuasion of plurality and fluidity of reality." We believe that the fluid nature of the roles that the two characters embody in their ever-changing relation provides a better indication of the fluidity of reality that Shahid (2018), correctly, refers to. Our view is, in this regard, much closer to Tait (2019).

1966 film *The Good, the Bad, and the Ugly* is emblematic in this respect. The good is not really that good and is often rather bad; the bad, besides being bad, is also at different points in time good and ugly; and the ugly is not that ugly and is both good and bad depending on the situation. Every character can turn into another. Once the structural determinism of the characters' rigidity/fixity is removed, characters are free to manifest their fluid self.

Graphic Novels

Graphic novels also witnessed the emergence of more fluid characters. Hugo Pratt's Corto Maltese is a perfect case in point. Recent studies, to some extent correctly, have suggested that "the politically subversive element of Corto Maltese comic books is not so much its manifest attention to the ideals of solidarity and affection for various marginalised groups… but rather the Deleuzo-Guattarian endless flows of meanings" (Stankovic 2019, 8) or what semioticians, Stankovic (2019) included, call endless or unlimited semiosis. Whether and to what extent unlimited semiosis is politically subversive is a question that extends beyond the remit of the present study. But reducing the subversive nature of Corto Maltese simply to the 'endless flows of meanings' leads one to neglect the equally important anarchic tendencies that Corto, with his allergies to hierarchy and authority, displays in each of the 29 adventures penned by Hugo Pratt. We do not wish to dispute either Corto Maltese's subversive tendencies or the unlimited semiosis that characterizes each of his adventures. We nevertheless get the impression that both accounts of what is subversive in Corto Maltese stories fail to capture what is truly subversive in the Corto Maltese saga: Corto Maltese is a fluid character and the Corto Maltese stories document the tension—one is tempted to say the *conflict*—between structure (and the structurally induced rigidity of roles) and the fluid self. There is no structural determinism in the Corto Maltese stories because Corto Maltese is not simply the product of structural conditions. His character is fluid because he is open or ready to do anything and its opposite. The fluid nature of Corto Maltese emerges with some clarity in his relation with Rasputin. Like the relationship between Vladimir and Estragon, the relationship between Corto and Rasputin is not static, it is dynamic and ever changing. Acts of great friendship alternate with egregious betrayals, efforts to save one another are intermixed with efforts to kill one another. The fluidity of this character (Corto Maltese) is subversive because the structures (not only of meaning)—upon which political order rests—no longer hold.

Art

In the realm of visual and plastic art, the movement Fluxus also provided an indication of the fact that our societies were becoming increasingly fluid. The movement was called Fluxus because it was expected to produce a tide or a wave. So while, in the intention of its founder(s), Fluxus was not necessarily intended to represent a venue for the expression of a fluid self, Fluxus ended up nonetheless as an agent of fluidity. Fluxus changed or attempted to change what could be considered as 'art.' It created works that were never ending and hence constantly in flux and finally took steps to destroy the (structural) separation between the artist and the spectator: spectators were allowed, invited, and even encouraged to contribute to art work. In 1961 Yoko Ono created—we cannot say painted because the artwork required more than just painting—an artwork entitled "Painting to Hammer a Nail" and visitors/viewers were allowed to hammer a nail in the canvas; thus breaking down the structural division between art producers and art consumers. Art had become more fluid. It had become a manifestation of the growing fluidity in society; art broke down the structural barriers between artists and spectators, thus securing and displaying the greater fluidity of their roles.

Popular Music

Pop and rock music were also instrumental in the removal of structures and barriers that had defined roles and given them rigidity. While white middle-class teenagers in the United Kingdom in the mid-1960s discovered and promoted the Delta Blues, Mick Jagger's sensuality challenged gender roles, identities, and orientations (Norman 1984). In the years in which Inglehart (1971) was writing about the rise of post-material values and the importance of self-realization, David Bowie legitimized the notion of what has alternatively been defined as gender transgression (Perrott 2017), gender bending (Coates 1997), gender variability (Halberstam 2017), or gender fluidity (Bradley and Page 2017).

The Rise of the Fluid Self and Political Science

Theater, movies, comics, art, and pop music to some extent reflected and to some extent promoted the rise of the fluid self and, conversely, the obsolescence of structure. The above brief and oversimplified review of how popular culture promoted the notion of fluidity has some obvious, yet important, implications for the social sciences in general, and political science in particular. First, it reminds us that political phenomena can only be understood in relation to, or in the context of, the cultural settings in which they manifest themselves (Morgan 2013). Second, and more specifically, it shows that the structures that had regulated the functioning of political systems and our lives, with the rise of the fluid self and fluid societies were (at risk of) becoming, or were about to become, outdated.

This transformation has not gone undetected. Bauman (2010), in what became an instant classic, noted that modernity had reached a new stage; that we had experienced a transition from solid to liquid modernity; that structures had become anachronistic because of their inability to provide adequate answers to the questions that liquid modernity brings with itself. The liquid modernity that Bauman theorized is a modernity characterized by an ubiquitous uncertainty, the separation of power from politics, by obsessively ongoing modernizing trends and efforts. There are obvious similarities between the liquidity that Bauman (2010) so forcefully brought to our attention and the notion of fluidity that we present here. Like Bauman, we also believe that the old structures and solutions are unable to cope with the challenges of the current phase of modernity. Like Bauman, we also wonder whether the phase that we are living in is a transitional phase between what was before and what has not yet arrived or whether what we are experiencing is instead the new phase. And we also agree that the current phase is characterized by growing uncertainty.

But our notion of fluidity differs in significant ways from Bauman's (2010) liquidity. For Bauman, liquidity was/is connected with the liquidation of old structures whose obsolescence had been brought about by proximate causes, such as deregulation, and ultimate causes such as the consumerist tendencies of contemporary societies. Along with the marketization of society that Polanyi (1943) had already identified with the great (and pernicious) transformation, such causes are responsible for all the changes that, for Bauman (2010), and earlier for Deleuze and Guattari (2008), are so problematic. For Bauman, the source of change and the causes of liquidity are structural—as in the Marxian/Marxist sense of the term— and operate at the macro level. In Bauman's (2010) account, there is no room for agency and whatever room is granted to culture is not more than what, for example in the Marxist tradition, has been granted to superstructural conditions— which, when they experience some kind of change, do so as a result of a change at the structural level.

Our approach is in many ways antithetic to Bauman's (2010). The obsolescence of structures and institutions (at the macro level) is primarily the result of the cultural changes associated with the emergence of a liquid self. Unlike Bauman, we attempt to provide a micro-level foundation for macro-level changes: structures change and/or become obsolete because they no longer manage to satisfy the demands, the needs, and the preferences of the individuals whose lives and activities they are supposed to structure and regulate. Society changes and structures become obsolete because individuals changed.

From the Rise of the Fluid Self to the Crisis of Party

For Maslow (1943), and later for Inglehart (1971), there is a sort of a hierarchy of needs, such that once lower-level needs are satisfied, the individual seeks to find satisfaction for higher-order needs. In explaining the rise of post-material values, Inglehart (1971) noted that it had occurred as a result of a betterment in the material conditions that Western societies experienced in the postwar era and increasingly in the 1960s. Whether the emergence of the fluid self would have occurred in the West if it had failed to achieve the kind of material wellbeing that it enjoyed in the 1960s (and more so in the following decades) or not is a question beyond the scope of the present analysis and for which we do not have a response.

But what is clear is that, with the rise of the fluid self—that is, with the emergence of a fluid individual with complex, possibly contradictory, or conflicting desires and with greater levels of instability and/or changeability that the rise of those complex conflicting desires had brought about—the old structures were no longer properly equipped to satisfy in an adequate manner the demands of these new individuals. The case of political parties was, and is, in this respect, rather emblematic.

Struck by the fact that the party systems of the 1960s were virtually identical to those of the 1920s in spite of all that happened in between, Lipset and Rokkan (1967) suggested that the stability of party systems was a byproduct of the stability of the cleavage structure. Lipset and Rokkan (1967) argued that, at several critical junctures, specific revolutions had occurred and that these revolutions had created politically divisive social cleavages. They likewise claimed that the format of the various party systems depended on and reflected the number of cleavages that were still salient when universal suffrage was granted and that the resemblance between the party systems of the 1920s and the 1960s was (or could be) explained by the fact that, in that timeframe, the cleavage structure had not changed. Writing in the 1960s, Lipset and Rokkan could not see or foresee how the emergence of the fluid self and the resulting transformation of Western societies in the 1960s would eventually transform the format of Western party systems. But, with the emergence of the fluid self, parties and party systems were set on their path toward greater change.

The appeal of parties to their prospective members declined. Katz and others (1992, 334) reported that the ratio between (party) Members and Voters (M/E) in the first election of the 1960s was 14.6 percent, by the last election in the 1980s the percentage had declined to 10.5 percent. Mair and van Biezen (2001) showed that, by the end of the 1990s, the M/E ratio had dropped to 4.99 percent, while van Biezen, Mair, and Poguntke (2012, 28) showed that the downward trend had continued in the following decade in such a way that, at the end of the first decade of the new millennium, the M/E ratio had reached a modest 4.65 percent.

The first reason why party membership had declined so significantly was that the historical parties had lost their appeal. In the first election of the 1960s, the British Labor Party and the Conservative Party won, respectively, 44.1 and 43.4 percent of the vote and combined for a total of 87.5 percent of the vote. In the last elections held in the 1980s, the Conservative Party and the Labor Party won, respectively, 42.2 and 30.8 percent of the British vote and combined for a total of 73 percent of the vote. In the 23 years from the 1964 to the 1987 elections, Britain's main parties had lost 14.5 percent of the valid votes cast.

Moving to the Netherlands, in the 1989 elections the Labor Party (PvdA) and the Christian Democratic Appeal (CDA) won, respectively, 31.91 and 35.32 percent of the vote for a combined 67.23 percent. The performance of the PvdA in the 1989 elections was a little bit better than it had been in the first election of the 1960s, but the performance of the CDA was dramatically improved. In the 1963 elections the Catholic People's Party, the Anti-Revolutionary Party, and the Christian Historical Union, which would join forces in 1977 to form the CDA, had won, respectively, 31.88, 8.72, and 8.58 percent of the vote. This means that the electoral performance of CDA and PvdA in 1989 was 9.96 percent lower than it had been 26 years earlier.

In the 1961-89 period the combined electoral returns of the two largest parties in Norway (Labor and Conservative) declined by 9.6 percent from 66.1 to 56.5 percent. In the 1962-88 period the share of the vote of the two largest electoral blocs (Left and Right) in France declined from 99.12 to 89.39.

In Germany there was virtually no change in the electoral strength of its two major parties, the Christian Democratic Union-Christian Social Union (CDU-CSU) and the Social Democratic Party (SPD) from 1961 to 1987. In 1961 they won a combined 81.5 percent of the vote and 26 years later they won a combined 81.2 percent of the vote.

In Italy the electoral strength of the two main parties, the Italian Communist Party (PCI) and the Christian Democracy (DC) decreased by a mere 2.7 percent from 1963 to 1987. The DC and the PCI, which had won a combined 63.6 percent of the vote in 1963, won 60.9 percent of the valid votes cast in 1987. But, in 1992, following the transformation of the PCI into the Democratic Party of the Left (PDS)—and the split of the Communist Refoundation Party or PRC and the beginning of the Tangentopoli scandal that put an end to the party system of the so-called First Republic—the DC and the PDS combined for a mere 45.8 percent of the vote—a decrease of 17.8 percent in 29 years.

This evidence appears to sustain the claim that traditional/historical parties, to a lesser or greater extent, had lost some appeal. And the loss of electoral appeal could make party membership less appealing. But the loss of appeal of the historical parties was not compensated by the growing popularity of the newly emerged parties. The emergence of the parties of the New Left, most notably the Greens, the rise of the parties of what has alternatively been called the new radical right or the new extreme right, and the appearance of new regionalist parties failed to boost party membership in Western European polities. Parties had lost their appeal to members and, conversely, members had lost some appeal to the political parties.

According to Katz (1990) the decline in the number of party members was due to the fact that the benefits of party membership had decreased while the costs had increased for both parties and prospective members. Due to the introduction of state subventions to party finance, parties no longer valued as much as they once did the revenue that party membership could provide. Likewise, in the absence of a widespread, highly ideologized membership base, they could no longer enjoy a greater freedom of movement. Members, Katz (1990, 151) showed, were no longer the most loyal group of voters for a party. For members, the benefits such as the ability to influence policy making had decreased while the costs of party membership were magnified by the fact that, with the emergence of new forms of participation, prospective members had other and better opportunities to be politically active.

The analysis of the costs and benefits that parties may enjoy or incur because of party membership provides a compelling explanation for why party membership had become less attractive for political parties. Yet, the analysis of the costs and benefits that perspective members may enjoy or incur because of party membership, however convincing, is somewhat incomplete since it has largely neglected the fact that Western European voters and societies were significantly transformed by the rise of the fluid self. The rise of the fluid self created, if not a conflict, then at least a clear tension between structure and fluidity—and the decline in party membership levels and political parties' vanishing appeal were an inevitable byproduct of such tension.

The Rise of the Fluid Self and the Impossible Equilibrium between Supply and Demand

For many years since the publication of *An Economic Theory of Democracy* (Downs 1957), patterns of electoral competition and electoral choice came to be increasingly analyzed in spatial analytic terms. Downs (1957) famously suggested that, in a unidimensional political space, a voter would vote for the party closer to her position. The utility that a voter attached to a political party—and, subordinately, the decision to vote for that party—was a function of the proximity between the voter's and the party's position. The idea was quite simply that in political systems or in party systems there is a sort of super dimension, the left-right dimension, and voters' and parties' positions on that dimension provide an indication of all that voters and parties stand for. The preferences of voters and parties were, or at least were believed to be, consistent or homogeneous. Voters of the Left were (believed to) prefer a macroeconomic configuration characterized by lower unemployment and higher inflation to a macroeconomic configuration characterized by higher unemployment and lower inflation. Believing in or assuming a party's desire to provide proper representation to the demands and the preferences of their voters, Hibbs Jr. (1977) suggested that, once in government, parties of the Left would attempt to reduce unemployment while allowing inflation to rise, while parties of the Right would attempt to reduce inflation while tolerating higher levels of unemployment. The results of the static and the dynamic analysis presented by Hibbs Jr. showed that the Left reduced unemployment and the Right allowed unemployment to increase.

In the wake of the oil shocks, stagflation obviously constrained the ability of parties to manufacture macroeconomic policy. Instead, and for lack of a better word, they manipulated the government macroeconomic performance to maximize their electoral returns in the following election. By contrast, Sargent and Wallace (1976) suggested that, while parties may have wanted to manufacture macroeconomic outcomes, their ability to do so was constrained, reduced, neutralized, and nullified by the fact that voters and firms may anticipate their efforts. Stagflation, the manipulation of macroeconomic conditions, and the anticipation of government efforts to manufacture macroeconomic outputs called into question the ability of parties to give proper representation to their voters' macroeconomic preferences. But the emergence of the fluid self and societies reduced even more their ability to match voter preferences. This is because, while parties—especially parties in government—could only translate a macroeconomic preference into a single macro-economic intervention, the preferences of the voters were fluid, unstable, ever changing, and often self-contradictory and inconsistent. They therefore could not possibly be satisfied by the policy and political offers of governments and parties.

The emergence of the fluid self is, or was, a silent revolution that even Inglehart had failed to fully appreciate. For Inglehart (1971), materialist demands were replaced by higher-order demands, but the new demands were as univocal and single-peaked as the old ones. In Inglehart's (1971) framework for analysis, someone holding materialist values would prefer employment and economic growth to environmental protection, whereas someone holding post-materialist values would prefer environmental protection to employment and economic growth. Inglehart thought that the silent revolution occurred because new values and preferences replaced the previous ones, that such preferences could be pitted against one another or be depicted in oppositional terms. However, with the rise of the fluid self, voters rejected such dichotomies and oppositions. The fluid voter did not want either growth/employment or environmental protection; the fluid voter wanted growth/employment *and* environmental protection. The 1998 Dutch Parliamentary Election Survey (see Aarts, van der Kolk, and Kamp 2006) offers some support for the claims we have advanced so far. Dutch voters were asked to indicate on a 10-point scale (1= unimportant, 10 = very important) the importance of 15 issues. The mean response for the importance of unemployment (materialist demand) was 8.01, while the mean response for the importance of pollution (post-materialist concern) was 7.87.

What we have said so far has an obvious implication. Since policies inevitably reflect priorities and/or create trade-offs as well as winners and losers (Gourevitch 1986), no policy offer and no policy making could come close to satisfying the (inconsistent) demands of the new, fluid voter. Parties' inability to come up with policy offers that could satisfy voters' demands reduced their appeal in the eyes of the voters, was responsible for a weakening (if not vanishing) of the voters' allegiances, and created the conditions for party system change.

From Party Crisis to Party System Change

The literature has discussed several ways in which party system change could be conceptualized and measured. Party system change has been associated with party change, electoral change, change in the cleavage structure (Lispet and Rokkan1967), change in the patterns of inter-party competition (Sartori 1976) and, more recently, in the related patterns of alternation in office, access to government, and government formulae (Mair 1996).

One of the most recent proposals to better capture the changeability of party systems is represented by the Index of Party System Fluidity (Nwokora and Pelizzo 2018; Pelizzo and Nwokora 2016, 2018). This index computes the fluidity of a party system by combining the frequency, the scope, and the magnitude of party system change. The frequency of a party system change is calculated by dividing the number of party system changes by the number of elections held in a given country. The scope of party system change is estimated by computing the distance between the two most different types of party systems that a country experiences in the course of its political history, while the variety of party system change tracks the number of party systems that the analyst can detect in a country's history. The index of party system fluidity is computed on the basis of the following formula:

$$Fluidity = Frequency *(scope*variety)$$

As we have noted in previous work (see Nwokora and Pelizzo 2018; Pelizzo and Nwokora 2016, 2018; see also Katz et al. 1992; van Biezen, Mair, and Poguntke 2012), party system fluidity has been evident.

In Austria, the fluidity of the party system increased from 0.67 in the 1962 elections to 2.29 in 1990 and to 2.9 in 2017.

In Belgium, the fluidity of the party system increased from 0 (in the 1919, 1921, and 1925 elections) to 2.4 in 2019 with party system changes occurring in 1961, 1968, 1974, 1987, and 1991.

In France, the fluidity of the party system increased from 0 in the 1945 (and 1946) elections to 2.12 in the 2017 elections.

In Germany, the fluidity of the party system increased from 2.81 in 1961 to 5 in the 1990 election and dropped to 4.52 in the 2017 elections.

In the 32 elections held in Great Britain from 1906 to 2019, there were 11 party system changes and the computation of the index of volatility reveals that the fluidity of the British party system increased from 1 in 1906 to 2.06 in 2019. In the 53 years between the 1906 and the 1959 elections, the index of fluidity registered an increase of 0.5 while in the 60 years from 1959 to 2019 it recorded an increase of .56.

In Ireland, there was one party system change in the elections held in the 1938-52 period (the party system change occurred in the 1945 elections) while there were six party system changes in the 11 elections held in the 1959-2018 period.

In Italy, the highly fragmented and ideologically polarized party system lasted for 11 consecutive elections and was replaced by a moderate pluralist party system in 1994. The fluidity of the Italian party system increased from 0 in the 1948 elections to .16 in the 1994 elections and in the 2018 election was of about .11.

In Portugal, in the 40 years since democracy was restored and from the first democratic elections, there were three party system changes (in 1986, 1991, and 2016) and the fluidity of the party system increased from 0 in the 1976 elections to 1.33 in the 1986 elections, to 2 in the 1991 and 2016 elections.

In Spain, in the aftermath of Franco's authoritarian rule, there were 14 elections, five party system changes, and a growing scope and variety of party systems which resulted in higher levels of fluidity. Fluidity in Spain increased from 0 in the 1976 elections to 0.4 in the 1993 elections, to .66 in the 1996 elections, and to 2.14 in the 2019 elections.

The upward trend of party system fluidity, that we have just documented for a selection of West European countries, can also be detected in other Western democracies. From 1961 to 2019, Australia held 23 elections and experienced eight party system changes (1972, 1980, 1983, 1987, 1996, 2001, 2007, and 2019). The level of volatility increased from 0 in 1961 to .66 in 1996 and to .69 in 2019.

From 1960 to 2017, New Zealand held 20 elections and experienced nine party system changes (1966, 1972, 1981, 1984, 1996, 2008, 2011, 2014, and 2017). The level of fluidity increased from 0 in 1960 to 1.45 in the 1990 elections to 2.4 in the 2017 elections.

From 1962 to 2015, Canada held 18 elections and experienced seven party system changes (1963, 1968, 1979, 2000, 2006, 2011, and 2015). The level of fluidity increased from 0 in 1962 to .54 in the 1993 elections, and to .77 in the 2015 elections.

Even in the otherwise fairly stable U.S. party system, one can detect a modest increase in the level of volatility. From 1960 to 2016 the United States held 15 elections and experienced one party system change (in 1988). Volatility increased from 0 in 1960 to .25 in 1988 and was .13 in the 2016 elections.

The evidence presented here sustains the claim that, to different extents, and at very different paces, fluidity has increased in Western European and other Western settings. By the end of the second decade of the new millennium, the level of fluidity was still reasonably low; that is, below one in a handful of countries (.11 in Italy, .13 in the United States, .56 in the UK, .69 in Australia, and .77 in Canada). It was considerably higher—that is, above 2—in the other settings (2.12 in France, 2.14 in Spain, 2.4 in Belgium and New Zealand, 2.9 in Austria, and 4.52 in Germany).

The emergence of the fluid self was, ultimately, responsible for higher levels of party system fluidity and for the unfreezing of party systems that, according to Lipset and Rokkan (1967) had been stable or frozen for several decades. One of the claims we advanced in these pages was that the rise of the fluid self was responsible for the vanishing appeal of political parties (as evidenced by a marked decline in party membership levels) and that the vanishing appeal of parties was responsible for the increase in the levels of party-system volatility we have just documented. To test whether and to what extent our intuition was correct, we now correlate the levels of fluidity that West European party systems had reached in the new millennium with the decline in party membership levels from the early 1960s (Katz *et al.* 1992) to the first decade in the new millennium (van Biezen, Mair, and Poguntke 2012). By computing the difference in M/E levels from the first election held in 1960, for which Katz and others (1992) reported the data, to the levels from the elections held in the first decade of the new millennium (as reported by van Biezen, Mair, and Poguntke 2012), we find that M/E declined by .2 in Germany, by 2.28 in Belgium, by 7.12 in Italy, by 8.19 in Great Britain, and by 8.93 in Austria. By correlating these values with the levels of fluidity reported above, we find that the correlation yields a strong negative coefficient (r =-.76)—which suggests, *prima facie*, that the level of fluidity is inversely related to the magnitude of the decline in party membership figures. Visual inspection of the scatterplot in Figure 1 suggests instead that the relationship between party membership decline and party system fluidity is actually curvilinear—a finding that partially supports our claim that party membership decline and the fluidity of the party system go hand-in-hand.

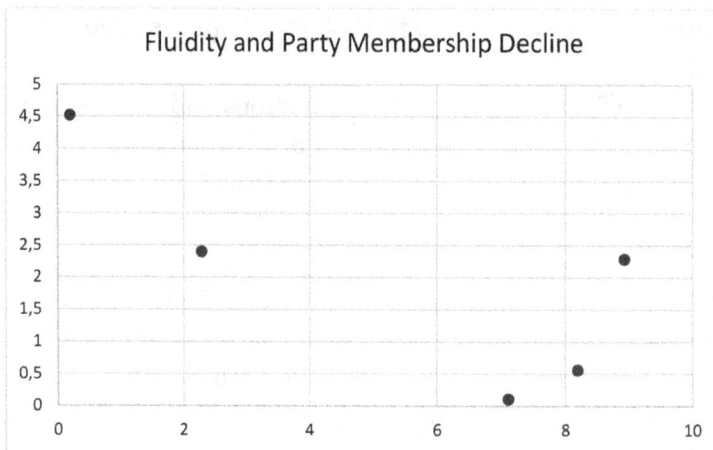

Figure 1. Fluidity and Party Membership Decline

Conclusions

The purpose of the present work was to explore whether and to what extent cultural change has been responsible for the increase in the level of fluidity of West European party systems. Our argument was that the rise of the fluid self reduced parties' appeal (as evidenced by the decline in party-membership levels) and that political parties' vanishing appeal had contributed to the destabilization of West European party systems. In the aggregate, the evidence presented here sustains our claim: 1960 witnessed the rise of the fluid self, parties lost voters and members, and the fluidity of party systems increased in each of the polities included in our analysis.

When we move, however, from the analysis at highly aggregate levels—that is, from what happens at the continental level—to what happens at the country level, the evidence in support of our claim is not as straightforward. Votes for the two largest declined in some cases (e.g., in the United Kingdom), but not in others (e.g., Germany). Party-membership levels declined considerably in some cases (Austria, Italy, the United Kingdom) but not so in others (Germany, and, to a lesser extent, Belgium). Furthermore, the analysis of the relationship between party membership levels and the fluidity of the party system reveals that the two variables are in a sort of curvilinear relation. In other words, above certain levels of party membership decline, the relationship between party membership decline and fluidity is as hypothesized—higher levels of party membership decline go hand-in-hand with higher levels of fluidity of the party system. Below a certain level of party membership decline, the relationship between party membership decline and the fluidity of the party system is antithetical with the claims that we advanced earlier on.

Concretely, this means that, while in some settings the vanishing appeal of political parties had a destabilizing effect at the party-system level, in other settings (Germany) the party system achieved high levels of instability (or fluidity) in spite of the fairly stable parties' appeal to prospective members or remained fairly stable in spite of a sizeable decline in membership figures (Italy). Be that as it may, the findings presented here show that, while party system change (and stability) can also be affected by cultural factors, cultural factors or conditions are not the sole determinant of party system change—either by themselves or through the mediation of some intervening variables such as party membership. Other factors do matter. And a comprehensive review of party system change and instability should attempt to identify as comprehensively as possible what exactly such factors may consist of.

About the Authors

Riccardo Pelizzo is an associate professor and the vice dean for research in the Graduate School of Public Policy at Nazarbayev University. A political development specialist, he holds a master's degree and a Ph.D. in political science from Johns Hopkins University.

Zim Nwokora is a senior lecturer in politics and policy studies at Deakin University, Australia. A comparative political scientist by training, he holds a bachelor's degree (in politics and economics), a master's degree (in comparative government), and a doctorate degree (in American politics), all from Oxford University.

References

Aarts, Kees, Henk van der Kolk, and Marlies Kamp. 2006. "Dutch Parliamentary Election Study, 1998 (ICPSR 2836)." *ICPSR*, January 18. Accessed on December 10, 2021. https://www.icpsr.umich.edu/web/ICPSR/studies/2836

Almond, Gabriel, and Sydney Verba. 1963. *The Civic Culture: Political Attitudes and Democracy in Five Nations*. Princeton, NJ: Princeton University Press.

Banfield, Edward C. 1965. *The Moral Basis of a Backward Society*. New York, NY: The Free Press.

Bauman, Zygmunt. 2010. *44 Letters from the Liquid Modern World*. Cambridge, UK: Polity.

Bradley, Peri, and James Page. 2017. "David Bowie–The Trans Who Fell to Earth: Cultural Regulation, Bowie and Gender Fluidity." *Continuum* 31 (4): 583-595. DOI: 10.1080/10304312.2017.1334389

Coates, Norma. 1997. "R(e)volution Now? Rock and the Political Potential of Gender." *Sexing the Groove: Popular Music and Gender* 50. Accessed on December 10, 2021. https://granolagradschoolandgoffman.wordpress.com/2017/06/26/coates-n -1997-revolution-now-rock-and-the-political-potential-of-gender/

Coëgnarts, Maarten, and Peter Kravanja. 2014. "On the Embodiment of Binary Oppositions in Cinema: The Containment Schema in John Ford's Westerns." *Image and Narrative* 15 (1): 30-43. Accessed December 10, 2021. http://www.image-andnarrative.be/index.php/imagenarrative/article/view/460

Deleuze, Gilles, and Felix Guattari. 2008. *Anti-Oedipus*. London: Continuum.

Downs, Anthony. 1957. *An Economic Theory of Democracy*. New York, NY: Harper.

Duverger, Maurice. 1954. *Political Parties: Their Organization and Activity in the Modern State*. New York, NY: Wiley.

Eco, Umberto. 1968. *La Struttura Assente*. Milano: Bompiani.

_____. 1962. *Opera Aperta*. Milano: Bompiani.

Eco, Umberto. 1965. "Le strutture narrative in Fleming. Il caso Bond. [Narrative Structure in Fleming: The Bond Case]." In *Il caso Bond*, edited by Oreste del Buono and Umberto Eco, 73-122 Milano: Bompiani

Gourevitch, Peter. 1986. *Politics in Hard Times: Comparative Responses to International Economic Crises*. Ithaca, NY: Cornell University Press.

Gupta, Suman. 2005. "Samuel Beckett's *Wating for Godot*." In *The Popular and the Canonical: Debating Twentieth-century Literature, 1940-2000*, edited by D. Johnson, 210-261. Abingdon, UK: Routledge.

Halberstam, Jack. 2017. *Trans: A Quick and Quirky Account of Gender Variability*. Vol. 3. Oakland, CA: University of California Press.

Hibbs, Jr., Douglas A. 1977. "Political Parties and Macroeconomic Policy." *American Political Science Review* 71 (4): 1467-1487. DOI: 10.2307/1961490

Ignazi, Piero. 1992. "The Silent Counter-revolution: Hypotheses on the Emergence of Extreme Right-wing Parties in Europe." *European Journal of Political Research* 22 (1): 3-34. DOI: 10.1111/j.1475-6765.1992.tb00303.x

Inglehart, Ronald. 1971. "The Silent Revolution in Europe: Intergenerational Change in Post-industrial Societies." *American Political Science Review* 65 (4): 991-1017. DOI: 10.2307/1953494

Katz, Richard S. 1990. "Party as Linkage: A Vestigial Function?" *European Journal of Political Research* 18 (1): 143-161. DOI: 10.1111/j.1475-6765.1990.tb00225.x

Katz, Richard S., and Peter Mair. 1995. "Changing Models of Party Organization and Party Democracy: The Emergence of the Cartel Party." *Party Politics* 1 (1): 5-28. DOI: 10.1177/1354068895001001001

Katz, Richard S., Peter Mair, Luciano Bardi, Lars Bille, Kris Deschouwer, David Farrell, Ruud Koole, Leonardo Morlino, Wolfgang Müller, Jon Pierre, Thomas Poguntke, Jan Sundberg, Lars Svasand, Hella van de Velde, Paul Webb, and Anders Widfeldt. 1992. "The Membership of Political Parties in European Democracies, 1960-1990." *European Journal of Political Research* 22 (3): 329-345. DOI: 10.1111/j.1475-6765.1992.tb00316.x

Kitschelt, Herbert, and Anthony J. McGann. 1997. *The Radical Right in Western Europe: A Comparative Analysis*. Ann Arbor, MI: University of Michigan Press.

Lévi-Strauss, Claude. 1955. "The Structural Study of Myth." *Journal of American Folklore* 68 (270): 428-444.

Lipset, Seymour Martin. 1959. "Some Social Requisites of Democracy: Economic Development and Political Legitimacy." *American Political Science Review* 53 (1):

69–105. DOI: 10.2307/1951731

Lipset, Seymour Martin, and Stein Rokkan. 1967. "Cleavage Structures, Party Systems, and Voter Alignments: An Introduction." In *Party Systems and Voter Alignments: Cross-National Perspectives*, edited by Seymour Martin Lipset and Stein Rokkan, 1-64. New York, NY: The Free Press.

Mair, Peter. 1996. "Party Systems and Structures of Competition." In *Comparing Democracies: Elections and Voting in Global Perspectives*, edited by L. LeDuc, R. G. Niemi, and Pippa Norris, 83-106. London: Sage.

Mair, Peter, and Ingrid Van Biezen. 2001. "Party Membership in Twenty European Democracies, 1980-2000." *Party Politics* 7 (1): 5-21. DOI 10.1177/13540688 01007001001

Maslow, Abraham Harold. 1943. "A Theory of Human Motivation." *Psychological Review* 50 (4): 370. DOI: 10.1037/h0054346

Morgan Margot. 2013. "Introduction: Political Theatre and the Theatre of Politics." In *Politics and Theatre in Twentieth-Century Europe: Critical Political Theory and Radical Practice*, edited by Margot Morgan, 1-17. New York, NY: Palgrave Macmillan: 1-17. DOI: 10.1057/9781137370389_1

Nordhaus, William D. 1975. "The Political Business Cycle." *Review of Economic Studies* 42 (2): 169-190. DOI: /10.2307/2296528

Norman, Philip. 1984. *Symphony for the Devil: The Rolling Stones Story*. New York, NY: Simon & Schuster.

Nwokora, Zim, and Riccardo Pelizzo. 2018. "Measuring Party System Change: A Systems Perspective." *Political Studies* 66 (1): 100-118. DOI 10.1177/00323217 17710568

Pelizzo, Riccardo, and Zim Nwokora. 2018. "Party System Change and the Quality of Democracy in East Africa." *Politics & Policy* 46 (3): 505-528. DOI 10.1111/ polp.12255

Pelizzo, Riccardo, and Zim Nwokora. 2016. "Bridging the Divide: Measuring Party System Change and Classifying Party Systems." *Politics & Policy* 44 (6): 1017-1052. DOI: /10.1111/polp.12188

Perrott, Lisa. 2017. "Bowie the Cultural Alchemist: Performing Gender, Synthesizing Gesture and Liberating Identity." *Continuum* 31 (4): 528-541. DOI: 10.10

80/10304312.2017.1334380

Polyani, Karl. 1943. *The Great Transformation: The Political and Economic Transformations of Our Time*. Boston, MA: Beacon Press.

Putnam, Robert, Robert Leonardi, and Raffaella Nanetti. 1993. *Making Democracy Work: Civic Traditions in Modern Italy*. Princeton, N.J.: Princeton University Press.

Sartori, Giovanni. 1976. *Parties and Party Systems*. New York, NY: Cambridge University Press.

Sargent, Thomas J., and Neil Wallace. 1976. "Rational Expectations and the Theory of Economic Policy." *Journal of Monetary Economics* 2 (2): 169-183. DOI: 10.1016/0304-3932(76)90032-5

Shahid, Afia. 2018. "Towards a Deconstructive Text: Beyond Language and the Politics of Absences in Samuel Beckett's Waiting for Godot." *International Journal of Cognitive and Language Sciences* 12 (1): 108-113. DOI: 10.5281/zenodo.1315607

Stanković, Peter. 2019. "Corto Maltese and the Process of Endless Semiosis." *Journal of Graphic Novels and Comics* (Early View). DOI: 10.1080/21504857.2019.1651359

Tait, Peta. 2019. "Striving, Falling, Performing: Phenomenologies of Mood and Apocalypse." *The Routledge Companion to Theatre and Politics*, edited by Peter Eckersall and Helena Grehan, 66-70. London: Routledge.

van Biezen, Ingrid, Peter Mair, and Thomas Poguntke. 2012. "Going, Going,... Gone? The Decline of Party Membership in Contemporary Europe." *European Journal of Political Research* 51 (1): 24-56. DOI; 10.1111/j.1475-6765.2011.01995.x

Weber, Max. 2002. *The Protestant Ethic and the "Spirit" of Capitalism and Other Writings*. London: Penguin.

Wright, Will. 1977. *Sixguns and Society: A Structural Study of the Western*. Oakland, CA: University of California Press.

Yacavone, Peter. 2018. "'Free from the Blessings of Civilization': Native Americans In Stagecoach (1939) and Other John Ford Westerns." *Film & History: An Interdisciplinary Journal* 48 (1): 32-44. Accessed December 10, 2021. https://www.muse.jhu.edu/article/701451

Featured Titles from Westphalia Press

westphaliapress.org

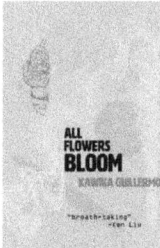

All Flowers Bloom
by Kawika Guillermo

"All Flowers Bloom is a beguiling book, with an inventive narrative unlike anything I have encountered before. This is an emotional journey through lifetimes and loves and losses." —Doretta Lau, author of How Does a Single Blade of Grass Thank the Sun?

Brought to Light: The Mysterious George Washington Masonic Cave
by Jason Williams MD

The George Washington Masonic Cave near Charles Town, West Virginia, contains a signature carving of George Washington dated 1748. This book painstakingly pieces together the chronicled events and real estate archives related to the cavern in order to sort out fact from fiction.

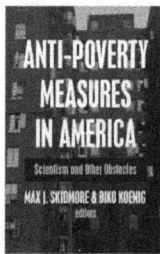

Anti-Poverty Measures in America: Scientism and Other Obstacles
Editors, Max J. Skidmore and Biko Koenig

Anti-Poverty Measures in America brings together a remarkable collection of essays dealing with the inhibiting effects of scientism, an over-dependence on scientific methodology that is prevalent in the social sciences, and other obstacles to anti-poverty legislation.

The Hope for Perfect People Leaders: Positive Psychology Education to Lead our Future Health, Happiness and Success by Dr. Lisa Miller

Dr. Miller provides a visionary strategic plan to educate and empower our future generations as luminaries of positive psychology. Leaders learn to dedicate themselves to the hope for higher humanism, while also producing prosperity.

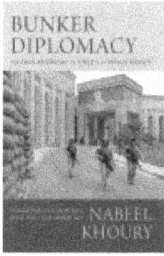

Bunker Diplomacy: An Arab-American in the U.S. Foreign Service
by Nabeel Khoury

After twenty-five years in the Foreign Service, Dr. Nabeel A. Khoury retired from the U.S. Department of State in 2013 with the rank of Minister Counselor. In his last overseas posting, Khoury served as deputy chief of mission at the U.S. embassy in Yemen (2004-2007).

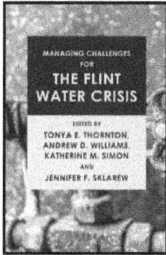

Managing Challenges for the Flint Water Crisis
Edited by Toyna E. Thornton, Andrew D. Williams, Katherine M. Simon, Jennifer F. Sklarew

This edited volume examines several public management and intergovernmental failures, with particular attention on social, political, and financial impacts. Understanding disaster meaning, even causality, is essential to the problem-solving process.

The Forgotten Army: The American Eighth Army in the Southern Philippines 1945
by Robert M. Young

History has produced many famous armies. It has also produced several that few knew even existed. The American Eighth Army of World War II is one such force. They saw action throughout the Southwest Pacific, specifically in the Philippines.

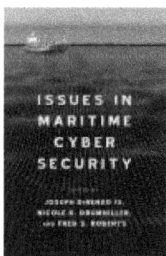

Issues in Maritime Cyber Security
Editors: Dr. Joe DiRenzo III, Dr. Nicole K. Drumhiller, Dr. Fred S. Roberts

The complexity of making MTS safe from cyber attack is daunting and the need for all stakeholders in both government (at all levels) and private industry to be involved in cyber security is more significant than ever as the use of the MTS continues to grow.

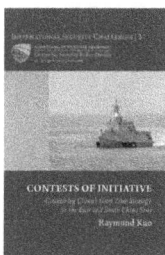

Contests of Initiative: Countering China's Gray Zone Strategy in the East and South China Seas
by Dr. Raymond Kuo

China is engaged in a widespread assertion of sovereignty in the South and East China Seas. It employs a "gray zone" strategy: using coercive but sub-conventional military power to drive off challengers and prevent escalation, while simultaneously seizing territory and asserting maritime control.

www.ingramcontent.com/pod-product-compliance
Lightning Source LLC
Chambersburg PA
CBHW081406270326
41931CB00016B/3397